HALLIBURTON'S ARMY

ALSO BY PRATAP CHATTERJEE

Iraq, Inc.: A Profitable Occupation

The Earth Brokers: Power, Politics and World Development

Nether Time

HALLIBURTON'S
ARMY

How a Well-Connected Texas Oil Company
Revolutionized the Way America Makes War

PRATAP CHATTERJEE

NATION
BOOKS

New York
www.nationbooks.org

Published by Nation Books
A Member of the Perseus Books Group
116 East 16th Street, 8th Floor
New York, NY 10003

Nation Books is a co-publishing venture of the Nation Institute and the
Perseus Books Group.

Books published by Nation Books are available at special discounts for
bulk purchases in the United States by corporations, institutions, and
other organizations. For more information, please contact the Special
Markets Department at the Perseus Books Group, 2300 Chestnut Street,
Suite 200, Philadelphia, PA 19103, or call (800) 810-4145, ext. 5000, or e-mail
special.markets@perseusbooks.com.

Design and typesetting by Cynthia Young.

Library of Congress Cataloging-in-Publication Data

Chatterjee, Pratap.
Halliburton's army : how a well-connected Texas oil company revolutionized the
   way America makes war / Pratap Chatterjee.
      p. cm.
   Includes bibliographical references and index.
   ISBN 978-1-56858-392-1 (alk. paper)
   1. Halliburton Company—History.   2. Petroleum products—
Texas—History.   I. Title.
TN872.Z6H353 2009
956.7044'31—dc22

                                          2008045876

10 9 8 7 6 5 4 3 2 1

To the cooks, cleaners, truck drivers,
and construction workers who make up
Halliburton's army, as well as the whistle-blowers
who came forward to tell this story.

CONTENTS

A Revolution in Military Affairs

Early on the morning of March 18, 2008, some four thousand raucous U.S. troops gathered at Holt Stadium on Logistical Supply Area (LSA) Anaconda, a giant U.S. military base located a little more than forty miles northwest of Baghdad near the town of Balad.[1] Named after the giant Amazonian river snake that is known for coiling its body around its victim and choking it to death, LSA Anaconda is really a small U.S. town in the middle of Iraq that houses the central command for all its military supply operations in the country. The soldiers who were gathered that cool spring morning were just a small fraction of the thirty thousand troops and contractors who work on the base.[2]

Some soldiers sat perched on top of the Humvees and Stryker fighting vehicles while others waved flags and chanted "USA, USA" when Brigadier General Gregory Couch, the commanding general of the 316th Expeditionary Sustainment Command, introduced the surprise guest who would mark the fifth anniversary of the 2003 invasion of Iraq.

Surrounded by plainclothes bodyguards, U.S. Vice President Dick Cheney strode in from the back of the stadium to meet and greet the troops, pin a Bronze Star on Staff Sergeant Shane Lindsey from Greenville, Texas, and Specialist Veronica Alfaro of Modesto, California, and give a speech. "The work that goes on at Balad and at Camp Anaconda, around the clock, seven days a week, is absolutely critical to the mission that America has undertaken here," he told the cheering soldiers. "Balad is one of the busiest airports anywhere, and it's the main staging area for the massive logistical operations we need in this theater."[3]

After the event, Cheney was ushered into one of the four major dining facilities on the base where he helped himself at a hot breakfast buffet to bacon, sausage, eggs, and hash browns and took a seat next to Shubra Bhattacharya-Jones, an Asian American lieutenant in the U.S. Army and others at a special table draped in black. Nearby, dozens of South and Southeast Asian contract workers kept busy, cooking and serving up food to fill the buffet that was being rapidly emptied by the thousands of hungry troops filing in after Cheney's speech.[4]

Later that day, Dick Cheney left Iraq the way he had come: holed up in a forty-foot silver trailer inside a C-17 aircraft, to continue his swing around the region—through Ankara, Jerusalem, Kabul, and Riyadh—before returning to Washington.[5] On this trip he packed a collection of World War II histories into a green duffel bag: *Washington Post* reporter Rick Atkinson's *The Day of Battle*, about the U.S. Army's campaign to capture Sicily and mainland Italy, and a collection of essays.[6]

Yet the war that Cheney had just visited could not be more unlike the history he was perusing where soldiers subsisted on canned Spam, powdered eggs, powdered milk, and powdered coffee.[7] The dining facility where he had just eaten (also known as DFAC), like most of the services on the sprawling nine-square-mile base—ranging from laundry to mail—are largely supplied and maintained not by soldiers, but by workers and subcontractors of Kellogg, Brown & Root (KBR), under a contract with the Pentagon called the Logistics Civilian Augmentation Program (LOGCAP).[8] KBR is a former subsidiary of Halliburton, a Fortune 500 company based until early 2007 in Houston, Texas.

This LOGCAP contract has netted KBR more than $25 billion since the company won a ten-year contract in late 2001 to supply U.S. troops in combat situations around the world. As of April 2008, the company estimated that it had served more than 720 million meals, driven more than 400 million miles in various convoy missions, treated 12 billion gallons of potable water, and produced more than 267 million tons of ice.[9] These staggering figures are testimony to the significant role that Halliburton/KBR has played in supporting the U.S. military in Iraq and other countries targeted in the Global War on Terror.

Cheney's 2008 visit stands in marked contrast to his brief trip to Iraq in early May 1991 as secretary of defense, when he clambered on top of a sand-colored Abrams tank to give a speech to U.S. troops who were camped out in tents in the southern desert just five miles north of the Kuwaiti border.[10] His visit was brief, just a few short minutes; he did not stay overnight nor could he expect to join the soldiers in a military mess similar to those back at home.

Most troops in Iraq at that time typically ate Meals Ready to Eat out of a pouch such as chicken stew, corned beef hash, and pork with rice and barbecue sauce washed down with a bottle of water, or the older-style A, B, or T rations that were prepared from semi-perishable or canned food by army cooks.[11]

Today's menus at large bases in the Middle East and Central Asia, particularly on festive holidays, are a far cry from the 1943 or even the 1991 menus. A 2003 Thanksgiving menu in Bagram, Afghanistan, featured glazed ham, turkey, roast beef, corn bread stuffing, simmered corn, giblet gravy, ground gravy, pumpkin pie, sweet potato pie, cheese cake, chocolate cake, blueberry pie, and hot fresh rolls.[12] Such menus have been possible only because of the unprecedented reliance on contractors: Approximately one in one hundred people on the Iraqi battlefield in the 1991 Operation Desert Storm were contractors, compared to today in Operation Enduring Freedom, where the numbers of contractors are roughly equal to those of military personnel.[13]

Much of this outsourcing was initiated by Dick Cheney himself when he was secretary of defense in the early 1990s to comply with U.S. Congressional demands to downsize the military and its bloated Cold War budgets.[14] Then, as CEO of Halliburton for five years before he became vice president in 2000, Cheney also oversaw the first major deployment of contractors into support services for the military in active battlefields in former Yugoslavia.

It was not the first time Halliburton or its subsidiaries had been involved in battle; indeed Brown & Root, then an independent company, built 359 warships that were actively involved in the Second World War, including amphibious assault ships, destroyer escorts, and submarine chasers.[15] During the Vietnam War, the company built most of the U.S. military bases in that country, but it was the first time that the contractors would allow soldiers to be wholly spared the dreadful monotony of cooking and cleaning up after themselves.

ENEMY NO. 1: PENTAGON BUREAUCRACY

Cheney was not alone—indeed the man who did most to implement the changes that he initiated after Operation Desert Storm, was one of his closest political allies and longtime friends—Donald Rumsfeld, who took over as secretary of defense under the new Bush-Cheney administration in 2001.

Rumsfeld heralded this little-noticed but seismic policy change in military logistics at a Pentagon event on the morning of September 10, 2001, precisely one day before three aircraft struck the Pentagon and the World Trade Center in New York. "The topic today is an adversary that poses a threat, a serious threat, to the security of the United States of America," Rumsfeld told the assembled senior staff who had gathered for the kick-off of the annual Acquisition and Logistics Excellence week. "This adversary is one of the world's last bastions of central planning. It governs by dictating five-year plans. From a single capital, it attempts to impose its demands across time zones, continents, oceans, and beyond. With brutal consistency, it stifles free thought and crushes new ideas. It disrupts the defense of the United States and places the lives of men and women in uniform at risk.[16]

"You may think I'm describing one of the last decrepit dictators of the world," he thundered. "The adversary's closer to home. It's the Pentagon bureaucracy. The technology revolution has transformed organizations across the private sector, but not ours, not fully, not yet. We are, as they say, tangled in our anchor chain."

Rumsfeld said that the Pentagon was wasting at least $3 billion a year. "We must ask tough questions. Why is DOD one of the last organizations around that still cuts its own checks? When an entire industry exists to run warehouses efficiently, why do we own and operate so many of our own? At bases around the world, why do we pick up our own garbage and mop our own floors, rather than contracting services out, as many businesses do?"

He outlined a series of steps to slash headquarter staffs by 15 percent in the next two years and promised even more dramatic changes in the years to come. "We will not complete this work in one year, or five years, or even eight years," said Rumsfeld. "An institution built with trillions of dollars over decades of time does not turn on a dime. Some say it's like turning a battleship. I suspect it's more difficult."

A little more than five years after Rumsfeld delivered that speech, he was asked to resign, but less than eight years down the road, when Cheney made his overnight stop at LSA Anaconda, Cheney would see that the transformation that Rumsfeld had demanded was complete.

No longer were U.S. soldiers picking up their own garbage and mopping their own floors, or cooking their own food or washing their laundry. Today, tasks like that are now done by an army of low wage contract laborers drawn largely from Third World countries. (Some senior Halliburton/KBR managers made considerably more money, particularly if they were willing to bend the rules.)

A HUNDRED TRIPS ACROSS IRAQ

A fortnight after Dick Cheney left Iraq, I visited the very same dining facilities and logistics operations at LSA Anaconda that he had toured. I flew south with the U.S. military to Kuwait city where I accepted an offer to meet with a group of Fijian truck drivers who worked for a local company named Public Warehousing Corporation (PWC) that was doing subcontract work for Halliburton/KBR.

My host was Titoko Savuwati from Totoya Lau (one of the Moala Islands in Fiji), who picked me up one evening in a small, white Toyota Corolla rental car. The sound system was cranked up to play country favorites and oldies.[17] Savuwati was six feet tall, with broad, rangy shoulders, short-cropped hair, and a French beard. A former police officer in Suva, he was fifty years old and had six children back in Fiji, whom he had not seen in four years. When he got out of his car, I noticed he had a pronounced limp, dragging one foot ever so slightly behind him.

We joined his friends at his apartment for a simple Anglican prayer service. Deep baritone voices filled their tiny living room with Fijian hymns, before they sat down to a meal of cassava and curried chicken parts and told me their stories. Each of them had made at least one hundred trips to Iraq, driving the large eighteen-wheeler refrigeration trucks that carry all manner of goodies for the U.S. soldiers, from ice to frozen steak and lobster, from Kuwaiti ports to bases like LSA Anaconda. They sleep in their trucks (they are not allowed to sleep in the military tents or trailers) and have to pay for their own food on the road.

Savuwati had arrived in Kuwait on January 14, 2005, as one of four hundred drivers, hoping to earn $3,000 a month. Instead, he discovered his real pay would be 175 Kuwaiti dinar (KWD) a month (US$640) out of which he had to pay for all his food and sundries, as well as rent. They were paid an extra 50 dinar ($183) allowance per trip. "I came to Iraq because of the large amount of money [the labor recruiter from Fiji] promised me," he says, sighing. "But they give us very little money. We've been crying for more money for many months; do you think my family can survive on 50 KWD?" He sends at least 100 dinar ($365) home a month, and has no savings to pay for a ticket home, which would cost him roughly US$2,500 round-trip.

I did a quick calculation. For every trip, if they worked the normal twelve-hour shift expected of them, the Fijians earned about $30 a day, or $2.50 an hour. I asked Savuwati about his limp, and he told me that in 2005, when he was on a trip to Nasariyah, his truck flipped, and he injured his foot. Did he get paid sick leave when he injured his foot? I asked. Savuwati looked incredulous. "The company didn't give me any money. When we are injured, the company gives us nothing." But he assured me that he had been lucky—a number of fellow drivers had been killed on the job.

The next day, I stopped by to see the Fijians again, and Savuwati gave me a ride home. I offered to pay for gasoline, and after waving me away, he quickly acquiesced. As he dropped me off, he looked at me a little sheepishly and said: "I've run out of money, do you think you could give me 1 KWD [$3.65] for lunch?" I dug into my pockets and handed over the requested money, but as I walked away I thought how ironic it was that the men who drove across a battle zone, dodging stones and bullets to bring fresh food and ammunition to the U.S. soldiers, had to beg for food themselves.

MILLION DOLLAR BRIBES?

The largest government-owned weapons manufacturing arsenal in the United States—the U.S. Army Rock Island Arsenal—is situated on Rock Island in western Illinois, the biggest island in the Mississippi River where Chief Black Hawk—the self-proclaimed political leader of the Sauk nation—was born.[18] The arsenal's modern stone buildings also house the offices of the Army Materiel Command from which Halliburton/KBR's multibillion dollar LOGCAP contract has been managed for the last seven years.

A week after I left Iraq, and less than a month after Cheney made his appearance at LSA Anaconda, a parade of former Halliburton/KBR junior and senior procurement managers from Kuwait and Iraq appeared to testify before a jury at the Rock Island federal courthouse, less than two miles from the arsenal across the 24th Street Bridge. Several of the witnesses were military veterans who had served in the Vietnam War in the 1970s and had traveled to the Middle East as employees of Halliburton/KBR. They had been summoned under subpoena for the case of USA v. Mazon et al. before Joe Billy McDade, an African American Republican judge from Texas, who was appointed by George H. W. Bush in 1991.[19]

The case to be heard in front of the jury was as follows: A million-dollar check had changed hands between Jeff Alex Mazon, Halliburton/KBR's procurement materials and property manager, and Ali Hijazi, a Kuwaiti-based businessman, in September 2003.The U.S. Department of Justice alleged that the check was a payoff for devising a scheme to defraud the taxpayers of more than $3.5 million related to the awarding of a subcontract to supply fuel tankers for military operations in Kuwait.

"The Department of Justice is committed to ensuring that hard-earned taxpayer dollars are not siphoned off or wasted in our defense procurement processes," Assistant Attorney General Wray charged in a press release. "Especially in a time of war, the relentless pursuit of those who would fraudulently divert money for their own benefit must be a high priority."[20]

J. Scott Arthur, Mazon's attorney, claimed that his client had made a simple mathematical error in overpaying Hijazi, blaming instead his former employers at Halliburton/KBR for making a scapegoat out of his client. "The mother ship—KBR and Halliburton—isn't going to take any responsibility," said Arthur. "They have the nerve to throw stones at people like Jeff Mazon [who] built Guantánamo Bay for the U.S."[21]

Mazon was the first of some thirty lower-ranked Halliburton/KBR managers, Pentagon procurement officials, and Middle Eastern contractors to go to jury trial. Almost every other person indicted has pled guilty to bribery charges.[22]

What was most astonishing was not the fact that Mazon accepted the million-dollar check, which is not in dispute, but that he claims that he did nothing wrong in accepting the money, which he says was a personal loan. The witnesses who were called to testify described similar offers of payoffs from local merchants as well as the tale of a party house where alcohol and women were made available to senior managers by a contractor. Robert Gatlin, the former project manager for all of Halliburton/KBR's contracts in Iraq, Jordan, and Kuwait, admitted to ordering multiple bottles of complimentary liquor from the Pakistani-American representative of a Saudi contractor to provide to David Lesar, then CEO of Halliburton, on his monthly visits to a company-leased townhouse at the Hilton resort in Kuwait—despite the fact that alcohol is strictly illegal in that country.[23]

PROFITS AND LOSSES

The rewards and punishments for Cheney and Rumsfeld's revolution in military affairs have been profound, not least for the soldiers who are now supplied with hot food and showers around the clock. For the Pentagon generals, it has meant that they can do far more with far fewer soldiers; the proverbial "tooth-to-tail" ratio has been reduced, so they can focus on training new recruits to engage primarily in warfare, instead of engaging in mundane logistics.

For military retirees, who take jobs with Halliburton/KBR, this new industry also represents a lucrative new career in which salaries and benefits far exceed what they might have made as public servants, while the profits for the company and its subcontractors run into the hundreds of millions of dollars.

Accompanying this new industry is the potential for bribery, corruption, and fraud. Dozens of Halliburton/KBR workers and their subcontractors have already been arrested and charged, and several are already serving jail terms for stealing millions of dollars, notably from Camp Arifjan in Kuwait.

The bulk of the workers like Savuwati, however, will not see anything close to that, as the pay for Asian workers starts at $300 and probably averages $1,000 a month, although this is still quite a bit greater than what they might have earned at home. Hardest hit are those who have been injured in the course of their work in the war and cast aside as noncombatants with no prospect of a medal, let alone medical care; or for those who have been killed and whose families have been left without a breadwinner.

These men and women make up Halliburton's Army, which employs enough people to staff one hundred battalions, a total of more than fifty thousand personnel who work for KBR under a contract that is now projected to reach $150 billion. Together with the workers who are rebuilding Iraq's infrastructure and the private security divisions of companies like Blackwater, Halliburton's Army now outnumber the uniformed soldiers on the ground in Iraq.

But without this private army of low-wage labor and highly paid managers, the invasion and occupation of Iraq would have been impossible: The U.S. simply did not have enough soldiers and reservists to maintain the supply lines to keep the combat troops alive. This book traces the history of the evolution of military logistics contracting since the Vietnam War, in parallel with the careers of Dick Cheney and Donald Rumsfeld, to explain the crucial decisions that were taken to make it feasible to implement George W. Bush's Global War on Terror.

Part 1

Riding the Catfish to Anaconda

CATFISH AIR must be the oddest little privately run airline in the world: It has no planes or pilots, charges nothing, and has no official schedule. The only way to get a ride is to call a phone number and ask to be placed on a flight to one of the military base destinations in Iraq. Its headquarters are on the west side of LSA Anaconda in a nine thousand square feet, sanitized, K-Span building. Unlike most airlines, which discourage passengers carrying liquids, it supplies one-liter bottles of cold water in the terminal that you are strongly advised to take with you (to prevent heat exhaustion). Cots are also provided for those who get stuck there with no available flights (this happens frequently and can last for days, as space on the free flights is subject to the hierarchical priorities of the military chain of command).[1]

Catfish Air operators can get passengers on the flight manifest for a Space-A (space available or stand-by, in civilian language) seat on a helicopter, which is the quickest and easiest way to move around Iraq. At its disposal are a fleet of more than U.S. Army 130 UH-60 Black Hawks and CH-47 Chinooks that typically deploy in pairs flying a few hundred meters apart—low and fast, often at night with no lights on. The U.S. Army pilots, who shuttle the aircraft around the country, frequently fire a flare and a burst of aluminum chaff on take-off as a decoy for heat-seeking missiles.

To the right of the main arrival/check-in desk at LSA Anaconda hangs a plastic replica of a catfish, which was placed there by members of the Mississippi Army National Guard's 185th Aviation Brigade, who set up the service back in 2004.[2] Behind the desk sit a half-dozen men and women in civilian clothes, whose attire seem to share just one thing in common: a red lanyard worn around their necks that secures their identification badges. On closer inspection, the strap can be seen to bear the initials KBR.

Indeed, for casual visitors to Iraq, the easiest way to find out how things work is to look for someone wearing a red KBR lanyard; they are usually the people in charge of everything from food service, laundry, bathrooms, and shuttle buses, to loading baggage on to the "break-bulk" pallets that are stacked on the back of a cargo plane.

THE RHINO RUNNER

Another popular service operated by the men and women of Halliburton/ KBR is the Rhino Runner service, which is housed in a low, wooden building with a porch that looks like it has been plucked straight out of a cowboy-and-western movie set and then dropped into the maze of concrete barriers, barbed wire, and port-a-potties that make up Camp Stryker, which is next to Baghdad International Airport. Appropriately named Stables, inside is a large, cool room, with two big TVs tuned permanently to the Fox network. Behind the counter are the ubiquitous South Asian workers and a supervisor with a KBR badge slung around his neck.

The Rhino Runner, manufactured in Ashdod, Israel, is a thirteen-ton, all-armored vehicle that resembles a very large black refrigerator on wheels with a small picture of a rhinoceros emblazoned on the front.[3] The windows are made of bullet-proof glass that is so tough it hurts one's knuckles to even tap on them. The passenger windows, which are angled in streamlined fashion, remind one of an old-time Greyhound bus and are supposed to be blacked out, but there are chinks through which one can see. A small fleet of these ugly buses that make the regular forty-minute ride to the Green Zone is protected by a vehicle that looks like a Humvee on steroids (it is literally the size of a small tank). This vehicle is an MRAP Cougar (Mine Resistant Ambush Protected vehicle) with various extra antennas and what look like square satellite dishes attached. It looks like something out of an apocalyptic sci-fi future battle.

Driven by Halliburton/KBR drivers, the Rhino Runner has the distinction of ferrying both Donald Rumsfeld and Saddam Hussein. It is the only safe way—other than by helicopter—to move diplomats, contractors, and others working for the government between the Baghdad airport and the Green Zone along "Route Irish," also known as "the Road of Death." (When a Rhino took a direct hit from a rocket-propelled grenade, "Nobody was hurt except for some minor bumps and bruises," said Army Major Sharon Smith of the Joint Area Support Group, who books the Rhino convoys.)[4]

DINING FACILITIES

Thirty minutes before midnight, every single night, three Ugandan men beckon forward a small cluster of U.S. soldiers at Camp Stryker just outside Baghdad's military airport. A trickle of men and women surges through, streaming past the slim and rather youthful-looking former African soldiers, personnel of a private security company named EODT. Soon there is a steady river of hungry people who complete the routine magazine check on their M16 carbines and head inside looking for a late snack—at an all-you-can-eat American buffet in the middle of the Iraqi night.[5]

Inside the vast and brightly lit Falcon dining facility that can seat more than one thousand people at once in three sections of fifty eight-seater tables, dozens of South Asian men with brown uniforms emblazoned in the orange colors of the Gulf Catering Corporation, a Halliburton/KBR subcontractor, serve up unlimited supplies of food to those who qualify: soldiers, government employees, and the media.

For the late-night snack, there were made-to-order omelets and hamburgers, breakfast food such as waffles, hash browns, sausages, and bacon, heartier food like pasta and meatballs, and no shortage of desserts from carrot cake to chocolate cake and pecan pies.

Falcon, like every major dining facility on a U.S. base in the region, has a salad bar, a soft drink station provided by Rastelli Global, a hot and cold food buffet, a soup station, drink fridges sponsored by Sprite and stacked with juices from Cargill, milk from Nada, a dessert bar, and ice cream freezers emblazoned with a Baskin Robbins logo (although the ice cream is Kuwaiti). On every table are the sauces that one might find at a roadside diner in the United States—Texas Pete Hot Sauce, A-1 Steak Sauce, and McIlhenny Tabasco. The orange marmalade and breakfast syrup is from Heinz of Pittsburgh, Pennsylvania, and the little honey packets are from Mason, Ohio. Peeking outside the dining facilities one can see the delivery vehicles—giant Mercedes Benz trucks with Thermo King Refrigeration containers driven by workers from countries as diverse as Egypt, Fiji, and Sri Lanka.

The scene at the Falcon mess is typical of dozens of dining facilities across Iraq and Kuwait, where contractors serve four full meals a day to the soldiers and contractors who work odd shifts (or for the plain hungry). One hour after midnight, the Falcon dining facility—the DFAC—will shut its doors but just to clean and prepare for the next rush, a much bigger throng of soldiers queuing up for breakfast at 5 a.m.

At another dining facility in LSA Anaconda, I met up with the chief warrant officer who ran it—Michael St. John of the Pennsylvania National Guard, who led me on a tour of the facility, pointing out little details that he was proud of such as the fresh romaine lettuce. He stopped at the dessert bar. "We added blenders to make milk shakes, microwaves to heat up apple pie, and waffle bars with ice cream." Next he led me to the "healthy bar" in the Carter room. "Here, we offer baked fish or chicken breast, crab legs, or lobster claws or tails."[6]

"Contractors here do all the work," said St. John. He explained that he had about twenty-five soldiers and six to eight Halliburton/KBR supervisors to oversee 175 workers from a Saudi company named Tamimi, feeding ten thousand people a day and providing take-away food for another one thousand.

"They do everything from unloading the food deliveries to taking out the trash. We are hands off. Our responsibility is military oversight: overseeing the headcount, ensuring that the contractors are providing nutritional meals . . . and making sure there are no food-borne illnesses. It's the only sustainable way to get things done, given the number of soldiers we have to feed."

These dining facilities are free to soldiers. Most big bases also have a "mini mall" where one can find U.S. fast-food chains serving in-between meals or a change from the Halliburton/KBR food. But even these Burger Kings, KFCs, McDonaldses, Pizza Huts, Subway sandwich shops, as well as Green Beans Coffee stores are run efficiently by polite Indian and Filipino migrant workers, who serve up espresso chai latte and mocha frappes or personalized pan pizzas and Whoppers to the soldiers. And at the military supermarket, operated by the Army and Air Force Exchange Service (AAFES), soldiers can stock up on anything from cookies to Bitburger nonalcoholic beer, Sony PlayStations, and even mountain bikes.

Sarah Stillman, a journalist with TruthDig, tells a story that she heard about a PowerPoint slide that's becoming popular in army briefings: "Back in 2003, the average soldier lost fifteen pounds during his tour of Iraq. Now, he gains ten." Stillman says that the first warning that many U.S. troops receive here in Baghdad isn't about the rampant IEDs (improvised explosive devices), or the RPGs (rocket-propelled grenades), or even the EFPs (explosively formed projectiles). It's about the PCPs: the pervasive combat paunches.[7]

INSIDE THE SCORPION'S DEN

At yet another military camp, whose name I am not allowed to reveal under military rules, the desert floor seems to extend forever. The pale brown color of the fine sand melds with the army tents and then the sky, which is the same muddy hue, even though it is 2 p.m. in the afternoon. If there were no gravel path between the sea of tents parked neatly in alphabetical rows, made out of light-grey pebbles, it would be hard to tell where desert merged with canvas and canvas merged with sky. Yet it is not too hard to find distractions from the gathering sandstorm.

Entering the "Scorpions Den"—a Morale, Welfare, and Recreation (MWR) tent run by Combat Support Associates, a Kuwaiti company that offers identical services to what Halliburton/KBR provides in Iraq—one is greeted by almost pitch darkness, the background music from a one-hundred-seater open theater, the soft glow of laptops, and the flickering lights of video games, which makes it feel as though one has just entered either a space station or a very large student recreation facility. A checkout desk allows anyone to borrow a movie for personal use (video-watching stations are available on a first-come, first-served basis). Small posters dangle over the desk for new films: *March of the Penguins*, *Georgia Rule*, *CSNY*, *Invisible*, and *Mission Impossible III*. There are also free popcorn, boxes and boxes of bottled water (Makkah water from Saudi Arabia, 550 ml), and a Dipping Dots ice cream machine ("Ice cream of the future").[8]

An MWR facility next door—a tent with a plywood floor covered in red carpets and white canvas walls punctuated by air-conditioning units—goes by the name of the "Sandbox." It hosts pool tables, table tennis, an Internet facility (thirty minutes free on a first-come, first-served basis), and it's also operated by either Indian and Filipino workers. Dozens of soldiers sit slumped into fake leather armchairs, playing war games or programs like Guitar Hero and watching a Star Trek movie. Festive decorations and clumps of green balloons from some forgotten party (it is three months after Christmas) hang from the ceiling.

It is a Friday night. The lights dim and a DJ has started spinning Latin music. One couple ventures onto the floor; they appear to have a rough idea of what they are doing. Other soldiers gawk: men and women, too shy to try. Soon enough, the first couple gets off the floor. But the ice has been broken and another couple follows. Soon the floor is filled with half a dozen army couples, men and women in identical blue shorts and grey T-shirts, gyrating to "*Corazon, Corazon.*"

THE FUSION CELL

How does this dizzying array of U.S. creature comforts find its way to Iraq? My answer came when I was invited to visit the "fusion cell," which is a coordination system housed inside a secure building on LSA Anaconda. At the time, this office was run by the 316th Expeditionary Sustainment Command from Coraopolis, Pennsylvania, near Pittsburgh, and it coordinates every piece of equipment from "beans to bullets" that is delivered in Iraq. Walking into the room, one feels transported to the command headquarters in the 1980s film *War Games*, or for that matter any recent Hollywood war thriller.[9]

The fusion cell resembles a small lecture theater with four tiers of benches rising from a large, polished wooden conference table at the front of the room. The room is divided by two aisles into three sections, each of which has swivel chairs that seat sixteen soldiers and the occasional contractor from Halliburton/KBR. There are transportation coordinators on the left, and munitions personnel to their left who keep track of everything from small bullets to missiles and supply and track everything from fuel and food, tanks, and their many spare parts, to uniforms and cots. A special desk at the far left has a small group called the route section that monitors truck convoys on every road in Iraq. Every soldier has a laptop flipped open, most of which are logged into the SIPRNet (Secret Internet Protocol Router Network) or NIPRNet (Unclassified but Sensitive Internet Protocol Router Network), and they can all watch four flat-screen TVs and two projection screens at the front of the room.

A sign at the back reads: "It's all about distribution management." Lieutenant Colonel Robert Harter and Major Michael Sharon, who run the fusion cell, explain that the term refers to the newest system of asset management in the military. "Rather than having large stockpiles to move on short notice, we now have smaller quantities throughout Iraq. We can't do "Just in Time" like Fed Ex, but we try to keep enough on hand to move it efficiently and in a timely fashion, to save money," says Sharon, a reservist whose civilian job is emergency coordinator at the State Department in Washington, DC. "Here at the sustainment brigade, we talk to the commanders in the battle space all the time to make sure the soldiers have what they need."

Sharon is also a firm believer in the use of contractors like Halliburton/KBR. "You don't necessarily have to have a soldier operating a dining facility," Sharon adds. "We try to gain efficiencies so that we are using our soldiers to focus on where we need the soldiers best. We decide on a case-by-case basis what jobs are not inherently military. In the battlefield, we might not have civilians run a dining facility."

FROM ROCK ISLAND TO CRYSTAL CITY

The Anaconda fusion cell represents the command central for logistics in Iraq once the supplies arrive in the theater. The supplies are actually ordered and paid for by a variety of military managers back in the United States, primarily working out of the LOGCAP office in Rock Island and the Defense Supply Center in Philadelphia, Pennsylvania, who in turn must answer to higher authorities like the Army Materiel Command (AMC) headquarters in Fort Belvoir, Virginia.[10]

You can find their civilian counterparts just twenty miles north in Crystal City, directly outside Ronald Reagan National Airport, a mile south of the Pentagon, in Arlington, Virginia. The complex is a small forest of sleek, white-and-brown commercial buildings that have sprung up to replace the junk-yards and low-rent motels that once dotted the neighborhood in the 1960s.[11] It now hosts some sixty thousand office workers during the daylight hours, a tenfold increase on the number of people who actually live there.[12] Most of those workers are military contractors who work for Boeing and Hallibur-ton/KBR. Walk down Crystal City Drive toward the airport and it is hard to miss the corporate logo of KBR in giant, red letters on the eleven-story build-ing at the far corner of Crystal Park. The company rents about 125,000 square feet at this property, which is one of its biggest offices in the Washington, DC, area—in addition to offices on North Kent Street and Wilson Drive in Arling-ton, where much of the company's military logistics work in countries from Afghanistan to Iraq is coordinated.[13]

Paul Cerjan, a retired army lieutenant general was one of the men who ran Halliburton/KBR's operations out of its offices in Kuwait, Texas, and Virginia. A former deputy commanding general of the U.S. Army in Europe who also led Pentagon delegations to China, he was hired by Halliburton/KBR in July 2004 to run its worldwide military logistics operation, a job he did for about one year. In an interview with Martin Smith of *Frontline* a public television news program—Cerjan described the services that Halliburton/KBR provides for U.S. forces in Iraq.[14]

"We're responsible for two significant areas. One that's base support ser-vices, which includes all the billeting, the feeding, water supplies, sewage—anything it would take to run a city. And on the other side, for the army in support, we handle logistics functions, which include transportation, move-ment of POL [petrol, oil, and lubricant] supplies, gas supplies—all class of supplies, as a matter of fact; all their spare parts, ammunition, anything they need to conduct the war. . . . It's like the Department of Public Works Plus."

Cerjan says that this was a complete contrast to when he served in Vietnam. "We erected our own tents; we put together our own dining facilities, etc. I spent my entire career watching soldiers pull 'kitchen patrol' in the kitchen. Why do we have to do that with soldiers? Why can't we outsource that mis-sion? We provide dining facilities that are very attractive and give soldiers all the nourishment they need. We give them MWR facilities so they can work out, see movies, etc. And we get their mind straight so when they go outside the wire to do their military job, they're sharp."

KEEPING A VOLUNTEER ARMY HAPPY

Tim Horton, the head of public relations for LSA Anaconda, and a former transportation officer for twenty years, has a simple explanation as to why the army relies so heavily on contractors to operate facilities today.

"What we have today is an all-volunteer army, unlike in a conscription army when they had to be here. In the old army, the standard of living was low, the pay scale was dismal; it wasn't fun; it wasn't intended to be fun," he says. "But today we have to appeal, we have to recruit, just like any corporation, we have to recruit off the street. And after we get them to come in, it behooves us to give them a reason to stay in."[15]

Horton points out that if the average soldier gets an average $100,000 worth of military training in the first four years, then the military has to spend another $100,000 to train every replacement soldier. "What if we spend an extra $6,000 to get them to stay and save the loss of talent and experience? What does it take to keep the people? There are some creature comforts in this Wal-Mart and McDonald's society that we live in that soldiers have come to expect. They expect to play an Xbox, to keep in touch by e-mail. They expect to eat a variety of foods."

A quarter century ago, Horton says, when he joined the army, all they got was a fourteen-day rotational menu. "We had chili-mac every two weeks, for crying out loud. What is that? Unstrained, low-grade hamburger mixed with macaroni. Lot of calories, lots of fat, lots of starch, that's what a soldier needs to do his job. When you were done, you had a heart attack." Today, says Horton, expectations are very different. "Our soldiers need to feel and believe that we care about them, or they will leave. The army cannot afford to allow the soldier to be disenfranchised."

"I treat myself to an ice-cream cone once a week. You know what that is? It's a touch of home, a touch of sanity, a touch of civilization. The soldiers here do not have bars; all that is gone. You've taken the candy away from the baby, what do you have to give him? What's wrong with giving him a little bit of pizza or ice cream?"

SUPPORTING AN ARMY OF ONE

The truth of the matter is that the U.S. military today is incredibly over-stretched. For the Bush administration to go to war, it needs an army of cheap labor to feed and clean up after its men and women who are sent into battle—who happen to be young U.S. citizens who have grown up in a world of creature comforts.

When did this symbiotic relationship between Halliburton/KBR and the Pentagon to support war come into being? For the answer to this question, we need to start at the very beginning—when Brown & Root first discovered how to turn on the spigot of dollars in Washington, DC. The man who taught them was the thirty-sixth president of the United States, a Democratic politician from Texas named Lyndon Baines Johnson.

Pampering the Soldier

A Fox reporter, Gregg Kelly, reported from a military dining facility in Taji, Iraq, in April 2005, that soldiers were very well taken care of. "You know, some of this looks like a brunch, you know, at a Marriott Hotel or something like that. It's pretty elaborate." The dining facility had "probably one of the few pastry chefs ever deployed to a combat zone—Chef Denzel from India," he added.[16]

In a report, a warrant officer named Joshua Gunter was seen eating a meal. He eagerly proclaimed, "KBR does an extremely good job." The food is so good, he says, that "we've been trying to hide it from our wives. . . . I was talking to my wife the other day. I was like, 'Baby, it's pretty rough over here.' I said 'they have only nine flavors of Baskin Robbins' (laughs)."

A Halliburton/KBR worker who asked to remain anonymous sent me the following description from his military base in September 2005: "I am a civilian working on a military base in Iraq. I find that most people in the States still have no idea what is going on over here. I get offers all the time: 'Do you need a care package, can we send you some snacks?' etc., but the shocking thing is that the bases over here are like upscale American cities."[17]

"I can talk only in general terms because I could get fired," he continued. "But it is no exaggeration that I live a higher lifestyle here on a base in Iraq than [I would] in the United States. We have free laundry, apartmentlike housing with unlimited, free A/C and electricity, hot water, various American fast-food outlets, lounges, free Internet, coffee shops, and a large PX [that sells thousands of CDs, DVDs, vacuum cleaners, junk food, steaks, etc., etc.—like a Wal-Mart]. Oh yes, and at lunch and dinner they serve Baskin Robbins ice cream out of huge tubs, and once a week we get steak and lobster. There is a lot more I am leaving out: karaoke night, all kinds of sports teams, and on and on and on.

"Yet just a few hundred meters outside the fence, little kids are begging for anything: food, bottled water. . . . The reality is very, very, very shocking. We are truly a pampered and spoiled culture."

*   *   *

But the general impression among the soldiers is that they could use a little more pampering, as the following memo (edited for length) indicates:

TASK FORCE ADLER–22D SIGNAL BRIGADE
CAMP VICTORY, IRAQ
17 May 2006

MEMORANDUM FOR RECORD
SUBJECT: Dining Facility Advisory Council Meeting

QUESTION: SPC R.: Asked if the dining facility could provide Belgium waffles, waffle cones, and more variety of ice-cream flavors.

RESPONSE: MR. L.: Explained that KBR is restricted by what it can order from the vendor's catalog, but stated that it does strive to provide a constant variety. These changes do take time to implement. We must take into consideration the ordering/delivering time.

QUESTIONS: LTC M.: Compliments the facility as one of the best he has ever seen. He expressed that when he and his soldiers have requested changes, they have been met: larger cups, onion and pineapples on the stir fry bar. He requested better pita bread for the gyros; the current ones tasted bad and fall apart too easily. LTC M. also requested chicken liver and asked if we could discontinue the live band performances. He considered the band to be too loud, and suggested that this may be the wrong forum for it.

RESPONSE: SFC W.: We thank you for your comment, and we will do our best to accommodate your requests.

QUESTION: Requests rye bread, bigger taco shells, and Jell-O without fruit or anything in it. He also stated that the salt and pepper shakers did not dispense enough salt and pepper, and many soldiers would need to unscrew the top to get enough.

RESPONSE: SFC W.: Explains that the shakers have just recently been purchased and that in order to get better ones, the military would have to provide funds to replace the existing salt and pepper shakers.

QUESTIONS: LTC M. expressed that the serving portions are too large.

RESPONSE: MR. L. states that they do train the servers on serving sizes; however, there is a language barrier issue with training the servers.

RESPONSE: SFC W.: The servers are briefed everyday on this issue. It is also put out that a diner should be specific on what he or she wants when at the serving line. The servers are very accommodating toward the diners' needs.

QUESTIONS: LTC M. informs the panel that the soap dispensers are unserviceable, and they have the wrong soap in them.

RESPONSE: MR. L. states that the new dispensers are on order, and that the soap currently used is the right soap for hand washing.

STATEMENT: PFC P.: The music in the dining facility is too loud. The soldiers cannot hear the televisions. I also would like to request more variety of fruit, with an emphasis on strawberries.

RESPONSE: SFC W.: The music issue will be addressed.

RESPONSE: MR. L. replies that travel time limits the type of fruit they can serve. We also can order only items that are available in the catalog.

QUESTIONS: SGT J. requests Spanish flan and more exits during the lunchtime hours as it is too crowded during that time for the one current exit.

RESPONSE: MR. L.: Flan is available almost daily.

QUESTIONS: SGT S.: Why does the DFAC let only the contractors/civilians get only one to-go tray, while military gets three?

RESPONSE: SFC W.: Three to-go trays are the absolute limit, and the policy is not strictly enforced, but there is a policy out there that states that civilians are authorized to dine in and take out only one to-go tray. For all customers, a written memorandum is required in order to take more than three trays. The restrictions are in place to keep the head count accurate.

RESPONSE: MR. L.: Each meal costs about fifty to sixty thousand dollars. KBR supports, but tries to control the cost of the meal while providing whatever it can to help morale. The DFAC gets its funding by a per-patron rate of $17.70 a day [BRK: $3.54 per patron; LUN: $7.08 per patron; DIN: $7.08 per patron].

QUESTIONS: SPC R.: This is for CSM H. What is the policy on having your weapon?

RESPONSE: CSM H.: MNC-I policy requires a weapon on you at all times, except when conducting PT. The guards have been instructed to turn away anyone who does not have their weapon.

QUESTION: LTC M.: Why not use the Air Force to fly fresh fruit and vegetables to the base?

RESPONSE: CSM H.: At this time, this is not feasible.

QUESTION: SGM A.: Can the lobster tails be cut in half?

RESPONSE: MR. L.: Due to the lack of proper equipment, this is not possible.

The advisory council meeting was adjourned at 1615 hours. The next council meeting will be held on 23 June 06.

//ORIGINAL SIGNED//

W. SFC, USA
Senior Food Operation Sergeant 18

Early Days of Brown & Root

IN 1937, LYNDON BAINES JOHNSON, the tall, lanky twenty-eight-year-old son of a five-term Texas state politician, ran for election to the U.S. Congress to represent Austin and the surrounding hill country. His campaign was based on the New Deal platform, a series of government-financed schemes to rebuild the economy after the economic disaster of the Great Depression.[1] LBJ won easily with the help of generous contributions from the Humble and Magnolia oil companies and immediately found himself courted by other local businessmen who wanted him to help them get New Deal dollars for their projects.[2]

George and Herman Brown, brothers and founders of a Houston construction company named Brown & Root that was less than twenty years old, were among the first in line. Before LBJ even left for Washington, he was invited to dinner with the Brown brothers to discuss getting federal money to build the Marshall Ford Dam on the lower Colorado River, the biggest project they had taken on to date.[3] LBJ agreed readily.

Weeks after he arrived in Washington, LBJ secured the money for the dam with the help of President Roosevelt, even though the project violated the work relief program that provided funding for government agencies to hire unskilled labor, rather than private companies hiring skilled labor. ("Give the kid the dam," Roosevelt is reported to have said.)[4]

LBJ and the Browns became friends forever after that day, and Johnson spent many nights at the Browns' house on 4 Niles Road at the edge of downtown Austin.[5] Later in his career, LBJ often visited the Brown Huntland estate in Middleburg, Virginia, where he once suffered a heart attack while on a secret visit in July 1955.[6]

"It was a totally corrupt relationship, and it benefited both of them enormously," said Ronnie Dugger, the author of *The Politician: The Life and Times of Lyndon Johnson.* "Brown & Root got rich, and Johnson got power and riches."[7]

"I remember asking Johnson once in the White House, 'Did you deal with cash?' And he said, 'It was all cash,'" Dugger recalled. "I mean, there were no records, so under those circumstances, there were plenty of politicians who were selling out to business interests."

After LBJ bowed out of the 1968 presidential election because of the immensely unpopular Vietnam War, he often stayed at the Lamar Hotel at 1000 Main Street in downtown Houston. (The building no longer exists; it was razed in 1983.) This hotel was then known as the "unofficial capital of Texas"—some eighty-eight of the hotel's three hundred fifty rooms were rented on a permanent basis by major figures in oil, politics, and banking. In particular, LBJ was a frequent visitor to Suite 8-F, which consisted of two rooms and a kitchenette, rented by Brown & Root.[8]

The room functioned as a meeting place for James Abercrombie (Cameron Iron Works), Hugh R. Cullen (Quintana Petroleum), Morgan J. Davis (Humble Oil), James Elkins (American General Insurance and Pure Oil Pipe Line), William Hobby (governor of Texas and owner of the *Houston Post*), Jesse H. Jones (multimillionaire investor in a large number of organizations and chairman of the Reconstruction Finance Corporation), Albert Thomas (chairman of the House Appropriations Committee), William Vinson (Great Southern Life Insurance), and Gus Wortham (American General Insurance Company).

BUILDING BROWN & ROOT

The Brown brothers did not start out rich. Like LBJ, they grew up in central Texas, where they initially struggled to make a living. Beginning in 1919 with contracts to build Texas roads, Herman Brown and his younger brother, George, a former miner, worked for almost two decades to build a construction business before they would strike it rich. (The name Root comes from Herman's brother-in-law, Daniel, who gave them some of their initial capital, but he was not involved in day-to-day business.)[9]

At first they did numerous small building projects, sometimes even resorting to selling pigs on the side and renting mules for transport to make ends meet. Dan Briody, author of *The Halliburton Agenda,* says the Brown brothers eventually learned how to get ahead in business: "At first, it was just taking out a commissioner for a nice dinner. Then they learned how to submit a low bid, then ratchet up costs over time. Finally, they became adept at the more sophisticated lobbying of public officials."[10]

The Marshall Ford Dam was just the first of many Brown & Root schemes to profit from taxpayer money. Another LBJ biographer Robert Caro reports that the Brown brothers made "an overall profit on the dam of $1.5 million, an amount double all the profit they had made in twenty previous years in the construction business" (roughly equal to $18.3 million in 2008 dollars).[11] And that was just for the first part of the dam; the second phase would net them millions more. George Brown would later explain that LBJ himself described the deals as a "joint venture" in which "Wirtz [Brown & Root's lawyer] is going to take care of the legal part. . . . I'm going to take care of the politics, and you're going to take care of the business side of it. . . . The three of us will come up with a solution that improves the status of all three of us."[12]

Dam building was quickly followed by more ambitious projects. In the spring of 1941, Albert Thomas, a U.S. Congressman from Houston who had gone to school with George Brown, helped them take over a contract from Platzer Boat Works to build what would eventually number 359 warships for the Second World War. This boom was worth $357 million at a facility on the Houston Ship Channel.[13]

What was remarkable about both the Marshall Ford Dam and the shipbuilding job was that the company had no experience in either field before they won the contracts; it was all based on lobbying the right politicians like LBJ and Albert Thomas. "We didn't know the stern from the aft—I mean the bow of the boat," George Brown would confess later about the shipbuilding deal.[14]

LBJ's support for Brown & Root in Washington was deeply appreciated by the Brown brothers. On May 2, 1939, George Brown wrote LBJ a letter: "I hope you know, Lyndon, how I feel reverence to what you have done for me, and I am going to try to show my appreciation through the years to come with actions rather than words if I can find out when and where I can return at least a portion of the favors."[15]

A few months later, he followed up with another letter dated October 27, 1939: "Dear Lyndon, In the past I have not been very timid about asking you to do favors for me and hope that you will not get any timidity if you have anything at all that you think I can or should do. Remember that I am for you, right or wrong, and it makes no difference whether you think I am right or wrong. If you want it, I am for it 100 percent."[16]

On February 27, 1940, LBJ replied, "I wish I could dictate as sweet a letter as you wrote me. . . . I really enjoyed being with Herman this time. . . . We had a lot of heart-to-heart talks and, I believe, know each other a lot better now. Knowing is believing, you know."[17]

That month, Brown & Root won a contract to build the Naval Air Station Corpus Christi, which was initially estimated to cost $23.4 million. James Forrestal, the undersecretary of the navy would later say that he "twisted a helluva lot of tails" to make sure that the contract would be awarded to one of "Lyndon's friends." George Brown himself would later acknowledge that LBJ helped them win the contract that was billed at "cost-plus," which meant that the company was paid a guaranteed profit on every dollar spent. When the project was finished, it had cost the taxpayer $125 million, making for a sizeable profit for Brown & Root.[18]

Briody explained that by the Second World War, the Brown brothers had become experts at getting taxpayer money: "The Browns knew then something that most government contractors understand now: Ninety percent of the work in government contracting is getting the job. Once you have the contract in hand, prices can be systematically ratcheted up and the government's costs for switching contracts midstream exceed the cost increases being handed down by the current contractor."[19]

Over the next three decades, the company went from strength to strength. They won contracts to construct air and naval bases in Guam, France, and Spain for the U.S. government worth $553 million altogether. In 1961, the company won the contract for the $200 million Manned Spacecraft Center, in Houston, and finally a $1.9 billion contract to build bases in Vietnam. Most of these contracts have been linked back to their ties with LBJ.[20]

(Construction projects were not the only way the Brown brothers profited at taxpayer expense—in 1947 they led a group of investors who put up $150,000 to acquire the Big Inch and Little Big Inch pipelines that the federal government had constructed to transport oil from Texas to the northeastern states after German submarines started to sink East Coast oil tankers. The pipelines were later incorporated as the Texas Eastern Transmission Corporation. When they offered an initial public offering, the brothers alone cleared some $2.7 million. Over the next four decades, Texas Eastern Transmission Corporation would supply Brown & Root with $1.3 billion in business.)[21]

BAGS OF MONEY

LBJ's ties to Brown & Root were well known and often remarked upon in the press. In August 1964, William Lambert and Keith Wheeler penned a lampoon of LBJ and President John F. Kennedy in *Life* magazine. Kennedy is described saying: "Now, Lyndon, I guess we can dig that tunnel to the Vatican." LBJ replies: "Okay, so long as Brown & Root gets the contract."[22]

The reason that LBJ was so helpful to Brown & Root was simply because they were very helpful to his political career. In addition to organizing rallies for their candidate, the Brown brothers reportedly began putting money into LBJ's campaigns in 1938, the year he ran for reelection to the U.S. House of

Representatives. Although citizens were not allowed to contribute to individual politicians, the Brown brothers created a group called Brown & Root for the Committee. This was the Democratic Congressional Campaign Committee to which LBJ was an informal advisor. Company employees and friends put in the maximum of $5,000 each, which LBJ then doled out to candidates around the country, buying future loyalty.[23]

Similar tactics were used to raise money for LBJ's 1941 U.S. Senate run. "Bags of cash, envelopes stuffed with $100 bills, accounting sleight-of-hand; all conceivable techniques of hiding the destination of the Brown's money were employed," writes Briody. "Lawyers would take bonuses from the Browns, pay the money to someone else in the law firm, take it back in cash, and give it away to the campaign." The bonuses also had the happy outcome of lowering company tax payments.[24]

LBJ lost the 1941 Senate bid, despite a campaign that was rumored to have cost as much as $500,000 (the limit at the time was $25,000). The lavish spending did not go unnoticed. In July 1942, the Internal Revenue Service (IRS) started an investigation into Brown & Root's books for tax evasion and criminal wrongdoing in funneling money to the campaign. What became quite clear, after eighteen months of investigations that involved testimony from senior executives, was that the company might be prosecuted. So LBJ asked for an audience with then President Franklin Delano Roosevelt on January 13, 1944, to discuss the matter. The next day, a new IRS agent was assigned to the case, who recommended a $549,972 fine for tax evasion and dropped the criminal charges.[25]

But Brown & Root allegedly continued to finance LBJ when he ran again for the U.S. Senate and won in 1948, after a primary battle that was widely considered to have been rigged. "That was the turning point. He wouldn't have been in the running without Brown & Root's money and airplanes. And the 1948 election allowed Lyndon to become president," says Dugger.[26]

Caro describes the aftermath of the 1948 U.S. Senate election: "Johnson flew back to Texas on the private plane of Brown & Root, the giant Texas construction company. When the Brown & Root plane delivered him to Texas, it delivered him first to Houston, where a Brown & Root limousine met him and took him to the Brown & Root suite in the Lamar Hotel. Waiting for him there, in Suite 8-F, were men who really mattered in Texas: Herman and George Brown, of course, oilman Jim Abercrombie, and insurance magnate Gus Wortham. And during the two months he spent in Texas thereafter, the senator spent time at Brown & Root's hunting camp at Falfurrias and in oilman Sid Richardson's suite in the Fort Worth Club."[27]

In the 1950s, LBJ went to Falfurrias to pitch for money. "I want to tell you fellows something. I'm thinking of running for president, and if I do, it's going to cost all of you a lot of money. So I want you to think about it." The Suite 8-F crowd ponied up. Ed Clark, a Brown & Root lawyer, would later tell Caro: "They would contribute substantially as hell if their friend, somebody who had helped them, had a political campaign."[28]

Decades later, telephone transcripts made public would clearly show that for more than twenty years the Brown brothers had indeed been contributing illegally to the campaign coffers of LBJ and his colleagues. "I have some money that I want to know what to do with. . . . I was wondering . . . just who should be getting it, and I will be collecting more from time to time," said George Brown in a conversation recorded with LBJ in January 1960 when his friend was U.S. Senate majority leader.[29]

ERLE HALLIBURTON

At the time that the Brown brothers set up Brown & Root, another Texas multinational was taking shape, founded on the new oil boom that was taking the country by storm. Although oil had first been struck in the 1860s, it wasn't until mass production of automobiles in the first decade of the twentieth century that gasoline (then a by-product of kerosene, which was used for stove fuel) would literally fuel a drilling frenzy in Oklahoma and Texas.

Erle Palmer Halliburton, of Henning, Tennessee, was a young jack-of-all-trades who landed a job working for Almond Perkins at the Perkins Oil Well Cementing Company in California in 1916.[30] There he learned how to use a technique called "oil well cementing" to protect the wells from contamination by underground water and lessen the danger of explosions from high pressure oil and gas. Basically a wet cement slurry was pumped down a pipe into a well under high pressure and forced up the gap between the wall of the hole and the pipe where it hardened. But Perkins fired Halliburton, and the young man traveled back East where he tried to sell the technique in Texas. Unable to get any customers, Halliburton moved his operations to Oklahoma where he quickly won business when he capped a well for the Skelly Oil Company, saving them millions in wasted crude.[31]

By 1921, Halliburton was dispatching crews and equipment to drilling sites in Arkansas and Louisiana from his headquarters in the town of Duncan, Oklahoma. Although he would later have to buy out Perkins for "borrowing" the techniques of oil well cementing, he deserves credit for improving upon the original idea. (He would be quoted as saying: "Don't ever tell me I cannot do something because it will infringe on somebody's patent. I started in business infringing.")[32] Halliburton followed up with a number of future inventions that the oil industry would come to rely upon such as the jet mixer—

a mechanized mixer that did away with hand-mixing of the minimum 250 bags of cement-and-water slurry needed for each well.[33]

In 1924, he incorporated as the Halliburton Oil Well Cementing Company or Howco. By 1926, the company was exporting cementing trucks to British companies, and by 1929, the company was using planes to deliver on contracts. In 1932, Howco was sending a total of seventy-five cementing and well-testing crews in red Halliburton trucks to sites in seven states. In 1940, Howco expanded overseas with the establishment of its first South American subsidiary in Venezuela.[34]

When the United States entered the Second World War, Howco joined the war effort like most other U.S. industries. Its oil drilling services were useful for a military that needed vast quantities of fuel for their operations. The company also used its expertise in the cement business to develop a soil/cement process that was used by the air force to make landing strips. Another technique that the company used for oil drilling was called "gun perforating" in which it lowered a cylindrical device into cemented oil wells to blast holes in the walls to allow the oil to flow. The company's engineering shops that built this equipment were easy to modify to build gun-mount bearings. Its engineering workshops were also soon turning out jigs, fixtures, and dies for the B-29 bomber as well as for the Boeing airplane plant in Wichita, Kansas.[35] Halliburton himself loaned his yacht (the Vida, named after his wife) to the navy to use as a weather station in the Pacific.[36]

When the war was over, Halliburton returned to its core work of designing and acquiring specialized equipment for the oil industry such as Hydrafrac in the late 1940s, which used jellied gasoline pumped under pressure into the bottom of a well to split the rock formation and rejuvenate many dwindling oil wells. The company rented and sold tools to obtain fluids and pressure readings from oil-bearing rock, wall cleaners, depth measuring equipment, and on-site services such as electronic logging and sidewall wellcoring and the transporting of cement and fracturing sands to drilling sites.[37]

The company soon outgrew Duncan, and Halliburton moved its headquarters to Dallas, Texas. By the time Erle Halliburton died in 1957, he had become one of the ten richest people in the United States.[38] The company continued to expand, however, making forays into new businesses such as airlines.

In 1962, shortly after Herman Brown died, Halliburton acquired Brown & Root. George Brown stayed on as chairman of the company until the end of the Vietnam War in 1975, after which he retired.[39] The new subsidiary would still operate under its own name for another three decades, until Dick Cheney became CEO of Halliburton and acquired Kellogg Industries, a competitor, and merged the two to create Kellogg, Brown & Root.

3

Brothers in Arms
Dick Cheney and Donald Rumsfeld

ON WEDNESDAY, MAY 11, 1966, a Fairchild C-123 "Provider" aircraft touched down on a newly installed, temporary runway in southern Vietnam. Once the VIP plane—originally designed as an assault glider aircraft—had rumbled to a halt, its distinguished cargo of six U.S. Congressmen, Agency for International Development (AID), and military officials disembarked. They were promptly whisked away by a Huey helicopter. It was 9 a.m. at Cam Ranh Bay, but 11 p.m. in Washington, DC, the city from which the group had departed five days prior on United Airlines flight 53.[1]

The Congressional delegation was led by John Moss of Sacramento, the Democratic chairman of the foreign operations and government information subcommittee of the House committee on government operations. (Moss was best known as the author of the Freedom of Information Act, and would later be known for chairing hearings on federal contracting abuses and then for initiating the call to impeach President Richard Nixon.)[2]

The youngest member of the group was Donald Rumsfeld, already on his second term in the U.S. House of Representatives from the state of Illinois, at the tender age of thirty-three. He was also one of just two Republicans (they were the minority party at the time) on the trip and it would be his first opportunity to see the work of Halliburton up close.[3]

Over the next three hours, the group listened intently as Major General Charles Eifler, the commanding general of the First Logistical Command, gave them a whistle-stop jeep and helicopter tour of a new base that was being constructed on what has been described as the most beautiful deepwater port facility in the entire world. A shimmering blue inlet of the South China Sea on the central coast of southeastern Vietnam, situated between the towns of Phan

Rang and Nha Trang, the facility stretched some ten miles long and twenty miles wide and was protected by a three-hundred-foot-high sand peninsula. A mile-wide strait linked it to the open ocean, allowing large ships to sail into the natural harbor and making it an ideal military base for the region.[4]

Hundreds of construction workers were laboring to transform the land around the bay that held two picturesque fishing villages, tropical scrub forest, and miles of perfect beaches into a major military supply installation practically overnight—a 1960s equivalent of LSA Anaconda. The workers were employed by a consortium named RMK-BRJ that was led by Brown & Root, the newly acquired subsidiary of Halliburton. (The acronym stood for Raymond/Morrison-Knudsen, Brown & Root, and J. A. Jones Construction.) RMK-BRJ was the sole contractor for the federal government for military construction projects in Vietnam, accounting for about 90 percent of the total share of all work.[5]

Building the base at Cam Ranh Bay was no easy task. The previous fall, construction crews worked through the rainy season to construct the very airfield that the Provider had landed on from the drift sand of the Cam Ranh Bay's central peninsula. The crews built a ten-thousand-foot aluminum mat runway, a parallel taxiway, an aluminum mat fighter apron, and a pierced steel plank cargo apron together with twenty-five thousand square feet of living quarters composed of Quonset huts (a military design invented by the British) that would house troops arriving from the U.S. Air Force. A million cubic yards of earth were moved by a workforce of U.S., Korean, Filipino, and Vietnamese workers. Following the construction of the landing strip, the consortium began work on a vast ammunition storage and the Dong Nai dredge arrived to build a U.S. Army port facility. Meanwhile, twenty miles away to the north, the crews were busy expanding a special forces airbase and an army field hospital at Nha Trang, just another of the two dozen major military installations that the company would build in the course of the decade.

Rumsfeld and his colleagues could not have arrived at a more chaotic time. That very week, workers on the Bess dredge had to abandon a project to place fill behind an army-troop-constructed bulkhead after excavating 120,000 cubic yards because the backwash was so great. An order to drill forty-two water wells had just been signed, and word had come through that yet another major order was about to be inked to build a new naval communications facility over three sites along the east coast of the peninsula.

After the tour of the port facilities in Cam Ranh Bay, the Moss delegation flew on to view the police training and civilian pacification programs in Vung Tau at the mouth of the Saigon River before returning to conduct hearings at the U.S. Agency for International Development (USAID) building in Saigon.

It took another two years for the Cam Ranh Bay military base to be finished, transformed from endless acres of "unbroken sand dunes" into an international air and sea terminal with substantial deep draft berth facilities, ample warehouse space, and many miles of new roads, including a new causeway.[6]

REINVENTING VIETNAM

U.S. military operations in Vietnam date back as far as 1950, when Washington began supplying small arms to the French military to combat communist expansion after the Second World War. This escalated in the late 1950s when the Chinese-supported North Vietnamese government ordered a military insurgency against the U.S.-supported South Vietnamese government.[7]

At the same time, the Soviet Union was expanding its sphere of influence with the takeover of Hungary in 1956 and the building of the Berlin Wall in 1961, putting pressure on U.S. politicians like President John F. Kennedy to pledge in his inaugural address to "pay any price, bear any burden, meet any hardship, support any friend, oppose any foe, in order to assure the survival and success of liberty."[8]

LBJ, who was Kennedy's vice president, flew to Saigon in May 1961 to declare support for the South Vietnamese government, and Washington began to send increasingly more "military advisors."[9] Raymond/Morrison-Knudsen was hired to help build bases with the U.S. Navy under a $15 million deal signed in San Bruno, California, on January 19, 1962.[10]

When Kennedy was assassinated in Dallas, Texas, in November 1963, LBJ took over the reins of government and continued the expansion of the war effort. On August 2, 1964, the USS *Maddox*, on an intelligence mission along North Vietnam's coast, reported that it had been fired upon by three North Vietnamese torpedo boats in the Gulf of Tonkin. Two days later, a second attack was reported on the USS *Maddox* as well as the USS *Turner Joy*.[11]

Coincidentally, these attacks occurred during the last few months before the presidential election. LBJ asked the U.S. Congress to approve a resolution "expressing the unity and determination of the United States in supporting freedom and in protecting peace in Southeast Asia . . . (that should express support) for all necessary action to protect our Armed Forces."

On August 6, Secretary of Defense Robert S. McNamara testified before a joint session of the Senate Foreign Relations and Armed Services committees, in which he stated that the *Maddox* had been "carrying out a routine mission of the type we carry out all over the world at all times." This was later revealed to be a lie. (The United States had been supporting covert operations of South Vietnamese commandos under a secret program called Operation Plan 34A.)

On August 7, 1964, the U.S. Congress voted unanimously to approve a joint resolution that authorized the president "to take all necessary steps, including the use of armed force, to assist any member or protocol state of the Southeast Asia Collective Defense Treaty requesting assistance in defense of its freedom" without consulting the U.S. Senate, as required by law.[12]

(Almost forty years later, on February 5, 2003, Secretary of State Colin Powell would repeat history in a speech to the United Nations in which he would lay out the case for war on Iraq: "Leaving Saddam Hussein in possession of weapons of mass destruction for a few more months or years is not an option," he told the international diplomats. The passage of time showed both McNamara and Powell had misled their audiences in order to make the case for war: LBJ tapes made public in 2005 proved that he knew that the Gulf of Tonkin incidents never happened.[13] That same year, Powell admitted that the speech was a "blot" on his personal record but claimed that he honestly believed the evidence he was given.[14])

Combat troops were rushed to Vietnam following the Gulf of Tonkin resolution; the covert support for the South Vietnamese was quickly turned into a full-blown war. From a mere sixteen thousand troops in mid-1964, the military had increased troops in the country to a quarter of a million by May 1966. Operation Rolling Thunder had been in effect for more than a year: an aerial bombing campaign was designed to destroy bridges, air defenses, and supply depots and was intended to destroy the will of the North Vietnamese to fight and to stop the flow of men and supplies down the Ho Chi Minh Trail.[15]

This sophisticated U.S. military operation that required fighter planes and radio technology was just not feasible in what was still principally a land of rice paddies and water buffaloes. So, as Secretary of Defense McNamara explained to U.S. Senate committee members, waging war "in a country of this sort requires the construction of new ports, warehouse facilities, access roads, improvements to highways leading to the interior of the country and along the coasts, troop facilities, hospitals, completely new airfields, and major improvements to existing airfields, communications facilities, etc."[16]

The U.S. Congress was convinced, and in 1966 it appropriated $1.4 billion for construction to be paid out to RMK-BRJ who grandly named themselves the "Vietnam Builders." Soon the consortium changed the very landscape of the country, according to James Carter, assistant professor of history at Texas A&M University—whose excellent book *Inventing Vietnam* is a comprehensive account of the Vietnam Builders.[17] Paul Harder, a photojournalist who visited the country at the time, described all of the activity in South Vietnam in 1967 as a "paradox of construction and destruction . . . Motor grader operators work with loaded carbines at their sides; . . . scrapers cut roads across the shadows of hastily prepared gun emplacements; a lean, tanned construction superintendent waxes enthusiastic over the future while helicopters stutter overhead looking for enemy guerillas."[18]

Cam Ranh Bay was just one of many projects that RMK-BRJ was hired to build in order to provide the infrastructure for prolonged military operations in Vietnam. The subcontractors that Brown & Root hired were primarily engineers and did not cook and clean or manage airlines and truck convoys as they would in Afghanistan and Iraq almost four decades later.

Over the life of the contract, the consortium boasted that it moved 91 million cubic yards of earth, used 48 million tons of rock product, nearly 11 million tons of asphalt, poured 3.7 million yards of concrete, enough to have built a wall two feet wide and five feet high completely around southern Vietnam, and moved an average of more than 500,000 tons of goods every month. A total of 150 million board feet of lumber, 3,600 prefabricated buildings, 11 million pounds of nails, 750,000 sheets of plywood, 98 million pounds of asphalt, plus nearly 2,000 trucks and tractors were used in the construction.[19]

Brown & Root's consortium negotiated a special payment system for themselves, changing from the standard cost-plus-fixed-fee (CPFF) type to a cost-plus-award-fee (CPAF) type. This allowed the Builders to earn an extra award of up to four-ninths of the fixed fee based on how well the job was done. For example, one specific project in 1966 cost $57 million. The base fee for the job was $975,000, and the maximum award fee was $433,000, which allowed the contractor to get a maximum profit of $1.4 million.[20]

Meanwhile, the escalating military operations conducted from the bases built by Brown & Root's consortium included sustained bombing campaigns in the countryside, which soon made life hell in rural Vietnam and caused villagers to flee to the cities. Once a nation of farmers and a leading rice exporter, South Vietnam went from a population of about 15 percent to 40 percent urban dwellers in the mid-1960s, and by the end of the war, it had become 65 percent urban. The country had to import nearly 500,000 tons of rice to feed its people, and 750,000 tons in 1967.[21] (The Moss delegation blamed this on the success of the Viet Cong in intercepting rice shipments from the Mekong Delta to Saigon and other cities.) A Senate subcommittee chaired by Senator Edward Kennedy suggested in 1965 that the war had resulted in 380,000 to 500,000 refugees; in 1966 this estimate had risen to 1.6 million, and on the eve of the Tet Offensive of early 1968, analysts estimated the number of uprooted Vietnamese had grown to approximately 4 million, or one out of four Vietnamese below the seventeenth parallel.[22]

The conditions under which the Vietnamese lived were wretched: a survey in 1967 revealed the rate of civilian war casualties ran at approximately one hundred thousand per year. A USAID public health official estimated that there was just one qualified doctor for every one hundred thousand inhabitants compared to one for every eighty-five hundred in nearby Thailand and one to every seven hundred fifty people in the United States. As a result, many of those injured and crippled by war received either inadequate medical aid or none at all. The number of cases of cholera in South Vietnam increased from a few hundred in 1963 to more than twenty thousand by 1965. A Congressional investigation concluded similarly: "The situation in South Vietnam is that there is just too much disease and too great a demand for medical services. Almost every disease known to man is present." [23] By 1968, an estimated thirty thousand to fifty thousand amputees awaited prosthetics that they would likely never receive. Another fifty thousand or more civilian war victims died each year before reaching understaffed, underfunded, and overcrowded hospitals.

Ironically, in the same time period that Brown & Root's consortium was paid $1.4 billion, historian Carter calculated that Vietnamese war refugees received a scant $22.5 million in aid, of which all but $3 million was actually designated for U.S. government official salaries, equipment, and logistics.[24]

"WASTE AND PROFITEERING"

When Rumsfeld returned to Washington, DC, in May 1966, he was more concerned that Brown & Root's projects seemed to be a payoff for financing LBJ, than with the plight of Vietnamese refugees. Three months after the delegation returned, Rumsfeld announced to his fellow politicians that the administration had signed contracts that were "illegal by statute." He urged a high-level probe into the "thirty-year association—personal and political—between LBJ as congressman, senator, vice president, and president" and the company's chairman, George Brown of Houston, who "had contributed $23,000 to the President's Club while the Congress was considering" whether to award yet another multimillion-dollar project to Brown & Root.[25] (Club membership could be bought for $1,000 in those days.)[26]

Rumsfeld noted that "under one contract, between the U.S. government and this combine, it is officially estimated that obligations will reach at least $900 million by November 1967. . . . Why this huge contract has not been and is not now being adequately audited is beyond me. The potential for waste and profiteering under such a contract is substantial."

When the subcommittee's full report from their investigations into how taxpayer dollars were being spent in Vietnam was delivered in October, Rumsfeld, together with fellow Republican subcommittee member Bob Dole of Kansas, issued a stinging, dissenting opinion, much to the dismay of Moss, who said he "confess[ed] disquiet over the negative tenor of my colleagues."

One quote from the Dole/Rumsfeld letter stands out: "I want this record and you gentlemen to know how disappointed I was at the discussions in Vietnam with AID personnel. Invariably the reason [our questions] could not be answered was because of the lack of records, the lack of audits, the lack of procedures whereby this information would be available. . . . I got the feeling . . . that the information is not available. . . . It is distressing for a . . . member of a subcommittee to be attempting to come to grips with these problems, and to be repeatedly told that necessary and basic information is not available."[27]

The $900 million turned out to be an underestimate. When the job was finished, the final bill for the ten-year-long "construction miracle of the decade" came to a cool $1.9 billion. And the General Accounting Office (GAO) discovered that over the course of the war, Halliburton/Brown & Root had lost accounting control of $120 million, and its security was so poor that millions of dollars worth of equipment had been stolen.[28]

The words of the junior Republican politician in the 1966 critique would sound remarkably familiar, indeed almost identical to those of Halliburton's critics from the Democratic Party following the invasion of Iraq in 2003.

PARALLEL CAREERS

Soon after Rumsfeld returned from Vietnam, he met a young intern who would eventually become his boss and paradoxically put the two men in the same position as LBJ: hiring Halliburton to help them support an unprovoked war. That man is, of course, Dick Cheney, and a brief review of the lives of the two men would show them to have followed a surprisingly similar path.

Both men dropped out of graduate school to work on Capitol Hill; both men married high-school sweethearts to whom they are still attached; both men served in the U.S. House of Representatives for several terms where they were known for their political conservativeness; both men served as chief of staff in the White House and as secretary of defense; both initiated campaigns to run for president; and both led invasions of Iraq. Both men also ran Fortune 500 companies in which they challenged the government of the time to open up markets that would make them millionaires many times over.

But the two men are also quite different in many ways. Rumsfeld was a wrestling champion who served in the military, unlike Cheney, who wriggled out of the draft. Cheney's career both as a businessman and as head of the Pentagon could arguably be characterized as mediocre by his critics, if not problematic. Where Rumsfeld's press conferences and speeches attracted media attention, Cheney shied away from publicity unless he really had no choice.

DONALD RUMSFELD

Donald Henry Rumsfeld was born on July 9, 1932, in Evanston, Illinois, and grew up in Winnetka, Illinois, on the North Shore of Chicago that borders Lake Michigan. His father, a real estate salesman, enlisted late in life into the navy at the age of thirty-eight, toward the end of the Second World War, when Donald was eight. The family then spent several years traveling from one military base to the next, ranging from North Carolina to California and Washington State, giving Donald an early glimpse into the government agency he would eventually run.[29]

The younger Rumsfeld studied at Princeton on a military scholarship, and then joined the navy in 1954. After he left the navy in 1957, he dabbled with the idea of a law career at Georgetown University in Washington, DC, but ended up working as an aide on Capitol Hill. Enamored by political life, he decided to try his chances in 1962, and despite his relative obscurity and youth, won a seat in the U.S. House of Representatives, with the help of his old schoolmates and the financial backing of local businessman Dan Searle, whose family owned the pharmaceutical giant GD Searle.

There are two sports that observers say explain Rumsfeld and his career: one is wrestling and the other is squash. Wrestling was something he took up early and helped him to distinguish himself at high school. He was then a wrestler at Princeton, and, finally, when he signed up for the navy in 1954, he won the title of All Navy Wrestling Champion.[30]

At Princeton, Rumsfeld was famous for his conditioning and determination (he would do one-armed push-ups for money) but especially as a relentless bulldog who never gave up. Roger Olsen, who co-wrote a book called *The Turning Point* about the 1953 wrestling season, explained to a *New Yorker* writer, "They've always built Rumsfeld up as being a great wrestler. . . . But he wasn't. Rumsfeld, I think, was just a plugger. He would keep coming after you, even when the final verdict was no longer in doubt."[31]

Two other wrestlers—Phil Harvey and Ken Hunt—told the magazine a story of a legendary fight between Rumsfeld and Hunt in the finals of the Eastern Intercollegiate championship in 1953. "The gym was packed—people were right down on the mats," Hunt said, "almost like the kids at Duke basketball games. It was quite a jovial get-together. But Don was quite serious. Even in those days, gosh, he was a very intense guy. . . . I think I was ahead eight-zip or eight-two," Hunt said. "And then I began to run out of gas. I had the feeling that he could taste blood, you know, if he could get me real tired—and I was getting tired."

Then Rumsfeld began "reversing" Hunt. "He exploited every possible tool," Hunt said. "I frankly don't remember the end of it. One of my best friends from high school was at the edge of the mat there, and I remember him saying, 'One more minute!' Don may have gotten one takedown toward the end—gosh, I don't remember. He had sheer will and determination."[32]

Rumsfeld took up squash when he worked in corporate America. He played it in a similar fashion to how he wrestled during his college days—relentlessly. Pretty much every day for six years, when he was running the Pentagon under President George W. Bush, he would take an hour off work in the afternoon, change into a T-shirt, sweats, and a headband, and play squash.

Rumsfeld plays a variation of the game known as "hardball," which requires less running and more quick hitting. "I think what struck me most was that Don never gave up on a point," wrote David Hiller, publisher of the *Los Angeles Times*. "His view was that every shot could be made, every game could be won, and he never surrendered until the last volley was played out. With me, he was usually right."[33]

"He hits the ball well, but he doesn't play by the rules," Chris Zimmerman, a Pentagon official in department of program analysis and evaluation, told the *New York Times*, noting that his boss would fail to get out of the way after hitting the ball, thwarting his opponent. (Zimmerman did not play with Rumsfeld but was often at the courts at the same time.)[34]

"There, no matter how the war in Iraq was going or how many Democrats were calling for his head, Mr. Rumsfeld could uncork his deadly drop shot, leaving his foe helpless and himself triumphant, at least for a moment," wrote David Cloud in the *New York Times*.

"In some ways, squash offers a window into Mr. Rumsfeld's complicated psyche, revealing much about his stubborn competitiveness and seemingly limitless stamina. Pentagon officials and employees say Mr. Rumsfeld's play closely resembles the way he has run the Defense Department, where he has spent six years trying to break the accepted modes of operating."

Indeed Rumsfeld himself has said that his military plans for invading Iraq were influenced by his squash playing. The same could be said of his political career. While in the U.S. Congress in the 1960s, he played hardball with the Democrats, challenging them relentlessly as he did on the Moss delegation, attracting a loyal group of young Republican followers on the Hill who were known as "Rumsfeld's Raiders."[35] This aggressive style also won the devotion of a quiet intern, Dick Cheney, who would work for Rumsfeld as an aide, then as a protégé, and eventually become a friend and, finally, Rumsfeld's boss.

RICHARD BRUCE CHENEY

Richard Bruce Cheney was born on January 30, 1941, in Lincoln, Nebraska, to a middle-class family like Rumsfeld's. But unlike his future mentor Cheney did not seek a military scholarship to get into an Ivy League college. Instead, he was sponsored by a local businessman named Thomas Stroock who introduced him to Yale. And, also unlike Rumsfeld, he did not do well, spending more of his time partying it up, drinking Thunderbird wine and Schaefer and Teals's beer ("Schaefer is the one beer to have when you're having more than one" went the jingle at the time). He got into trouble for playing pranks like throwing water balloons and disrupting the film society. Kicked out twice for poor grades, he initially gave up school to work in Wyoming as a groundman to lay power lines. His job was helping the "powder monkeys" who would transport explosives to blast rocks.[36] There he started to develop a serious smoking and drinking habit and was arrested twice for driving under the influence, once in Cheyenne and then in Rock Springs.[37]

Stephen Hayes, author of Cheney's biography, tells the story of how the future vice president sobered up after a night spent in the Rock Springs jail in June 1963, following the second run-in with the police, and less than four years after he started school at Yale. At the same time he was under pressure from his girlfriend, Lynne Vincent, who had graduated early from Colorado College with the highest honors, who let him know that he would have to finish school if he wanted to marry her. Cheney picked himself up, enrolled at Casper College in Wyoming, and finished his undergraduate degree. He then moved to Madison where he started doctoral studies in political science at the University of Wisconsin. He married Vincent and used his college attendance and eventually the birth of his first child to obtain five deferments from the draft.[38] (Rumsfeld did serve in the military but escaped serving overseas because he was too young to deploy to Korea and too old to serve in Vietnam, while most men of Cheney's age had to sign up for service and were often sent to Southeast Asia.)

While at school in Wisconsin, Cheney got an American Political Science Association fellowship to be an intern in Washington, DC, which brought him to live in the nation's capital just months after the assassination of Robert F. Kennedy in 1968. At twenty-seven, he was already older than most of the other interns, but he was determined to stay. He applied for a job with Rumsfeld, but the interview was a disaster. "It was one of the more unpleasant experiences of my life," Cheney would recall later. "The truth is I flunked the interview. After half an hour, it was clear to both of us that there was no possibility that I could work for him."[39]

He went to work, instead, for Bill Steiger, a U.S. Congressman from Wisconsin. Less than a year later, however, Cheney got another chance to work for Rumsfeld, an opportunity of his own making that would transform his career, propelling him swiftly into the White House, and starting a long political partnership that continues to this day. It began when he saw a notice on Steiger's desk from Rumsfeld looking for advice on an agency called the Office of

Economic Opportunity (OEO), a special office set up as part of Lyndon B. Johnson's War on Poverty. Rumsfeld was the newly appointed director of this agency, having resigned from his position in the U.S. Congress.[40]

The agency was not what one might have expected a conservative politician to want to work in: It provided grants to community-based programs such as the Middle Kentucky River Area Development Council and the East Oakland-Fruitvale Planning Council in California, groups filled with radical activists who were involved in the anti-war movement. But, indeed, that is exactly why President Nixon hired Rumsfeld; he figured that the abrasive politician would make short work of the trouble-causers.

Cheney dashed off a memo, suggesting close evaluations of each project, which caught Rumsfeld's eye and then had him summoned to the OEO office, which was in a rundown office building on 19th and M street in downtown Washington. When Cheney walked in for his second job interview with Rumsfeld, he noticed the rusty buckets arrayed in the room to catch rainwater as it dripped from the leaky ceiling. It was a very short meeting. "[Rumsfeld] didn't say: 'Hey, I liked your memo' or 'Would you like to come work for me?'" Cheney would later tell Hayes, his biographer. "He said: 'You, you're Congressional relations. Now get the hell out of here.'"[41]

Unexciting though the job was, it turned out to be Cheney's lucky break. He did Rumsfeld's dirty work, investigating radical programs and helping shut them down. By hitching his wagon to Rumsfeld at that crucial time in history, Cheney would quickly go straight to the top, bypassing the normal climb up the ladder.

It was tough going working for Rumsfeld, but Cheney persevered. A biographer would later write: "Rumsfeld was swaggering and super-ambitious, an ex-fighter pilot who would greet subordinates visiting his office with lines like 'You've got thirty seconds!' and would relentlessly needle the people working for him. 'Speak up, Dick! Don't talk into your sleeve!' he'd say to the very green Cheney when he'd go into his Western mumble in staff meetings."[42]

Two years after he took on the OEO, Rumsfeld was given another thankless job for a conservative: running a new agency called the Cost of Living Council that Nixon created to impose price freezes in order to stem rising inflation. By coincidence, Rumsfeld had written his senior thesis at Princeton about what happened when Truman seized the steel mills in the 1950s for refusing to accept the rulings of the Wage Stabilization Board. (The decision backfired on Truman when the Supreme Court ruled to limit the power of the president in 1952.)[43]

Rumsfeld was aghast when he was offered the job. "I don't agree with it; I don't believe in wage or price controls; I'm a market man," he told George

Shultz, who had been instructed to offer him the job. Shultz informed him that was precisely why they wanted him to do it.[44]

And so on Thursday, November 11, 1971, Rumsfeld and his crew worked through the night to draw up a list of what products would have price controls and what would not—the very antithesis of their own political beliefs. Cheney was assigned the job of typist for the twelve-page list that divided every product available in stores at the time into the two groups. For example garden plants, raw honey, and unpopped corn were exempt from price controls, but floral wreaths, processed honey, and popped popcorn were not. Cheney was not as upset as Rumsfeld about having to do the project; he says he simply followed orders. "At the time I didn't think much about it. Nixon had done it, so we were going to make it work."

When this list was finished, Cheney was put in charge of a small army of three thousand Internal Revenue Service agents who were to investigate and punish offenders, such as nine grain workers in Chicago who had been given pay raises above the 5.5 percent allowed under the law. The experience had a major effect on Cheney.

"I became a great skeptic about the whole notion of wage-price controls," he told Hayes. "The idea that you could write detailed regulations that were going to govern all aspects of the economy as big as the U.S. economy is loopy. . . . You know, all of a sudden the price of a hamburger was our problem."[45]

But doing Nixon's dirty work would give Rumsfeld and his sidekick much needed political experience for their résumés. Rumsfeld then got another unwelcome but lucky break. Nixon decided that Rumsfeld was getting too ambitious (Rumsfeld wanted to be vice president), so Nixon banished him to Brussels to serve as ambassador to the North Atlantic Treaty Organization (NATO). Although Rumsfeld was unhappy about this move, it allowed him a safe haven when politicians like Moss moved against Nixon in 1973.[46]

THE FORD ADMINISTRATION

On August 9, 1974, Dick Cheney, who had left government, when Rumsfeld departed for Brussels, was glued to the television like millions of other U.S. citizens, watching Nixon bid farewell to the White House. Partway through, Cheney left the live broadcast, got into his 1965 Volkswagen, and drove to the Dulles airport to meet his former boss who had returned under invitation from Gerald Ford to help lead the transition to a new administration. Cheney drove Rumsfeld back to Washington, where they harvested the fruit of the unexpected turn of events.[47]

As two of the very few Republican stalwarts who were close to Nixon but untainted by the Watergate scandal, Rumsfeld and Cheney were extremely valuable to the new president, Gerald R. Ford. By late September, Rumsfeld was asked by Ford to become chief of staff, and he, in turn, asked if Cheney could share his job as a special "consultant." (Officially they used the terms staff coordinator and deputy staff coordinator because Rumsfeld did not like the term chief of staff). From then on, Rumsfeld and Cheney became a team working in Ford's inner circle to the anger of other Republicans who felt pushed aside.

It was a political ascent akin to a miracle. It had been little more than thirteen years since Cheney had been kicked out of Yale, eleven years since his night in jail as a drunk, blue-collar groundman in Rock Springs, Wyoming, and just six years after he had been rejected as an intern. Now, Cheney was suddenly Rumsfeld's deputy and an advisor to the president! The appointment was almost canceled when the FBI learned of the DUI arrests, but fortunately for Cheney, Rumsfeld stood up for him. "It impressed the hell out of me that he was willing to stand by me," Cheney said.[48]

Cheney took his work seriously and soon gained the confidence of Ford, such as drafting memos for the president on how to respond to Seymour Hersh's explosive investigative bombshell in the *New York Times* that the CIA was spying on U.S. citizens. Cheney would also become deeply involved in Ford's "Sunday Morning Massacre" on November 2, 1975, when the president fired William Colby as head of the CIA, Henry Kissinger as national security advisor, and James Schlesinger as secretary of defense. On Air Force One, en route with Ford to a meeting with President Anwar Sadat of Egypt, Cheney had the distinct pleasure of calling his former boss to offer him the job of Secretary of Defense, making Rumsfeld the youngest man to be offered that post. When he accepted, Cheney took over as chief of staff.[49]

On January 4, 1976, Cheney, then just thirty-four years old, was grilled about budget and unemployment issues by reporters on CBS Evening News' *Face the Nation*.[50] He had finally arrived as a political leader, but not quite in the way he wanted; he much preferred to be anonymous, helping write the president's speeches and write talking points. When Ford decided to run for reelection, Cheney stayed involved with the media, but the voters, angry with the slow economy and his pardon of Nixon, voted Ford out.

BEACH VACATION IN THE BAHAMAS

With Ford out, and Jimmy Carter installed in office in early 1977, Cheney and Rumsfeld were out of jobs. But Cheney was no longer a hapless would-be intern; he had become Rumsfeld's friend and colleague, evidenced by the fact that the two men took that opportunity to take a vacation together with their wives. They flew to Eleuthera, a small remote island in the Bahamas that the wealthy often used as a hideaway. (Robert de Niro and the Prince and the Princess of Wales became frequent visitors to the island.) Cheney had rented a beachfront house and Rumsfeld, his guest, took it upon himself to teach Lynne how to play tennis.[51]

After a week of holidaying in the Caribbean, the two men went their separate ways. Cheney decided to emulate his mentor and get some experience as an elected official, so he returned to Wyoming, where he had spent his teenage years, to try his luck running for the U.S. Congress. In November 1978, Cheney was elected to Wyoming's sole seat in the U.S. House of Representatives, where he would serve for most of the 1980s.[52]

During Cheney's tenure in the House, he rose to become Minority Whip for the Republicans, the second spot under the Minority Leader, and made a name for himself as one of the most conservative members of the U.S. Congress in history.[53]

DONALD RUMSFELD, CEO

While Cheney was voting against just about any progressive bill in Congress, Rumsfeld, for his part, had returned to Illinois to work for the former finance chair of his Congressional campaign, Dan Searle, as chief executive officer of Searle's family pharmaceutical business. Fresh from Washington where Rumsfeld had run the Pentagon for more than a year, he was seen as an ideal candidate to shake up Searle who had fallen on hard times with a $28 million loss in 1977 and shares at a low of $10. The company had been very profitable in the past with drugs like Metamucil (once the top-selling laxative), Dramamine (the first motion-sickness pill), and Enovid (the first contraceptive of its kind to reach the market). But a series of acquisitions, the expiration of a number of patents, and a failure to get new drugs to market was causing the company to lose money.[54]

Rumsfeld played hardball from the day he stepped into Searle's headquarters in Skokie. He disposed of twenty-five businesses with a net worth of $400 million soon after he arrived, fired 150 staff, and moved a similar number out to regional offices, then he hired his high-school friend John Robson who had been his issues director on his run for Congress. The following year, the company made a profit of $72.2 million.

Next, Rumsfeld turned his attention to a product that Searle had spent $30 million developing and trying to get to market: a controversial new product called aspartame. The Food and Drug Administration was reluctant to approve it because two of Searle's hypertension drugs called Aldactone and Aldactazide had recently been discovered to have ingredients that were considered carcinogenic. The Justice Department had opened an investigation into allegations that Searle had withheld evidence about the dangers of the ingredient, which in turn "led the FDA to question the integrity of all of Searle's research work," despite the fact that the company had been given approval for developing aspartame in 1974.

Rumsfeld took unprecedented action—ignoring the legal advice he had been given—and sued the government to force them to approve the drug. On July 15, 1981, the new Republican government of Ronald Reagan conceded. Rumsfeld and Robson immediately called a press conference the following day.

"The lemonade was free. The strawberries and the chewing gum were, too. These confections, offered at a press conference by G. D. Searle and Company yesterday, are just a few of the food items that will contain the company's new low-calorie sweetener," wrote a *New York Times* reporter who attended.[55]

"The sweetener is aspartame, a food additive approved Wednesday by the Food and Drug Administration. Many believe the additive will eventually steal away much of the existing $115 million annual demand for saccharin, currently the only substitute for sugar in the United States, and possibly convert some sugar users as well."

And indeed aspartame, which had by then cost the company an astronomical $70 million, became a runaway best-seller, making the company $336 million in 1983. Rumsfeld was hailed as Outstanding Chief Executive Officer in the Pharmaceutical Industry from the *Wall Street Transcript* in 1980 and *Financial World* in 1981.

(Incidentally, aspartame remains a controversial product despite its ubiquitous availability. *Food and Chemical News* reported that aspartame complaints represented 75 percent of all reports to the U.S. government of adverse reactions to substances in the food supply from 1981 to 1995. A number of studies have recommended further investigation into the possible connection between aspartame and diseases such as brain tumors, brain lesions, and lymphoma. The U.S. Air Force even issued an alert in 1992, warning air force pilots about drinking diet drinks containing aspartame before flying.)[56]

In 1985, Rumsfeld sold off the Searle Company at $65 a share for $2.7 billion to Monsanto, pocketing $12 million for his part in the turnaround. He continued to work in the private sector, while accepting a number of government advisory positions such as on the General Advisory Committee on Arms Control and as a special envoy for President Reagan, including a controversial trip to Iraq, where he met with Saddam Hussein. In 1990, Rumsfeld took over as CEO of General Instrument, a military contractor, until he took the company public in 1993, making yet another fortune.[57]

FALL OF THE SOVIET UNION

While Rumsfeld was making his millions, Cheney was following his former mentor's footsteps in Washington. When George H. W. Bush was elected president in 1988, Cheney was invited to become Secretary of Defense to fill in for John Tower, who was unable to get confirmation from the U.S. Congress. The senior Bush knew that Cheney could be relied on to do his bidding and keep his mouth shut, just as he had done for Ford. Cheney was also well liked in the Pentagon for his unflagging support of weapons' systems. "As a member of Congress [I] voted for every single defense program—I never saw a defense program I didn't like," Cheney once said.[58]

Nor did he take any risks trying to shake up the bureaucracy. The day he was sworn in, he arrived at his new office at the Pentagon and asked an aide to fetch the agency's organization chart, a mammoth diagram that "sort of fell off both ends of the desk," he told Hayes. "I rolled it up and stuck it in the trash and never looked at it again. I decided right then and there I wasn't going to spend a lot of time trying to reorganize the place."[59]

History intervened shortly after he took office. Pro-independence movements in Estonia, Latvia, and Lithuania began organizing protests against Moscow. The Berlin Wall was torn down in 1989, and finally, the Soviet Union crumbled in 1991, bringing the end of the four-decade-old Cold War and with it, the expectations of a peace dividend.

For a man who had claimed to never have voted against a weapons system, Cheney was suddenly faced with demands to cut the budget. He didn't think too hard apparently; he simply axed projects in the districts of David Bonior, Thomas Downey, and Jim Wright, all high-profile Democrats. Jane Mayer of *The New Yorker* says that a Democratic aide on the House Armed Services Committee told her that Cheney developed a contempt for Congress, which he regarded as "a bunch of annoying gnats." Meanwhile, his affinity for business deepened. "The meetings with businessmen were the ones that really got him pumped," the former aide told Mayer.[60] He also downsized the military, cutting troop levels about 19 percent, from about 2.2 million in 1989 to about 1.8 million in 1993.

These cuts also paved the way for new thinking about the future of warfare in a world without another superpower. To that end, the Pentagon awarded a $3.9 million contract to draw up a strategy for providing rapid support to twenty thousand troops in emergency situations. The company that was given the contract was Halliburton. After reading the initial report, the Pentagon paid Halliburton another $5 million to draw up detailed plans for outsourcing support operations, setting the stage for multibillion dollar contracts in future wars.[61]

PERSIAN GULF WAR

Cheney's time as Secretary of Defense was also marked by another event almost as significant as the fall of the Soviet Union: the invasion of Kuwait by Saddam Hussein in 1990. It would also have an enormous influence on his future.

Cheney was dispatched by President Bush on a whistle-stop tour of Middle East capitals to help negotiate access for troops preparing for the 1991 Persian Gulf War. Cheney did not have to actually plan the war itself—that was left to General "Stormin" Norman Schwarzkopf and General Colin Powell. Cheney did make some suggestions, such as Operation Scorpion—a plan to send U.S. troops into the desert west of Baghdad—which was scuttled by Schwarzkopf, who thought his boss was getting too big for his boots. "Put a civilian in charge of professional military men, and before long he's no longer satisfied with setting policy but wants to outgeneral the generals," he would later write scornfully in his memoirs.[62]

Six weeks after the war began on January 17, 1991, Saddam Hussein had been defeated, and less than three months after it ended on February 28, the last troops pulled out of Iraq to return to the United States.

A victory parade was called for New York for June 10. Cheney, Powell, and Schwarzkopf rode at the head of the parade in matching red, white, and blue convertibles, as grand marshals. It began at Battery Park at the very tip of Manhattan Island at 11:30 a.m. and lasted for four hours as an estimated 4.7 million people gathered along Broadway under warm, summer skies to watch twenty-four thousand marchers, including 4,761 uniformed soldiers, sailors, and marines make their way to City Hall.[63]

There were Humvees, there were Patton tanks mounted on flat-bed trucks, there was a woman painted in pale green and dressed as the Statue of Liberty. After the parade, lower Manhattan was illuminated that night by a patriotic fireworks display that included a simulation of an Iraqi Scud missile being blasted out of the sky by a Patriot missile.

Paper floated down from the skyscrapers lining the "Canyon of Heroes" like winter snowflakes, including some five hundred pounds of donated ticker-tape, ten thousand pounds of multicolored confetti, 140 miles of shredded yellow ribbon and streamers, and U.S. flags.

But despite the outpouring of support, Bush Senior was not able to stave off defeat in the 1992 election, and so eighteen months later, Dick Cheney found himself looking for a new job.

DICK CHENEY, CEO

If there was a sport that defined Cheney, it was fishing. Although he would later gain infamy as a hunter for going shooting with Supreme Court Justice Antonio Scalia in southern Louisiana in 2003, and later when he accidentally shot his friend Harry Whittington, in February 2006 on a southern Texas ranch, he was most at home wading into a river and casting for fish. He learned the skill at age sixteen when he went on a backcountry trip with his friends in Wyoming's Powder River Basin.[64]

A wry portrait of the man appeared in *The New Yorker* magazine in 2001, shortly after he became vice president. "If I were entering a contest to win a dream date with Dick Cheney, here is what I would say: We would definitely go fishing. Not bait fishing, which is for amateurs, a category that does not include Cheney, but fly-fishing," wrote Nicholas Lemann.[65]

"Way up in the Wind River Range of Wyoming, someplace beautiful and remote like that. We'd make camp, and then we'd get up before dawn and go out on the river. You have to be cool and patient and quiet to be a good fly fisherman—that's Cheney. We'd spend the whole day out there, just working the pools, not talking. With Cheney you do a lot of not talking. Maybe every hour or so, I'd ask him a question, and he'd answer with a 'yep' or a 'nope' or a 'little bit,' nothing more. Any fish we caught, we'd throw them back."

"Then at the end of the day we'd build a fire, and Cheney would make dinner—he's a really good cook, just basic American stuff, though, spaghetti and chili and stew. But I would tease him about how bad his cooking is. That's one of the rules with Cheney: He won't tease you, but you can tease him—under that masculine proviso by which you can express affection only through patently unmeant insults—and he kind of likes it."

So it isn't that surprising that his next lucky break would come when he was out fishing with his buddies on the remote Miramichi River, in New Brunswick, Canada. One of the fishermen was Thomas Cruikshank, the CEO of Halliburton, who was "impressed" with Cheney. Cruickshank would say later: "When you're isolated for about a week, fishing and sitting around the dinner table at night, you get to know people a little better."

Two stories are told about what happened next. Lemann writes in *The New Yorker:* "After a long, silent day, he decided to turn in early. The businessmen were sitting around talking and the conversation turned to how Halliburton needed a new CEO. After a while, somebody said, 'What about ol' Cheney?'

Since he was asleep in the lodge, he couldn't gruffly protest that he'd never worked in business, but his mysterious silent magic was permeating the place—so that was it, he got the job."

Hayes tells it differently. He says that the fishing trip that Cheney and Cruickshank took was in August 1994, and that the Halliburton CEO did not think of recommending Cheney for the job until the following spring. "A lot of the things that he was overseeing as secretary of defense would be similar to the things he would be overseeing at Halliburton," said Cruickshank. "Big infrastructure. A lot of foreign operations. Long-range planning. Logistics planning. Budgeting. Personnel management. Technology management."[66]

In reality, of course, Cheney had no experience in the oil business or in any kind of corporate management, for that matter, but he did have a far more valuable education: the ways of Washington and access to the corridors of power among the sheikhs and kings, presidents and politicians, bureaucrats and generals who really controlled the purse strings, particularly as a result of his involvement in negotiating access during the Persian Gulf War. "The members [of the search committee] believed that Cheney had a good reputation with their customers in the oil-rich Middle East," wrote Hayes. He had another advantage—he knew Congress and the White House as well as the Pentagon, where Halliburton/Brown & Root often shopped for contracts.

And it had been done before, after all. Rumsfeld had gone from government to the private sector and worked wonders. So the committee called Cheney up, and he agreed to fly from Jackson, Wyoming, to Dallas to meet with them over an informal lunch at Cruickshank's house on a Sunday afternoon in July 1995. The very next day, Cruickshank offered him the job and Cheney accepted a few days later and moved to Texas in August of 1995.[67]

Cheney at the Helm

HIGHLAND PARK is an expensive and quiet neighborhood nestled in the heart of Dallas. It is surrounded on all four sides by the big city, but this community has its own mayor, gathers its own taxes, and oversees its own services. The houses are often palatial, resembling those of Beverly Hills in California. Here and there Jaguars, Lexuses, and new model Mercedes Benzes dot the streets, quite a few of which are named after Ivy League colleges like Dartmouth and Harvard.[1]

In the mid-1990s, Dick Cheney bought a home[2] that practically sits on Turtle Creek, a stone's throw from Prather Park, a charming little city escape with winding, stone-walled paths and bridges. There is a city-owned swimming pool and children's playground, although much of this is invisible to the inhabitants of Cheney's home at 3812 Euclid because of the twenty-foot-high white walls that surround the forty-seven-hundred-square-foot home. At the entrance, two green statues of women pouring water flank the stairs and three giant jars top the gate. Walk around past the bamboo and ferns and you can peek inside the compound through ivy-entwined, white lattice work that punctuates the walls on either side.

It was here, in this quiet enclave in the heart of a city, after a twenty-five-year career in the nation's capital, that Cheney came to live and work while the Democratic party ruled the country under President Bill Clinton.

A fifteen-minute commute from his house was Lincoln Plaza, right in the heart of downtown Dallas. A forty-five-story skyscraper that is painted alternate gold and dark brown, the building has a nice little old clock outside and broad steps sunken into the sidewalk leading downstairs to a posh restaurant named Dakota's. Water cascades over the walls of the sunken area, through decorative plants.[3] Next door is the Fairmont Hotel, where Cheney's Halliburton would hold its annual meetings, until it moved to Houston in 2003.

It was out of these offices that from 1995 to 2000 Dick Cheney ran Halliburton, primarily helping the company win new business around the world as well as unprecedented loans and credit guarantees from the U.S. government. "What Dick brought was obviously a wealth of contacts," David J. Lesar, Halliburton's subsequent CEO would later tell the *Baltimore Sun*. "You don't spend twenty-some years in Washington without building a fairly extensive Rolodex."[4]

During his tenure, Cheney personally intervened or lobbied to change U.S. government policy in Azerbaijan and Russia, while the U.S. government intervened directly to help Halliburton in Angola. Cheney's statements on Iran and Halliburton's work in that country suggest that he was not above figuring out loopholes in the law for financial benefit, while the company's dealings in Nigeria suggest that its executives knowingly broke the law and paid out multimillion-dollar bribes.

AZERBAIJAN

While he was head of Halliburton, Cheney cultivated a number of friendships with heads of states, including dictators. One such notable leader was Heydar Aliyev, who was president of Azerbaijan, a former Soviet Politburo member, and head of the local KGB, and whose country had been subject to stringent sanctions from the U.S. Congress beginning in 1992. This was because of alleged human rights violations in presiding over the latter half of a vicious war and blockade against the Armenian enclave of Nagorno-Karabakh and because of the ethnic cleansing of the country's Armenian population.[5] But Azerbaijan was also one of the key states that controlled access to oil in the Caspian Sea, which led to potentially lucrative contracts with Halliburton.

Cheney lobbied in Washington to repeal the aid embargo against Azerbaijan and to sell oil-drilling equipment there, which he claimed would further America's national interest by bolstering Azeri independence from Russia. In 1997, Cheney gave a speech to the U.S.-Azerbaijan Chamber of Commerce, in which he said: "I believe that our current policy prohibiting U.S. assistance to Azerbaijan is seriously misguided. In my experience, this kind of unilateral sanction, based primarily on U.S. domestic political considerations, is unwise.[6]

"The Caspian may be the first world-class oil province to open up since the North Sea," he continued. "Azerbaijan is among the countries on the frontlines of this global competition as nations and commercial interests now jockey for influence over the Caspian's vast oil and gas resources. We in the petroleum industry have an obvious interest in seeing that the word goes out that Azerbaijan and the Caspian region are indeed of vital interest to the United States."

Indeed, his efforts on behalf of the Central Asian country were so impressive that, in addition to being named honorary advisor to the U.S.-Azerbaijan Chamber of Commerce, Cheney was given a "Freedom Support Award."[7]

In 1998, Cheney reiterated the same concept in a broader fashion when he said the following, quite unequivocally, at a foreign policy conference: "The good Lord didn't see fit to put oil and gas only where there are democratically elected regimes friendly to the United States. And so occasionally we have to operate in places where, all things considered, perhaps we'd rather not operate, but that's where the business is."[8]

Later, when he became vice president, Cheney made sure to promote Azerbaijan at every possible opportunity, such as in the national energy policy paper of May 17, 2001 (also known as the Cheney Report after the vice president refused to release the names of the people he consulted for it), when he included Azerbaijan among the "high-priority areas." "Proven oil reserves in Azerbaijan and Kazakhstan are about twenty billion barrels, a little more than the North Sea." His recommendation to the president was this: "Ensure that rising Caspian oil production is effectively integrated into world oil trade."[9]

The State Department dutifully conveyed the message to Azerbaijan's capital city, Baku. Steve Mann, the Caspian energy advisor to the State Department, was keen to tell the media about Cheney's strong interest in the country at a briefing at the U.S. embassy in Baku in June 2001. "I had a very good meeting with Vice President Dick Cheney last Friday in Washington. The vice president is very knowledgeable about the Caspian and Central Asia area, and he is very interested in energy developments in this region. And he has asked me to bring to the region the message that he personally fully supports the project we have on the way." [10]

In January 2002, President George W. Bush announced that the sanctions against Azerbaijan would be dropped.[11] Cheney stayed in touch with President Aliyev when the Azeri president came to the United States for prostate surgery at a clinic in Cleveland, Ohio, in February 2002. While he was recovering, Cheney would call to chat about the two countries' common interests.[12]

So when the United States announced its plans to invade Iraq in early 2003, Aliyev publicly, albeit cautiously, supported the idea. It was an important gesture on his part, given that the people of Azerbaijan were mostly Muslim. In return, he was given a half-hour meeting with President Bush in the Oval Office in February 2003,[13] an important political signal that the U.S. supported him. (Aliyev was running for re-election.) At the meeting Aliyev asked Bush to help him get money from the World Bank for the Baku-Tbilisi-Ceyhan oil pipeline. The International Financial Corporation, a division of the bank, approved the project in November 2003 in the face of bitter opposition from environmental and human rights groups.[14]

That very afternoon Aliyev was invited to the State Department to witness the signature of a bilateral agreement, granting immunity for both countries' citizens from possible prosecution by the International Criminal Court (ICC) in The Hague. The document was signed by Azerbaijani envoy to the United States, Hafiz Pasayev, and the U.S. assistant secretary of state for European and Eurasian Affairs, Elizabeth Jones.[15]

RUSSIA

Russia provides an excellent example of how Cheney personally intervened in contracts, according to an account by investigative reporter Aram Roston in *Mother Jones*. In February 2000, Cheney visited Alan Larson, then undersecretary of state for economic affairs at the State Department, to discuss the department's decision to block $500 million in federal loan guarantees to a Russian company called Tyumen Oil.[16] Larson had apparently been directly responsible for blocking these loans, which he had done in response to warnings from British Petroleum and the CIA that Tyumen and its owners—a Russian conglomerate called the Alfa Group—were deliberately driving the company into bankruptcy and attempting to steal its assets in a rigged auction.

Halliburton was hoping to get nearly $300 million of the federal subsidies to refurbish a Siberian oil field, so the hold-up was bad news for the company. In lobbying for the loans to go through, Cheney reportedly told Larson that American jobs at Halliburton were at stake. Within two months of the meeting, the State Department agreed to release the money.

The following January, Larson appears to have been rewarded by the new administration—he kept his job as undersecretary of state for economic affairs, the only one of thirty-seven undersecretaries from the Clinton era to remain. (State Department officials denied that there was any quid-quo-pro. A senior official told *Mother Jones* magazine that "questions of loans, contracts, or individual companies were never raised nor even considered.")

Larson and Tyumen would later play crucial roles in providing support during the planning period for the invasion of Iraq in 2003. Worried that war might disrupt Iraqi oil supplies and send prices soaring, the Bush-Cheney administration put in place a series of contingency plans in the summer of 2002. First the White House signed a deal with the Alfa Group to explore a series of oil projects in Russia. And in October of 2002, Tyumen became the first Russian company to deliver 285,000 barrels of oil to the Strategic Petroleum Reserve, which is an emergency fuel store of petroleum maintained by the United

States Department of Energy. Second, at the very same time that Tyumen shipped its oil across the globe, Larson was dispatched on high-profile missions to Saudi Arabia and other oil-supply nations to secure a commitment for increased production if war were to begin with Iraq.[17]

IRAN

Cheney's dealings with Iran are possibly the most curious, given the fact that the Bush-Cheney White House would later impose harsh sanctions on that country. At an earlier conference in February 1997, in Washington, Cheney told an audience that sanctions were a bad idea, in keeping with his long-standing opposition to sanctions. "The unintended result of our policy toward Iran is to give Russia more leverage over the independent states of central Asia and the Caucasus by blocking export routes toward the south," he said.[18]

The following year, Cheney lobbied the Clinton administration to ease sanctions on Libya and Iran. "I think we'd be better off if we, in fact, backed off those sanctions [on Iran], didn't try to impose secondary boycotts on companies . . . trying to do business there," Cheney told an Australian television interviewer in April 1998.[19]

Halliburton has had long-standing ties with Iran: Howco set up an office in Tehran as early as 1957, and the company won an $800 million contract in 1975 to build a naval base for the Iranian Army.[20] But Cheney didn't have to worry too much about sanctions as the company had figured out a loophole to continue to do business with Iran—by using foreign subsidiaries that were not subject to U.S. law. When ABC Television's Sam Donaldson confronted Cheney, pointing out that the practice was "a way around U.S. law," Cheney replied, "No, no, it's provided for us specifically with respect to Iran and Libya."[21]

Halliburton claimed that its work in Iran was legal because the contracts were signed by a foreign-owned subsidiary based in the Cayman Islands. Yet investigative reporters would later discover that this might have just been a matter of legal convenience.

When a crew from the CBS television program 60 Minutes visited the Cayman Islands address where Halliburton Products and Services was incorporated, it discovered a "brass plate" operation. The reporters "weren't allowed to enter the building with a camera. So we went in with a hidden camera and were introduced to David Walker, manager of the local Caledonian Bank, which is where the subsidiary is registered." [22]

Walker told 60 Minutes that while Halliburton Products and Services was registered at this address, there was no actual office, no employees on site, and if any mail for the Halliburton subsidiary came to that address, it was forwarded to Houston. "If you understood what most of these companies do, you would know they're not doing any business in Cayman per se. They're doing business, international business," Walker told the reporters. "Would it make sense to have somebody in Cayman pushing paper around? I don't know. And some people do it. And some people don't. And it's mostly driven by whatever the issues are with the head office."

Halliburton responded by saying that its Cayman Island subsidiary was actually run out of Dubai. So *60 Minutes* visited Halliburton's office in Dubai where it learned that the Dubai operation shared office space, and phone and fax lines with a division of the U.S.-based parent company—which raises the question about whether it was truly a separate foreign operation that was not subject to U.S. laws.

A federal grand jury was convened to look into whether the company or its executives knowingly violated a U.S. ban on trade with Iran.[23] The U.S. Department of Justice subpoenaed company documents in the fall of 2004 but took no subsequent action. In April 2007 Halliburton succumbed to pressure from the U.S. government and pulled out of Iran after completing its contracts.[24]

ANGOLA

Angola provides another example of the U.S. government support that Cheney was able to help engineer for Halliburton. The company had a $200 million contract with Chevron and its partners in the enclave of Cabinda, a province of Angola that is geographically distinct from the rest of the country.[25] In Cabinda Halliburton services more than 330 wells in thirty oil fields that are located between one and forty miles offshore, which provide 8 percent of U.S. oil imports—more than even Kuwait provides, and which is 80 percent of the Angolan government's revenue.[26] Tourists report that the once beautiful sandy beaches of Cabinda have turned black from the pollution, and the smell of petroleum hangs everywhere.[27]

Then Secretary of State Madeline Albright personally flew out to Chevron's Takula Oil Drilling Platform in Cabinda, on December 12, 1997, to announce that the Export-Import Bank of the United States was "finalizing an innovative loan of nearly $90 million to develop new oil fields here, and it is discussing with SONANGOL [the state oil company] and Chevron a further $350 million package to support purchases of American equipment."[28]

A follow-up cable from the U.S. embassy in Angola to Albright in 1998 explains the help it gave Halliburton: "Our commercial officer literally camped out at the offices of the national oil company, petroleum ministry, and central bank, unraveling snag after snag to obtain the transfer of funds. The bottom line: thousands of American jobs and a foot in the door for Halliburton to win even bigger contracts." That memo detailed how the embassy helped Halliburton "in tough competition with foreign firms" by allaying the Export-Import Bank's concerns and removing "barriers" to the $68 million loan package.

David Gribbin, the vice president of government affairs for Halliburton, told the Associated Press that the helpful diplomat in Angola was "a guy who was enthusiastically doing his job. God bless him. I'm sure probably a lot of our folks, when they are working in these countries, will get to know the commercial attaché and vice versa. You can call any company that is a global business, and they will tell you this."[29]

NIGERIA

Halliburton was implicated in a bribery scandal in Nigeria in the late 1990s. In 1994, a consortium known as TSKJ was incorporated in Madeira, Portugal, that consisted of M. W. Kellogg (it was not yet a part of Halliburton at the time), Technip of France, Italy's Snamprogetti, and Japan Gasoline Corporation. The partnership submitted a bid to Nigeria LNG, a company partly owned by the Nigerian government, to work on a multibillion dollar natural gas liquefaction complex and related facilities at Bonny Island in Rivers State. In December 1995, TSKJ was awarded the contract.[30]

A little more than two years later, M. W. Kellogg was acquired by Halliburton and merged with Brown & Root to create Kellogg, Brown & Root (KBR), an acquisition directed by Dick Cheney. Albert Jack Stanley, the chairman, president, and chief executive officer of Kellogg, was appointed to head up the new company. Cheney told the *Middle East Economic Digest* in 1999, "We took Jack Stanley . . . to head up the organization, and that has helped tremendously." [31]

Investigators would later reveal that between 1995 and 2002, Stanley's business associates had paid more than $166 million in "advisory fees"—part of which was paid out during Cheney's time at Halliburton. Notes written by M. W. Kellogg employees during the mid-1990s mention bribing Nigerian officials, evidence that, according to the *Financial Times*, "raises questions over what Mr. Cheney knew—or should have known—about one of the largest contracts awarded to a Halliburton subsidiary."[32]

Stanley stayed in his job as chairman of KBR until December 2003 when he retired, at which point he became a consultant to Halliburton. In June 2004, Halliburton fired Stanley after investigators turned up evidence that he had violated the company's "code of business conduct" by accepting "improper personal benefits" of $5 million, related to construction work in Nigeria.[33]

The official Halliburton 2006 annual report acknowledged that people employed by Halliburton and/or its predecessors made illegal payments to Nigerian officials: "Information uncovered in the summer of 2006 suggests that, prior to 1998, plans may have been made by employees of the M. W. Kellogg Company to make payments to government officials in connection with the pursuit of a number of other projects in countries outside of Nigeria. We are reviewing a number of recently discovered documents related to KBR activities in countries outside of Nigeria with respect to agents for projects after 1998. Certain of the activities discussed in this paragraph involve current or former employees or persons who were or are consultants to us and our investigation continues."[34] In September 2008, Stanley pled guilty to participating in the decade-long scheme to pay $182 million worth of bribes.[35]

It is difficult to ascertain who knew what at the time, but Stanley, as chairman of KBR, was definitely part of Cheney's inner circle. Stanley reported directly to David Lesar, Halliburton's president and chief operating officer at the time, who in turn reported to Cheney. Neither Lesar nor Cheney have so far been charged in association with the Nigeria case.[36]

LEAVING DALLAS

At 6:22 a.m. on Tuesday, July 25, 2000, the phone rang at Cheney's Euclid Avenue house in Dallas.[37] It was Texas Governor George Bush offering Dick Cheney the vice presidential spot on the Republican ticket. Within minutes the media had the house staked out and pretty soon were rewarded by his daughter Liz who peeked out of the gates to take some pictures of the assembled photographers and reporters. Cheney immediately took a leave of absence from Halliburton and joined the race.

Ironically, Cheney was not officially in the running for the job as he had been the head of Bush's vice presidential selection committee. One obstacle Cheney faced in pursuing the V.P. position was that his primary residence, his place of work, indeed his driver's license, were all registered in Texas. This was constitutionally problematic because the president and the vice president are supposed to come from different states. But Cheney was already hard at work on solving that problem: the previous Friday he had flown to Wyoming to have his voter registration changed. Some consider he put the Euclid house up for sale so that he could say that his real residence was in the gated community in Jackson Hole where he had a vacation home. (Dianne T. Cash, a wealthy Republican Highland Park resident who had contributed $200,000 to the party committee, bought the Euclid property soon after the election. This completed the legal process to void a lawsuit that challenged Cheney's appointment.)[38]

After a long, grueling battle over the results of the 2000 election, the Supreme Court effectively handed the election to Bush on December 12. Cheney quit Halliburton and set up a transition office for the new Bush-Cheney administration on Anderson Road in McLean, Virginia, to begin the process of moving back to Washington.[39]

Halliburton's chief financial officer, David Lesar, took the reins from Cheney. Things looked good at the time—the company's share price had doubled from $21 in August 1995 to $43.56 in the five years between Cheney's appointment in August 1995 until his resignation.[40] Although it would later emerge that Cheney had made a number of extremely rash decisions that would force the company temporarily into bankruptcy,[41] what the investors at the time saw was the rich seam of government finance and contracts that Cheney had brought to the company.

In the five years before Cheney joined Halliburton, the company received $100 million in government credit guarantees. During Cheney's five-year tenure, this amount jumped to $1.5 billion with sweetheart deals from the U.S. Export-Import Bank and the Overseas Private Investment Corporation. The company also won $2.3 billion in direct U.S. military contracts, almost double the $1.2 billion it earned from the government in the five years before he arrived, which is the subject of the next chapter.[42]

- -

Golden Paydays

Cheney made a fortune when he took over as chief executive of Halliburton in 1995. In the five years that he worked at the company, he received $12.5 million in salary. He also held $39 million worth of stock options when he quit the company in 2000—a fortune for a man with no previous experience in running a multinational company. In addition, Halliburton's board of directors voted to award him early retirement when he quit his job, even though he was too young to qualify under his contract. That flexibility enabled him to leave with a retirement package, including stock and options, worth millions more than if he had simply resigned.[43]

Halliburton made payments of $205,298 to Cheney in 2001, $162,392 in 2002, $178,437 in 2003, $194,852 in 2004, and $211,465 in 2005, in the form of "deferred compensation" (to avoid excessive taxes) that was on par to his 2005 vice presidential salary, which was worth $205,031.[44]

Cheney cashed in his remaining stock options gradually, starting with selling one hundred thousand Halliburton shares in May 2000 to rake in an immediate profit of $3 million. In 2005, Cheney exercised most of what remained of his Halliburton stock options for a $6.9 million profit, all of which he donated to charity. (Most of it was donated to the Richard B. Cheney Cardiac Institute at George Washington University.) The remaining stock options that he held in the company were also "irrevocably" committed to charity.[45] However, it appears that Cheney invested his previous earnings from Halliburton well, as his net worth was reported be as high as $99 million in May 2008.[46]

A report by the Congressional Research Service, at the request of Senator Frank Lautenberg, a New Jersey Democrat, says that the deferred compensation that Cheney receives from Halliburton, as well as the stock options he possesses, "is considered among the 'ties' retained in or 'linkages to former employers' that may 'represent a continuing financial interest' in those employers, which makes them potential conflicts of interest."[47]

This contradicts Cheney's statement made September 14, 2003, on NBC television's *Meet the Press*: "I have no financial interest in Halliburton of any kind and haven't had, now, for over three years. . . . I've severed all my ties with the company, gotten rid of all my financial interest."[48]

. . . But Workers Get Stiffed

A federal investigation of Halliburton's pension plans showed that the company had charged some costs of Halliburton's top bosses' pension and bonus plans to the workers' pension fund, spending about $2.6 million in total between June 1, 1999, and January 1, 2004. Two such violations took place when Cheney was the company's CEO.

The company also failed to pay out part of the pensions that were owed to employees who came to work at Halliburton when Cheney bought up Dresser Industries, in marked contrast to the former CEO's early retirement package. When the workers complained to investigators at the Department of Labor, Halliburton returned the money to the affected people and returned the money it had spent from the workers' pension funds.[49]

The Birth of LOGCAP

IN THE FIVE YEARS that Cheney jet-setted from "New Delhi to Cairo and all points in between," cutting oil deals,[1] his company was also deeply involved in a remarkable experiment to transform the U.S. military. To truly understand how the traditional practice of military quartermasters—soldiers who pulled kitchen patrol and day laborers from surrounding communities at U.S. bases around the world from Germany to Vietnam—were replaced by an international pool of migrant workers under a single corporate logo belonging to Halliburton, we need to explore the introduction of major logistics contractors to the Pentagon. The planning for this effort began a few years after the end of the U.S. war in Vietnam, at a time when the suspension of the draft was starting to cause a drop in walk-ins to military recruitment stations.[2] The tragedies in Southeast Asia were already retreating in national consciousness, and a hawkish new president was seeking a return to the global stage to undertake interventions in far-flung trouble spots such as Grenada. But military planners knew that it was going to be tough.

Time magazine highlighted the logistical hurdles that the planners were confronting for such campaigns in a November 1983 article titled "How Much Can America Do? Its power is vast, but its global commitments are breathtaking."[3] George J. Church, the reporter, summed up the problem: "As long as trouble on opposite sides of the globe can be met by deployments the size of those in Lebanon and Grenada, there is no strain. . . . But a pair of widely separated major confrontations—a Soviet threat to the Persian Gulf oilfields, say, and a blowup in Korea—would pose a real problem," noting that the real problem would be sustainment as "the U.S. would be hard pressed to fly or ship in the fuel, food, and ammunition."

One of the men Church interviewed for the article was General John A. Wickham, then U.S. Army chief of staff under President Ronald Reagan.

Wickham was already working on creating light infantry divisions for possible rapid "contingency missions" in the Third World and in the forested and urbanized regions of Western Europe. He also ordered his staff to determine what might have to be done if U.S. troops were ordered into a hostile situation in Central America.[4]

But Wickham's most important legacy was a short, thirteen-page order that he signed on December 16, 1985, that set out the concepts, responsibilities, policies, and procedures for using civilian contractors to replace soldiers and recruiting local labor during wartime.[5] This order—which described a new military doctrine called the Logistics Civilian Augmentation Program (LOGCAP)—became the umbrella under which Halliburton has been contracted by the Pentagon: to provide support services to the U.S. military in conflict zones like Iraq. The LOGCAP regulations remained on a shelf for several years before planners would take the next step to turn them into a contract for industry to bid on. They would not be used in any major way until after the 1991 Persian Gulf War highlighted how hard it was for the post–Cold War military to deploy quickly to distant battlefields.

Wickham gave an interview to the *Washington Post* when he retired in 1987, in which he noted that despite the creation of the quick reaction forces, the army would be able to fight for only three months before running out of supplies and would have to wait nine months before industry could start delivering replacements for destroyed tanks and guns, particularly in the Persian Gulf, where even the dovish [President] Carter had promised to protect the critically important oilfields by "any means necessary."

One answer to this, Wickham believed, was to place supplies on Diego Garcia—an island in the Chagos Archipelago in the Indian Ocean that had been vastly developed over the previous decade to house a U.S. and UK navy base. Another answer was to build up bases in friendly countries like Turkey and Saudi Arabia, where Wickham was advocating that the Air Force could deploy F-15 fighter planes.[6]

These military base expansion proposals would prove immensely lucrative to Halliburton, after its mentor, LBJ, had lost power in the White House. Halliburton led a consortium that won a contract to expand Diego Garcia in 1982, and it also created a joint venture to provide catering and maintenance services on U.S. bases in Turkey in 1988, picking up one of the first contracts in the arena of logistical support.

DIEGO GARCIA

Diego Garcia is an atoll in the middle of the Indian Ocean, about one thousand miles south of India and Sri Lanka in the Chagos Archipelago. It was initially settled by the French in the eighteenth century who established copra plantations by using slave labor, but the island passed into British control after the Napoleonic wars in the early nineteenth century.[7]

In 1967, the British bought up and closed down all the plantations. In 1971, the British handed over control of the island to the United States in exchange for a $14 million discount on a purchase of Polaris missiles. The two thousand Chagossians—descendants of Indian workers and African slaves—were deported to Mauritius, an island off the east coast of Africa.[8]

U.S. Navy engineers, who are also called Seabees, then began an eleven-year construction project to turn Diego Garcia into a military base for operations by the United States and the United Kingdom. In 1982, the U.S. Navy awarded a contract to a consortium of Houston-based Raymond International Builders, Brown & Root, and Mowlem International of Middlesex, England (RBRM) for a major new expansion—consisting of 128 projects at a cost of more than $452 million—to be built over five years that would expand the harbor and the runways to allow bigger aircraft and ships to be received.[9]

Halliburton/Brown & Root's expansion of Diego Garcia has allowed the U.S. military to base long-range U.S. Air Force bombers like B-1Bs, B-2s, and B-52s on the island for quick strikes on strategic targets, without refueling, anywhere in the Middle East, or Central or South Asia. It was used during the Persian Gulf War in 1991 and during military missions in Afghanistan during Operation Enduring Freedom in 2001. And the island was also used to carry out the initial aerial bombardment on Baghdad, Iraq, on March 22, 2003.[10]

TURKEY

The Incirlik military base in eastern Turkey is about an hour's drive inland from the Mediterranean coast and about seven miles from the city of Adana. Incirlik—which means "place of the fig orchard"—was transformed from its fruit growing origins in 1951 when a company named Metcalfe, Hamilton, and Grove was hired by the U.S. military to build the original base. Initially, it provided a base for CIA spy missions in the 1950s when U-2 aircraft were launched from extremely high altitudes to photograph ground installations and eavesdrop on electronic signals from the Soviet Union and the Middle East.[11]

Incirlik also provided a major staging post for thousands of sorties flown against Iraq and occupied Kuwait during the Persian Gulf War in January 1991, dropping more than three thousand tons of bombs on military and civilian targets. Following the end of that war, approximately fourteen hundred U.S. soldiers continued to be stationed there—to staff Operation

Northern Watch's Air Force F-15 Strike Eagles and F-16 Fighting Falcons, monitoring the no-fly zone above the thirty-sixth parallel in Iraq.

Catering and housing services for the pilots were provided by a consortium named Vinnell, Brown & Root (VBR), a joint venture between Halliburton and the Vinnell corporation of Fairfax, Virginia, under a contract that was first signed on October 1, 1988, which also includes two more minor military sites in Turkey: Ankara and Izmir.[12]

(Vinnell Corporation was founded by the late A. S. Vinnell in 1931 to pave roads in Los Angeles. Since then, the company has handled a number of large, private as well as government projects, not unlike Brown & Root. The company was the major contractor for U.S. military operations in Okinawa, overhauled air force planes in Guam in the early 1950s, and sent men and equipment onto the battlefields of the Korean War. It also won a contract to train the Saudi Arabia National Guard.)[13]

Cheap labor was the primary reason for outsourcing services, said Major Toni Kemper, head of public affairs at the base. "The reason that the military goes to contracting is largely because it's more cost effective in certain areas," she told my colleague Sasha Lilley. "I mean there were a lot of studies years ago as to what services could be provided via contractor versus military personnel. Because when we go to contract, we don't have to pay health care and all the other things for the employees; that's up to the employer."[14]

Approximately twelve hundred VBR employees work on the base at a cost estimated in the late 1990s of about $30 million a year.[15] "We provide support services for the United States Air Force in areas of civil engineering, motor vehicles transportation, and in the services arena here—that includes food service operations, lodging, and maintenance of a golf course. We also do U.S. customs inspection," explained VBR site manager Alex Daniels, who had worked at Incirlik for almost fifteen years when Lilley interviewed him in early 2003.[16]

About eleven hundred of the employees are local. They travel to work at the main gate at Incirlik by shuttle bus or *dolmus*, a popular Turkish private bus service that ferries people from the center of Adana down the E5 highway. All visitors are greeted by armed Turkish sentries who do a casual check of identification cards before waving the vans through.[17]

Before one gets to the base, visitors must pass a mile-long commercial strip that houses restaurants, gun shops, carpet sellers, tailors, and bars, offering goods ranging from Mexican burritos to pirate copies of the latest James Bond movies on DVD to homesick soldiers. Local women may often be seen leaving the premises of the Cheers Bar or the Happy House Restaurant on the arm of a soldier to make a quick ride back to a cheap hotel on Innonu Caddesi in Adana before curfew closes the main base gate at 11 p.m.

Company employees try to keep a low profile, though. In early 1991, gunmen from a militant, underground Marxist group killed two VBR employees: Bobbie Eugene Mozelle was killed at Incirlik, while director John Gandy, a former U.S. Air Force officer, was shot to death by gunmen who boldly walked into the VBR offices in Istanbul after overpowering several employees. These incidents caused the company to shut down its multistoried offices in downtown Adana and move onto the base itself.[18]

Despite the attacks, jobs on the base in Adana have always been much sought after by the local population—at the base exchange, bowling alley, minimart, fast food restaurants such as Burger King and Taco Bell, clubs, the golf course, library, movie theater, and post office. Indeed, these jobs are so sought after that they have invited petty graft, according to former VBR employee Mehmet Aziz (not his real name), whom I met in late 2002. In the privacy of his home in Adana, he sipped his tea—which was served Turkish style without milk in a glass thimble with a couple of cubes of sugar—recalling the twenty years he worked on the base as a driver before he retired the prior year.[19]

"Everybody in Adana wants jobs at the American base because they pay so well. Starting salaries for a driver are $500 a month, twice as much as you can get from other companies. Both the Americans and Turkish people working at VBR know this, and they make good money charging people to get hired. Today, people pay as much as $5,000 to get a job on the base," he told me.

Another reason for the demand for jobs on the base is the ability to buy goods at U.S. prices and then smuggle them out to the Amerikan Pazari (American market) in central Adana where perfumes and jeans could fetch two to three times the original price.

Company officials do not deny that there may have been incidents of corruption in the past. "I'm not saying it was impossible that people did or did not buy jobs in the past, but I can tell you the way it is today," said site manager Alex Daniels.[20] "Today, our processes are that we gather most of our applicants through the Adana Labor Exchange; that's a government agency. If you have a requirement, let's say a carpenter for example, we would go to that government agency and say we would like applicants for a carpenter position. They would provide us with ten to twenty applicants, and then we would interview those folks.

"The closest we come to nepotism is I'm sure some of our workers recommended family members as references on applications, and those people are considered, you know, just like any other company would consider an application from somebody that's working for them," he added.

Despite the demand for jobs, VBR employees repeatedly expressed dissatisfaction with the company. Kenan Durukan, president of Harbis (the war workers union in Turkey) in 1989, charged the company with carelessness toward the health of Turkish employees, who were suffering from respiratory diseases and eye and ear disorders from working in the company cold storage in Izmir, where the temperature was kept at thirty degrees below zero Celsius.[21]

The base has also been a target for three major union strikes since VBR took over. The first strike began in August 1990 when Harbis asked for more job security and pay raises proportional to inflation. The strike was postponed when Iraq invaded Kuwait. The second month-long strike, in July 1998, ended when the company threatened the workers. Izzet Cetin, head of Harbis at the time, said: "We strongly criticize the employer who threatened and broke the strike by telling that the Turkish-American relations would be destroyed."[22]

The latest strike occurred in December 2002, but it too was called off. Orhan Sener, the president of Harbis, told me, "We asked for pay reviews [to keep up with the galloping inflation in Turkey] every three months in our collective labor agreement with the air force, but they agreed only to a review every six months. So after consulting with my head office, I personally refused to sign the new agreement." At the time, Sener was a twenty-year veteran on the base who started at the bottom as a freight handler.[23]

Daniels says he believes the workers got the upper hand in the arbitration that followed the strikes. "I think it had to do primarily with—how can I say this—the home-field advantage, the union being Turkish, and the people that are negotiating are the U.S. government, for all practical purposes, and Uncle Sam has the [money] pot."[24]

OPERATION DESERT STORM

The Incirlik contracts were probably the first to employ single contractors to provide support services to the U.S. military, such as food and general maintenance, predating the use of LOGCAP by at least four years. LOGCAP was also used briefly in July 1989 to help maintain two oil pipelines in the Middle East. However, it was not employed in any major way during Operation Desert Storm in 1991, when the U.S. led a multinational coalition to kick Saddam Hussein out of Kuwait, which his army had invaded in August 1990.[25]

Instead, in the Saudi desert, suppliers and construction companies were hired on hundreds of separate contracts to provide logistics support with uneven results, which frustrated military planners.[26] These concerns would cause planners to give Halliburton/Brown & Root a $3.9 million contract to figure out if it would be possible for the military to use a single contractor under LOGCAP to coordinate rapid support to twenty thousand troops over 180 days in emergency situations at thirteen different "hot spots" around the world.[27]

Simultaneously, soldiers who served in Operation Desert Storm were also complaining bitterly about the harsh living conditions, leading the army to turn to its research lab in Natick, Massachusetts, after the end of hostilities, to figure out a better way to support troops in the field. The lab decided to expand on an existing system pioneered by the U.S. Air Force, called Harvest Eagle and Harvest Falcon, of prefabricated military bases. This would become a cornerstone of LOGCAP.[28]

THE BASE IN A BOX

Natick's new design was called Force Provider: It is a one-size-fits-all, prefabricated base-in-a-box that was designed to make military operations more efficient. This off-the-shelf package can be shipped or airlifted anywhere in the world in a standard container. It comes with complete instructions so that anybody can assemble it, eliminating the need for specialized, trained engineering battalions and paving the way for private contractors to set up the bases.[29]

Each $5 million module is capable of housing 550 soldiers in comfortable climate-controlled tents with showers, laundry rooms, and complete kitchens as well as eighty thousand gallons of water storage and distribution, forty-thousand-gallon fuel storage and distribution, 1.1 megawatt power generation and distribution, and waste water storage units. The set is designed to work in weather ranging from fifteen below zero or 120 above. The ten-acre base camp, which takes about ten days to assemble, needs fifty support staff to set it up and run it.

By the end of the 1990s, the army possessed twenty-seven of these Force Provider modules, each consisting of one hundred or so containers, at multiple locations around the world, ready for shipment at a moment's notice.

"These kits benefit soldiers. It's a better way of life. It keeps them off the dirty ground. They've got just about everything you've got at home, except a wife," says William Oliver, a supervisor at the Defense Depot in Albany, Georgia, where some of these kits are stored. Michael Gallagher, Force Provider's program manager at Natick, says officials recently visited troops overseas who were living in the modules. "They were getting handwritten notes from the troops, saying, 'I've never deployed in conditions as good as this.' That's what it's all about."[30]

One of the more unusual components of the Force Provider is a "containerized chapel," a multidenominational religious center catering to Christians, Jews, and Muslims, which can be set up in six hours out of a box that measures eight by eight by ten feet. Complete with its own altar power supply, electric piano, and a digital hymnal, the chapel is sixty-four feet long and comfortably seats one hundred people. "We like to say that we not only take care of the soldier's body, but of his spirit. We're great defenders of the right of everyone to express their faith," says Ben Richardson, the chaplain at Natick Labs who helped develop the containerized chapel.[31]

According to U.S. Department of Defense statistics at the time, of the 470,000 soldiers in the army, about 40 percent were Protestant, 20 percent were Catholic, while Jewish, Muslim, Buddhist, and Hindu all made up less than 1 percent. (The rest presumably are atheists or unaffiliated to a religion.) The Catholic kit, for example, includes a heavy metal cross and chalice. The Islamic kit has ten *kufis* (male prayer caps), *kimaras* (female head coverings), prayer mats, and Korans. The Jewish kit includes ten yarmulkes and camouflage prayer shawls.

SOMALIA

In August 1992, the U.S. Army Corps of Engineers issued the first global LOGCAP contract known as LOGCAP I.[32] The contract gave the government an open-ended mandate and budget to ask Halliburton/Brown & Root to go anywhere in the world to support military operations. That opportunity would arise almost immediately when President George H. W. Bush offered to lead a military operation to enforce United Nations Security Council Resolution 794 "to create a protected environment for conducting humanitarian operations in the southern half of the Republic of Somalia," following the collapse of the government of General Siad Barre and the subsequent civil war.[33]

In December 1992, working under LOGCAP, Halliburton/Brown & Root began providing support to U.S. troops assigned to Somalia, putting employees on the ground within twenty-four hours of the first U.S. landing in Mogadishu. Bob Burroughs, the military logistician who oversaw the contract, was pleased with what they did, although he suspected that money may have gone astray. "I had an unlimited budget because of what we were doing there, and I'm sure they overcharged me on some things. But I would have been in real trouble if they hadn't been there," he would later tell Dan Briody, author of *The Halliburton Agenda*. "I don't know how they did it . . . but Brown & Root got whatever we needed."[34]

There was one minor problem, though. To get things done in Somalia, Burroughs says that Halliburton/Brown & Root was paying off the "bad guys" who the United States was supposed to be fighting. Warlord Mohammed Farrah Aidid's finance man was arrested with "a bunch of Brown & Root checks in his pocket." He looked the other way, though, as he believed that "sometimes you have to work with the devil to make things work."

By the time Halliburton/Brown & Root left, in 1995, it had become the largest employer in the country, having outsourced most of the menial work while importing experts for more specialized needs. For this job in Somalia, Halliburton/Brown & Root was paid $107.3 million by the U.S. government, but when the company left the country, it simply dumped its temporary labor, causing riots to break out.

A Reuters reporter in Mogadishu described the incident thus: "A demonstration by Somali workers at the United Nations compound to protest the dismissals of local laborers by an American construction company was broken up today with clubs and tear gas. The workers who were dismissed had been employed repairing roads. . . . United Nations spokesperson, Eugene Forson, said that ninety Somali workers were laid off [but] Somali sources had said that five hundred employees had been dismissed. Mr. Forson said that after fruitless negotiations, United Nations troops rushed the workers at the United Nations compound in Mogadishu with batons and tear gas."[35]

After Somalia, Halliburton/Brown & Root continued to be tasked with LOGCAP duties in U.S. military interventions throughout the 1990s, such as the following:

- **Rwanda:** "Operation Support Hope," August 1994, $6.3 million. Water production, storage, and distribution.
- **Haiti:** "Operation Uphold Democracy," September 1994, $150.1 million. Base camp construction and maintenance; food service and supply; laundry; bulk fuel receipt, storage, and issue; airport and seaport operations; and transportation services.
- **Saudi Arabia/Kuwait:** "Operation Vigilant Warrior," October 1994, $5 million. Food service and supply; transportation; Arabia/convoy support; shuttle bus service; Kuwait laundry; and off loading and storing containers from ships.
- **Italy:** "Operation Deny Flight," September 1995, $6.3 million. Base camp construction.[36]

YUGOSLAVIA

The first major LOGCAP operation took place in former Yugoslavia shortly after Dick Cheney took the helm at Halliburton. The very month he started working in Dallas, NATO began bombing Bosnia-Herzegovina in Operation Deliberate Force to undermine the military capability of the Bosnian Serb Army that was attacking UN-designated "safe areas" in Bosnia.

Following the bombing, a peace conference was held in late November in Dayton, Ohio, between Serbian President Slobodan Milošević, Croatian

President Franjo Tudjman, Bosnian President Alija Izetbegović, and Bosnian Foreign Minister Muhamed Sacirbey. "Operation Joint Endeavor"—a U.S.-led NATO peacekeeping force—deployed days after the Dayton Peace Accord was signed in Paris, France, on December 14, the first commitment of forces in a wartime environment in NATO's history.

Brown & Root was hired to deploy with the troops, and the initial results were mixed. Major James P. Herson, Jr., the executive officer of the 181st Transportation Battalion ("The Road Warriors") was one of the first to call upon them because he was hard pressed to move supplies into Bosnia. His battalion had been cut from six truck companies in 1990 to three in 1995, with one of them shuttered as late as September 1995. So he came up with the idea of asking Brown & Root to dispatch civilian drivers to pick up goods that would be delivered by rail to Dombovar, Hungary, from where they could be driven into Bosnia.[37]

While Brown & Root attempted to put together a civilian truck fleet, Herson worked frantically to speed up the bureaucracy to get his own military truck drivers on the road at short notice. He was able to issue the military drivers American Express credit cards to cover the cost of fuel, roadside emergencies, and unscheduled billeting to drive from Mannheim, Germany, through Austria into Hungary en route to Bosnia in early December, but Brown & Root was unable to assist him with any additional trucks.

"Ultimately, this novel approach proved untenable for several reasons," Herson would later recount in *Army Logistician*. "The M911 HET's [Oshkosh trucks] and M747 trailers were in poor condition; it would take weeks of maintenance to get them fully mission capable. Considerable contracting and host-nation support negotiations would have been needed to ready the Dombovar base. Brown and Root would need several weeks to get drivers to Hungary and would not be able to meet the timeline. Difficulties in finding sufficient hardstand parking for HET systems and adequate maintenance facilities in Dombovar finally doomed the idea."

Food for the troops was dispatched from the Defense Distribution Depot Europe in Germersheim, Germany, in standard twenty-foot containers of breakfast and dinner T-rations. Initial plans for Brown & Root to supply the food were also scrapped because it would take too long to issue the contracts.[38]

Brown & Root was more successful in working with the Force Provider life-support systems, if only because the company was given more notice. The day after the first U.S. tank platoons crossed the Sava River into Bosnia on December 30, 1995, over a just-completed pontoon bridge, crawling in at three miles per hour, Brown & Root contractors were at Kaposvar, Hungary, working to move Force Provider sets to house them in the Tuzla Valley in Bosnia.[39]

Two months earlier, the Pentagon's Military Traffic Management Command in Alexandria, Virginia, had initiated planning discussions with Brown & Root to get the Force Provider systems up and running. In anticipation of a possible deployment, the first Force Provider containers shipped from the Sierra Army Depot in Herlong, California, for the port of Beaumont, Texas, on November 8. A total of 355 items were radio tagged—248 twenty-foot containers, ninety 100-kilowatt (kW) generator sets, twelve M85 laundries, and five latrine-servicing trucks—collectively weighing more than twenty-five hundred tons. These were loaded onto a U.S. Navy ship, the *American Condor*, to set sail for Rotterdam, where it arrived on December 3. As soon as the agreements were signed, the containers were dispatched to Kaposvar, Hungary, where C-5 and Boeing 747 aircraft could land and take-off. During the month of January 2006, the containers arrived, some by air, to build three base camps in Bosnia's Tuzla Valley: Comanche Base (Tuzla West), with a population of seventeen hundred soldiers; Steel Castle Base (Tuzla East), also seventeen hundred soldiers; and Lukavac Base (also known as Gotham City), with fifteen hundred soldiers.

Eventually, as the Pentagon got over its teething problems, Brown & Root took over much of the operations, providing a dizzying array of services: base camp construction and maintenance; showers; latrines; food service and supply; sewage and solid waste removal; water production, storage, and distribution; shuttle bus service; bulk fuel receipt, storage, and issue; heavy equipment transportation; mail delivery; construction material storage and distribution; railhead operations; and seaport operations.

As the peacekeeping operations expanded, Brown & Root would be able to support the military more smoothly. In the spring of 1999 NATO jets pounded targets in Yugoslavia for seventy-eight days in Operation Allied Force to stop President Milošević from evicting ethnic Albanians from the province of Kosovo. Brown & Root was hired to help build Camp Bondsteel in a wheat field near the town of Uroševac in the eastern part of Kosovo and eighteen miles south of the capital of Pristina. It would be the biggest base that the United States had constructed from the ground up since the days of the Vietnam Builders.[40]

In the summer of 1999, more than one thousand Brown & Root construction workers completed construction of Camp Bondsteel. The finished 955-acre base, with a perimeter measuring seven miles, looked like a veritable fortress on top of a series of small hills. Inside, it was no different from bases back in the United States with a hospital, library, two gymnasiums, a volleyball court, and two chapels.[41]

By contrast, the soldiers from the other thirty nations participating in the NATO-led peacekeeping force lived in existing apartment blocks and, in some cases, factories. But U.S. commanders were learning that U.S. soldiers expected to be treated like they were at home. "We need to get these guys pumping iron and licking ice cream cones, whatever they want to do" when not on duty, Colonel Robert McClure, commander of the 1st Infantry Division engineers, told *USA Today*.[42]

By 1999, the Brown & Root staff practically ran Bondsteel. They met soldiers on arrival, assigned them to barracks, and told them where to pick up their gear.[43] "We do everything that does not require us to carry a gun," David Capouya, Brown & Root's regional manager for the service contract in Kosovo, would tell *Government Executive* magazine. Colonel Vincent Boles of the Army Materiel Command in Rock Island, who oversaw LOGCAP, agreed. "By having contractors in the rear," he said, "we can move soldiers to the front."[44]

Just as in Turkey and Somalia, the bulk of the employees were local—some five thousand out of the company's fifty-five hundred workers were from Kosovo, and the company had more than fifteen thousand applications for vacancies. The company also used some two dozen subcontractors for specific tasks like building fences. Once again, the workers were paid at local rates of $1 to $3 an hour. "We can't inflate the wages because we don't want to over-inflate the local economy," said Capouya.

The Pentagon dispatched twenty-one military and civilian workers to supervise the contract, under the aegis of the Defense Contract Management Agency (DCMA). "Our job is to be the Johnny-on-the-Spot wherever our war fighters need a contractor service," army Brigadier General Edward Harrington told *Government Executive*.[45]

In fact the company was no longer being called upon as a last resort; it had become indispensable and impossible to fire. When Halliburton/Brown & Root officially lost the competition for the second LOGCAP contract (LOGCAP II) in 1997 to DynCorp, another private military contractor that was better known for hiring out former soldiers and police officers for training and security operations, the U.S. Army carved out the Yugoslavian portion of the contract and awarded the "Balkans Support Contract" back to Halliburton/Brown & Root on a sole-source (no-bid) basis in May 1997.[46]

The Balkans Support contract grew to a size that was probably ten times bigger than any previous LOGCAP project, although it was smaller than the kind of work the company had done in Vietnam. Halliburton/Brown & Root made sure that the managers on the ground knew the ropes—most senior managers like Capouya had worked at one time or another for the military and knew how to get projects done and troubleshoot problems. For example, Capouya's man in charge of engineering and construction was fifty-five-year-old Robert Bruce "Butch" Gatlin from Tennessee, who had worked for the

Army Corps for thirty-two years, including several years as the commander for the agency's Texas coastal district, which includes Houston. There he had to face off with local groups that wanted to preserve the Sheldon Lake wetlands for the recreational use of inner-city kids, instead of allowing developers to divert local water into Lake Houston, and songbird enthusiasts who wanted to prevent the filling of wetlands near Lake Jackson to build a golf course. Gatlin rarely gave into the pressure, favoring the engineering works over the interests of environmental activists.[47]

At Bondsteel, Gatlin was also tasked with making decisions about water resources. He hired a Greek company to dig for water and they eventually struck an aquifer about seven hundred feet below ground. All told, eight wells were completed to supply the camp, although most soldiers refused to use it for drinking. At the time, Gatlin said the water well project was the largest ever dug by the military on a base.[48]

In time, Gatlin would be called to head up an engineering project that was ten times bigger than Bondsteel: the building and supply of military bases in Kuwait for the 2003 invasion of Iraq. That project would tax even his experience, and he would resign in anger from the company.

But for the time being, his supervisors were happy. U.S. Army officials were full of praise for Halliburton/Brown & Root whom they said had finally licked the problems of short-staffing as well as the complications encountered in using multiple contractors in the 1991 Persian Gulf War.

Under the terms of the contract, the company was guaranteed a 1 percent profit and up to 8 percent more if it did a good job. Between 1995 and 2000, Halliburton/Brown & Root was given the full amount for five evaluation periods, 99 percent twice and 98 percent once.[49] In fact, the Logistics Management Institute (LMI), a military think tank, claimed that LOGCAP contractors employed 24 percent fewer personnel and were 28 percent less expensive than using the military itself.[50]

Other government agencies were more skeptical than LMI. "It is convenient to contract a lot of this work out. The problem is that the government doesn't do the best job of oversight," Neil Curtin, director of operations and readiness issues at the Defense Capabilities and Management Team at the GAO said.[51]

A February 1997 study by the GAO showed that the 1996 estimate presented to Congress of $191.6 million had ballooned to $461.5 million a year later. Examples of overspending included billing the government $85.98 per sheet of plywood, which cost $14.06 per sheet in the United States. The company also billed the army for its employees' income taxes in Hungary.[52]

A subsequent GAO report, issued in September 2000, noted that army commanders in the Balkans were unable to keep track of contracts as they were typically rotated out after six months, erasing institutional memory. For example the GAO pointed out that "half of the crews had at least 40 percent of their members not engaged in work," despite the fact that jobs like office cleaning were being performed four times a day. The GAO also faulted Halliburton/Brown & Root in its over-zealous purchasing of power generators at great expense and employing far more firefighters than necessary. (The company wanted to hire 116 firefighters, but army engineers concluded that sixty-six would be sufficient. Eventually the two would compromise with seventy-seven firefighters.)[53]

Pentagon officials were able to identify $72 million in cost savings on the Brown & Root contract simply by eliminating excess power generation equipment that the company had purchased for the operation. The company also eventually settled allegations of fraud: In November 2006 Halliburton/Brown & Root paid the government $8 million to resolve lawsuits brought under the False Claims Act for double-billing, inflating prices, and providing unsuitable products during the construction of Camp Bondsteel.[54]

"Was there waste in Bosnia?" General William Nash, the former U.S. commander in Bosnia and the UN administrator in Kosovo told Briody. "Of course there was. When you come in on the leading edge of an operation, you've got to expect that there will be some degree of less-than-perfect organization. To some extent, it's the cost of doing business. There were a lot of scams that people could run. The fact that they got over on some portion of the contract, I can't deny. Life is real."[55]

And the reality was contractors had become an institutional part of the battlefield. By the time the Clinton administration's tenure in office drew to a close, contractors were called in even to take part in war game exercises such as Operation Restore Order, which took place at Fort McPherson, Georgia, and the Diamond Reserve Center in Louisiana in July 2000. There, troops were deployed at the request of the embattled (and fictional) "Vogarian" government in Africa, which was under siege because of political and economic instability as well as factional fighting outside the capital of Queenstown, to prevent large-scale famine and disease among displaced civilians.[56]

Fort Ord

In February of 2001 Halliburton paid out $2 million to settle a lawsuit with the Justice Department, which alleged that the company defrauded the government during the closure of the Fort Ord military base in Monterey, California, in the mid-1990s. The allegations in the case first surfaced when Dammen Gant Campbell, a former contracts manager for Halliburton turned whistle-blower, charged that between 1994 and 1998 the company fraudulently inflated project costs by misrepresenting the quantities, quality, and types of materials required for 224 projects. Campbell said that the company submitted a detailed "contractors pricing proposal" from an army manual containing fixed prices for some thirty thousand line items.[57]

Once the proposal was approved, the company submitted a more general "statement of work," which did not contain a detailed breakdown of items to be purchased. Then, according to Campbell, Halliburton intentionally did not deliver many items listed in the original proposal. The company defends this practice by claiming that the "statement of work" was the legally binding document, not the original "contractors pricing proposal."

"Whether you characterize it as fraud or sharp business practices, the bottom line is the same, the government was not getting what it paid for," explained Michael Hirst, who litigated the case for the U.S. attorney's office in Sacramento. "We alleged that they exploited the contracting process and increased their profits at the government's expense," Hirst added. "Kellogg, Brown & Root was very cooperative and eager to settle. They said they wanted to maintain a good relationship with the government."[58]

Meanwhile, Campbell's attorney, Dan Schrader, was pleased with the settlement, but he wondered why the company was so eager to compromise. "If the company was indicted, I suspect that it might have been far more difficult for them to get new government contracts," he said.[59] The 2001 annual report says precisely that in its notes on the settlement of the lawsuit: "Kellogg, Brown & Root's ability to perform further work for the U.S. government has not been impaired."[60]

Part 2

Supporting the War on Terror

ON THE SECOND FLOOR OF 1150 18TH STREET—a white, ten-story office building between L and M streets, in the heart of the Washington, DC's, "Golden Triangle" business district—are the discreet offices of Halliburton's staff lobbyists.[1] Their job is to make sure that the company continues to win large federal contracts such as the giant multibillion dollar LOGCAP contract under which the company has been supporting the "Global War on Terror" by building and maintaining military bases from Bagram in Afghanistan to Guantánamo Bay, Cuba, and all points in between, not least of which are the fifty-odd bases in Iraq.

These offices housed a few of Cheney's closest aides at the Pentagon when he took over Halliburton. The first of these aides to come on board was Charles "Chuck" Dominy, a former three-star general with the Army Corps of Engineers (the agency that awarded the LOGCAP contracts).[2] Next to arrive was David Gribbin, who had served as Cheney's assistant secretary of defense for legislative affairs.[3] Finally, Admiral T. Joseph "Joe" Lopez, who had served as Cheney's military aide while he was secretary of defense, was brought in on July 1999, although his main base of operations would be at the Houston headquarters.[4]

Dominy told *National Public Radio* in December 2003, "Mr. Cheney made it very clear to me when he arrived that he would not be engaged in the government side of our business. He said, 'You're on your own. I don't want any perception that as a former secretary of defense I influenced government work.' This was direct conversation."[5]

The job could not have been easier for Dominy, who grew up on a farm in Fairfax, Virginia, and spent thirty-three years in the army. The job of meeting with Army Corps staffers in charge of the LOGCAP contract at the Pentagon in Arlington was like meeting up with old friends. During his career he had served as an Army Corps colonel in Savannah, Georgia, and as a brigadier general at the Army Corps Missouri River Division, before becoming director of the army staff, where he was responsible for the management and organization of the army staff and coordinated the activities of all agencies reporting to the chief of staff. He also served as the chief legislative liaison responsible for all army activities related to the U.S. Congress (i.e., he was the army's lobbyist on Capitol Hill).[6]

For Gribbin, who joined Halliburton in 1996, the job of chief lobbyist at the 18th Street offices where he had to represent Cheney in Washington, DC, was also a natural step. Gribbin had shadowed Cheney for most of his life after the two met at Casper's Natrona City High School in the mid-1950s. Both men married their high school sweethearts, graduated from the University of Wyoming together, and despite losing touch for a short time in the 1960s, they worked together again in the 1970s. Gribbin helped Cheney move out of his house in a rented Ryder truck in 1977 when he lost his job at the White House and drove him back into Washington in a Volkswagen in 1979 to his new job as Congressman. (The two men initially found themselves locked out of the office because they hadn't brought a key.) When Cheney was sworn in at the Cannon Building on Capitol Hill as secretary of defense, Gribbin was invited to jump into the blue Cadillac limousine with a red light on top for the seven-minute ride to the Pentagon in Virginia.[7]

Gribbin's Capitol Hill résumé was not limited to working for Cheney. He worked as chief of staff to former House of Representatives Speaker Newt Gingrich and Senator Dan Coats after Cheney left the Pentagon in 1993. While with Coats, Gribbin took a brief sabbatical to teach a seminar on the U.S. Congress at the Naval Postgraduate School in Monterey, California, before coming to work for Halliburton.[8]

With friends like Dominy and Gribbin lobbying Capitol Hill and keeping Cheney out of the public eye for a possible conflict of interest over the Balkans contract, Cheney then hired Admiral Joe Lopez. Cheney and Lopez had a long-standing relationship that dated back to the days of Operation Just Cause—the Panama invasion in 1989—when Lopez was part of the Crisis Action Team that reported directly to Cheney under Lieutenant General Thomas W. Kelly, director of operations for the Joint Chiefs of Staff. (Lopez actually came up with the name Operation Just Cause to replace the slightly ridiculous original name, Blue Spoon.)[9] Lopez had just retired as commander of all U.S. and Allied Bosnia Peace Forces where his job included meeting with Serbian President Slobodan Milošević in Belgrade.[10] Lopez was asked to run Brown & Root Services, which he was very familiar with already, as the company had provided support to his troops in the Balkans.

This close group of comrades was split up when Cheney left Halliburton in 2000. Gribbin was the first to leave; he quit his job at the company as chief lobbyist at the same time Cheney quit his post. At first he followed his mentor, joining Cheney at his McLean office to work as director of Congressional relations for the White House transition team, where he managed the confirmation process for newly nominated cabinet secretaries.[11] Eventually, in June 2001, Gribbin left Cheney's immediate orbit and took a job as managing director of a Washington, DC, lobbying firm named Clark & Weinstock.[12] Both Dominy and Lopez, however, stayed with Halliburton, with Dominy taking over Gribbin's job as chief lobbyist.[13]

LOGCAP III

When Cheney and Gribbin left Halliburton and Dominy took over the 18th Street offices. The company's lobbying budget plummeted. It went from $600,000 in 1998 and 1999 to $300,000 in 2001 and stayed down there to the present day (with the exception of 2004, which is the year that the company was hauled over the coals in the U.S. Congress to explain allegations of overcharging).[14]

Yet despite this, Halliburton's winning streak did not abate. The Army Corps of Engineers, Dominy's previous employer, issued a new LOGCAP contract to replace the one that DynCorp controlled. LOGCAP III, issued on December 14, 2001,[15] was an "unlimited firm-fixed-price/cost-plus-award-fee/cost-plus-fixed-fee order" to perform "selected services in wartime and other operations." The contract was for one year, but the Pentagon was able to extend it every year for a maximum of nine years, until January 31, 2012. The contract was awarded after three competing bids were reviewed.

"The Halliburton Company wins their work on the merits of our capabilities. It's all about competence. Our history of working for the Department of Defense goes way back to World War II. We have won work building ships. We've won work building airfields in Vietnam," Dominy told CNN later. "We are the only company in the United States that had the kind of systems in place, people in place, contacts in place, to do that kind of thing."[16]

"We've had multiple contracts successfully done in places like Somalia, Rwanda, Haiti, Bosnia, and Kosovo. We win work in Republican administrations. We win work in Democratic administrations. This is a company that has great capabilities, worldwide reach, lots of talent, and we like to compete. And we're ready to compete on any given field."

Asked whether the fact that Dominy had once been a senior staffer at the Army Corps had helped them win the contract, he told *60 Minutes,* "I wish I could embed [Halliburton's critics] in the Department of Defense contracting system for a week or so. Once they'd done that, they'd have religion, just like I do, about how the system cannot be influenced."[17] Later he told *The Hill* newspaper, "There was never any profiteering. There was never any gouging. Everybody says, 'Oh, you had this sweetheart deal, it was no bid.' There is zero—zero—cronyism associated with our work."[18]

But it's hard to convince people that the company had no influence when your entire upper management once worked for the very agencies that awarded the contracts. As Charles Lewis, the executive director of the Center for Public Integrity, said: "This is not about the revolving door, people going in and out. There's no door. There's no wall. I can't tell where one stops and the other starts. They're retired generals. They have classified clearances, they go to classified meetings and they're with companies getting billions of dollars in classified contracts. And their disclosures about their activities are classified. Well, isn't that what they did when they were inside the government? What's the difference, except they're in the private sector?"[19]

AFGHANISTAN AND UZBEKISTAN

A month after the attacks on the World Trade Center in New York and the Pentagon on September 11, 2001, a thousand light infantry troops from the U.S. Army's Tenth Mountain Division were dispatched to an old Soviet air base named Khanabad, after permission was granted by President Islam Karimov in October 2001.[20] The base is near the town of Karshi in southern Uzbekistan, about ninety miles north of the Afghan border. Supplies to set up Camp Stronghold Freedom on the Uzbek airbase were first dispatched by giant military cargo planes like the C-130 and the C-17 Globemaster and then by rail from Bremerhaven, Germany. At the base, the 164th Transportation Contract Supervision Detachment arranged for these supplies to be driven across the Afghan border in private, ten-ton Super Kamas trucks rented from local merchants.

As of mid-April 2002, Major David Cintron, the 164th detachment team leader, estimated that they had sent six hundred contracted trucks south to Bagram in Afghanistan carrying approximately forty-two hundred tons of cargo. "Some of the obstacles transporters have encountered along the way include delayed bridge crossings, avalanches, blizzards, flooded tunnels, one-way traffic alternating daily, and administrative delays," he wrote later in *Army Logistician* magazine.[21]

But help was on the way. With the new LOGCAP contract in hand, planners at the Army Materiel Command in Rock Island, Illinois, were already issuing task orders to Halliburton/KBR to provide support at Camp Stronghold Freedom.[22]

On April 26, 2002, three employees of Halliburton/KBR arrived at Khanabad to begin operations at the U.S. military base in the Afghanistan "theater of operations." Within two weeks the numbers of Halliburton/KBR employees had swelled to thirty-eight, and by June 10 these men replaced the 130 military personnel that previously oversaw day-to-day support services at the two Force Provider prefabricated military bases that housed the Tenth Mountain Division.[23]

New troops arriving at the base were soon being assigned sleeping quarters by the Halliburton/KBR employees who wore khaki pants, black or blue golf shirts, and baseball caps to distinguish themselves from the soldiers. In addition the Halliburton/KBR employees were made responsible for laundry, food, and general base camp maintenance as well as airfield services, taking on the same tasks as their colleagues at Camp Bondsteel and Incirlik.[24]

The contract was soon extended to Afghanistan. When the United States seized Bagram from the Taliban in 2001, there was no sewage system, no running water, or electricity. So Halliburton/KBR employees were set to work drilling and sawing, installing these basic services, putting up new buildings and heated tents, running laundry services, showers, and the Camp Viper mess hall at Bagram.[25] In August and September 2002, Halliburton/KBR was awarded two new task orders that would yield $216,263,785 and $144,864,959, respectively, to provide similar services for troops at bases in both Bagram and Kandahar in Afghanistan. A third task order issued in 2003 yielded $68,511,111.[26]

Most of the supervisors Halliburton/KBR hired were former military personnel. In 2003 an army reporter interviewed three contractors working at Bagram for an article on the dining facilities that Halliburton/KBR was operating: Dean Brunn, Glenn Lee, and Willie Mickens estimated that Halliburton/KBR was spending about $1.5 million a week to feed thirteen thousand troops at five dining facilities in Bagram airfield and in Kabul, and importing meats from Philadelphia, fruits and vegetables from Germany, and sodas from Saudi Arabia and Bahrain.[27] "A lot of the guys working here are prior military," said Mickens, who retired from the army in 1994. "We've been there and done that too, so this is like we're giving back. I remember what they're going through."

On Thanksgiving Day in 2003, the Halliburton/KBR crew served up a menu which included glazed ham, turkey, roast beef, corn bread stuffing, simmered corn, giblet gravy, ground gravy, pumpkin pie, sweet potato pie, cheese cake, chocolate cake, blueberry pie, and hot, fresh rolls. A military reporter interviewed three Halliburton/KBR workers—Derryel Clarke of Orlando, Florida; and Jerry Gross and Ronald Waters of Killeen, Texas—about the meal. "This is something I've been looking forward to since I arrived with Brown and Root in support of the military," said Waters, a food service manager. "I know how important this meal is, considering I served twenty-one years in the food service in the military." [28]

Fariba Nawa, an Afghan American reporter from Fremont, California, agreed to visit Bagram on my behalf in late 2005. She emailed me a report from the military base: "Halliburton/KBR hires Afghan laborers who are paid ten dollars a day, three times the local rate, but sources inside the base said that they seem to be employing more and more from outside the country such as Bosnians, Kyrgyz, and Indians. A group of Afghan men working for Halliburton/KBR unloaded garbage from a truck into a large bin in their orange jackets. They said they work twelve hours a day, six days a week. The men said there are too many unemployed Afghans who need work, and they did not understand why foreigners were being hired instead. They pointed to the dozens of Afghan laborers standing outside the base, waiting for employment."[29]

Rick Scavetta, Nawa's military tour guide, a former journalist at a small paper before he came on duty, was quite candid. "It frees up soldiers to do what we do best—kill the enemy," he said matter-of-factly. "When KBR shows up, the troops know they get a hot shower, a chess game, a clean toilet. They work tirelessly to support us."

Nawa described how Scavetta took her to the food court and bazaar of the base where a big Burger King sign was painted on the side of a blue building, next to a Subway sandwich shop. Souvenir shops sold Afghan and Central Asian merchandise for prices ten times higher than in the stores in Kabul. The workers in these restaurants were mainly from Kerala, India, who spoke English. Binu, who worked at Green Bean Coffee, told Nawa that he had been in Bagram for nine months. He received $600 a month and free food and housing. "I like it here," he said.

"[When] the tour was over, Scavetta dropped me off right outside the base where I witnessed a startling contrast of lifestyle," wrote Nawa. "Scrawny vendors looking tired and ragged sold fruits and vegetables in carts. Women shopped in their *burqas,* haggling with the vendors. Off the main road, all the streets were dirt, and a couple of men sat on a corner complaining about the lack of electricity and water in their homes. This was life in the Bagram town outside the base."

PRISON CELLS ON GUANTÁNAMO

Beginning in 1996, the U.S. Navy also put in place a program that was nearly identical to LOGCAP. Named Contingency Construction Capabilities (CONCAP), it was created to help the Naval Facilities Engineering Command's ability to respond to emergencies anywhere in the world.

The company first hired for CONCAP was Perini, based in Framingham, Massachusetts. Perini was first deployed to Camp Lejeune when Hurricane Bertha hit North Carolina with sustained winds of 100 mph on July 12, 1996. Over the next couple of years the contract was used in the Caribbean, the Florida Keys, Mississippi, and Virginia. CONCAP was also used to design a road between Grozde and Sarajevo in Bosnia during 1996; to build a sewage treatment plant, holding tank, and pumping stations in Souda Bay, Crete; and for urgent runway repairs at Aviano, Italy, in 1999, and in Morocco in 2001.[30]

In 2001, Perini lost the contract with Halliburton/Brown & Root. In March 2002 Halliburton/Brown & Root was tasked with building new detention facilities to replace the ramshackle Camp X-Ray where Al Qaeda suspects who were picked up in Afghanistan were being held in Guantánamo Bay, Cuba.[31] For those with long memories, the contract would bring back thoughts of Vietnam, when Brown & Root was hired to replace the infamous Tiger Cages built by the French to hold Vietnamese prisoners.[32]

To do the Camp Delta job, Halliburton/KBR hired 199 Filipino welders, fabricators, and carpenters through a Manila-based company named Anglo-European Placement Services (AEPS). In less than twenty-four hours, AEPS was able to obtain their travel and working papers (a bureaucratic process that normally takes two to three months) when the Philippine Overseas Employment Administration received a phone call from the U.S. Embassy and the Philippine ambassador in Washington, DC, to expedite approval.

Rick Rocamora, a Filipino American journalist, accidentally discovered the story of the workers when he met some of them at the San Francisco airport in California. He told the story of Jojo (last name omitted for security reasons), a thirty-five-year-old carpenter, in the *Philippine Daily Inquirer*.[33]

Jojo says he was flown to Cuba on a chartered DC-10 registered to Electra Airlines in Greece, with refueling stops in Dubai, Greece, and Portugal. "We were not allowed to leave the plane during stopovers and traveled for thirty-two hours, longer than the time our travel papers were processed by the Philippine government," he said.

Once Jojo and his fellow workers arrived at Guantánamo Bay, they were housed in enormous tents, where they were not allowed access to television, radio, or newspapers, and were allowed to call their families for no more than two minutes at a time. They were paid $2.50 an hour for twelve hours a day, seven days a week, but they lived like prisoners. "We had our own guards and could not leave our compound," he said. Indian engineers and British managers supervised them.

A small shop was set up to sell the workers cigarettes, toiletries, chocolates, and Gatorade on credit while they were supplied working clothes, safety goggles, helmets, and working shoes. A cook was provided to prepare Filipino meals of beef, chicken, pork, and fish. They were also given two cans of beer at the end of each work day.

Jojo and his co-workers built the Guantánamo prison cells out of shipping cargo containers, removing three walls and replacing them with plastic-covered cyclone fencing. A hole was cut in the roof for ventilation, and a ceiling fan was installed in each unit. A small window was also cut into each door, and each door was reinforced with big bars and heavy-duty padlocks. Plumbing was placed underneath the units that were elevated four feet off the ground.

Each container was divided into six small cells with a toilet, a bed, and a sink. Special air-conditioned cells were built as interrogation rooms, and an exercise area was also built near the units. Around the complex, the workers also constructed five layers of security fence four meters apart as well as a high-perimeter fence with six layers of security fence with razor-sharp edges.

After almost two months in Guantánamo Bay, the Filipinos were given a certificate of employment, but the location of work was not recorded on the grounds that it might jeopardize their chances of getting jobs in the Middle East.

Jojo and his group took a small plane to Jamaica, and from there they flew on American Airlines to San Francisco via Miami before being put on a Philippine Airlines flight to Manila. In San Francisco, the group was kept in a small room where immigrations officials insisted on escorting them at all times, even when they went to the bathroom, made phone calls, or bought food. One of them got so upset with the treatment they received that he shouted, "Why are you doing this to us, keeping us like prisoners? You should treat us better; we were the ones who built the prisons of your enemy."

The man in charge of the CONCAP contract at Guantánamo was Jim Spore, an engineer with a master's degree from the Georgia Institute of Technology and a graduate of the U.S. Naval Academy.[34] He would later advertise his accomplishment on his résumé when he got a job in Kuwait as "Program General Manager [for a] special four-hundred-person, $15 million detention facility complex on a remote island in just fifty-four days, later expanding to a twelve-hundred-person prison, troop housing, hospital, and related infrastructure in excess of $60 million in just eight months." (Like his workers, he probably omitted the name Guantánamo in case it stirred up any resentment in the Middle East.)[35]

When he retired from the navy, he would be invited to work for Halliburton/KBR in northern Iraq, to oversee, among other projects, the expansion of the Balad airbase to create LSA Anaconda. With him, he would bring the men who had helped supply the Filipino workers, so as to avoid having to hire local workers.

Camp Delta was not the last CONCAP contract that Halliburton/KBR would be awarded in Guantánamo, whose work on the island approaches $100 million. In July 2005, Halliburton/KBR was awarded a contract by the Naval Facilities Engineering Command to build a new prison on the island, named Detention Camp 6 and costing $30 million. The two-story prison was designed by Miami Correctional Facility Superintendent John VanNatta, who is also an officer in the U.S. Army Reserves, and was intended to house 220 men and include exercise areas and medical and dental wards, as well as a security control room.[36]

"The future detention facility will be based on prison models in the United States and is designed to be safer for the long-term detention of detainees and guards who serve" at Guantánamo, a Pentagon statement said. "It is also expected to require less manpower."[37]

INVADING IRAQ

While Jojo and his comrades were building Camp Delta under the supervision of Jim Spore, and Major David Cintron was working to dispatch trucks from Camp Stronghold Freedom in late April 2002, General Tommy Franks was at Camp David with President Bush describing possible options for a future military operation, code-named Operation Polo Step—a possible invasion of Iraq.[38]

The internal discussions among the senior members of the Bush administration for dealing with Saddam Hussein can be traced back to the days when Cheney's team was still making the transition from Anderson Road in McLean to Pennsylvania Avenue in Washington, in 2001. In January that year, Cheney sent a message to then Secretary of Defense William S. Cohen who was preparing to leave office. "We really need to get the president-elect briefed up on some things . . . [such as a] discussion about Iraq and different options," he wrote, according to Washington Post journalist Bob Woodward. Woodward also noted in his book Plan of Attack that between May 31 and July 26, 2001, Deputy National Security Advisor Stephen J. Hadley had convened four meetings of the "deputies" (the advisors to the administration's national security "principals"—Dick Cheney, Colin Powell, Secretary of State George Tenet, the head of the CIA, and National Security Advisor Condoleezza Rice) on how to weaken Hussein diplomatically, which resulted in a paper presented to their bosses on August 1. The topic of attacking Hussein was also raised briefly by Secretary of Defense Donald Rumsfeld on the afternoon of September 11 after the destruction of the World Trade Center in New York and the attack on the Pentagon.

Serious planning for an invasion began, however, only in late November 2001, when Rumsfeld flew down to Tampa, Florida, to direct General Tommy Franks, the head of Central Command, and his operations director, Air Force Major General Victor "Gene" Renuart, to revise an existing document code-named Op Plan 1003 that had been written in 1996 for a possible intervention in Iraq.

Op Plan 1003 called for a seven-month buildup for a military force of five hundred thousand, a scheme not dissimilar to the 1991 Persian Gulf War. Rumsfeld was not happy with this plan; he wanted a much smaller group that could be dispatched in weeks, not months. "Let's put together a group that can just think outside the box completely," ordered Rumsfeld. "Certainly we have traditional military planning, but let's take away the constraints a little bit and think about what might be a way to solve the problem."

The successful invasion of Afghanistan, just two months prior, was a major stimulus. On the one hand, the fact that a military force had been put on the ground within weeks, and the country taken over in a matter of days, made any future military operation seem feasible. On the other hand, Rumsfeld and his military planners knew that the first boots on the ground were from the CIA, not the much-vaunted Special Forces, so the Pentagon had to save face in any future operations. Franks, in particular, was acutely aware that Saddam's military was far superior to anything the Taliban had in Afghanistan.

Franks and Renuart set about their task somewhat reluctantly as they were still knee-deep in overseeing the Afghan operations. Indeed the battle for Tora Bora had only just begun when Rumsfeld ordered the two men to start planning for Iraq. Over the next nine months, they struggled to come up with a plan that would please Rumsfeld. Operation Polo Step, which envisioned two hundred fifty thousand soldiers, was just one of several plans that they would present to Rumsfeld, only to be shot down and told to come back with a plan that would involve smaller numbers.

The final plan that would win tentative approval was called the Hybrid (although the actual invasion would be given the code name Cobra II) that Franks and Renuart would present to the National Security Council at 4:30 p.m. on August 4, 2002, in the White House Situation Room. The presentation consisted of 110 slides.

One of the key concepts that the Hybrid plan envisioned was a buildup of infrastructure in Kuwait. In the years after the 1991 Persian Gulf War, the United States had maintained a small force in the country and had agreed with the Kuwaitis on a joint plan to improve the country's airfields, in a manner very similar to what the United States had done in neighboring Saudi Arabia. Two Kuwaiti bases—Ahmed Al Jaber and Ali Al Salem—were to be built up with Kuwaiti money. However, the Kuwaitis had deferred the funding, so

Franks figured it would be easy to provide U.S. funds to pay contractors to do the work without the Iraqis suspecting that this was a covert operation for a U.S. invasion.

The two bases also already had foreign personnel working on them. Al Jaber "The Jab" was used for Operation Southern Watch, a decade-long reconnaissance mission of overflights to protect Southern Iraq. DynCorp contractors worked on the base providing support to the Kuwait Air Force. Ali Al Salem, which was the first base to be overrun by Saddam's troops in August 1990, was shared with the UK's Royal Air Force.

Some thirty projects worth $700 million to upgrade the Kuwaiti bases were quietly approved by Bush by late July 2001 without notifying the U.S. Congress. This included converting ramp space at the two bases to make way for storage. Franks also signed a series of contracts with the Kuwaiti oil ministry to clean out some existing fuel pipelines close to the bases to allow an invading force to get a continuous supply of fuel from Kuwait's refineries on the coast.

Bush would later tell Woodward that the buildup of the infrastructure was a smart plan by Franks and Rumsfeld: "It was, in my opinion, a very smart recommendation by Don and Tommy to put certain elements in place that could easily be removed, and it could be done in such a way that was quiet so that we didn't create a lot of noise and anxiety."

Although Congressional approval for an invasion of Iraq would not be given until October 12, 2002, the first ships started delivering the military equipment into Kuwait in August 2002, following the approval of the Hybrid concept, and the first Halliburton/KBR managers would be hard at work by September, starting on the building of brand new bases for the invasion.[39]

In many ways, the use of Halliburton/KBR and contractors for the buildup in Kuwait was but a logical next step from previous interventions such as in Bosnia, where Halliburton crews were just days behind the initial invading force, and in Cuba and Kosovo, where they were used for building "sustainment" bases and facilities such as Camp Delta on Guantánamo Bay and Camp Bondsteel in Uroševac.

Still the use of contractors six months in advance of an invasion was highly unusual—but it was also the only way that Franks and Renuart could possibly begin to implement what Rumsfeld kept demanding: an invasion force numbering just one hundred fifty thousand. Ultimately the number of troops that would fight under the banner of the "Coalition of the Willing" in March 2003 would be three hundred thousand, closer to the number that Franks had recommended in the May 2002 version of Operation Polo Step.[40] Later, as the number of troops was drawn down to half the initial strength, it would be Halliburton/KBR that would expand to take up the slack.

7

Operation Restore Iraqi Oil (RIO)

DEEP IN THE BOWELS OF THE PENTAGON, in a secure room, accessible only to those with high-level military clearance, the military engineer looked around the vast conference table to see who had arrived. Lieutenant General Carl Strock looked worried.[1]

It was a cold, blustery Wednesday in late February 2003, and war was in the air. Less than two weeks prior, the world's largest mobilization had taken place—from estimates of well over a million in London to a small gathering of five scientists bundled in red parkas and woolen hats at the South Pole, protesting U.S. plans to break international law and oust Iraq's dictatorial ruler, Saddam Hussein.[2]

But neither the protestors nor the impending war worried Strock. He had, after all, led battalions from the 82nd Airborne Division through Operation Just Cause in Panama, Operations Desert Shield, and Desert Storm in Saudi Arabia and Iraq.[3] Indeed the army was his life; he had been born into a military family in Georgia. No, his chief concern was what was described in the papers the group was about to discuss: a new kind of military operation, a kind that his agency had never undertaken before.

He was director of military operations at the U.S. Army Corps of Engineers, an agency that had built and repaired a wide range of public projects for a little more than two centuries, from dams to emergency shelters after earthquakes. The Army Corps has had long ties to the Middle East, particularly in Kuwait, where as far back as the Second World War, Army Corps engineers had supervised the assembly of prefabricated barges used to transport war materials up the Tigris and Euphrates rivers. A special office called the Middle East/Africa Projects Office (MEAPO), headquartered at Winchester, Virginia, had coordinated the building of some $14 billion in Saudi military infrastructure such as the King Khalid Military City; King Faisal Military Cantonment and King Abdulaziz Military Cantonment; Jubail and Jeddah naval bases; and Khamis Mushayt, Taif, and Tabuk air bases.[4] But today the Army Corps was being asked to take a special lead on fixing oil fields, a subject on which Strock and the Army Corps had little or no experience at all.

Seated close to Strock was the Corps' chief procurement officer, Bunnatine "Bunny" Greenhouse, a former mathematics teacher from Louisiana. Broad shouldered, with short, dark hair, and a few years older than Strock, she too had a lot of military experience, starting out as a military wife, and then working her way up the chain of command as a civilian employee at the Pentagon. Like Strock, she was part of both Operations Desert Storm and Desert Shield, albeit in the procurement arena, not in the battlefield. She was the person who was responsible to sign off on the contract that was on the table that day.

"It was a snow day," Greenhouse would later recall in her quiet, understated fashion. And indeed, for the first time in a week, the temperatures had dropped below freezing in the Washington, DC, area. Visibility was down, a northeasterly wind had picked up, and the light rain was predicted to turn to snow. The weather was marginally better than in Texas, where a strong winter storm had been building over the week to bring a mix of rain, sleet, freezing rain, and snow to the region. The day before, the Dallas/Fort Worth airport had canceled more than 220 flights, tree limbs and power lines snapped across the state, while motorists were trapped for up to ten hours on slippery, crash-filled highways.[5]

Joining Strock and Greenhouse around the conference table were representatives of a slew of government and military agencies. From Secretary of Defense Donald Rumsfeld's office there was Gary Vogler, who had a background in both the military and in the oil business, a West Point graduate who had just retired from Exxon-Mobil,[6] and Clarke Turner, the director of the Rocky Mountain Oilfield Testing Center, in Casper, Wyoming. Both of them had been working for Rumsfeld for almost six months and were called in to help with the war plans.[7]

From the office of the under secretary of defense, there was Stephen Browning, who had been in charge of reconstruction after Hurricane Mitch and the World Trade Center collapse[8] and Barbara Glotfelty, a procurement analyst who was writing the new Pentagon purchasing regulations.[9]

From Central Command at the MacDill Air Force Base in Florida, there was Colonel Gary Tregaskis. Then there were several officials from USAID and the State Department.

All of them were acutely aware that war was just days away in Iraq, which was halfway across the world, even though the White House continued to deny that a final decision had been made. European diplomats were scuttling across the world in an effort to influence a pending United Nations Security Council resolution to avert war on the one hand while U.S. officials were doing precisely the opposite. In Washington that week senior White House and Pentagon officials were already making presentations on reconstruction plans for after the war.

Then the door opened. Greg Badgett and Mary Wade of Halliburton/KBR were ushered into the room, apologizing profusely for being just a little bit late. The men and women who were gathered around the table nodded; everybody knew how difficult it was to get around in the nation's capital in winter.

On the table was a proposal that Halliburton/KBR had drawn up for what to do in case Saddam Hussein set ablaze Iraq's southern oilfields, as his troops had done in Kuwait when his army was routed in 1991. (More than six hundred wells were booby-trapped with plastic explosives and set on fire, causing millions of barrels to burn every day, which took months to put out.)[10] Then there was the even bigger question of who would fix the Iraqi oil fields, known to be in a state of disrepair after decades of war and sanctions. This contract, which was named Restore Iraqi Oil, or RIO for short, had yet to be put out to bid, as is the normal procedure, but it was clear to the Halliburton/KBR officials, who had just arrived, that they were in the running.

As the meeting, chaired by Strock, got under way, Greenhouse sat back, stunned. Under this plan, Halliburton/KBR had drawn up the contingency plan in November 2002 for fixing the oil fields, for which it had billed the taxpayer $1.9 million. (This was done at the direction of Michael Mobbs—a special assistant to U.S. Undersecretary of Defense Douglas Feith.) But in such cases, the contractor that draws up a plan for a project is rarely allowed to bid on the job itself because that company would know insider details that would give them an unfair advantage. In any case, there were a number of other international engineering companies that were qualified to do the job—Bechtel, Fluor, Parsons—all of which had previously worked for the military and were known to be interested.

"KBR came to give an update on where they were, you know, in the planning session. They provided that update, but they were allowed to continue to stay on, you know, within the meeting," recalled Greenhouse.

"I was just flabbergasted," she continued. "I got up and whispered in the ear of the lieutenant general that it was time KBR left the meeting. If you know I've got a budget for $200,000, you're going to give me [a bid of] $199,000 plus some cents."[11] It was instantly clear that this was a setup because exactly a week prior, Gordon Sumner (no relation to Sting), a Pentagon lawyer, had sent Greenhouse an e-mail asking for her opinions on no-bid contracts with Halliburton/KBR.[12]

What's more, it was also obvious that the contract was to be "cost-plus"—that is to say that Halliburton/KBR would submit bills for all expenses, and the government would pay every penny back plus guaranteed profits ranging from 2 to 7 percent. Indeed, this was exactly why Greenhouse had been so critical in the past, because of absurd bills from the conflict in Yugoslavia where the company had billed $85.98 per plank of plywood.

Reluctantly, Strock complied with her request, asking Badgett and Wade to leave the room, but even after they left, Strock seemed adamant that Halliburton/KBR would get the job on the grounds of "compelling emergency." All Greenhouse could do was insist that the contract be limited to one year.

She left the Pentagon that evening feeling deeply troubled. The question on her mind was why were they breaking all the rules to negotiate this contract? "I sensed that the entire contracting process had gone haywire," she said later. "The Corps had absolutely no competencies related to oil production. . . . No aspect of the contracting work related to restoring the oil fields following the 1991 Persian Gulf War was undertaken by the USACE, and there was no reason why USACE should take over the function for the prosecution of the Iraq War. Restoration of oil production was simply outside the scope of our congressionally mandated mission. How then, I asked, could executive agency authority for the RIO contract be delegated to the USACE?"[13]

If she had a crystal ball to look a few weeks into the future, then she would have seen many of the men and women whom she had conferred with around the table that day, congratulating each other in springtime in Baghdad at the chandelier-illuminated Republican Palace, at Saddam Hussein's former residence. Walking the Italian marble corridors was Stephen Browning, now number two to Paul Bremer, the de facto governor of Iraq who ran the Coalition Provisional Authority (CPA) in Baghdad. Working across the river at the vast, sand-colored Ministry of Oil, there was Gary Vogler, Clarke Turner, and Barbara Glotfelty, coordinating the RIO contract with Halliburton/KBR.[14]

Less than six months later, in the middle of Baghdad's fierce summer heat, Greenhouse would have seen Gary Vogler go cap in hand to ask a powerful group of CPA officials in Baghdad to ask if it was OK to use Iraq's own money to pay for the very U.S. military-issued contract she was being asked to sign *before* the war. And lo and behold, she would have seen Strock appear, almost as if by magic, at a hastily called emergency meeting, to vote on behalf of *Iraq's* government in favor of the payment to Halliburton/KBR, even though Strock had almost never attended any of the meetings in the past. Nor would there be a single Iraqi at the table to consult on those decisions. And once again the argument would be this: There's no time for competition.[15]

Eighteen months down the road, with the same crystal ball, Greenhouse would have seen Strock, back in Washington, DC, now promoted to commander of the Corps, attempting to get her demoted, even though she had stellar internal evaluations. And two years down the road, in the early summer of 2005, she would have seen herself in the U.S. Senate, testifying against these men, before Strock finally demoted her.[16]

PREPARING FOR THE INVASION

While Greenhouse was battling Strock in Washington in February 2003, former Colonel Ray Rodon was already working on the contract in Kuwait for Halliburton/KBR. The day before the Pentagon meeting, Rodon had already taken delivery of firefighting equipment from Boots and Coots, a Texas company, despite the fact that the contract to put out the oil well fires had yet to be signed.[17] The company had agreed to charge $3,500 a day for each of their employees in Kuwait and $5,000 a day in Iraq once the team got across the border.[18]

Like Strock and Greenhouse, Rodon had a wealth of military experience. He was formerly deputy director of operations for the Defense Energy Support Center, at Fort Belvoir, Virginia. The Center was responsible for crude oil purchases for the Department of Energy's Strategic Petroleum Reserve, a program used to store crude oil as a buffer against potential national energy emergencies.[19]

There Rodon had helped set up an electronic Web-based system in late 1999 to process fuel orders and provide receipts and invoices for deliveries to the Pentagon, eliminating the previous labor-intensive paper-tracking system. He had often spoken of the need to make the military work more like a business, working closely with oil companies to help them eliminate annoying government inspections on their fuel deliveries.

He did have one little problem though—his Kuwaiti contacts were a little too helpful. More than pleased that the United States was coming back to fight Saddam Hussein, who had despoiled their country a little more than a decade prior, the Kuwaitis had offered to help put out the oil well fires for free.[20] This was highly unorthodox and might compete with the Boots and Coots men, who were scheduled to come in and stay at the Crowne Plaza Hotel. It's hard to make a profit on a cost-plus contract if you have locally based labor who work for nothing.

Leading the Kuwaiti team was Aisa Bou Yabes, the chief firefighter for the state-owned Kuwait Oil Company. Aged forty-six, he sported a long, graying beard, and a shiny metal hard hat, ornately inlaid with galloping horsemen.[21]

He was a contrast to the clean-cut, wraparound sunglass-clad Rodon, whose green metal hard hat had no such decoration.

The Kuwaiti's generous offer was also very practical. Kuwait also wanted to prevent pollution risks and damage to the underground oil reservoirs, which it shares with Iraq. Then there's the macho factor. Bou Yabes had worked side by side with Brian Krause, the president of Boots and Coots, when Iraq's departing army set fire to Kuwait's oil fields back in 1991. Krause then worked for the legendary Paul "Red" Adair, who decorated his Houston headquarters in plush red carpet and kept a fleet of red company Cadillacs. The two were rivals back then, when the Texan team bet that Yabes and his men couldn't put out one particularly nasty tower of flame and smoke in Kuwait's burning fields.[22] But they did, and they were now willing to take care of business again.

Halliburton/KBR went one step further. Instead of leasing the equipment from Boots and Coots, which is the normal procedure, Halliburton/KBR's bosses bought the equipment, which ended up being much more expensive.[23]

THE WAR BEGINS

On March 6, 2003, less than two weeks before the invasion and the day after Greenhouse signed the RIO document, it was sent up the chain of command. An e-mail dispatched by an Army Corps official described securing "authority to execute RIO" after "DepSecDef [Paul Wolfowitz] sent us to UnderSecPolicy [Under Secretary of Policy Douglas] Feith and gave him authority to approve" [the RIO contract].[24] The final contract stated that the company could be awarded as much as $7 billion in repair work.[25]

The war began on March 19, 2003. In the hours and days before the United States and Britain invaded Iraq, a team of British Petroleum (BP) engineers in Kuwait led by Robert Spears taught combat troops from the 516 Specialist Team Royal Engineers how to run the oil fields in southern Iraq.[26] U.S. oil executives who served as reserve officers also trained soldiers and combat engineers in West Texas oil fields in preparation for the attack. ("We leveraged the private sector," U.S. Brigadier General Robert Crear, the commander of the Southwestern Division of the Army Corps who was put in charge of RIO, commented to the *Wall Street Journal*.)[27]

Lieutenant Colonel Fred Padilla of the First Marine Division Alpha Company was the first to enter Iraq after two days of "shock-and-awe" bombing of Baghdad, driving across the Kuwaiti border up Shoe Road—a service road for the oilfields—before dawn on March 21, to capture three Gas Oil Separation Plants (GOSPs) in Rumaylah. He was followed by oil engineers who checked to see that the plants were not rigged to self-destruct. They also seized Pumping Station 2 by firing cluster bombs that killed the Iraqis assigned to guard it. "The battalion came upon . . . grisly proof of the weapon's effectiveness: a red film and body parts," a reporter would write later.[28]

Lieutenant Colonel Sam Mundy's battalion followed Padilla to seize more GOSPs, at which point Iraqi soldiers tried to repel them with artillery and small arms fire, while lighting fire trenches in the oil fields to create a haze of fire and smoke to confuse the helicopters. They were no match for the superior military technology of the U.S. Marines. By daylight an infantry battalion and a tank battalion had followed to capture the rest of the GOSPs in Rumaylah and head onto the Zubayr oil fields. The next day an oil complex that was dubbed the "crown jewel" was taken rather easily by Lieutenant Colonel Chris Conlin of the 1st Battalion, 7th Marine Regiment.

With the oil fields secured without much of a fight, and the regime of Saddam Hussein defeated in less than three weeks, the amount of work originally envisioned under RIO was significantly cut back as only seven wells were set on fire. But it quickly became obvious that there was a lot more work that needed to done because the oil fields and refineries were in a desperate state of disrepair.

There was another problem: the widespread looting that took place after the invasion. In May 2003, a reporter from *National Public Radio* described the looting at the Zubayr oil fields thus: "Inside the gate, four men are stripping what little is left of a large generator. Like jackals dining on a carcass, the looters look up briefly, then go back to their prey, uninterested in Hasan [the drilling manager]. Around the men are the skeletal and charred remains of equipment and buildings that once housed important archives and data about Iraq's southern oil fields."[29]

The report quotes Mustafa Al-Bader, the chief engineer and manager of the state-run Iraqi Drilling Company (IDC): "They took all the engines. They took all the pumps. They took all the motors. They destroyed all the rigs. The parts which they don't use, they just broke, and all of it because no protection, no security from the soldier, from the American or the British soldier."

T. Christian Miller of the *Los Angeles Times* says this was no accident. "Much of the looting, American officials came to believe, appeared to have been an inside job: Looters took specific equipment and instruments, and accessed the most sensitive locations. In one case they managed to penetrate the country's largest gas refining complex, make their way to a command room hidden deep inside, and smash control panels—hardly spontaneous behavior. The looting was the functional equivalent of the oil well fires that Iraqi commanders ignited when retreating from Kuwait in 1991. It crippled oil production, made repairs difficult, and caused debilitating loss of oil revenue."[30]

IMPLEMENTING RIO

Weeks after the February 26, 2003, Pentagon meeting at which the first RIO contract was drawn up, Strock and Crear were hard at work with Halliburton/ KBR crews at the Zubayr oil fields in southern Iraq.[31]

Halliburton/KBR dispatched Charles "Stoney" Cox to take charge of the RIO contract.[32] Like most other senior Halliburton/KBR managers, he was ex-military—a retired Army Corps deputy commander of the Middle East/Africa Projects Office (MEAPO). In fact, during Operation Desert Storm in 1990, Cox was in charge of building emergency facilities such as field latrines and sunshades for Blackhawk helicopters.[33]

Dan Baum described the arrival of Cox's oil engineers in late April 2003 at the lavish Crowne Plaza Hotel in Kuwait City in the *New York Times Magazine*: "No sooner does the lobby restaurant open at 5 a.m. than a line of middle-aged men in jumpsuits, golf shirts, and identical tan caps forms at the breakfast buffet, eschewing the mezzeh and labneh for French toast, home fries, and beef bacon. Outside, a couple of dozen silver SUVs are lined up, and after a quick breakfast the men are off in a swift northbound convoy, each car marked with the sideways V of duct tape that designates American and British vehicles."[34]

Armed with clipboards, calculators and cell phones, the engineers soon arrived at the border, where the Kuwaiti guards waved them across. On the other side, Jim Koockogey, a KBR security coordinator, arranged for armed soldiers to join them. "For they are the legions of Kellogg, Brown & Root subsidiary of the oil-services giant Halliburton," wrote Baum. "Most have spent years toiling in the raw, scraped, and sometimes violent places where oil lurks, and each hews to the oilie's ethic: No place is a hardship. How were your twelve years in Algeria? 'Not bad.' Your six years at Prudhoe Bay? 'Not bad.' Your fourteen years in Nigeria? 'Not bad.' Southern Iraq—searing, bleak, lawless—is an assignment like any other. Also, they are very well paid."

Meanwhile Iraqi oil workers feared that they would soon lose their jobs. A *Washington Post* reporter who was traveling in the region at about the same time, described them thus: "The oil workers stood listlessly in front of the plant, hair blown brittle by a dusty wind, as they shared cigarettes and bitterness for lack of anything else to do. They complained about the looting that has left them without a chair to sit on, let alone a tool to wield. They worried about whether the state oil company can continue to pay them."[35]

When Jim Humphries, a KBR manager, arrived in a sparkling GMC Yukon with Kuwaiti license plates, he was accosted by the workers. "You should cooperate," scolded Mohammed Mohee, an instrument technician, speaking in Arabic, as Humphries shrugged, backed away, and then got in his car and drove off. "KBR just comes and gives orders, but they don't do anything," Mohee continued. "They don't give us anything to work with. This is our oil. This is our city, our company. Our country. We want to clear away the damage and move forward. We have no tools, no instruments. No spare parts. They do nothing. They just look and leave."

Immediately after Humphries left, a British desert-camouflage military jeep and a silver sport utility vehicle pulled up, carrying six soldiers—some American, some British, and all holding assault rifles. They demanded Mohee's name and asked whether he worked there, leaving only after he showed them his identification card.[36]

Three months after the invasion, a major three-day workshop was held in Baghdad, from July 6 to 9, 2003, by Task Force RIO, to figure out the next steps. More than one hundred technical experts and military officials from the Pentagon, USAID, Bechtel, and Halliburton/KBR drew up a priority list of 226 major projects to be completed by March 31, 2004, at a cost of $1.14 billion.[37]

SHOCK AND AWE IN FORT WORTH

Meanwhile, there was a public outcry in the United States over Strock's secretive sole-source contract, which caused the Pentagon to alter course somewhat. The contract was re-opened for competitive bidding—on January 16, 2004, two new contracts were awarded (also known as Project Restore Iraqi Oil II or RIO II): an additional $1.2 billion to Halliburton/KBR for work in the southern oil fields of Iraq and $800 million to a Parsons-Worley team for work in the north. The RIO II contract was for two years, with three one-year extension options. By September 2004, Halliburton/KBR had already billed the government $2.5 billion for all RIO work.[38] U.S. authorities in Baghdad, who had complete control of Iraq's oil revenues and who seized assets for the first fifteen months of the occupation and no oversight, were happy to pay more than half of the value of those invoices with the Iraqi cash.

But competing contractors were not that happy—they argued that even the new bidding process for RIO II had been rigged in favor of Halliburton/KBR. Sheryl Tappan, chief negotiator for Bechtel of San Francisco, wrote and self-published a book in April 2004 entitled *Shock and Awe in Fort Worth: How the U.S. Army Rigged the "Free and Open Competition" to Replace Halliburton's Sole-Source Oil Field Contract in Iraq.* In the book, Tappan details the bidding process and exposes a number of problems.[39]

"The irony is the 'Sons of RIO' [aka the RIO II] competition turned out to be far more corrupt than the secret sole-source award," she wrote, adding, "Pentagon officials, up and down the chain of command, lied and cheated Halliburton's competitors and broke federal laws to ensure Halliburton kept all of the Iraq oil work. They include generals and high-level political appointees at the Pentagon, as well as lower-level contracting staff at the Army Corps' Southwestern Division/Fort Worth District, who conducted the RIO II competition."

Tappan alleges that critical information about the bid (from the plan drawn up by Halliburton/KBR itself) was withheld—against federal law—until only thirteen days before their proposals were due on August 14, 2003. And the final work plan that was put out to bid required that all subcontracts and purchases of equipment and materials had to go through Halliburton/KBR's procurement and accounting systems, even for projects managed by Iraqi Ministry of Oil personnel, allowing Halliburton/KBR to receive a fee and profit from virtually everything done in the Iraq oil fields.[40]

Tappan's book was the first public criticism of the RIO process. She was invited to testify before the U.S. Congress on September 10, 2004, but not everybody was convinced—she did after all work for a rival company. The next whistle-blower, however, would be more compelling.

BUNNATINE GREENHOUSE

"Bunny" Greenhouse, the woman who authorized the RIO contracts, grew up in Rayville, Louisiana, a segregated cotton town. Her parents had never completed high school. A deeply religious woman who has clear ideas of what she believes is right and wrong, she is still heavily involved in her local Catholic church where she sings in the choir every Sunday. ("There's not a dishonest bone in her body," her former boss, Joe Ballard, says.)[41]

She has a drive to be the best she can be, like her brother Elvin Hayes, a National Basketball Association all-star. Early in her sixteen-year career as a mathematics teacher, she was named one of the Outstanding Young Women of America in 1975. And like her two siblings who went on to complete doctorates, Greenhouse has strong academic credentials. She studied mathematics at Southern University, and has three master's degrees: in business management, engineering, and national resources strategy. She got her first job in 1967 at a high school in Louisiana, where she was the first black teacher. Aloysius, her college sweetheart and now husband, was a military procurement officer, and after fourteen years of following his career, she decided to get into the same business herself.[42]

In 1996, General Joe Ballard, became the Army Corps' first black chief engineer. He brought in Greenhouse, an African American woman, as the Corps' top procurement official, to challenge the "good old boy" network that controlled the contracting system. Ballard left in 2000, but Greenhouse stayed on. (And unlike his colleagues who went to work for big engineering companies like Howard, Needles, Tammen & Bergendoff [HNTB], Ballard refused to cash in on his senior position.)[43]

From the day she stepped into the job, Greenhouse worked with Halliburton, Brown & Root, and eventually KBR, on the logistics contracts for the military. Although Cheney was CEO of the company at the time, she never dealt with him directly, but mostly with his chief lobbyist, Charles Dominy, a former three-star general in the Army Corps, who would later leave Halliburton to work for IAP.[44]

She was required to sign off on every contract valued at more than $10 million. On more than fifty of the documents she signed, she added clauses and conditions to make sure competitive bidding rules were upheld. "When our officers don't understand that a decision is giving one company an exceptional advantage, when they don't understand that a decision doesn't protect the public trust, then it's my job to make them understand it," she would say later.[45]

On March 5, 2003, when the Halliburton/KBR RIO contract was presented to her, she signed, but she recorded her concerns by writing next to her signature on the contract a warning that the length of the deal could convey the perception that limited competition was intended: "I caution that extending this sole source contract beyond a one-year period could convey an invalid perception that there is not strong intent for a limited competition." It was this memo that would bring her to public notice, when Adam Zagorin, a veteran reporter at *Time* magazine, read it. (The army sent Zagorin the documents after he requested them under the Freedom of Information Act.)[46]

She wrote similar complaints on the $1.2 billion follow-on contract to the RIO agreement that summer and on a $165 million extension to the Balkans contract because each included serious violations to acquisition regulations and ignored competition requirements, she says.

Later, at a public hearing convened by Democratic members of the Senate in the summer of 2005, she was categorical: "I can unequivocally state that the abuse related to contracts awarded to KBR represents the most blatant and improper abuse I have witnessed" in twenty years working on government contracts.[47]

The Corps' commanders realized they had a serious problem brewing, so they conspired to get around her in order to ensure that Halliburton/KBR could keep working. She was assigned a new deputy, Lieutenant Colonel Albert Castaldo, who confessed in an e-mail later that: "It was discussed, well known, and even expected by the USACE Command Group that I would have to take adverse positions against Ms. Greenhouse's desires in order to protect the command and accomplish certain actions for the best of the command mission."[48]

For weeks, Greenhouse says, Castaldo waited. On Thursday, December 18, 2003, she caught bronchitis and called in to say that she would be taking the rest of the week off. This was the golden opportunity for management, and they took it.

On Friday that week, a waiver for Halliburton/KBR was drawn up in the Corps' Dallas office by contracting officer Gordon Sumner. It was then couriered the same day to Washington to be signed by Army Corps Lieutenant General Robert Flowers, who was chief engineer for the Corps. Greenhouse returned to work, but she was unaware of the waiver until the news broke the next month because Sumner failed to give it a tracking number and enter it into the Corps' computer system.

Meanwhile, an exasperated Robert Griffin, the deputy commander of the Corps, asked Greenhouse to stop writing comments directly on the contracts and, instead, attach them in a cover letter. Greenhouse refused to do so, believing that the cover letters might conveniently get lost. This refusal to obey orders proved to be her undoing because it triggered a negative performance rating.

On October 6, 2004, Griffin asked her to come to his office. He told her that he was demoting her to the government rank of GS-15, citing negative performance reviews. He also gave her the option to retire with full benefits. She was informed that her two most recent performance ratings had been "less than fully successful." This despite the fact that in 1997 and 1998 Greenhouse had been described as "absolutely committed . . . totally loyal." She "has no equal when it comes to technical issues," the report said.[49]

In a twelve-page letter sent to the army on October 21, 2004, Greenhouse alleged that she repeatedly objected to the handling of a number of Halliburton/KBR contracts, but that other Pentagon officials regularly dismissed her concerns. Her complaint cited a sworn declaration made by Ballard, her former boss, who stated that Greenhouse "strictly followed the Federal Acquisition Regulation (FAR) for contracting and approached her work with high ethical standards," but that pressure from individuals "associated with favorite companies" resulting in "Greenhouse's strict and ethical application of the FAR work[ing] against her when it should have been viewed with high regard."[50]

Greenhouse then called Michael and Stephen Kohn of the National Whistleblower Center, who arranged a meeting with Zagorin and with Erik Eckholm of the New York Times, and they took her story to the public. But Greenhouse had waited too long—the Republicans pounced upon her testimony and dismissed it as Democratic election propaganda. On August 24, 2005, she was finally demoted. "They stuck me in a little cubicle down the hall, took my building pass," she told the Washington Post. "It's all about humiliation."[51]

EVALUATING RIO

Halliburton/KBR spokesperson Wendy Hall says that the company was well qualified to win the original RIO contract based on its work after Operation Desert Storm in 1991. "Halliburton crews helped bring 320 wells in Kuwait under control in less time than was expected, following the Gulf War. More than one hundred ninety thousand work hours were incurred on this project without a lost-time accident. Originally scheduled as an eighteen-month project, Halliburton's crew assisted in extinguishing 90 percent of the blowouts within one year of the beginning of operations."[52] Tappan disputes this. "It was Bechtel who managed the entire firefighting and oil field reconstruction program in Kuwait—in half the time experts said it would take," she said.[53]

A report by the Special Inspector General for Iraq Reconstruction (SIGIR) would later conclude that the no-bid contract that Strock had Greenhouse sign on March 5, 2003, was not illegal because it was signed by the appropriate officials, namely the Assistant Secretary of the Army for Acquisition, Logistics and Technology.[54]

Stoney Cox testified to the U.S. Congress on June 15, 2004, that the company had done well, noting that first oil flowed from the southern Iraqi oil fields on April 23, 2003, just five weeks after the assignment began and exports restarted in June of 2003. "[We] produced some $12 billion in revenues for the Iraqi people in one year's time. And on December 30, three months ahead of schedule, Iraq reached its pre-war production levels of 2.4 million barrels per day," he said.[55]

But memos released by Congressman Henry Waxman's office indicate that throughout the RIO project, Pentagon oversight officials had serious concerns over the company's performance. On December 31, 2004, just days before the RIO II contract was issued, the Defense Contracting Audit Agency sent out a "flash report," alerting various Pentagon agencies about "significant deficiencies" in Halliburton/KBR's cost-estimating system that "could adversely affect the organization's ability to propose subcontract costs in a manner consistent with applicable government contract laws and regulations." It also stated: "We recommend that you contact us to ascertain the status of [Halliburton's] estimating system prior to entering into future negotiations."[56] This advice was ignored.

Twice in the first half of 2004, Halliburton/KBR was informed that its "reporting needed to show changes that have been made in the last six months to visibly demonstrate we are not repeating past mistakes of the [first] RIO contract." On August 28, 2004, the Iraq Project and Contracting Office (PCO, an office housed at the U.S. Embassy to solicit and award bids for approved reconstruction schemes) sent Halliburton/KBR a sharply worded "letter of concern" that it was "accruing exorbitant indirect costs at a rapid pace," and also complaining that Halliburton/KBR had denied the government access to its electronic cost reporting system.[57]

One major complaint was that after the RIO II contract was signed in January 2004 and detailed task orders were issued in June, Halliburton/KBR did not start actual work until November 2004, while charging the government millions of dollars at a rate far above that of its counterparts.

A SIGIR comparison of five such contracts issued at the same time concluded that Halliburton/KBR's overhead costs were by far the highest—other contractors showed overhead costs as low as 11 percent.[58] The Parsons joint venture (with Worley of Australia) for RIO II oil infrastructure work was also issued a contract in January 2004, given detailed task orders in June, but started work in July 2004. The SIGIR estimate pegs the Parsons joint venture overhead at 43 percent, while Halliburton/KBR's $296 million bill included at least 55 percent overhead.

Halliburton/KBR pointed the finger of blame at the government, saying that it had failed to issue specific administrative task orders after the workers were deployed. "It is important to note that the special inspector general is not challenging any of KBR's costs referenced in this report," Halliburton/KBR spokesperson Melissa Norcross wrote. "All of these costs were incurred at the client's direction and for the client's benefit."[59]

Major General William McCoy, who was in charge of the Army Corps, publicly supported Halliburton/KBR at the time. He said that work such as "waiting for concrete to cure" could still be taking place during what seem to be periods of inactivity, so a quiet period "does not mean that the project is not moving forward."

But internal memos uncovered by Waxman show that the PCO took the extreme step of issuing a "cure notice" on January 29, 2005, which notified Halliburton/KBR that its part of the RIO II contract could be terminated if the ongoing problems were not cured. On February 20, 2005, Halliburton/KBR presented its "Corrective Action Plan" for addressing cost reporting deficiencies identified in the cure notice, but the following month the contracting officer also expressed "sheer frustration with the consistent lack of accurate data." By late May 2005, the contracting officer detected improvements in cost control and reporting.[60]

Eventually the company received about $57 million in award fees or 52 percent of the maximum possible for the original RIO project. In this case the amount of the award paid out ranged from 4 to 72 percent of the fee available. No data to date has been released on the award fees paid out under the RIO II contract. (A committee of military officials determines if contractors should get "good" performance bonuses. Typically 60 percent of the grade is based on the company's performance such as adhering to schedule, quality of work, and problem-solving, and 40 percent is based on cost control.)

What did Halliburton/KBR actually accomplish under the two RIO contracts? After all the mudslinging on how the contract was issued, it appears today that the company's work ended up being both expensive and not very effective. There were three key components of the job: fixing the dilapidated and looted oil fields, fixing the oil meters to make sure that oil smuggling was stopped, and providing refined fuel to the Iraqi population for domestic consumption—all of which Halliburton/KBR seems to have botched.

DAMAGE TO OIL FIELDS

Red shadows rippled across the desert sand of southern Iraq as gray tendrils of smoke billowed from the sheet of flame dancing bright orange over the twelve outstretched chimneys. It sounded like a jet engine from almost a hundred feet away, and if I looked into the flames I could feel my skin burn. I stepped back, glad of the cool, blue sky around me that allowed me to rest my eyes before I gazed back into the hypnotic fire. Over by the turbines that pump the oil from the wells to the port of Basra, I met a crew of Indian and Pakistani workers, dressed in the blue uniforms of the Al Kharafi Company, a Kuwaiti subcontractor working for Halliburton/KBR. It was December 2003, at the tail end of the first RIO contract. The following year, I traveled up north to Kirkuk to inquire into the RIO II project.[61]

I was welcomed by Army Corps engineers who told me that they were delighted with Halliburton/KBR's work, handing me a series of documents and even a promotional CD boasting about the innovative engineering being undertaken at the Al Fatah Bridge.[62] Yet over the subsequent years, it turns out that they were badly mistaken. An astonishing series of blunders (Halliburton is widely regarded as one of the leading equipment providers to the oil industry worldwide) impeded oil production in the first couple of years and may have permanently damaged the largest of the country's vast oil fields.

The news of this colossal failure was first broken in September 2005 by T. Christian Miller of the *Los Angeles Times*, who revealed that Halliburton/KBR and/or its overseers at the Army Corps had created three major problems:[63]

- **Qarmat Ali water treatment plant in southern Iraq:** Natural pressure in the sands causes oil to flow upward, but as this oil is tapped, the pressure declines, making extraction more difficult. So Iraqis inject water into the earth to maintain the pressure in the oil field. At Qarmat Ali, the water is treated to make sure particles or bacteria don't block the holes in the soil that allow the oil to rise. Halliburton/KBR rebuilt motors, refurbished pumps, and installed electrical generators and chlorination and anticorrosion systems but failed to fix the leaky pipelines carrying water to the fields. Another unexpected problem was local farmers who tapped the pipeline to get water for their tomato crops.[64]

Halliburton/KBR was tasked with rebuilding motors, refurbishing pumps, and installing electrical generators, chlorination, and anticorrosion systems. The Army Corps however, did not ask the company to fix the pipelines. Thus when Halliburton/KBR officials opened the taps to send the treated water to the Rumaylah oil field in August 2004, the pipes burst repeatedly, causing the pressure to decline early and the oil to sink. No money was provided to maintain the equipment, so a year after the project was completed, just two of the five pumps fixed were still working. A machine used to add cleaning chemicals was broken.[65]

Bob Todor, the senior U.S. advisor to Iraq's Oil Ministry at the time, said that by the time the problem became apparent, most of the money available in the south had already been spent on other projects.

One Iraqi engineer blamed Halliburton/KBR for the whole problem, saying that the company had installed substandard equipment and had not provided sufficient training. "It's useless. We have material . . . but we don't have documents on how to use it," he told the *Los Angeles Times*.[66]

Company officials just shrugged their shoulders. "KBR is not responsible to support with the ongoing maintenance and repair of these facilities unless tasked to do so," said Stephanie Price, a Halliburton/KBR spokesperson, in response to questions e-mailed by the *Los Angeles Times*. The Iraqis, meanwhile, failed to put any money into further repairs, allocating their revenue instead toward fuel subsidies and salaries.

• **Southern oil well repairs.** A $37 million project to do thirty "well workovers"—cleanup jobs that can improve the productivity of oil wells—was canceled after Halliburton/KBR refused to proceed without a U.S. guarantee to protect it from possible lawsuits. Had any contractor effectively undertaken the repairs, Iraq could be producing up to five hundred thousand additional barrels a day, according to some estimates. Since Halliburton/KBR did not accept the task order or get paid for the work, it is hard to blame the company for this failure. The end result however, for which U.S. planners bear the bulk of the responsibility, was that the work was not done. This poses a catch-22 situation for Iraq planners though, as many old and new projects may never be completed in Iraq because the contractors face the risk of lawsuits. Since no insurance company would ever cover such risk, either, it may be an insurmountable obstacle unless one resorts to more daring contractors possibly with less experience, a risky proposition for the Iraqis. There is also the possibility that the U.S. government should have provided the insurance guarantees to make sure that the work gets done.

In hindsight, it is obvious that fixing taps is useless if the pipes are near the end of their useful life, but Halliburton/KBR officials are also correct to point out that they were never asked to fix the pipelines. The problem was that the Army Corps planners had no experience in managing oil field repair, so the task orders that were issued and modified by contracting officials were based on faulty assumptions and could never have been successful. This problem could have been fixed if a proper assessment was conducted with outside experts. The next example, however, shows that even prior assessment is open to failure if the outside advice is ignored.

· **Kirkuk to Beiji pipelines:** Halliburton/KBR was awarded a major contract to rebuild a pipeline network in northern Iraq from the Kirkuk oil fields to Beiji, one of the main refineries in the north. One of the most important elements was to reconnect a maze of sixteen pipelines at the Al Fatah Bridge that had delivered crude and other petroleum products. The pipelines, which ran over the river, had been bombed and destroyed by U.S. jets during the 2003 invasion. The bridge project was expected to take ten weeks and cost $75.7 million.[67]

Gary Loew, a Army Corps official, told the *New York Times* that Halliburton/KBR officials decided it would be quicker to run the pipelines under the riverbed using a technique known as horizontal directional drilling instead of repairing the bridge, despite warnings against such a route made by Fugro South, a geotechnical consultant hired by Halliburton/KBR before the project began. Fugro submitted a written report that stated repeatedly that the project should not begin without extensive field exploration and laboratory testing of the area because of "past tectonic activities near the site." A Halliburton/KBR pipeline expert, who also saw a preliminary design before the drilling began, advised the company "that the project would probably fail."[68]

Fugro South noted that the soil under the river was comprised of rocks, which could shift, rather than clay—where such drilling techniques might be more likely to work. Some of the on-site managers also expressed reservations about proceeding, but these were ignored as senior Army Corps officials decided that finishing this project quickly would showcase U.S. good intentions and bring much needed revenue into Iraq. "There is an urgent and compelling need to accomplish this feat as soon as possible," Douglas Lee Cox, the northern Iraq project manager for the Army Corps, wrote in a memo on June 9,

2003. Colonel Emmett H. Du Bose Jr., who took charge of the project in December 2003, says that Halliburton/KBR provided him with optimistic assessments nearly to the very end. "In hindsight, knowing what I know today, I would have probably said we need more geology information before we start drilling those holes," Colonel Du Bose told the *New York Times*.[69]

Trouble began soon after the project started in January 2004. "The analogy for drilling through cobble and gravel is poking a finger into a jar of marbles and expecting the hole to remain when the finger is removed," wrote the SIGIR investigators.[70]

Under the contract, Halliburton/KBR explicitly did not forbid the subcontractors from talking to the Army Corps, nor did the company relay these problems to the government. "Typically when you manage a project, you have people who can tell you that you've got so much of your project finished and this much money that has been spent," said Gary Vogler, who was now an advisor working at the Iraqi Oil Ministry. "We couldn't get anything like that."[71]

The problems were first discovered when Bob Sanders, a geologist with a Ph.D. from the University of Oklahoma, was dispatched by the Army Corps to find out what was happening at the site in July 2004, almost a year after it began. By then the company managed to install only six of the pipelines originally planned. The Iraqis were forced to reinject some two hundred thousand barrels of oil per day back into the ground that once again may have damaged the fields by plugging fissures through which the petroleum flows.[72]

Sanders first tried to get the Army Corps to change course but had no luck. He then called SIGIR to lodge a complaint, but by that time all the money had been spent. Halliburton/KBR's contract was canceled (in any case, it had spent its entire budget by then), and a joint venture between Parsons of Los Angeles and Worley from Australia was hired to finish the project using a less risky method in which the pipelines are laid down in a trench dug into the river bottom and encased in concrete.[73]

The Al Fatah Bridge was the most glaring blunder in the Kirkuk to Beiji pipeline but not the only one. The government-owned State Company for Oil Projects failed to complete the crossings at the Riyadh and Zegeton canals. The company work was supposed to have been overseen by Halliburton/KBR, but at the request of the company, which feared attacks if U.S. personnel visited their worksites, the supervision was never conducted. Project managers say that the work is 80 percent complete, but SIGIR puts the figure at closer to 10 percent.

Jaafar Altaie, a former senior planner at the oil ministry who moved to Amman, told Miller, "I think we had the worst quality of U.S. service, staff, and companies. We had maximum rhetoric and minimum results on the ground."

Far more costly, however, was the opportunity cost—that is to say the potential revenue lost from reduced oil production and exports. This adds up to a staggering $14.8 billion, according to calculations made by SIGIR.[74]

MYSTERY OF THE MISSING METERS

The line of ships at the Al Basra Oil Terminal (ABOT) stretches south to the horizon, patiently waiting in the searing heat of the Northern Arabian Gulf as four giant supertankers load up. Close by, two more tankers fill up at the smaller Khawr Al Amaya Oil Terminal (KAAOT). These two offshore terminals, a maze of pipes, and precarious metal walkways, deliver some 1.6 million barrels of crude oil—at least 85 percent of Iraq's output—to buyers from all over the world. If the southern oil fields are the heart of Iraq's economy, its main arteries are three forty-plus-inch pipelines that stretch some fifty-two miles from Iraq's wells to the ports.[75]

Guarding both terminals are dozens of heavily armed U.S. Navy soldiers and Iraqi marines who live on the platforms. They spend their days at the oil terminals, scanning the horizon, looking for suicide bombers and stray fishing *dhows* (boats).[76]

Meanwhile, right under their noses, smugglers were suspected to be diverting an estimated billions of dollars worth of crude onto tankers. Rumors were rife among suspicious Iraqis. "Iraq is the victim of the biggest robbery of its oil production in modern history," blazed a March 2006 headline in *Azzaman*, Iraq's most widely read newspaper. A May 2006 study of oil production and export figures by Platt's *Oilgram News*, an industry magazine, showed that up to $3 billion a year is unaccounted for.[77]

"Iraqi oil is regularly smuggled out of the country in many different ways," an oil merchant in Amman told *The Nation* magazine. "Emir al-Hakim [the head of the Supreme Council of the Islamic Revolution in Iraq] is spending all his time in Basra, selling oil as if it were his own. People there call him Uday al-Hakim, meaning he is behaving the same way Uday Saddam Hussein was acting. Other merchants like myself have to work through him with the big deals or smuggle small quantities on our own. The petroleum is now divided among political parties in power."[78]

Indeed Lieutenant Aaron Bergman, the U.S. Navy officer in charge of Mobile Security Squadron 7 at ABOT, even admitted that they had no idea how much was really being exported because the actual sales at the terminal were "guesstimated" with a back-of-the-envelope formula: Every centimeter a tanker lowers into the water equals six thousand barrels of oil cargo. "So you can imagine," he said to *Stars & Stripes*, a newspaper serving the U.S. military, the numbers could be off. "A couple of inches could equal 180,000 barrels of fuel." (Mathematics was probably not his strength at school!)[79]

"I would say probably between 200,000 and 500,000 barrels a day are probably unaccounted for in Iraq," Mikel Morris, who worked for the Iraq Reconstruction Management Organization (IRMO) at the U.S. embassy in Baghdad, told KTVT, a Texas television station.[80] Yet there was no reason why this situation should have occurred.

For almost five years after the invasion, fixing the meters at the oil terminals was part of the work order issued to three U.S. companies under the RIO contract: Halliburton/KBR and Parsons of Pasadena, California, and the company hired to oversee them, Foster Wheeler, failed to complete the job. The three U.S. contractors have long played a key role in the repair and upgrading of Iraq's oil infrastructure, going back more than forty years. Brown & Root began work in Iraq in 1961 shortly before it was acquired by Halliburton,[81] while Parsons dipped into Iraq's oil sector in the 1950s. Foster Wheeler dates its work in Iraq to the 1930s.[82]

Halliburton built the ABOT terminal, then known as Mina al-Bakr, in the early 1970s.[83] After it was damaged during the Iran-Iraq war in the 1980s, Halliburton repaired the terminal before it was bombed yet again during the 1991 Persian Gulf War.[84] The Khor al-Amaya oil terminal also saw a similar cycle of destruction and rebuilding. Built with Halliburton's help in 1973, it was heavily damaged by Iranian commandos during the Iran-Iraq war, then again during Operation Desert Storm in 1991, and most recently in May 2006 by a major fire that destroyed 70 percent of its facilities.[85] During the sanctions, Ingersoll Dresser Pump Company, a Halliburton subsidiary, had a secret contract to sell Iraq spare parts, compressors, and firefighting equipment for the refurbishment.[86]

MEASURING THE OIL

The kinds of meters they were supposed to repair or replace at ABOT are commonly found at hundreds of similar sites around the world. Three kinds of meters are used around the world today: positive displacement, turbine, and ultrasonic. A displacement meter measures the rate at which compartments of known volume are filled with the liquid or gas; a turbine meter is simply a pipe with a spinner that measures the volume that passes through it, while an ultrasonic meter uses sound frequencies to measure flow rates. Each has advantages and disadvantages.[87]

Before the 1991 Gulf War, ten turbine meters were installed on ABOT's platform A, while ABOT's platform B got sixteen positive displacement meters.[88] In the late 1990s, the United Nations hired Saybolt International, a Dutch company, to make sure that Saddam Hussein was selling crude only under the Oil-for-Food program. However my interviews with UN inspectors indicated that the inspectors could not rely on the meters at the time because they were not calibrated. Instead Saybolt relied on a simple and effective way of determining how much was being shipped: It measured the amount of crude loaded into the tankers.[89]

After the invasion, all the meters were turned off. While Halliburton/KBR worked on several projects to fix the oil terminals, the metering work seemed to be a low priority for all concerned. One excuse that U.S. embassy officials offered for the delay was that the job of calibration requires special devices to assess the current meters, and security issues make importing these devices problematic. Yet that and other security-related explanations fall apart given that the oil terminals are under twenty-four-hour high-security guard, lie more than fifty miles offshore, and are accessible only by helicopter or ship.

In mid 2005, Halliburton/KBR was taken off the project. Finally in January 2007, Parsons Iraqi Joint Venture installed ultrasonic meters to verify the older meters. The meters were eventually certified in July 2007, according to an e-mail update to me from Kimberly Mielcarek, a spokesperson for the Army Corps.[90]

FUEL SUPPLY OVERCHARGES

The U.S.-led occupation ran into an unexpected problem almost as soon as it took the reins in Baghdad: Iraq had very little refined fuel! For a country with one of the largest supplies of crude in the world, where gasoline is sold for pennies on the dollar, this was the last thing on anyone's mind. But immediately after the invasion, the wave of looting had destroyed whatever fragile refining capacity existed.

The CPA asked the Army Corps and Halliburton/KBR to use the RIO contract to arrange for an emergency supply of fuel from Kuwait for Iraqi gas stations.[91] The U.S. ambassador to Kuwait, Richard Jones, who also served as a deputy to CPA chief Paul Bremer, recommended that Halliburton/KBR sign a deal with a company named Altanmia, which it later transpired was not an oil transportation company at all, but an investment consultant, real-estate developer, and agent for companies trading in military and nuclear, biological, and chemical equipment. The company's lead shareholder, it was reported, was Najeeb al-Humaizi, a member of a prominent Kuwaiti family.[92]

The KBR managers at the Khalifa allegedly asked Altanmia's general manager, Waleed Al-Humaidi, to pay a kickback, according to a complaint lodged with an embassy staffer. "Al-Humaidi caveats this by requesting that we not address 'kickback' issues with KBR directly," a U.S. embassy memo cautions. "He fears being blacklisted by KBR." The memo further reports that Al-Humaidi believes Halliburton/KBR executives plan to "find a reason" to fault Altanmia for poor performance on an earlier fuel contract, while Altanmia claims were exceeding Halliburton/KBR's expectations. Any shortcomings were blamed on Halliburton/KBR's failure to obtain tanker trucks and to secure military escorts for the convoys to Baghdad through war-torn Iraq.[93]

In fact, the memo says, Altanmia believed that it was really Halliburton/KBR that was failing to meet contract requirements, such as racking up more than $23 million (7 million KWD) in unpaid bills owed to the Kuwait company. Another embassy memo summarizes a list of allegations made by Altanmia officers who maintained that it was "common knowledge" that "KBR officers are on the take."

For its part, Halliburton/KBR has repeatedly claimed that it was pressured into doing business with Altanmia. One December 2003 e-mail from Ambassador Jones backs up Halliburton/KBR's claims. "Please tell KBR to get off their butts and conclude deals with Kuwait NOW!" Jones demanded to an official whose name has been deleted from the documents. "Tell them we want a deal done with Altanmia within twenty-four hours and don't take any excuses." Jones concludes that if Bremer hears that Halliburton/KBR is "dragging its feet," then he "will be livid."[94]

Halliburton/KBR managers have also claimed that, according to State Department documents, Altanmia refused to meet competitive pricing or open its books to justify its higher prices for fuel. Indeed, when the Pentagon got the bill from Halliburton/KBR, the numbers were definitely high—an average of $2.64 a gallon and as much as $3.06 on occasion.[95]

By comparison, the Defense Department's Energy Support Center (DESC) had been doing a similar job supplying fuel to the U.S. military at $1.32 a gallon. And the State Oil and Marketing Organization (SOMO), the local Iraqi oil company, was doing the same work for just $0.96 a gallon. The total bill for 61 million gallons of fuel from Kuwait and about 179 million gallons from Turkey, between May and late October 2003, was $383 million, over $100 million more than what local providers, or even the DESC, would have charged.

("I have never seen anything like this in my life," Phil Verleger, a California oil economist and the president of the consulting firm PK Verleger LLC told the *New York Times*. "That's a monopoly premium—that's the only term to describe it. Every logistical firm or oil subsidiary in the United States and Europe would salivate to have that sort of contract.")[96]

A letter written by Mary Robertson, a senior contracting officer at the Army Corps, suggested that the U.S. embassy in Kuwait was putting pressure on Halliburton/KBR to hire Altanmia. "Since the U.S. government is paying for these services, I will not succumb to the political pressures from the [government of Kuwait] or the U.S. embassy to go against my integrity and pay a higher price for fuel than necessary," the letter states.[97]

Wendy Hall, the Halliburton/KBR spokesperson, denies that there were any problems. She says, "The facts show that KBR delivered fuel to Iraq at the best value, the best price, and the best terms and in ways completely consistent with government procurement policies. It is important to the company that clients, suppliers, and host countries know Halliburton's Code of Business Conduct is expected to be followed in every country in which the company operates," she said. She added that one of the reasons the cost was so high at the time was because the company had more than twenty trucks damaged or stolen, nine drivers injured, and one driver killed when making fuel runs into Iraq.[98]

SPENDING IRAQ'S OWN MONEY

Minutes from high-level meetings of the CPA suggest that one major reason that Richard Jones and Paul Bremer were not worried about the fuel overcharges was the fact that it wasn't their money in the first place. Most of the money that the CPA spent in the first year of occupation was Iraq's own money that the United States had effectively seized.[99] On March 20, 2003, President Bush issued an executive order moving all Iraqi assets, held in U.S. banks and frozen since Iraq's invasion of Kuwait, into a special account established at the Federal Reserve Bank of New York. Then in May 2003, UN Security Council Resolution 1483 established the Development Fund for Iraq (DFI), which would include proceeds from all Iraqi oil sales, Iraqi assets frozen in bank accounts outside of the United States, and the $8.1 billion in funds remaining in the UN Oil-for-Food Program. Under the terms of the Security Council resolution, these funds were to be used "in a transparent manner to meet the humanitarian needs of the Iraqi people . . . and for other purposes benefiting the people of Iraq."[100]

Over a period of thirteen months, cargo jets airlifted this money into Iraq in "cashpaks" of $100 bills. All told, 281 million individual bills, weighing 363 tons, were flown into the country.[101] Twice a week, in the first year after the invasion, a group of up to a dozen officials met in the Green Zone to vote on how to spend what would eventually total $19.6 billion of DFI funds. This ad-hoc group of people named the Program Review Board (PRB) was coordinated by Sherri Kraham, a young twenty-nine-year-old State Department official who was assigned to be their staff person. The meetings would often be attended by as many as twenty other people, typically CPA officials, lobbying to get a share of the money.[102]

Almost all of the people who attended the meetings were from the United States, and many were either military or ex-military. There were two or three non-U.S. citizens with voting powers: typically, Neil Mules, representing Australia; Yusaf Saimullah, representing Britain; and Marek Belka, a Pole who represented the rest of the "coalition." Sometimes, there weren't enough voting members present to get a quorum, and Kraham would be dispatched after the meeting to get signatures to authorize the disbursement of the money. (On other occasions she was even allowed to vote, which made a mockery of what little democratic process existed.)

Two or three Iraqis attended occasionally, but quite often none were present. When Iraqis did attend, exactly one representative from the Iraqi Ministry of Finance was among the eleven people officially allowed to vote on how the money was disbursed. (In 2004 a second person from the Ministry of Planning was also given a vote.) Minutes from the meetings showed that the Iraqis were confused by the proceedings because they were rarely consulted or briefed, so they had to have matters explained to them. Pretty soon, the Iraqis stopped coming altogether.

U.S. officials don't appear to have worried about the lack of Iraqi participation. With oil production limping along and stocks of gasoline in the country running low, a series of oil ministry officials, led by Gary Vogler, the ex-Exxon staffer who had advised Rumsfeld on the invasion, made a pitch to the PRB in early July 2003 to spend the Iraqi money on the urgent needs of fuel production and supply.[103]

In a series of decisions, beginning July 12, 2003, Vogler told the PRB that the Ministry of Oil needed to spend $3 million a day of Iraq's cash reserves to continue importing liquefied petroleum gas and benzene. He explained that the amount needed would diminish as refinery capacity was built up, from $90 million in August to $30 million in October, but right now he needed cash, and he needed it fast.[104]

The minutes indicate that Gary Vogler's requests were met with some concern by even the U.S. officials present. Peter McPherson, an old friend of Cheney from the Ford White House in the 1970s, was the chair of the meeting. A former administrator of the Agency for International Development who had also managed a $600 million account at Bank of America as executive vice president, McPherson was now being asked to authorize expenditures in the billions for an entire country.[105] At first, he was worried that the absence of competition for Vogler's proposal might land them in hot water down the road especially because the contract would effectively make Halliburton/KBR the biggest recipient of Iraq's oil money, with no input from the Iraqi people.

The minutes also indicate that when Kraham was asked why Halliburton/KBR was selected to do the work, she defended the company saying that it was the only company on the ground but was unable to provide any answers as to whether any competitive bidding had actually been done in the first place.

Vogler returned again and again to this body over the course of the next few months to ask for increasingly large sums of money to pay Halliburton/KBR. On July 29, he requested $300 million for Halliburton/KBR, and on August 30, he asked for $711 million to be paid out. An emergency meeting was called to consider the large sum of money. But on September 1, the money was approved after a new member joined the Program Review Board: none other than Carl Strock, Bunny Greenhouse's boss, who had previously approved Halliburton/KBR's no-bid contract before the war in Washington, DC, despite the fact that he had never attended previous meetings.

All told, Halliburton/KBR was paid $1.66 billion from the Iraqi money, primarily to cover the cost of importing fuel from Kuwait. Mohammed Aboush, who was a director general in the oil ministry at the time, told the *Washington Post* that he and other Iraqi officials were not consulted about the Halliburton/KBR contract, adding that the Iraqis had told their "advisors" that Halliburton/KBR's performance had been inadequate and that he'd prefer that another company take over its work. "I am old enough to know the Americans and their interests, and they are not always the same interests as the Iraqi interests," he said.[106]

"One of the advantages of the Iraqi accounts was that money could be delivered faster," Walt Slocombe, the CPA's special advisor on security and defense, told the *Financial Times*. "Bremer took the position under legal advice that he was in charge of the money—that he could spend it without rattling what he affectionately called 'the Washington squirrel cage.'"[107]

COLLECTING THE MONEY

The Iraqi money that Vogler spent on Halliburton/KBR's oil imports became a matter of considerable acrimony but was eventually settled in Halliburton/KBR's favor in September 2006 when the Army Corps agreed to pay the company nearly all of $263 million in costs in Iraq and Kuwait that were criticized as "unreasonable" or "unsupported" in official audits of the company.[108] The settlement allowed Halliburton/KBR to keep $253 million of the $263 million in oil reconstruction and distribution costs paid by the Pentagon but disputed in the audits. About $208 million of the disputed charges were related to the fuel import program.

"[T]he contractor is not required to perform perfectly to be entitled to reimbursement," Rhonda James, a spokesperson for the Army Corps said in response to widespread criticism of the Pentagon's reimbursement decision.[109]

(Actually 55 percent to 75 percent of costs criticized by Pentagon auditors are ultimately withheld from contractors. In this case, the army withheld from Halliburton/KBR only 3.8 percent of the $263 million in disputed costs).[110]

The army did release the audits of the disputed costs to the public.[111] But at the request of Halliburton/KBR, the Pentagon heavily redacted from public view sentences such as Halliburton/KBR "did not demonstrate the prices for Kuwaiti fuel and transportation were fair and reasonable," that Halliburton/KBR "was unable to demonstrate the proposal was based on actual costs," and Halliburton/KBR "was unable to reconcile the proposed costs to its accounting records." The censored sentences were discovered later when an original copy of the audit was leaked to Waxman.[112]

A second group that attempted to deny Halliburton/KBR the fuel overcharges also failed. Under United Nations Security Council Resolution 1483, the CPA was required to work with an International Advisory and Monitoring Board (IAMB) that would provide independent, international financial oversight of all Iraqi oil spending. The IAMB was to consist of representatives from the UN, the World Bank, the International Monetary Fund and the Arab Fund for Economic and Social Development as well as the government of Iraq.[113]

The IAMB first met in October 2003, six months after the invasion, so it had to make up for much lost ground. Several meetings a year have since been held in Amman, New York, Paris, and Washington. They ran into problems right away—initially, they had a hard time getting the CPA to cooperate. Finally in April 2004, the Bahrain office of KPMG was allowed to come in and inspect CPA books on behalf of the IAMB, a full year after the CPA and PRB had taken charge of Iraq's billions, and shortly before the CPA itself was to be dissolved.[114]

In November 2005, the IAMB recommended that the United States "expeditiously" repay as much as $208 million, saying that the work was either carried out at inflated prices or done poorly.[115] But this recommendation was set aside, oddly enough, when the auditors hired by the IAMB—KPMG—were informed that they faced a conflict of interest because they had contract work with Halliburton/KBR. In order to resolve this, another international auditing firm, Crowe Chizek of Chicago, was hired to investigate Halliburton/KBR while KPMG was tasked with investigating the non-Halliburton/KBR no-bid contracts.

In November 2006, Halliburton/KBR won the last word over the $208 million repayment request, when Crowe Chizek issued a statement stating that the "the settlements were reasonable," although it severely criticized Halliburton/KBR for leasing a fleet of tanker trucks from Altanmia, at a cost of up to $25,575 a month for each truck "irrespective of the number of deliveries" to

Iraq. Between two hundred and eighteen hundred trucks racked up charges that "in some instances, were as high [as] 86 percent" as they sat idle for long stretches on the border.[116]

(Despite the fact that the costs were paid, there were some consequences of the investigations. Under the RIO II contract, this fee was slashed to 52 percent, with some individual contracts being given as little as 4 percent. By comparison, during the Balkans deployment, Halliburton/KBR always received at least 98 percent of the maximum award fee, even though some grumbled about the waste.)[117]

Lloyd Owens International

Halliburton/KBR eventually lost the fuel delivery contracts when the Coalition Provisional Authority officially relinquished Iraq on June 28, 2004. The newly appointed government of Iraq awarded a contract to Lloyd Owens International (LOI), a British company, and Geotech Environmental Services of Kuwait to help deliver the fuel. Remarkably, this new company, which provided fuel over the next year in Iraq, a far more dangerous time period, emerged almost unscathed from the experience, and charged just eighteen cents per gallon to supply the same sites.[118]

Alan Waller, the chief executive officer of LOI, described how Halliburton/KBR often thwarted them by delaying their passage into the country or failing to help them when their drivers were in danger. He described how every morning 120 of his trucks lined up at the Kuwait-Iraq border to deliver gasoline from Kuwaiti refineries. The drivers, who were TCNs who had to cross at dawn because if they waited too long, Halliburton/KBR managers who operate the border post during the day, subjected them to rigorous checks that effectively shut down the deliveries. "The only way we can cross the border is to arrive before KBR," says Waller of his fleet of seven hundred trucks, which he has hired from five different subcontractors.[119]

"For eleven months we provided fuel to all of southern Iraq. We lost only one truck to theft and not one driver was killed in hostile action. We responded to civil uprisings in Najaf, Hilla, Karbala, Kut, and Nasariya within twenty-four hours to provide fuel to the public. Our role has become instrumental in normalizing relationships between Iraqi authorities, the population and coalition forces."

But all that changed on June 9, 2005, when a convoy of LOI trucks, on its way to deliver construction materials for a Halliburton/KBR dining facility to a U.S. Army base near Fallujah, Iraq, came under attack. Three drivers—two Egyptians, and one Turk—were presumed killed, and six trucks were abandoned.[120]

When the survivors limped into the Al Taqaddum military base, they were expected to receive support from the Halliburton/KBR staff. Instead they got the cold shoulder. When the drivers tried to leave the country, they hit a roadside bomb, and another Bosnian staff member was killed.

Reading from an e-mail, apparently sent by a Halliburton/KBR manager, Waller said that the company staff was ordered not to help them: "Many people volunteered to help but were told no by management." He also noted that Halliburton/KBR had failed to inform them that two other convoys had been attacked in the same area in the previous week.

Waller and his business partner, Gary Butters, a former London police detective, delivered this information at a Senate Democratic Policy Committee hearing on June 27. The two men flew to the United States to testify after they were twice refused an audience with the U.S. embassy in Iraq to resolve the situation.[121]

Asked to respond to the LOI testimony, Cathy Gist, the Halliburton/KBR spokesperson, e-mailed this brief statement: "KBR does not control ANY borders in the Middle East or any other country." Waller offered to prove his statement to me the next time I was in Kuwait.

Crossing the Border

Alan and his security chief Trevor, a forty-nine-year-old Brit, picked me up from my hotel at 3:30 a.m. one April morning in 2006 to take a trip to the border and see their operations. We were also joined by Somo, Alan's dog, a stray that he had picked up in Iraq and named after the Iraqi oil company, who barked at me initially and then got friendlier over time. A disciplined dog, he did not seem like an attack or guard dog. Neither man carried guns, although they may have had concealed weapons.[122]

Driving down the flat, black ribbon through the night, broken only by the twinkle and dull roar of passing long-haul trucks, it was easy to imagine that our Chevy SUV was driving through the California desert. The smooth highway allowed us to cruise easily at 85 mph, making it hard to imagine that we were less than an hour away from the mayhem in Iraq.

As we sped through the night, Alan explained the various corruption schemes in the oil business. Indeed, the day before, he received a call from a man who said he had gotten permission to set up twenty-six private gas stations in southern Iraq; would Alan deliver gasoline to them? Now,

Alan had never agreed to deliver gas to individual stations, insisting that his agreement was to deliver only sealed tankers to the depots because he was well aware that the stations could report that only part of the gasoline had arrived and siphon off the rest—this happened routinely to his predecessors. "I don't blame them, the gas station attendants have to make a living," he said. "But I'm not willing to be part of such a scheme."

Alan explained that the corruption on the Turkish border was even more blatant—four out of six trucks that crossed the border would turn right back and then be declared "missing." The ministry would pay for oil dispatched, although not delivered, and whoever organized the scheme would collect the excess. These mishaps did not stop with imported gasoline or fuel; it was also done openly with crude. Tankers would load up and drive their cargo to Iran or load them into ships at the main terminal where they would be diverted; no attempt was made to cover this up because there was no one who could monitor the shipments.

We drove past the Al Muthla Ridge where the U.S. troops carpet-bombed surrendering Iraqi troops in 1991, past a few buildings that had been destroyed by the invading Iraq Army in 1990. On our way back, in daylight, we would see the occasional Bedouin tent and sheep herders as well as more elaborate tents used by Kuwaitis for partying and drinking on the weekends, out of sight of prying eyes.

Just before 5 a.m., as the sun was rising, we arrived at the border. There were two crossings. One was a civilian post that would open at 9 a.m., where trucks were lined up for a half a mile or more, four deep, to cross into Iraq. Then there was the military crossing that would officially open at 6 a.m. but allowed the fuel trucks to cross at 5 a.m. Today, Alan had fifty-six trucks ready to go.

We drove past a British army post to find the office where permits were issued for traffic to cross the border, called the Movement Control Team (MCT). This office was staffed by three older Americans, each of whom had badges slung around their necks, clearly identifiable by the red straps that said KBR.

Corruption in Kuwait

THE SPEARHEAD—A GLIMMERING, SILVER, Australian-built catamaran[1]—nosed into the port of Shuwaik in Kuwait in August 2002. A four-engine, ninety-eight-meter, high-speed vessel that could travel four times faster than the army workhorse Logistical Support Vessel was one of the first arrivals in the much-anticipated invasion of Iraq.[2]

Able to deliver military equipment and personnel like Patriot missile battalions directly into shallow water ports, the Spearhead was brought in to assist much larger and heavier ships like the USNS *Watson* to haul supplies from Camp As Sayliyah in Qatar (the largest prepositioning site for the U.S. Army in the world) to Camp Doha, just west of Kuwait City, a distance of some 250 miles as the crow flies. Contract workers from ITT, the company that helped manage Camp As Sayliyah, also traveled to Kuwait to help stage and maintain Camp Doha.[3]

For Colonel Carl Cartwright of the Combat Equipment Group-Southwest Asia, who had arrived in July on behalf of the army and Coalition Land Forces Component Command to figure out how to stage this new war, using the Spearhead was an experiment as the army had never used catamarans before. Cartwright needed all the help and speed he could get. Before the major combat was over, the Command would ask him to bring in 6.4 million MREs, 66,000 tons of ammunition, 324 tanks, 374 Bradleys armored vehicles, 9,426 Humvees, and 7,074 other trucks into Kuwait.

But using the Spearhead would not be the first or the only experiment. Pretty soon it became obvious that much more innovation would be necessary particularly because Camp Doha, which was located on a property leased from a Kuwaiti company named Public Warehousing Corporation (PWC) near the port next to a huge water desalination plant and an electrical plant, had no room for expansion to handle this influx of tens of thousands of troops and their heavy equipment. The second problem was that Secretary of Defense Rumsfeld wanted to limit the number of troops who would take part in the invasion to just one hundred forty thousand—less than one-eighth of the number who had taken part in Operation Desert Storm.

Lieutenant General David McKiernan, who was in charge of the ground war, would tell the planners that "The guys back in Washington and the guys back in Central Command in Tampa are probably not going to understand this—but the biggest concern we have is logistics. If we can't sustain the force on the battlefield, we're wasting bringing the force over here. A tank without ammunition and fuel is just a piece of metal. You guys have got to make us succeed. Without you we can't succeed."[4]

So in August 2002, the 377th Theater Support Command, which was charged with running the logistical side of Operation Iraqi Freedom, decided to do what had never been done before: use a contingency contractor to set up for war (in both Afghanistan and former Yugoslavia they worked on sustainment operations after the initial land and air war). Halliburton/KBR was notified that LOGCAP support would be needed to construct new bases. For the company, which had just started work in Afghanistan, Cuba, and Uzbekistan—not to mention existing work at Incirlik in Turkey and Camp Bondsteel in Kosovo—it meant they would have to ramp up quickly.

By September, Halliburton/KBR started to divert experienced managers from other operations to Kuwait to recruit local labor and suppliers and hire hundreds of new people for what was already clearly going to be their biggest military contingency operation ever. Gatlin was one of the first to arrive from Halliburton/KBR's Government & Infrastructure corporate office in Arlington, Virginia, bringing with him about a dozen contract managers from the head office as well as others from prior Halliburton/KBR missions in the Balkans and Cuba.[5] He was appointed LOGCAP project manager for Kuwait and was eventually put in charge of Iraq and Jordan, too. This was a challenge that he relished, even more than digging water wells in Kosovo. "When we got here, there was no power or water, I had a thousand people working here in twenty-four hours; the army can't do that," he boasted to a *New York Times Magazine* reporter later.[6]

A new military headquarters to replace Camp Doha started to come together in the desert an hour away to the south—Camp Arifjan—where workers poured gravel roads and set up massive shelters to house the trucks, Humvees, and Chinook helicopters that were being delivered by ship. The workers also erected Force Provider tents and fast-food outlets like a Burger King, Subway, and Baskin-Robbins, vending machines, and a Nautilus-equipped gym.[7] Within a matter of weeks, a series of complementary smaller temporary camps were set up across the desert near the Iraqi border and were named after the states associated with the attacks of September 11, 2001: Camp New York, Camp Virginia, and Camp Pennsylvania.

Joyce Taylor of the U.S. Army Materiel Command's Program Management Office at Fort Belvoir, Virginia, arrived to supervise Gatlin and his crew, which soon numbered more than eighteen hundred workers. Once again, they looked for the cheapest labor—but this time they did not hire local citizens as they had done in Bosnia, Kosovo, and Somalia. Instead, following the tradition of most oil-rich sheikhdoms, they hired South and Southeast Asian workers. "We can quickly purchase building materials and hire third-country nationals to perform the work. This means a small number of combat-service-support soldiers are needed to support this logistic aspect of building up an area," explained Lieutenant Colonel Rod Cutright, the senior LOGCAP planner for all of Southwest Asia.[8]

THE KHALIFA RESORT

Overlooking a private beach on the Persian Gulf, some forty miles south of Kuwait city, just east of Camp Arifjan, is the Khalifa Resort. The hotel Web site claims it has no less than a dozen swimming pools and offers guests activities such as windsurfing, banana boat rides, and deep-sea fishing. Every single one of the eighty-four air-conditioned villas faces the pools.[9] Halliburton/KBR took over the entire resort as a makeshift office headquarters and residence for middle managers once the project got underway.[10]

Senior managers stayed at the more luxurious Kuwaiti Hilton a few miles to the north, which had its own private, mile-long white sand beach, garden chalets, and a "presidential villa" that was occasionally stocked with (illegal) alcohol for the special occasions. The Hilton's pride and joy was a famous Thai restaurant named Blue Elephant, set right on the beach, where many Pentagon deals were discussed and sealed with a handshake.[11] The total hotel tab soon reached $1.5 million per month.

When the Halliburton/KBR managers arrived in Kuwait, the country was still a bit of a backwater. Unlike cities in neighboring countries like Dubai or Bahrain, alcohol was strictly forbidden, although it was generally available at the homes of wealthy Kuwaitis or at a steep price on the black market. Downtown Kuwait City looked more like a sleepy, somewhat ramshackle Indian town, rather than the capital of one of the world's wealthiest countries, partly because most Kuwaitis had chosen to keep their money overseas, ever fearful of another invasion by Saddam Hussein, than invest in building up their own country.[12]

In time, with the ouster of Saddam and the influx of tens of billions in U.S. military dollars, Kuwaitis would start to build flashy new suburbs populated with hundreds of apartment buildings and gleaming office skyscrapers to house the new contractors, but in 2002 it was still hardly a party town. There were no discos or nightclubs; the only entertainment was smoking *sheesha* (a scented-tobacco water pipe), shopping by the seaside at the Sharq or Marina mall, drinking coffee at Starbucks, and steering clear of the joyriding Kuwaiti population who seemed to have no idea how to drive safely on freeways. ("I have never seen so many cars go airborne," an army officer said to me one day.)

Indeed there didn't even seem to be many Kuwaitis to meet. Almost everything in town was actually run by South Asian workers, typically Bangladeshi, Indian, Pakistani, and Sri Lankan. Food service jobs and housekeeping were done by Filipino women, while Egyptians and Lebanese served as managers, being fluent in Arabic—unlike the migrant workers from further east. These transient workers, many of whom had lived in the country for decades, understood the Kuwaiti bureaucracy and how to bend the rules.

These local suppliers knew right away that the Halliburton/KBR managers had billions to spend, and to get a piece of that pie they had to work in the lobby of the Hilton or the Khalifa. Documents from the U.S. embassy in Kuwait suggest that it was common knowledge "that anyone visiting their seaside villas, who offers to provide services, will be asked for a bribe," according to a August 6, 2003, memo that quoted officials from a local Kuwaiti company named Altanmia.[13]

Three of the lower-ranked contract managers who arrived to work at the Khalifa in the first six months—Stephen Lowell Seamans, Jeff Alex Mazon, and Anthony J. Martin—would eventually be arrested. Their charge sheets and guilty pleas would shed light into what really happened at the seaside villas. Over the course of the next eighteen months, each of them chose a similar path, accepting money and gifts from the willing suppliers who were knocking on their doors looking for contracts. The companies they would help included Tamimi, already a prominent Saudi contractor; La Nouvelle, a fast-food operator in Kuwait; and two virtual unknowns named First Kuwait Trading Corporation and Public Warehousing Corporation (PWC), both of whom were fairly small companies in Kuwait with revenues in the millions of dollars that would expand quickly into billion-dollar players in the space of just three years.

A little more than five years later, all three men would appear in the federal court in Rock Island, Illinois, to answer charges of bribery. Two would plead guilty and serve time in jail, but one would deny the allegations. The indictments suggest that these men were either novices or amateurish at best, not really sure how to funnel the payoffs without getting caught.

The higher-ranked Halliburton/KBR managers, as well as their counterparts in the military who had typically worked in the system long enough, figured out a better scheme. Once they discovered how easy it was for companies to submit bids and win work, they quit their jobs and either went to work for the competition, or even set up their own companies to bid on the very contracts they had supervised for Halliburton/KBR or the military itself. None of this was illegal, but a few overstepped the boundaries.

Three former Halliburton/KBR senior managers would stand out: Terry Hall who would get busted for paying army contracts officers millions of dollars after he quit Halliburton/KBR to start his own companies; his boss, Butch Gatlin, the man whom Halliburton/KBR hired to prepare for the invasion, who would also set up his own company and apply to Halliburton/KBR for the very work he used to supervise; and, finally, Gatlin's boss Al Neffgen, who would go to work for IAP, a Halliburton/KBR rival, and would be exposed for failing to treat veterans at the Walter Reed Army Medical Center in Washington, DC.

The corruption took its toll on a number of military officers also: At least two of the army contract managers who accepted bribes later committed suicide—Lieutenant Colonel Marshall Gutierrez and Major Gloria Davis—others would end up in jail like Major John Cockerham and Chief Warrant Officer "Pete" Peleti.

STEPHEN LOWELL SEAMANS

The first to arrive and the first to be offered a bribe was Stephen Lowell Seamans of Crofton, Maryland, a former contracting specialist for the air force in Phoenix, Arizona, who had worked for Halliburton/Brown & Root on the Balkans contract in Macedonia. He was initially dispatched for a six-week stint from the company's Arlington, Virginia, offices in October 2002, to negotiate subcontracts with suppliers and manage materials and property.[14]

Days after he arrived, Mohammed Shabbir Khan, the Pakistani-born director of operations for Tamimi, a Saudi Arabian company, threw a forty-first birthday party for Seamans at another Tamimi worker's house on Wednesday, October 9, 2002. There, Khan arranged for the Halliburton/KBR manager to meet a prostitute. When the party was over, Khan, a naturalized U.S. citizen who was just four years older than Seamans, offered to drive the younger man home.

The U.S. Congress was already debating a resolution to authorize the war in Iraq, which would pass a few days later. Franks and Renuart had won approval in August of the Hybrid plan, so the Pentagon wanted Halliburton/KBR to start the construction of Camp Arifjan in Kuwait's northern desert.

One of the first projects commissioned for the camp was the construction of a dining facility. As Shabbir Khan drove Seamans back home, he suggested that

Tamimi could do the job. The proposal was not an outrageous one—Tamimi was a major conglomerate in Saudi Arabia, after all, with interests in bus transportation and trucking, hotels, oil field services and supplies, power generation, road construction, and supermarket chains. A fifty-year-old family-owned company, Tamimi had started out as a major parts supplier to oil giant Saudi Aramco and then diversified to work with General Electric and Safeway. Most importantly, it acted as distributor for Halliburton in Saudi Arabia.[15]

A plea agreement submitted four years later would detail what happened next. Khan offered to pay Seamans a kickback. Seamans reportedly accepted the offer, and on Saturday he sent an e-mail to his superiors requesting that Tamimi get the contract, providing the "essential documents" to justify his recommendation. By Monday the deal was approved; Seamans and Khan signed the official documents, awarding Tamimi a $14.4 million contract to build the dining hall.[16]

Over the next year, Khan arranged for approximately $133,000 to be transferred to Seamans, starting with about $30,000 in cash. On October 29, Khan wired $2,965 to a bank account in the name of someone identified as "M. S." in Maryland. The next month, Khan paid off Seaman's car loan in the amount of $20,965 by wiring money to an account in Georgia.

In November, Seamans went back to Arlington, returning to Saudi Arabia only at the end of March 2003 when the invasion was launched. Iraq's military crumbled almost overnight, and the camps that Halliburton/KBR had built for the troops were soon obsolete. Instead, suddenly the U.S. military needed living and dining facilities in Baghdad, and fast. Seamans turned to his new friend and "provided Khan with bid information, including the price Tamimi needed to bid to secure the award, for another dining facility services subcontract at a palace in Baghdad, Iraq," officials from the U.S. Attorney's office reported later.

On April 14, 2003, five days after the city of Baghdad fell to the U.S. troops, Seamans issued a $2 million contract to Tamimi that was later increased to $7.4 million on May 21. Once again, Khan started making payments to Seamans. Over the course of the next five weeks, Khan made nine wire transfers from Bahrain and Kuwait to a bank in Maryland totaling almost $70,000. A final payment of $9,965 was made on October 2, 2003, almost a year after the birthday party.

Tamimi went on to win hundreds of millions of dollars more in dining facility contracts, bringing in the necessary equipment, hiring laborers, and running the daily operations in Kuwait and Iraq, eventually getting contracts directly from the army. Indeed, to this day Tamimi is one of the largest providers of workers to the military camps, such as at LSA Anaconda, where its workers run the dining facilities.[17]

Seamans was offered payoffs from other contractors also. Just before he left in November 2002, he issued a cleaning contract for Camp Arifjan to a company named La Nouvelle for a little more than $98,000. When he returned in May 2003, he upped the La Nouvelle cleaning contract to $2.3 million, despite the fact that Butch Gatlin had called Hijazi in to tell him that he was canceling the contract for poor service. Around the same time Seamans quit his job and was approached by Ali Hijazi—La Nouvelle's managing partner—who happened to be visiting the Khalifa. Hijazi offered Seamans a job as a consultant to La Nouvelle at a salary of $1.2 million a year, which he accepted.[18]

Hijazi was a well-known businessman and longtime resident of Kuwait. He ran several local food chains—La Baguette, Star Juice, and the local Domino's Pizza franchise.[19] His business partner was Al Homoud, and his U.S.-born wife, Wendy Stafford, often represented the company. She wore elegant, tight clothes, with expensively teased hair and "lots of jewelry—diamonds, diamonds, diamonds."[20]

His company, La Nouvelle, had been in existence for a little more than five years, providing services to multinational companies from Pizza Express to Starbucks in the Middle East. The U.S. Army had also hired the company to provide logistical support to thousands of marines who had flown in from Twentynine Palms in California to hastily constructed Camp Coyote in Kuwait, which was about thirty miles from the Iraqi border and was known as "the tip of spear" in the March 2003 invasion.[21]

The day before the expanded cleaning contract was awarded, Hijazi paid Seamans a $300,000 advance, but the consulting job Hijazi promised him never materialized, and neither was Seamans asked to pay back the $300,000.[22]

SHABBIR KHAN

About three years after the second contract was signed, federal investigators were becoming suspicious and began making inquiries. In April 2005, Seamans received an e-mail from Zubair Khan, an associate of Shabbir Khan. Seamans called back, and Shabbir Khan answered the phone, telling him that the U.S. embassy in Bahrain had recently inquired about the wire transfers.[23]

Seamans and Shabbir Khan realized that they needed to come up with an explanation, so they decided to claim that the money was given as part of a business deal with Zubair Khan—who also worked at Tamimi—to jointly buy an armored car in the United States for sale in the Middle East. They also agreed to claim that the business deal had fallen through, and Seamans was simply late in repaying the money.

On April 11, 2005, Zubair Khan sent Seamans an e-mail, inquiring about the money: "Would you please send me the details and when you can shift it to me." Four days later, Seamans replied: "Sorry I was not able to respond immediately. It has been a very busy week. I am glad that you are finally able to contact me. I have your funds in escrow. I am not operating my business any longer, and would like to return the funds to you."

Zubair Khan replied right away: "Thanks for your e-mail and it is OK if it didn't work this time. I feel comfortable when you said you are going to transfer my fund, though it didn't work this time but I will be more than happy to have business in the future with an honest person like you."

Over the next week, Seamans unsuccessfully tried to wire Zubair Khan $60,000 so that it would appear as if he was trying to return the money that he had received in the past. Shabbir Khan also obtained a document suggesting that a Tamimi manager had approved the 2003 transaction.

On August 30, Zubair Khan sent Seamans another e-mail that stated, "What is going on man, I am still waiting for the transfer." Seamans followed up about a week later with, "I am still waiting for your reply about my money to be transferred back."

That month, Brian L. Berntson from the U.S. Internal Revenue Service and Jeffrey G. Jackson from the U.S. Federal Bureau of Investigations traveled to Kuwait to interview Tamimi employees, including Shabbir Khan and Zubair Khan, on August 26 and 28 at Camp Arifjan. Shabbir Khan denied that he or Tamimi had paid any kickbacks to the former Halliburton/KBR manager. But unknown to Shabbir Khan and Zubair Khan, Seamans, who was being questioned simultaneously in the United States, had broken down and confessed. On September 9, he agreed to help Berntson and FBI agent Anne M. Hefel catch Shabbir Khan in exchange for a lighter sentence.

Soon after, on October 8, 2005, a devastating earthquake hit the Kashmir region of Pakistan. Shabbir Khan rushed to the region where he arranged for blankets, building materials, food, and tents for the victims, earning praise from local people who called him "a ray of hope."

On returning from Pakistan, Shabbir Khan sent Seamans a plane ticket to fly to London so that they could meet up and coordinate their alibis. On October 28, Seamans arrived in London and met with both Shabbir and Zubair Khan at the Cumberland Hotel, overlooking Hyde Park on the corner of Oxford Street and Park Lane. The three men sipped cognac and whiskey in a quiet lounge as they discussed their cover stories that explained the 2002 and 2003 money transfers. Unknown to the two Tamimi employees, Seamans was wearing a secret recording device, which had been approved by British authorities on behalf of the U.S investigators.

A week after the London meeting Zubair Khan continued the subterfuge, as previously agreed. On November 4, he wrote to Seamans: "Thanks for your mail and I am glad to have an honest friend like you which is rare. . . . No problem for the failure of our plan but there is always a next time to do some business."

Almost five months later, the U.S. Attorney's Office in Rock Island asked Shabbir Khan and his lawyer, James Koch, for a meeting to discuss the transactions. Shabbir Khan and Koch agreed to travel to Rock Island on March 22, 2006. The terms of the interview were set forth in a letter stating that Shabbir Khan would not be arrested for any activities that had occurred prior to his arrival in the United States. But there was a catch: The letter also stated Shabbir Khan could be charged with any criminal conduct while in the United States, such as making false statements.

At the March 22 interview, Shabbir Khan was told again that any false statement made by him during the interview could be considered a federal crime for which he could be prosecuted. Believing that Seamans had his back, Shabbir Khan fell for the trick and repeated the fictitious story about an armored vehicle business deal. He also swore that he had not paid Seamans for the Tamimi contracts and that he had not met with Seamans since 2003. At that juncture he was arrested for lying.

In June Shabbir Khan pled guilty. Koch asked the judge to sentence Shabbir Khan to home detention, supervised release, no restitution, and then allow him to return to Kashmir and work on the rebuilding effort. "Mr. Khan has already faced ruination—losing his livelihood and his personal reputation—as a result of his criminal conduct. Indeed, Mr. Khan is now a man without a country. He is persona non grata in Kuwait, and his plea to bribing the U.S. government renders him virtually unemployable in the United States," Koch told a local newspaper.[24]

Instead on December 1, 2006, both men were sentenced to time in prison. Seamans was ordered to spend a year and a day in prison, and Shabbir Khan was sentenced to fifty-one months in prison. Seamans was released early on September 27, 2007, for good conduct, and now works as a commodities manager for Aggregate Industries in Crofton, Maryland, while Khan is expected to serve in jail until March 1, 2011, unless he can get out earlier on good conduct also.[25]

ANTHONY J. MARTIN

Anthony J. Martin of Houston, Texas, a Vietnam vet in his mid-fifties, who had spent fifteen years at the company working his way up the ladder from the construction division, arrived from Turkey to work in Kuwait in February 2003. He worked for Halliburton/KBR for about a year, initially, under

Seamans where he was expected to solicit bids for LOGCAP subcontracts. Starting at Camp Arifjan, Martin eventually moved into the Khalifa Resort, where he wrote out paperwork for goods that the military needed, calling up buyers, soliciting bids, and then issuing fulfillment orders. Often the buyers would come to the Khalifa and offer him special deals, ranging from cut prices on goods to support when he quit his job.

Among those who approached him were Ali Hijazi who suggested "maybe he and I could be friends," Martin would testify in court later. "I took it as possibly leading into something, that he would wait for me to respond to something," which made him feel uncomfortable.[26]

In mid-June 2003, Martin was tasked with finding fifty semi tractors and fifty refrigeration trailers for the "Theater Transportation Mission" for a six-month period.[27] Martin says he was soon offered a kickback by Wadih al-Absi,[28] a Lebanese-born Christian who grew up in Beirut and moved to Kuwait to escape war in his home country in the late 1970s, where he says he started work as a laborer installing drywall.[29] In 1996, al-Absi set up a company named First Kuwaiti General Trading & Contracting (FKTC). Al-Absi, along with Mohammed Maaraf, at first won minor electrical wiring jobs for residential buildings in Salmiya, which was followed by a multimillion-dollar job to build a college of administration at the university near the port of Shuwaikh.[30]

Most of First Kuwaiti's projects were fairly small; many were less than $1 million, with only one exceeding $10 million. When the invasion began, al-Absi lined up with the other contractors to visit the managers at the Khalifa to get work, but he was having a hard time making headway against bigger contractors like Tamimi. He initially won a half-dozen small projects from Halliburton/KBR to provide light sets, dumpsters, and laundry services at prices ranging from $21,216 to just over $407,000.

Martin says al-Absi offered him a deal: al-Absi would pay 50 KWD (approximately US$170 at the time) per semi tractor per month for any government subcontract that Martin awarded to First Kuwaiti. A $10,000 advance was agreed upon and paid out in cash and stuffed into an envelope for Martin. Later Al-Absi bought Martin a round-trip ticket from Kuwait to the United States.[31]

On June 15, Martin sent out an e-mail, inviting bids for a number of potential subcontractors, including al-Absi. Four bids were made, and on June 17, Martin awarded a $4.67 million subcontract to First Kuwaiti. Under the kickback agreement, Martin expected to get payments of approximately $50,240. On July 11, Martin put up another bid request for three hundred semi tractors and three hundred fuel-tanker trailers over a six-month period, which al-Absi won again when he offered to supply them at 2,950 KWD per semi tractor per month. Martin subsequently awarded him an $8.9 million contract on July 18. Once again, Martin says al-Absi agreed to pay him a kickback of 50 KWD per semi tractor per month. Under the second scheme, Martin would have received an additional $150,265 in kickbacks.[32]

Martin handed the $10,000 advance to a woman named Kelly Klmudaynn, a U.S. citizen who worked for a company called Actel. She deposited the funds in her Kuwaiti bank account and handed him an ATM card. Two days after issuing the contract, Martin left for a short vacation in the United States. With him, he carried the ATM card, which he used to withdraw approximately $9,100 between July 20 and July 28, 2003.[33]

On returning to Kuwait, Martin felt guilty and says he told al-Absi that he was not going to take any additional money under the kickback agreement. But al-Absi was on a roll by then. He started to get more subcontracts from Halliburton/KBR—such as an $81 million contract to supply trailers at LSA Anaconda and a $63 million contract to supply trailers to Camp Victory in Baghdad on October 16. All told, al-Absi won a total of well over $300 million in contracts from Halliburton/KBR. Eventually, al-Absi got the biggest prize of all—a gigantic $592 million contract directly from the U.S. State Department to build an embassy in Baghdad—the largest, most fortified embassy in the world. For First Kuwaiti, this was a major leap. In less than a decade, the company had grown from doing odd jobs like fixing electrical wiring in Kuwaiti residential complexes in 1996 to competing against the biggest construction companies in the world, all because of the invasion of Iraq.[34]

Two years later, in 2005, al-Absi met over coffee at the Four Seasons Hotel in Washington with my co-worker David Phinney to discuss labor conditions on the embassy project. The former drywall worker was dressed in a finely tailored suit and a shirt that had French cuffs, and he spoke of sending his children to American universities and enjoying the fruits of being a newly minted millionaire. "I love America," he said simply.[35]

On July 17, 2007, Anthony J. Martin, who had taken up a job managing refinery construction contracts with Jacobs Engineering in Houston, Texas, pleaded guilty at the Rock Island court, and was eventually sentenced in June 2008 to one year in jail and a $200,000 fine.[36] Al-Absi's name was left out of the documents, but when a court document was accidentally unsealed, reporters quickly figured out where the bribes allegedly came from.[37] First Kuwaiti and al-Absi immediately denied the allegations. "Martin made his allegations to receive a reduced sentence. First Kuwaiti's work is always subject to the oversight of the U.S. government, and we welcome their review," the company said in a statement issued in October 2007.[38]

JEFF ALEX MAZON

In December 2002, Jeff Alex Mazon of Country Club Hills, Illinois, a thirty-year-old, six-year veteran of Halliburton/Brown & Root operations in Bosnia and Guantánamo Bay, arrived from Arlington where he was appointed chief of procurement, material, and property under Gatlin.[39]

There were a little more than a dozen managers working for Halliburton/KBR in Iraq, and everyone worked fifteen-, sometimes twenty-four-hour days. Some business associates describe Mazon as a "high-energy guy" who was always flashing a smile.[40] Others, like Anthony Martin, would later testify that he would see Mazon frequently fall asleep at his computer and even become incoherent. Martin was so concerned that he called Tod Nickles, a senior Halliburton/KBR manager, to tell him that Mazon needed help because his health was being affected by the workload.[41]

In February 2003, U.S. Air Force captain Denise Bentle, the administrative contracting officer, asked Mazon to solicit bids from potential subcontractors to supply three-to five-thousand-gallon fuel tanker trucks at a U.S military facility adjacent to Kuwait International Airport for a six-month period from March through August of 2003 to fuel up the vehicles and trucks that were being airlifted into Kuwait. The estimated cost for this six-month contract was about $685,080.[42]

Mazon sent out a solicitation for bids on February 2 and got at least two bids by February 8—one from Saleh Huwaidi of TWG Kuwait for about $1.9 million and another from Ali Hijazi of La Nouvelle, who offered to do the job for less than $1.7 million. (A third bid from National Contracting Company was declared invalid.) Mazon called Seamans and asked him about his dealings with Ali Hijazi whom Seamans had been dealing with on the cleaning contract.

What happened next is the matter of some dispute. Mazon submitted the paperwork to his boss, Butch Gatlin, the former Army Corps commander who had run engineering projects at Camp Bondsteel. The documents Mazon turned in stated that the value of the bids was $6.2 million for TWG and $5.5 million for La Nouvelle. Mazon maintains it was an accounting error. (Indeed, if the bids were in Kuwaiti Dinar, they would have converted into dollars at the value he turned in.) Gatlin signed the papers late one night without asking any questions. "He was the procurement manager," Gatlin said later. "I took his word."[43]

On February 14, Mazon and Hijazi signed a contract for 1.67 million KWD or US$5.5 million. The payments for services rendered were paid out on September 15, 16, and 27, as well as on December 17, 2003. In June 2003, Mazon quit his job and went to work for another company—Science Applications

International Corporation—which had won a contract to provide security cameras to the Olympic Games in Athens, Greece.[44] (SAIC is a major CIA contractor that had been hired to create radio and television propaganda in Iraq at the time, but that's another story. For more details on that, see Chapter Four of my previous book, *Iraq, Inc.*[45])

Three months after leaving Halliburton/KBR, Mazon received a $1 million payment from La Nouvelle, ostensibly for Mazon to open a McDonald's franchise in the United States. Mazon expressed some worries, but Ali Hijazi told him to calm down. "Nervous don't be. Confidence is you," Hijazi wrote. "You were the king of procurement in KBR with $500 million under your management."[46]

One September 24, Ali Hijazi sent Mazon an e-mail, which stated that Hijazi considered "this whole lown [*sic*] as totally your money. . . . "[47]

Mazon called Seamans again to ask his advice. "Jeff said that he wanted to buy a McDonald's franchise and that his mother was not feeling well and he wanted to plant himself in Chicago," Seamans told the Rock Island jury when Mazon went on trial in April 2008. "And I asked him how much. He told me a million dollars. And I asked him why he was asking me this. And he told me, well, I know that you had a deal with Ali, referring to—it was common knowledge that I was going back to work with La Nouvelle. And at that point I told Jeff that I had no deal with Ali Hijazi, that we had agreed to terminate, and I have no relationship with LaNouvelle any longer."[48]

Mazon flew to the United States. He showed the check to his mother and his ex-wife, who later testified that he did not attempt to hide the money. He then opened bank accounts in Chicago and New York and attempted to deposit the check on October 1, along with a promissory note from Hijazi that indicated it was a loan at 0 percent interest.

Cardell McCollum, an Axa financial advisor, questioned the first version of the loan agreement. Mazon re-presented the same agreement with 7 percent interest. McCollum then asked Mazon specifically as to whether the check was a "kickback."[49]

Mazon replied: "In Kuwaiti culture, they like to share their wealth with people who have helped them build wealth." The bank called Mazon's new employer, SAIC, who turned the matter over to one of its senior company lawyers named Susan Frank. After Mazon failed to get banks in Chicago and New York to accept it, he returned to Greece to try to deposit it in an offshore account, but they turned him down also.

"They're all asking too many questions about the origin of the money," he wrote, according to court documents. "They all look at me like I am some kind of criminal since I have a fried [*sic*] from the mid east that wants to help. They throw words, like money laundering, and terrorist's money in my face. The world is soooooo ignorant about the whole Muslim community now that it is disgusting. Whatdya think?"[50]

On October 9, Hijazi told Mazon to open three different offshore accounts and to tell them that he expected to deposit about $300,000 in each one from "consultancy work, business assoicates [sic], salaries abd [sic] bonuses, or any other reasoning." Mazon grew increasingly worried. "This whole situation has become more impossible to manage and I would like to cancel . . . ," he e-mailed Hijazi.

But Mazon was already too late. Harold Norman, an ex-cop and an investigator for Halliburton/KBR, called him up and asked to meet with him at the Ramada Inn near O'Hare International Airport in Chicago, along with Chris Heinrich, KBR's chief counsel. Mazon started a series of desperate e-mails to explain what was going on. "Maybe there is more in the file that explains that erroneous figure in the monthly charge column," Mazon wrote an hour after the interview concluded. The next day Mazon called Norman again to explain how he arrived at the calculations for the bid. The second voicemail told the Halliburton/KBR investigator to ignore the previous message.[51]

Meanwhile SAIC's Susan Frank asked a private investigator, Tom Maslin, to travel with her to Greece to meet with Mazon and get to the bottom of the million-dollar check. In Athens, Frank and Maslin asked Mazon about whether he had any dealings with subcontractors, which he denied. Frank and Maslin then showed him faxed copies of the check and loan agreement.

Mazon appeared "shocked," Frank testified later. "My impression was he felt like he just got caught," Maslin said. "He had a clear understanding of what he was doing . . . was illegal."

Six weeks later, Hijazi and his partners were called in for a meeting with KBR investigators. The next day, November 13, a worried Hijazi sent an e-mail to Mazon that stated: "Please when you call your ex-friends in kuwait [sic] please be very carreful [sic] on what you say."

On March 16, 2005, Mazon was arrested in Norcross, Georgia, just outside the city of Atlanta and charged with four counts of major fraud and six counts of wire fraud. He waived his right to appear before an Atlanta court the next day and was sent to Rock Island.

Hijazi was charged but refused to appear. He continued to live at large in Kuwait, even briefly turning himself into the local authorities, but he did not travel to the United States. Indeed, I was able to track down his cell phone number and chat with him briefly in January 2007. He seemed amused at my questions, but he refused to answer anything and referred me to his lawyer Ty Cobb at Hogan & Hartson in Washington, DC.[52]

Cobb filed a motion to have the case dismissed. "The U.S. Attorney for the Central District of Illinois is not the world's Prosecutor General, and the

United States can no more pass a law to bind the rights of the whole world than can the Island of Tobago," he wrote to the judges. "We are aware of no successful prosecution under the charging statutes of a foreign citizen based on foreign conduct."[53]

Kuwait's ambassador to the United States, Abdullah Al-Jaber Al-Sabah, a member of the Kuwaiti royal family, also asked the Department of Justice to drop the charges. "We are aware of no bilateral agreements between the State of Kuwait and the United States that cover cases such as this one and that permit the United States Government to intervene, investigate, and prosecute Kuwaiti companies, nationals, and residents based on American law for actions committed within the territory of Kuwait," he wrote to Bruce Schwartz, deputy assistant attorney general for the Department of Justice.[54]

The Defense Cooperation Agreement between the two countries "states clearly that the United States will limit its attempt to extend its criminal jurisdiction to only American military personnel within Kuwait." He concluded with a request: ." . . that the United States consider the amicable relations between our two countries by taking all necessary actions to discontinue and dismiss the legal action. . . . "

The judge replied that the charges might be dropped if Hijazi appeared in court. Instead, Cobb filed a second motion. "This prolonged legal limbo has significantly affected his reputation, livelihood, freedom to travel, and family relationships," Cobb wrote. "Being accused of fraud by the U.S. Government has put a black mark on Hijazi's good name and been disruptive to his business. Hijazi has not been able to visit his father, who lives in another country in the Middle East and is in very poor health. Hijazi cannot leave Kuwait for fear that he would be subject to extradition or else forcibly brought to this country by the U.S. Government outside of any legal process."[55]

In April 2008, Mazon appeared at the trial in Rock Island. Seamans, who had been released from jail, and Martin, who was on his way to jail, both testified about their relationships with Mazon and with Ali Hijazi, who had offered both of them large sums of money when they worked at the Khalifa. Butch Gatlin and the investigators Susan Frank and Tom Maslin also testified. Mazon, however, did not say a word during the trial. When the jury met to discuss the case, they deadlocked so the judge declared a mistrial and scheduled a new trial for September 2008.[56]

THE WHISTLE-BLOWERS: MARIE DEYOUNG

On August 2, 2003, Pentagon auditors issued an internal report titled "Report on Audit of Billing System Internal Controls" that found "significant deficiencies" in the billing methods of Halliburton/KBR. The deficiencies "have adversely affected the organization's ability to record, process, summarize, and report billings." Unless the company fixed its billing system, the auditors warned, "the result is significant over-and under-billed costs" to the government.[57]

On December 3, 2003, Joe Lopez, the former admiral who was now the Houston-based head of procurement, issued an angry memo to senior management calling them together for a 9:30 a.m. conference call to address the problems of lack of paperwork. On the list for the call were Gatlin, Halliburton/KBR lawyer Chris Heinrich, and Jim Spore (the former navy officer who was in charge of the Camp Delta construction project in Guantánamo Bay and who had been hired by Halliburton/KBR), as well as senior manager of Middle East operations Tom Crum, and Al Neffgen, chief operating officer for government operations at Halliburton/KBR. Lopez explained to them that they could easily become "toast" unless they fixed the system quickly: "This is an enormous gorilla we are dealing with, and the normal handshake and wink deal we're asked to cover with are way over any ever experienced."[58]

The company dispatched a "Tiger Team" of auditors to clean up the mess. One of them was Marie deYoung, of Philadelphia, Pennsylvania. On first meeting her, one could mistake her for a missionary or a salesperson. She's friendly but dogged; she won't let go of you once she thinks you can help her cause. And indeed she was the first female chaplain for several combat units in the U.S. Army and was a chaplain resident at the Hospital of the University of Pennsylvania in 1991 and 1992. She first joined the army in 1983 where she trained to serve in rapid deployment forces. In addition to her religious and military service, she has also operated a childcare center for the military and counseled soldiers. Out of this experience, she has written two books, *Women in Combat: Civic Duty or Military Liability* and *This Woman's Army: The Dynamics of Sex and Violence in the Military.*[59]

She worked briefly for Halliburton/Brown & Root at Camp Bondsteel in Kosovo in mid-2003 and then went to work for the company at Camp Udari in Kuwait as well as at the Khalifa Resort. An occasional folksinger, she has written a song entitled "KBR Trucker Daddy" to honor friends who have died in Iraq since she left Kuwait in May 2004.[60]

Paid $100,000 a year, she arrived in Kuwait on December 14, 2003, where she was assigned to check up on hundreds of Halliburton/KBR subcontracts for work being done at the camp. The first twenty-seven subcontracts she looked at were complete chaos: The goods bought could not be found, bills were paid without paper work, and indeed many of the staff who wrote the contracts appeared to have no bookkeeping skills at all. "I believe that [Halliburton/KBR] defrauded the government by staffing high-paid, high-skilled positions with unskilled personnel . . . based on family and personal relation-ships," she later testified before a U.S. Senate Democratic Policy Committee. "Very often, Third [World] nationals from the Balkans, India, and Pakistan had stronger literacy, engineering, and construction, operations, and book-keeping skills than those who held the high-paying KBR jobs."[61]

By late February 2004, deYoung was at the Khalifa Resort where she was put in charge of 519 subcontractors who appeared to her to be in no better shape than the first twenty-seven. She immediately noticed how well the Hallibur-ton/KBR staff was living at the taxpayer expense in posh waterfront hotels and traveling in expensive SUVs. The Tiger Team was also housed in the five-star Kempinski Hotel for $10,000 per employee, per month. Her estimate of the cost of supporting Halliburton/KBR managers in Kuwait City was an eye-popping $73 million a year. "Their objective was not to set up clean accounts or justify costs. Their No. 1 objective was to close the books because they were operating under the assumption that if the books were closed they wouldn't be subject to auditing." She described the Tiger Team as a "social gang," where "insiders were rewarded with fancy digs . . . and promises of promotion. . . . Typically, the high-ranking guy would go to a young, inexperienced person and use him to award this contract to the subcontractor of choice. If the young person refused, he'd be threatened: 'You have twenty-four hours to make a decision.' If he was adamant, he'd either be sent home or to Iraq. Which was to say they'd put his life in danger."[62]

DeYoung says she immediately spotted major cost inflation that made her very suspicious. "The subcontractor would come in with bills for four or five times the expected cost, which had to do with under-the-table payments." She does say that she never saw money change hands, but managers in the subcon-tracts department changed so often (twelve times in one year) that it was physically impossible to track what was really going on. "We were instructed to pay invoices without verifying whether services were delivered. I personally told a KBR Tiger Team member not to pay an invoice that I knew was a double billing, [but] the long-term KBR employee told me I didn't know what I was doing," said deYoung.[63]

Ali Hijazi's company, La Nouvelle, for example, came under her scrutiny. On one contract, La Nouvelle had been tasked to deliver 37,200 cases of soda at $1.50 a case, but delivered only 37,200 cans, resulting in charges that were six times the normal wholesale cost for the drinks. She also discovered that Halliburton/KBR paid La Nouvelle $100 per bag for laundry services at some locations—four times more than the military was paying elsewhere to the same company. The overcharges on that alone added up to more than $1 mil-lion per month, she claimed. La Nouvelle was also billing Halliburton/KBR

$1.1 million a month for fuel trucks that it rented from another company, which a fellow manager discovered represented 500 percent inflation on the actual cost. By contracting directly with the original vendor and bypassing La Nouvelle, KBR was able to reduce its costs to less than $200,000.[64]

On March 16, 2004, deYoung asked for a meeting with La Nouvelle. Ali Hijazi, Al Homoud, and Stafford showed up. She asked the group for documentation on the expensive laundry contract. Stafford and the others said there wasn't any. DeYoung said she'd already found the paperwork herself and that she believed that Halliburton/KBR and La Nouvelle were together overcharging on the laundry by about $1 million a month. DeYoung showed her documents to Ali Hijazi, whom she says then e-mailed a Halliburton/KBR vice president. "Within twenty-four hours, I was told I was off the La Nouvelle account," she would tell a reporter later. "The Halliburton corporate culture is one of intimidation and fear," deYoung said. "I had been advised by subcontract administrators who quit the company that employees get moved around when they get too close to the truth. I personally observed and experienced this as a routine company practice. Ironically, other previous managers who tolerated bad practices were promoted to better-paying jobs in Iraq or Houston or Jordan."[65]

DeYoung quit Halliburton/KBR in July 2004 and returned to the United States to try her luck at a number of things, including running for state representative in Pennsylvania. Eventually, she became principal of a school in Louisiana that she helped restore after Hurricane Katrina.[66]

THE MANAGERS: ROBERT GATLIN

For Gatlin, who was proud of his record running the Army Corps in Houston and building both Camp Bondsteel and Camp Arifjan up from scratch, the contracting mess had become untenable by the time he got the e-mail from Lopez at headquarters in late 2003.

Like Seamans, Gatlin had attended Shabbir Khan's "Tamimi Party House." In fact he had gone further just by hanging out with Khan. When Gatlin's senior bosses Crum, Drew Bacon who worked in Arlington, and Don Gavin from Houston came to Kuwait with David Lesar, the CEO of Halliburton, for monthly meetings to check up on the contract, Gatlin would call up Shabbir Khan and ask him to deliver two or three bottles of liquor to the two five-bedroom townhouses that were reserved for management at the Hilton so that his staff and bosses could enjoy a drink or two after work, despite the fact that alcohol is illegal in Kuwait.[67]

Gatlin later testified at Mazon's trial that Khan delivered up to five bottles of liquor on as many as fifteen occasions, between February 2003 and February 2004, but no money ever exchanged hands. Asked why he never paid for the liquor, he claimed that he never thought about it. "It's a long day, getting ready to follow troops into war, and there was a lot of stress, and at the end of the day we felt like just having to relax and getting a little off our mind before starting the next day," said Gatlin. He also admitted accepting a rug from Khan as a Christmas present in 2003 but says he left it behind.

Perhaps he realized that trouble was inevitable, or because he realized that he could make more money if he set up his own subcontracting company, on February 15, 2004, Gatlin sent a terse letter to his bosses, which read: "This project has grown to such proportion and the issues and problems which have ensured [sic], I feel my leadership and management are ineffectifve [sic] and nonproductive. I therefore request to tenure [sic] my resignation with this project, effectife [sic] immediately."[68]

On April 10, 2004, less than two months after his resignation, Gatlin wrote to his boss, reiterating his resignation as a Halliburton/KBR employee and simultaneously asking for work as a subcontractor, causing a ripple of concern at the company. Gatlin then set up his own company, GKL—"a life support and contracting construction company" with an office in Surra, Kuwait—and started bidding directly for U.S. military contracts initially with Halliburton/KBR and then directly with the U.S. military.[69]

"I am generally pretty skeptical about doing business with a former employee," Halliburton/KBR lawyer Heinrich wrote in another internal memo. "There is not a law or a company policy that prohibits us from doing so, but we need to be sure about what kind of business [Gatlin] is starting and who he is aligned with. He must have a Kuwaiti sponsor or he cannot have a business. We need to have him fully disclose all the pertinent info regarding his business and then decide if we will allow him to bid on work."[70]

Pretty soon the money started flowing in. Gatlin won contracts primarily at Camp Taji, some twenty-five miles north of Baghdad. In April 2008, when he testified at Mazon's trial, Gatlin stated that he had won two construction contracts, a fuel contract, a food service contract, a maintenance contract, another contract to provide trash, garbage, water, and wastewater services, and another to provide "scaled and unscaled leather" for the soldiers.[71]

TERRY HALL

Gatlin was not the only senior manager to jump ship at the time. Terry Hall, a former army sergeant from Rex, Georgia, in his mid-thirties, arrived with the first wave of contract managers and was put in charge of dining facility contracts with Tamimi and Gulf Catering Corporation from Saudi Arabia, another major dining hall contractor (that was later acquired by PWC).[72]

Hall quit in 2004 and set up several companies of his own: Freedom Consulting and Catering Co., U.S. Eagles Services Corp., and Total Government Allegiance. (State records show Freedom Consulting and Catering was incorporated in Lithonia, Georgia, in May 2004, with Hall as the chief financial officer, CEO, and secretary.) From January 2005 to the fall of 2006, Hall's companies received more than $20 million in revenue from the military for miscellaneous items like bottled water. Everything Hall did seemed above board; he even testified before a grand jury about another procurement fraud case in 2005.[73]

On March 25, 2006, Hall ordered one of his employees to transfer "110K" in kickbacks from a U.S. Eagles account in Kuwait to an account in the Philippines, and the same month he personally delivered $100,000 in cash kickbacks to a "co-operating witness" at the Atlanta airport. Another $100,000 payment followed a few months later. All told, a Department of Justice prosecutor estimated that Hall made more than $2.5 million in bribe payments.[74]

Major John Cockerham, of Castor, Louisiana, one of the contracting officers at Camp Arifjan who Hall paid off, has emerged as one of the top recipients of bribes in Kuwait. Together with his wife Melissa, and his sister, Carolyn Blake, Cockerham allegedly raked in about $9.6 million in bribes, which they stored in cash in safe deposit boxes at banks in Kuwait and Dubai before they got caught.[75]

A *New York Times* profile of Cockerham suggests that he grew up dirt poor. "From outside the family's run-down, four-room house, it is hard to see where he got the nerve to dream. Growing up, the boys slept in one room, the girls in another, said his brother Charles. They lived on grits in the morning and corn bread at night. For water, he said, the children hauled buckets from a nearby stream."[76]

His former schoolmates defended him. "He's a country boy, just like the rest of us," Mark Plunkett told the newspaper. "You throw a suitcase with a million dollars in front of us, who knows what we would do?"

Cockerham was arrested in late July 2007 after his house was searched at Fort Sam Houston in San Antonio, Texas. And Hall was arrested in November of that year when he went to buy concert tickets near his home in Fairburn, Georgia, an Atlanta suburb.[77]

IAP

While lower-ranking managers like Martin and Seamans have been convicted of taking small bribes, and Terry Hall was arrested for giving large bribes, the higher-ranked managers were able to collect much greater sums of money by creating legal businesses to either subcontract or compete with Halliburton/KBR. For example Gatlin kept his nose clean by setting up GKL, while many of his colleagues simply went to work for rivals.

A good example of this is Al Neffgen, chief operating officer for KBR Government Operations, who testified to the U.S. Congress on behalf of the Halliburton/KBR in July 2004. "We have performed, and performed well, for our soldiers and our country," he told the U.S. House of Representatives Committee on Oversight and Government Reform. "While we have undoubtedly made some mistakes, we are confident that KBR has delivered and accomplished its mission at a fair and reasonable cost."[78]

One month later, he quit the company to go run Florida-based IAP Worldwide Services in December 2004. In January 2006, IAP won a $120 million "cost-plus" contract for support services and facilities to manage the Walter Reed Army Medical Center in Washington, DC.[79] The company inherited an organization that had been losing employees in droves; some 240 of the 300 workers doing non-medical work such as facilities management, patient care, and guard duty had quit rather than face an uncertain future under private management. According to Congressman Henry Waxman, the company replaced the sixty remaining federal employees with just fifty contractors when it took over on February 4, 2007.[80]

His company hit the front pages of the newspapers in February 2007. He found himself back in the hot seat in the U.S. Congress, when a *Washington Post* investigation found ghoulish conditions of neglect at the ninety-eight-year old hospital. "Signs of neglect are everywhere: mouse droppings, belly-up cockroaches, stained carpets, cheap mattresses," wrote Dana Priest and Anne Hull. "On the worst days, soldiers say they feel like they are living a chapter of *Catch-22*. The wounded manage other wounded. Soldiers dealing with psychological disorders of their own have been put in charge of others at risk of suicide. Disengaged clerks, unqualified platoon sergeants, and overworked case managers fumble with simple needs: feeding soldiers' families who are close to poverty, replacing a uniform ripped off by medics in the desert sand, or helping a brain-damaged soldier remember his next appointment."[81]

Neffgen was not the only one to jump ship and join IAP—indeed the company's senior management team read like a who's who of former Halliburton and KBR employees. Chuck Dominy, Halliburton's chief lobbyist who had worked closely with Gribbin and Cheney in 1990s, quit to go to IAP, as did David Roh, director of KBR's operations for military logistics who became director of IAP's global strategy; David B. Warhol, Halliburton's director for Americas Region Staffing and Resource Development became IAP vice president of Human Resources; Craig Peterson, vice president of KBR's Contingency and Homeland Operations became IAP senior vice president for Major Programs (including bidding for LOGCAP work); and David Swindle, vice president of business acquisition and national security programs for KBR, became IAP president.[82]

In early 2008, Neffgen was replaced as CEO of IAP, although much of his original team remained on payroll: Dominy, Swindle, and Warhol were still at the company in July 2008.

COLLECT $200; GO TO JAIL

By the middle of 2008, the Department of Justice had indicted several dozen people for fraud at Camp Arifjan, of whom roughly half were connected to Halliburton/KBR. Both Anthony J. Martin and Stephen Lowell Seamans got off relatively lightly for cooperating with the government, serving just one year in jail each. Indeed Seamans had been released from jail by the time Jeff Alex Mazon faced his first jury trial in April 2008. Shabbir Khan expects to be in jail until 2011, unless he gets out earlier for good behavior.

On January 31, 2008, the Cockerhams pleaded guilty, and on June 24 they were both sentenced to up to twenty years in prison.[83] (Cockerham's co-worker, Major Gloria Davis, who worked on several contracts with Cockerham at Camp Arifjan, killed herself in December 2007, a day after admitting to army investigators that she took $225,000 from a different contractor—Lee Dynamics International.)[84]

Some of the smaller companies who paid bribes were suspended or debarred from work with the military. Remarkably, most of the bigger companies whose executives paid the bribes did not lose work. First Kuwaiti's revenues have gone from tens of millions in 2003 to well over a billion dollars in 2008, with the majority of the money coming from U.S taxpayers. Tamimi of Saudi Arabia, which was already a large conglomerate, continued to do well. La Nouvelle's businesses in Kuwait aren't doing badly at all, but it is embroiled in a number of disputes with Halliburton/KBR, and Ali Hijazi remains under indictment for his role in the Mazon case (although not in the Seamans case).

Yet First Kuwaiti, La Nouvelle and Tamimi, are not the biggest "success" stories on the block. That honor has gone to PWC, the operator of the warehouses that the U.S. military leased in the mid-1990s to create Camp Doha.

PUBLIC WAREHOUSING CORPORATION (PWC)

There are eleven Sultan Centers located at or near some of Kuwait's fanciest shopping malls.[85] From Horizon Organic milk flown in from the United States ($22 a half gallon!) to mangosteens from Thailand, tents for desert camping to a shoe store, they offer one-stop shopping twenty-four hours a day to wealthy Kuwaitis and expatriates (as well as their maids who trail behind them, pushing over-laden shopping carts).[86] Operated by the family of Jamil Sultan al-Essa, a Kuwaiti family whose heritage has been alternately described as southern Iraqi and Saudi, they opened Kuwait's first self-service store near the Shuwaikh Port, focusing on hardware and do-it-yourself products, in 1981.[87]

The family, like many wealthy Middle Eastern families, has its hand in numerous businesses, each operated by a sibling or cousin with overlapping ownership and often senior government positions. One, Abdul Aziz Sultan al-Essa, was chairman of Kuwait's Gulf Bank. Another, Kamal Sultan, ran the local franchise for Apple. Yet another, National Real Estate corporation, bought up 25 percent of the shares of a state-owned company—Public Warehousing Corporation (PWC)—a moribund state agency created in the 1970s to develop and lease out government property, when it was privatized in 1997.[88]

PWC was given to Abdul Aziz's son, Tarek Sultan al-Essa, whose mother and wife were both U.S. citizens.[89] Tarek Sultan, who is also a U.S. citizen, grew up partly in the United States and attended the University of Pennsylvania's Wharton School of Business. When Tarek took over PWC, the company was already making some money renting the 1.6 million-square-meter property near Shuwaik port for Camp Doha (the rental fee was less than $60,000 a month).[90]

In the late 1990s Tarek hired Toby Switzer, a twenty-year veteran of the navy supply corps, who was more than familiar with U.S. military logistics.[91] When the invasion of Iraq began, Switzer, like Shabbir Khan and Ali Hijazi, started to visit the U.S. military bases on a regular basis to offer services to the military. As a former soldier, Switzer was able to gain access easily; indeed, he was invited to events like the Naval Supply Corps birthday party at Camp Patriot in May 2003 with his former comrades in the military supply business.[92]

Tarek and Toby hired a man by the name of Kevin Reulas, who recruited dozens more ex-soldiers through Eric Stagliano of the Lucas Group in Atlanta to trawl for business and write up bids to send to the military contract managers at Camp Arifjan and their Halliburton/KBR equivalents at the Khalifa Resort. (A former PWC employee told me: "It's much easier for a former soldier with a crew cut and shiny shoes to get a contract than any foreigner, even a wealthy Arab.")[93] PWC officials also started to wine and dine army officials at five-star hotels like the Hilton Resort in Kuwait. One official—"Pete" Peleti—was treated to the Super Bowl game in Detroit, Michigan, in January 2006, by Dan Crighton of PWC. (Peleti was also a regular visitor to the "Tamimi Party House" and accepted cash from Shabbir Khan as well as a job for his girlfriend at the time.)[94]

The first major contract PWC made a bid for was a multibillion dollar annual contract in March 2003 called Prime Vendor Subsistence to supplement LOGCAP by supplying all the food eaten on U.S. military bases in this region, that is, up to half a million meals a day for the one hundred fifty thousand troops and a similar number of contractors.[95] (Halliburton/KBR cooks the food and serves it, but it does not provide the food supplies.)

When the contract came up for bid, Tarek had no experience in food supply, nor did he have a personal track record with the U.S. military. So he asked his cousin Kamal to create a joint venture with him to provide the "experience" required to bid on the contract because Kamal had a minor toilet-cleaning contract on Camp Doha. (Once Tarek won the contract, he dropped his cousin from the work. Kamal, who related this story to me, has spent years suing Tarek in Kuwaiti courts for his share of the profits.)[96]

The next major contract that PWC won was a $130 million contract in June 2004 to manage the Abu Ghraib and Umm Qasr warehouses, near Baghdad and Basra respectively, two of the biggest supply depots for the U.S. military in Iraq.[97] Then in June 2005 PWC won part of the $1.5 billion Heavy Lift 6 contract to move all the military equipment from the Kuwait ports to Baghdad, sharing the award with IAP, Al Neffgen's company.[98] In October 2006, PWC bought up a company called Taos from Alabama, allowing it to become the main supplier of guns to the Iraqi army and police force.[99]

The Heavy Lift 6 contract, which is worth about a billion dollars a year, was awarded to PWC as a result of a sweetheart deal cooked up between two ex-101st Apache helicopter pilots who were in the same class at West Point. Major Anthony Kramm was the military official in charge of the deal, and John Arnold was one of the Lucas recruits who was bidding on it at PWC. Kramm gave Arnold the draft documents in late 2004, four months in advance of the published bid. What's more, Arnold hosted dinners for Kramm and his staff at resorts in Kuwait, three months before they published the request for proposal (RFP).[100]

Trouble was, once again, PWC didn't have the capacity to do the job. So the company basically borrowed "low-boy," "reefer," and "flat-bed" trucks and parked them on their property to pretend they were able to do the contract (reefers are refrigeration trucks, and low-boys have low beds). They were supposed to have forty reefers, but they had only ten. Once they won the contract, PWC paid Mercedes to set aside an entire assembly line for four months in Stuttgart to build eighteen hundred trucks.[101]

In addition to the "bait-and-switch" tactics used to win the contracts, PWC allegedly worked with shell companies and subcontractors to overcharge the military by millions of dollars for food supplies, using a system called "prompt payment discounts."[102] This system is best explained with an example: Let's say

Company A (a shell company) buys a pound of chicken for one dollar and gives it to Company B (like PWC) along with a bill for $1.10. Then Company B sells it to the military for $1.10 plus the agreed-upon overhead and profits that are documented on paper. Then Company B pays Company A $1.10 and and receives from Company A ten cents in prompt payment discounts. In this case, Company B has effectively earned the agreed-upon (and legal) profits from the military plus an extra ten cents that the military would never have paid if they bought it directly from company A. At the very least, this is a waste of taxpayer money. And if Company A and Company B are actually owned by the same people, and there is no actual reason to sell it from A to B, this is fraud.

PWC spokesperson Jim Cox told me that the prompt payment discounts were written into the contract and therefore there is nothing illegal about the prompt payment discounts, and that's completely true.[103] In fact, the military even offers contractors the same terms, although the discounts are typically quite a bit smaller (on the order of 2 percent). But if it is true that the Sultan family partially owns some of the suppliers, such as the Sultan Center that provides $200 million in food per year to the military via PWC, then this starts to look like a scam. (Tarek and Jamil are indeed on each other's boards. Jamil and four other Sultan family members are the largest stockholders in Sultan Center and also control a large stake in PWC.[104] Cox told me that this cross-ownership is common in Kuwait and there is nothing illegal about it.)

What makes the scheme look like a good-old-boys network is the web of former military officials who now work for PWC's suppliers. For example, PWC has been buying chicken breast, turkey breast, ham and sausage, and bakery products from Sara Lee of Illinois since 2003. Sara Lee has paid back to PWC 5 percent of the purchase price on these orders. The agreement was negotiated by a Sara Lee executive in charge of military sales, Paul Simmons, who was previously a chief warrant officer for the army. One of his counterparts on the military side is David Staples, a senior procurement official at the army who formerly worked at Sara Lee's Jimmy Dean Sausage unit.[105]

Staples went to work for the army after his predecessor, Emily Prior, quit. Prior now works for Quantum Foods, in Illinois, which supplies beef to the troops in Iraq. She also represents Perdue chicken, which also sells food to the military.

The first prime vendor contract has since been extended and re-bid, and the total amount of money that PWC had earned by the end of 2007 exceeded $6 billion. However, that looked set to change because in early 2007 the Defense Supply Center in Philadelphia, which is in charge of the contract, began a series of investigations into the company's pricing practices, alleging that the company overcharged the Pentagon by as much as $374 million "by inserting a related company to inflate the amount billed."[106]

Other PWC suppliers that are being investigated include American Grocers Inc., which provides food stuff like Smucker's peanut butter to the Sultan Center for resale to PWC in Iraq. The company, which is run by a Lebanese-American businessman in Houston, Samir Itani, is being investigated for tacking on "bogus trucking charges." Another company under scrutiny is Ocean Direct LLC, which is owned by Richmond Wholesale Meats Inc. of California, and supplies raw coldwater lobster tails to the military for about $21 a pound (the average price for the same product on the wholesale market at that time was between $17.60 and $18.75 a pound) for a total of about $2.3 million a month.[107]

Rory Mayberry, a Halliburton/KBR food production manager for a dining facility at Camp Anaconda, made similar charges when he testified before Congress in June 2005. "For example, tomatoes cost about $5 a box locally, but the PWC price was $13 to $15 per box. The local price for a fifteen-pound box of bacon was $12, compared to PWC's price of $80 per box. PWC charged a lot for transportation because they brought the food from Philadelphia," he said.[108]

TAMIMI FIGHTS BACK

PWC's explosive growth attracted the attention of its rivals. One contractor that appeared jealous was Tamimi that assumed it would win a bigger chunk of the military contracts. Indeed Tamimi's business model is similar but older than that of PWC.

For example, among the Saudi Arabian conglomerate's subsidiaries is Tamimi Markets, which opened its first store in 1979, and was the pioneer of the modern supermarket concept in Saudi Arabia, just as the Sultan Center had been in Kuwait. The founder of the business group was Sheikh Ali Abdullah Tamimi who graduated from the American School in Bahrain and then dispatched his children to study abroad, as do most wealthy Arab families. "We all studied in America, which is why we created and established joint ventures with U.S firms, not just because we understand their business philosophy but moreover we communicate easily with them," Tariq Tamimi, the current president would later explain to his company magazine.[109]

Tamimi Real Estate is very similar to National Real Estate in Kuwait—it owns, manages, and develops real estate throughout Saudi Arabia, from executive housing compounds for expatriates to commercial centers, office buildings, showrooms, warehouses, and industrial buildings.[110] Tamimi also has a history of working with the U.S. military as far back as Operation Desert Storm when U.S. troops set up camp in Saudi Arabia and even in Kuwait, notably as the operator of the main 1,140 square-foot dining facility at Camp

Doha and as the operator of a fast food outlet on the base called "Frosty's," which provides hot dogs, hamburgers, and sodas to soldiers after lunch hours.[111] Finally, Tamimi is closely allied with Halliburton/KBR as an exclusive distributor of its products in Saudi Arabia.[112]

Tamimi officials in Kuwait, such as Shabbir Khan and Zubair Khan, therefore assumed that they would easily win major contracts for the 2003 invasion and during any aftermath. Initially, things went well, as Shabbir Khan worked with Steve Seamans to secure Halliburton/KBR subcontracts to build dining facilities first in Kuwait and then in Iraq.

But as one contract after the next went to PWC—Prime Vendor in May 2003, the Abu Ghraib and Umm Qasr warehouse management contracts in August 2004, Heavy Lift 6 in spring 2005—Shabbir Khan realized that they were becoming the underdogs. Then as inquiries started to come in about the payments to Seamans, he realized he had to do something quickly, so he decided to talk with an up-and-coming officer, Lieutenant Colonel Marshall Gutierrez.

MARSHALL GUTIERREZ

Gutierrez, who was appointed director of logistics at Camp Arifjan in 2005 was from the little town of Las Vegas in the foothills of New Mexico's Sangre de Cristo Mountains. He was a descendant of the original farmers who received Spanish land grants to settle the area.[113]

Gutierrez was already suspicious of PWC's prices. He wanted to know why PWC was charging the army $8 a pound for green beans and $90 for five-gallon bags of Coca-Cola syrup when they could be bought in the United States or in Kuwait City for $10 and for $40, respectively.[114]

At that point Shabbir Khan had already been questioned by Berntson from the IRS and Jackson from the FBI. In his own way, Khan decided to co-operate with federal authorities—not by admitting his own guilt, but by providing Gutierrez and other officials with information on his rivals—such as a spreadsheet comparing PWC's prices to the local market. A week after he received the spreadsheet from Khan, Gutierrez wrote a memo to his bosses. "I have started looking at the items we are purchasing from Public Warehousing," he wrote to the camp's commander. "We are being charged way too much for food."[115]

At that juncture, a PWC advisor realized that things could go very wrong, and quickly. Professional Contract Administrators of Albuquerque, New Mexico, a consulting firm that was working for PWC, sent an e-mail marked "urgent" to PWC to advise Switzer to "fire somebody, blame it on them, and cover up" by revising the local market prices. "ASAP—THIS IS VERY SERIOUS."

Switzer agreed to come in and meet with Gutierrez on February 12, but he wasn't able to satisfy the director of logistics. A month later, Shabbir Khan was arrested in Rock Island. In May, Gutierrez started to turn over contracts to Tamimi.

This alarmed Mike Abdul Rahman, PWC's Iraq country manager under Switzer, who decided to take matters into his own hands. A former vocal-graphic analyst for a special division of the U.S. Marine Corps, he claims that Gutierrez was on the take. One of his colleagues later told a Kuwaiti newspaper: "[Gutierrez] suggested we start an intern program and then put forward the name of his son and his son's girlfriend to participate. When the son arrived and was found to be a slacker, we couldn't get rid of him because of his father's position. We had to shuffle him through three different departments instead. There had always been things, like the fact that the floors of his building at Camp Arifjan had been redone with marble or the mysterious appearance of a $10,000 Persian rug in his outer office on camp."[116]

Abdul Rahman says that Gutierrez suddenly asked him for a loan of 1,000 KWD (approximately US$3,500) every week to finance his affair with a young Kuwaiti woman plus buy an occasional air ticket for his family. The PWC manager relayed this information to Switzer who called Brigadier General Mason at Camp Arifjan.[117]

On August 18, a sting was arranged. A little before midnight, the two men met at Diva's restaurant in Kuwait City to smoke *sheesha*. Diva's is a popular place and is adorned with pictures of U.S. movie stars such as Marilyn Monroe and John Travolta. "I was fitted with a wire and accompanied by PWC lawyer Sam McCahon, who arrived first and waited nearby with CID [the local police]," Abdul Rahman would relate later. "Gutierrez arrived shortly after with an eighteen-year-old woman he introduced as his Kuwaiti girlfriend, but court records identify her as his second wife and of Iraqi descent carrying an Austrian passport. The same court records indicate that Gutierrez became a Muslim before entering into a prenuptial agreement to pay his second wife a $20,000 settlement in the event of a divorce."

Gutierrez offered Rahman a ride home. When they got in the vehicle, Rahman offered Gutierrez the requested 1,000 KWD. As soon as Gutierrez told him to put it in the car's center console, agents surrounded the car and arrested both men.

Gutierrez was locked in a steel cage next to some soldiers who were accused of murdering Iraqi detainees. He tried to commit suicide a couple of times but was caught. A week later he was released to await court-martial proceedings. A few days later, on the morning of September 4, Gutierrez was found dead in his quarters from swallowing ethyl glycol, the active ingredient of antifreeze. There was no note.

AGILITY IS BORN

"Pete" Peleti, the army official who PWC had taken to the Super Bowl, was arrested in 2006 when he flew back to the Dover Air Force Base from the Middle East with a duffel bag stuffed with watches and jewelry as well as about $40,000 concealed in his clothing.[118]

Major Anthony Kramm is still under investigation, while John Arnold has returned to the United States and is now reportedly attending the Wharton Business School, the university of choice for PWC executives. A number of PWC recruits from Kevin Reulas's team were fired. A number of them found other jobs in Kuwait, and a few continue to battle the company in local courts for back pay.

In December 2006 PWC announced that it was changing its name to Agility. In 2007, the company announced it had taken in $3.5 billion in revenue, with profits of $585.2 million. In 2008, the company announced revenues of $6 billion, a staff of 32,000 employees with 550 offices on 100 countries around the world.[119]

From managing a few warehouses in 2003, Agility was suddenly in the same league as global logistics giants FedEx and DHL. It operated ports in Dubai and ran shipping companies out of New Orleans. The company boasted to the *Los Angeles Times* that it was capable of "hauling giant mining equipment through the jungles of Papua New Guinea or erecting stage sets in Asia for touring rock groups such as the Doobie Brothers."[120]

Fraud Outside Kuwait

- Kevin Andre Smoot, of Woodlands, Texas, the managing director of the freight forwarding station of Houston-based Eagle Global Logistics (EGL), conspired with Christopher Joseph Cahill, EGL's regional vice president for the Middle East and India who was stationed at its regional office in Dubai, to inflate invoices for military shipments to Baghdad in 2003 and 2004, in order to earn higher bonuses.[121]

The shipping company had been subcontracted by Halliburton/KBR to transport military equipment, ranging from "armor-plated vehicles to trash bins" from Houston to Iraq for two years. The company brought the equipment by sea into the port of Dubai and then used Russian cargo planes to fly the material to Baghdad. After a rival company's plane was shot down in November 2003, Cahill asked to be paid a "war risk surcharge" that supposedly had been imposed by Aerospace Consortium, which supplied aircraft to EGL.

Federal investigators in Texas were informed by a whistle-blower that the extra fifty cents per kilogram of cargo added for 379 air cargo shipments were in fact, phony. All told, some $1.14 million in fraudulent surcharges were added into a total invoice of $13.3 million.

In order to win contracts from Halliburton/KBR, Smoot also provided kickbacks such as meals, drinks, golf outings, and tickets to rodeo events, and baseball and football games to five Halliburton/KBR employees worth approximately $25,337, on approximately ninety different occasions, plus another $8,494 through a colleague.

Cahill and Smoot pled guilty on February 16, 2006, and July 20, 2007, respectively.[122]

- Glenn Allen Powell, from Cedar Park, Texas—a Halliburton/KBR contract manager in Iraq—was arrested for accepting more than $110,000 in kickbacks from an Iraqi subcontractor he selected in July 2004 to renovate buildings in Iraq. The subcontractor agreed to pay Powell 20 percent of the $609,000 contract, but Powell was caught by KBR security in January 2005 before the full amount could be paid out. He pled guilty on August 19, 2005.[123]

- Wallace A. Ward, of Spring Lake, North Carolina, a Halliburton/KBR employee who worked at the Bagram Airfield in Afghanistan, pled guilty to accepting payments from Red Star Enterprises drivers who were transporting jet fuel to the military base between May and September 2006. After being given documents falsely showing that the truckloads of fuel had been delivered to the airfield, the drivers resold the fuel to parties outside the airfield. More than eighty truckloads of fuel involving more than 784,000 gallons valued at more than $2.1 million were in fact diverted for sale outside the airfield between May and September 2006. Ward pleaded guilty on January 25, 2008. On May 9, 2008, James N. Sellman, from Arnold, Maryland, pleaded guilty to being part of the same scheme.[124]

Camp Anaconda

THE LINEUP OF PARKED MIG and Mirage jets at the old Iraqi airbase at Balad in northern Iraq would have embarrassed any self-respecting air force captain. Cannibalized for souvenirs, decorated with red or black graffiti that read "Hi Ma" and "East Liverpool, Ohio" and "Sgt. Paredes," they were rusting hulks of their once-proud former selves. To the east of this motley collection of aircraft were two major runways that formed an incomplete V. To the west past a third dirt runway was a twin-engine turboprop that was clearly destroyed in a bombing raid, probably by the United States. It was smashed in the middle, and one wing had broken off.

Arriving at the base in June 2003, Laszlo Tibold drove out past the ruined aircraft and the runways to the western edge of the base where he was assigned to work for the next few months. When he first visited, all he could see was dirt, bushes, and scrub, with the occasional outcrop of dead ordnance or an abandoned oxygen tank. His task was to help figure out how to procure the material needed to turn this desolate land into a modern version of Cam Ranh Bay—a huge housing complex of prefabricated buildings where many of the thirty-five thousand soldiers assigned to northern Iraq would live.[1]

There were certainly some similarities to what happened at Cam Ranh Bay when Donald Rumsfeld visited it in 1965. Like the Vietnamese base, the land itself would eventually be completely transformed in northern Iraq. Some fifty acres would be paved with an eight-inch-thick asphalt pad, and another twenty acres would be cleared and smoothed down with gravel. On this gravel base would rise thousands of six-bunk, modular-housing units on block piers. And there would be one other similarity: at night, just as in Cam Ranh Bay, in Vietnam, the darkness would be broken with sporadic mortar and automatic weapons' fire.[2] Every so often the alarm would sound and workers would have to scramble for the nearest bunker.

This time around, Halliburton/KBR was hired to create what would eventually become the central logistical hub for all of Iraq: LSA Anaconda. Like Cam Ranh Bay and Camp Bondsteel, LSA Anaconda would include a postal distribution center, power distribution, drinking and waste water treatment, and it would be watched by forty-foot-tall steel guard towers equipped with sensitive surveillance equipment. But for all the similarities, there was one major difference: unlike Tibold's predecessors almost exactly thirty-eight years prior, he would not enjoy picturesque views of the ocean or days on the beach.

Laszlo Tibold had plenty of experience in the construction business. In July 1965, when Brown & Root crews were building the Cam Ranh Bay base, Tibold had just signed up to earn a mechanical engineering degree at the California State University at Pomona in Southern California. After graduating as a qualified mechanical engineer, Tibold worked for two major engineering corporations for a good part of his working life—Fluor and Parsons. He had worked on the Trans-Alaska Pipeline System (TAPS), and he had worked in Isfahan, Iran, during the last days of the Shah, and in Chelyabinsk, Siberia. And he had help in understanding the military: his boss was Jim Spore, who previously worked for the navy, managing the CONCAP contract to construct prisons in Guantánamo Bay.[3]

When the two men got to work, they had no physical office, let alone any systems or real instructions on how to do the job. Beginning with a laptop, a satellite phone, and a folding table with two chairs that they set up under the blazing sun, they got to work.

The first hurdle was getting workers. Getting Iraqis on the base was well nigh impossible. "We should have started work at 4 a.m., before it got too hot, but that was impossible. Iraqi workers were not allowed to stay on base at night, and it took four hours to enter the base in the morning, so unless you got to work at midnight. . . ." recalls Tibold. So Spore called up his two friends who had helped him at Guantánamo—Neal Helliwell and Toby O'Connell— who were starting up a company called Prime Projects International (PPI). Helliwell and O'Connell said they could get Filipino workers to Iraq in a matter of weeks, just as they had done in Cuba. Two weeks later, the first private plane to land at the base touched down with workers from the Philippines.

The next problem was supplies; they needed gravel and stone to lay a base on which to construct the new facilities. "We didn't have any way to issue competitive bids, so we took what we could get," says Tibold. So they accepted a bid from the first guy who offered to get them the needed supplies. His name was Ali Dijaily (popularly known as "American Ali"), a naturalized U.S. citizen who grew up in Tikrit. Later Tibold would realize that Dijaily was ripping them off by sending half-filled trucks with substandard gravel, so Tibold switched to a better supplier, a Bosnian who showed up on the base, who filled his trucks with the appropriate quality of gravel.

For the first three months that they worked there was not even a cloud in the sky. Then one morning when Tibold awoke, he noticed something unusual in the sky. He called out to his co-workers, and they all looked up in wonder as the first patches of white were clearly outlined at the horizon. He snapped a picture of all of them staring into the heavens.

Gradually they put together housing and dining facilities. A picture of the finished buildings shows the soldiers lined up in the rain for a Thanksgiving meal, while Halliburton/KBR workers entertained them with a pageant, dressing up as pilgrims and Native Americans, complete with long, black robes for the pilgrims and feathers for the natives.

Tibold left Iraq in frustration in December 2003. "We were getting half a dozen mortar attacks a day," he said. Down in Kuwait, while on leave, he started to reflect on the dangers of life in Iraq and decided it was not worth returning.

Almost a year after Tibold and Spore had started building Camp Anaconda, a dispatch from *Houston Chronicle* reporter David Ivanovich, in April 2004 claimed that it was still dangerous at Anaconda. He wrote: "As the Halliburton employees' plane landed at Camp Anaconda, insurgents launched a rocket attack on this U.S. military base. Hurried away from the airstrip, the new Halliburton recruits stared as a 'dust devil'—think mini-tornado—swept through the camp in a twenty-foot-high swirl of sand and grit. And as the forty-three new arrivals gathered for their evening muster, under a sky awash with stars, the sirens wailed again. A rocket had landed inside the camp, injuring two soldiers."[4]

The new recruits were greeted by Tadeusz Kowalski, Halliburton/KBR's head of human resources, who was clad in a flak vest, carrying a Kevlar helmet. "We have just been under attack," he told them. "We've had a few mortars come in just off to our right. Yesterday, we had a suicide bomber at the north gate. We've had mortar attacks. We've had shots." Security chief Scott Metzdorf told them not to make friends with local Iraqis. "You keep a working relationship with them. That's it."

The men and women who came were not always at the top of their professions, nor were they familiar with the language, the culture, or even the history of the country. The common refrain was that they were unemployed and desperate. "I was laid off in October," Gene Chaney told the *Chronicle*. He was a thirty-nine-year-old electrician from Mount Enterprise, who left behind a wife and three children. "There was no hesitation," he said.

They came because they were paid well, to the tune of at least $80,000 a year, tax free, with free accommodation and semi-annual paid leave. The lack of skills was often not a hindrance as many of them were generally not expected to do much except supervise menial labor from Third World countries. No U.S. citizens were assigned menial work such as cooking, cleaning, or manual labor—Steve Powell, a former Halliburton/KBR supervisor from Azle, Texas, who worked at Camp Diamondback until May 2005, says U.S. citizens "weren't supposed to get our hands dirty."[5]

The workers whom they oversaw, however, rarely got to leave the country unless they were fired or quit their jobs. These workers were often paid less than a twentieth of their U.S. supervisors—salaries as low as $3,000 a year were commonplace and in high demand in countries from Pakistan to the Philippines.

THIRD COUNTRY NATIONALS

On U.S. Army bases in other parts of the world such as Camp Bondsteel in Kosovo thousands of local people are hired to cook and clean for the troops, but in Iraq the fear of infiltration was too high to take that risk. Instead Halliburton/KBR hired what the army calls Third Country Nationals (TCNs) through a complex layer of companies working in Iraq.

At the top of the pyramid-shaped system is the U.S. government, which assigned billions of dollars in contracts to prime contractors like Halliburton/KBR. Below them are dozens of medium-sized companies—largely based in the Middle East—including PPI of Dubai, Kulak from Turkey, First Kuwaiti Trading & Contracting and PWC of Kuwait, Gulf Catering Company, and Tamimi of Saudi Arabia. Under these companies are small, local recruiters such as MGM Worldwide Manpower and General Services, Anglo-European Placement Services (AEPS) in the Philippines, and Subhash Vijay Associates in India.

The TCNs are mostly from Asian countries such as India, Nepal, Pakistan, the Philippines, and Sri Lanka, and they are paid monthly salaries between $200 and $1,000. They work as truck drivers, construction workers, carpenters, warehousemen, laundry workers, cooks, accountants, beauticians, and other such blue-collar jobs for the U.S. military.

Halliburton/KBR's own estimate of the number of the TCNs in Iraq is thirty-five thousand out of the total forty-seven thousand employees on company payroll. There is no official figure. Indeed the Government Accountability Office (GAO), an investigative arm of the U.S. Congress, concluded in April 2005 that it is impossible to accurately estimate the total number of U.S.

or foreign nationals who work in Iraq. "It is difficult to aggregate reliable data," said the GAO report, "due in part to the large number of contractors and the multiple levels of subcontractors performing work in Iraq."[6]

AEPS

One of PPI's principal suppliers was AEPS from Makati, which is a major municipality that makes up the city of Manila in the Philippines. AEPS operates out of a small, two-story white stucco building with fancy wrought-iron fencing hidden away in a back alley of a residential neighborhood.

Inside the patio/waiting room, dozens of job listings are tacked to a stucco wall. Two large picture frames hang on either side of a mounted AEPS logo, which are filled with photos from Iraq, one of which is titled Anaconda. The Anaconda frame includes pictures of kitchen staff, posing in their aprons and hats, and there are others, smiling over plates of food. On a large cork board the company has posted its license from the Philippines Overseas Employment Administration (POEA). AEPS was the very first company to receive an official license—so their license number is 001. Posted among the various licenses is an article by Jerome Aning from the *Philippine Daily Inquirer* with the headline "25,000 workers wanted for Iraq."

In the waiting room, a couple of women and a handful of men (whose ages range from twenties to forties) wait on cushioned wooden benches to be interviewed. All are neatly dressed, mostly in collared shirts and slacks. They carry plastic folders that contain their résumés and passports, and most smoke nervously to pass the time. At the top of a narrow flight of stairs, behind a large desk covered in piles of paper, sits Gilbert C. "Nicky" Arcilla. The walls of his office are covered with dry erase boards with lists of job assignments overseas.

At an interview in late 2005, Arcilla told Lee Wang (a New York filmmaker, who directed *Someone Else's War*—a documentary about migrant workers in Iraq) that he is responsible for 95 percent of the Filipino workers in Iraq. Arcilla explained that he has been supplying workers to Helliwell in Saudi Arabia for more than twenty-five years, including the ones who were dispatched to build the prisons in Guantánamo Bay and LSA Anaconda in Iraq.[7]

Arcilla says he didn't even have to advertise when the job orders came in for Iraq in the summer of 2003, he just relied on word-of-mouth and was quickly overwhelmed by applicants. "You could say it was the most popular job," he said, noting that he got one hundred to two hundred applicants every single day, four thousand applicants a month. People would sleep outside on the streets just waiting for an interview. They would come on a Monday from provinces like Pampanga (Arcilla's home province, which is also the home province of the president). Some came from as far away as the southern island of Mindanao just for a chance to interview, borrowing the fare for the trip from fellow villagers.

Arcilla says his staff was working twenty-four hours a day in 2003, sending as many as two flights to Iraq everyday. "There were so many people outside of his office, he could barely get through the door. He jokingly tells us that he considered getting a helicopter so he could fly in to work," Wang wrote in an e-mail to me.

His biggest complaint was that people don't understand what work is actually like in Iraq. Arcilla told Wang: "The problem is that the public is misinformed about this. You tell someone on the street I'm going to work in Iraq, and they think no way. Now there are bombs and explosions. They don't know these people are working inside U.S. military bases, well protected. It's safer than walking the streets of Manila. Not even a mosquito could get through the gate." (When Wang asked Arcilla if he had ever visited Iraq, he said no.)

A comparison is in order: Russell Gold of the *Wall Street Journal* reported on an identical situation halfway across the world, in Houston, Texas, in February 2004, where hundreds were lining up outside a Halliburton/KBR office waiting to interview for a job. "They are unemployed and underemployed workers with few jobs in a U.S. economy that isn't producing many jobs," he wrote. Gold interviewed men lining up for the training sessions, citing the example of one typical applicant whose previous job was transporting chickens for $12 an hour. When he arrived in Iraq, his navy-blue U.S. passport earned him a tidy sum of money: between $7,000 and $8,000 a month, generous paychecks even by U.S. standards. In return, he had to work twelve to fifteen hours a day, seven days a week, often living in a tent and subject to blinding sandstorms as well as temperatures exceeding 130 degrees.[8]

In other words, these companies that pay $200 for Indians and $8,000 for Texans are like any other industry in the world. Despite common perceptions that sweatshop jobs are the least-liked jobs in most countries, multinational companies pay more than local companies (if they are available), making them attractive to the local population. Three hundred dollars a month is a small fortune for a poor worker in India, and $8,000 is what engineers earn in the United States.

Yet this was not just a two-tier system of wages where the supervisors were paid well and the workers made minimum wage. In fact, salaries were tied to the country of origin. Thus, a Bangladeshi cleaner would be paid less than a Pakistani, a Georgian truck driver more than a Fijian, and a white South African security guard would make more than an Indian for doing the very same job. The poorer the country of citizenship, the less the workers were paid, which is not unlike the caste system in India or the apartheid system in South Africa before the African National Congress came to power.

TRAFFICKED TO IRAQ

At dawn the muezzin's call to prayer echoes across Dubai's empty streets. At Terminal Two of the city's international airport, right across from a giant mosque where a few faithful and religious gather for the morning ceremony, taxis arrive to drop off the first passengers of the day. Unlike its sister building several miles away, this terminal does not have banks of gleaming silver escalators, no advertisements for duty-free shopping, seven-star resorts, or even for the famous gold *souks* (markets) of the city. Nor do its departure and arrival screens flash data from any of the more popular destinations: London, Paris, New York, or Bangkok.[9]

No, the flights that depart from this terminal are destined for Beshehr (which houses an Iranian nuclear reactor), Bossaso (smuggling-central in Somalia), and Baku (oil capital of the Central Asian state of Azerbaijan). But by far the most popular destinations on the list are Baghdad and Kabul via airlines like African Express, Al Ishtar, and Jupiter. Flights are announced on a regular basis, but some have no check-in gates and simply vanish off the screens after staying up for a short time. Most flights arrive and depart several hours after schedule.

This is one of the world's most mysterious airports. Every morning, from dawn until about noon, passenger flights leave for Iraq and for Afghanistan, together with a dozen or so private cargo flights, making this possibly the busiest commercial terminal in the world for the "global war on terrorism." Tickets to either destination go for about $400 a seat, round-trip; cargo travels for about $2 a kilogram.

Most of the passengers at this terminal are Afghan or Iraqi, but every morning a few U.S. citizens, Indians, and Filipinos arrive, often accompanied by "minders" to make sure that they catch their flights: some from the U.S. embassy or military, others like Lloyd D'Costa of Skylink, who subcontracts to Halliburton/KBR.

One of the key players in this supply of labor to Iraq is located in a skyscraper that overlooks Dubai Creek, twenty minutes from the airport. On the fifth floor one of these Twin Towers, behind the dark steel-blue glass windows that reflect the sun as it sets over the ocean, are the offices of Neil Helliwell and Toby O'Connell—Prime Projects International (PPI), the company that provides the bulk of Gilbert "Nicky" Arcilla business at AEPS.

On Saturday, December 10, 2005, African Express Airways flight XU 106, officially based in Nairobi, Kenya, was scheduled to take off from Terminal Two in Dubai for Mosul, in northern Iraq, when immigration caught eighty-eight Filipino workers preparing to leave on the early morning flight after arriving in the country on tourist visas. Arrested along with the eighty-eight workers was Jordanian national Mah'd Moh'd Ahmad Hamza, also known as "Khalid." Hamza was issued a temporary visitor's visa to the Philippines by the country's consulate in Dubai on September 19, 2005, on behalf of a labor recruitment agency named Tierra Mar of Manila. The workers say that they paid the agency between 40,000 to 70,000 Philippine pesos (PHP) each (US$760 to $1,330 at the time) for the jobs.[10]

The eighty-eight workers were deported back to Manila the following week, and Tierra Mar was placed under investigation. However, government officials said the incident might just be the tip of the iceberg. "United Arab Emirates seems to be a favored jump-off point because of the facility for obtaining a visit visa to this country," Philippine Labor Secretary Patricia Santo Tomas told reporters.[11]

Ironically, a more senior government official seemed to appreciate the work of the companies that exported Filipino workers to Iraq. On November 10, 2005, Philippines President Gloria Macapagal-Arroyo gave a special "International Employer Award" at Malacanang Palace in Manila to Neil Helliwell as chief executive officer of PPI. The award was for "displaying continuous preferences for Filipino workers and providing them with excellent career advancement and a generous package of employment benefits."[12]

RUDE SHOCK AWAITS

Not everyone on those planes from Dubai realized that they were destined for Iraq. For example, dozens of young Indian men from the northern state of Punjab traveled to Dubai in early 2005 enticed by promises of salaries of $750 a month to work as drivers in Kuwait. Like the Filipinos, they too were following a dream that millions have pursued over the last three decades: the hope of making a fortune in the oil-rich Middle East, or at least creating a small nest egg. For this dream, they each paid $2,700, typically borrowed from a loan shark whom they thought they could pay off in a matter of months.

But the youth were in for a rude shock when they touched down in Dubai. Packed into a thirty-five-seater plane soon after they arrived, they discovered that they were being flown, not to the staid safety of Kuwait, but to Baghdad and Mosul, two of the most dangerous locations in Iraq. They were unwitting victims of a scam by unscrupulous employment agencies.

Baljinder Singh and Karanpal told Indian newspapers later that they "were locked up in a small area, which had heavy wiring all around. We were made to do menial tasks for U.S. soldiers like picking up their excreta, washing their clothes, picking up their cigarette butts—all this for US$50 a month, and a plate of boiled rice once a day. If we raised our voice, we were tortured." [13]

"We were made to drive trucks right into the areas where bombs were being dropped. We could not protest either, for our passports were with the company authorities," said another worker named Dharampal of Siala village in Punjab.

Rescued after eight months by sympathetic Indian embassy staff, the men returned to India, their dreams shattered and deeply in debt. In late December 2005, several went public with the help of a former minister.

FIRST KUWAITI

One major subcontractor accused of trafficking is Wadi al-Absi's company—First Kuwaiti—which is one of PPI's leading rivals in the business of importing TCN labor. First Kuwaiti had approximately a billion dollars in army contracts including a $500 million contract to build the U.S. embassy in Baghdad.

Like PPI, First Kuwaiti was hired by Halliburton/KBR to supply unskilled labor, whom they would recruit through third-party agencies. One of these men was Ramil Autencio, who had signed with MGM Worldwide Manpower and General Services in the Philippines. The thirty-seven-year-old air-conditioning maintenance worker thought he would be working at Crowne Plaza Hotel in Kuwait for $450 a month. "I had no idea that I would end up in Iraq," he told my colleague David Phinney of CorpWatch. [14]

Autencio arrived in Kuwait in December 2003, only to discover that First Kuwaiti had bought his contract. The company, which now holds U.S.-funded contracts valued in the neighborhood of $1 billion, threatened that unless he and dozens of other Filipino workers went to Iraq, the Kuwaiti police would arrest them, he says. "We had no choice but to go along with them. After all, we were in their country."

Once in Iraq, Autencio found that there were no air-conditioners to install or maintain, so he spent eleven hours a day "moving boulders" to fortify the camps, first at Camp Anaconda and then at Tikrit. Food was inadequate and workers were not getting paid, he says. "We ate when the Americans had leftovers from their meals. If not, we didn't eat at all."

Working and living conditions were so bad that in February 2004 Autencio escaped with dozens of others. A U.S. soldier born in the Philippines helped them leave the camp, and sympathetic truck drivers working for Halliburton/KBR offered them rides through the country. By the time the Filipinos reached the Kuwaiti border, Autencio said the number of fleeing workers was so great that the border police let them pass through without proper papers.

First Kuwaiti general manager Wadi al-Absi claims Autencio was lying. His proof was a working agreement, purportedly signed in the Philippines by Autencio. He claimed that unscrupulous recruitment agencies do sometimes misrepresent jobs and take money from people eager to work, but he provided Autencio's undated contract with First Kuwaiti that identified the job site as both Kuwait and "mainly" Iraq.

The agreement also laid out the salary: $346 a month for eight-hour days, seven days a week, plus $104 a month for a mandatory two hours overtime every day. Al-Absi insists that Autencio was paid in full. "He sued me in court over this, and he lost," al-Absi said. "He doesn't have a case against us."[15]

Nepalese worker Krishna Bahadur Khadka told a similar story of false recruitment by the same company in a September 7, 2004, news report in the *Kathmandu Post.* After being recruited for a job in Kuwait, he says, he arrived only to be told by First Kuwaiti that if he and 121 other workers refused work in Iraq, they would be sent back to Nepal. "I was not happy, at first, as my contractors did not provide me a job as heavy vehicle driver as pledged. But they had offered 175,000 Nepalese rupees (NPR) (US$2,450), and one would not be able earn half that amount in Kuwait. So I signed the papers," Khadka said, adding that he had already invested $1,680 as payment to an agent in Nepal.[16]

Al-Absi claimed that Khadka's allegation, too, is a lie and that Khadka misrepresented his skills. Again al-Absi presented a contract identifying the work site as "mainly Iraq." It bore Khadka's signature and fingerprint.

"Khadka is a troublemaker who was trying to organize the workers," al-Absi said, claiming that thousands of TCNs working for First Kuwaiti have renewed their contracts with raises. "We treat our workers with excellent care," he said.

First Kuwaiti contract to build the U.S. Embassy

On July 26, 2007, Rory J. Mayberry, an emergency medical technician who worked for First Kuwaiti, made the following statement about the construction of the U.S. Embassy in Baghdad (edited slightly for length) to the Committee on Oversight and Government Reform Subcommittee on National Security and Foreign Affairs in the U.S. House of Representatives:[17]

"I reported to First Kuwaiti managers in Kuwait City, where I signed my paperwork and received photo identification. Nothing led me to be concerned at this point. A few days later I was given my flight information to Baghdad. At this time, First Kuwaiti managers asked me to escort fifty-one Filipino nationals to the Kuwait airport and make sure they got on the same flight I was taking to Baghdad. Many of these Filipinos did not speak any English. I wanted to help them make sure they got on their flight okay, just as my managers had asked. We were all employees of the same company after all.

"But when we got to the Kuwait airport, I noticed that all of our tickets said we were going to Dubai. I asked why. A First Kuwaiti manager told me that because Filipino passports do not allow Filipinos to fly to Iraq, they must be marked as going to Dubai. The First Kuwaiti manager added that I should not tell any of the Filipinos they were being taken to Baghdad.

"As I found out later, these men thought they had signed up to work in Dubai hotels. One fellow I met told me in broken English that he was excited to start his new job as a telephone repair man. He had no idea he was being sent to do construction work on the U.S. Embassy.

"Well, Mr. Chairman, when the airplane took off, and the captain announced that we were headed for Baghdad, all you-know-what broke loose on that airplane. People started shouting. It wasn't until a security guy working for First Kuwaiti waved an MP-5 in the air that people settled down. They realized they had no other choice but to go to Baghdad.

"Let me spell it out clearly. I believe these men were kidnapped by First Kuwaiti to work on the U.S. Embassy. They had no passports because they were confiscated at the Kuwait airport. When the airplane touched down at Baghdad airport, the Filipinos where loaded into buses and taken away. Later, I found that they were being smuggled into the Green Zone. They had no IDs, no passports, nothing. They were being smuggled in past U.S. security forces. I had a trailer all to myself in the Green Zone. But they were packed twenty-five to thirty in a trailer, and every day they went out to work on the construction of the embassy without the proper safety equipment.

"I went out to the construction site to watch. There were a lot of injuries out there because of the conditions these people were forced to work in. It was absurd—I had been hired based on my experience with OSHA [Occupational Safety and Health Administration] guidelines and compliance, and I saw guys without shoes, without gloves, no safety harnesses, on scaffolding thirty feet off the ground, their toes wrapped around the rebar like a bunch of birds. One guy, he was up there intoxicated on pain killers, and I had to yell and scream for ten minutes until they got him down."

On April 14, 2008, the company announced that the new U.S. Embassy in Baghdad was complete. "Despite the ongoing insurgency, compromised supply routes, and unrelenting risk to the lives and safety of First Kuwaiti workers, the project was completed in just over two years within the original fixed price budget of $474 million, an unprecedented achievement."

The finished project consisted of a 104-acre, twenty-seven-building compound—a complete, self-supported city-within-a-city, the largest U.S. embassy in the world, which includes 619 apartments for employees, office space, restaurants, indoor and outdoor basketball courts, a volleyball court, and an indoor, Olympic-sized swimming pool.

TAMIMI AND GULF CATERING

Indian newspapers reported a similar scheme involving Subhash Vijay Associates, which supplied workers to Gulf Catering in Kuwait, a subcontractor to Tamimi in Saudi Arabia. In early May 2004, a news story surfaced that contractor Subhash Vijay Associates offered Abdul Aziz Hamid and his younger brother Shahjahan, from southern India, two-year contracts to work as butchers on a military base in Kuwait for an $1,800 fee.[18]

The men were promised salaries of $385 a month, a small fortune for a laborer in India, so they mortgaged a relative's house and land, paid the fee, and flew to Kuwait in August with two of their friends. Within days the brothers were taken, without their passports, to a U.S. military base in northern Iraq. Their supervisor, who had taken their passports in Kuwait, told them they were required to work on the base for six months and could not leave. Their work consisted of washing dishes and cleaning up after U.S. soldiers for $150 a month. "We were in hell. I told my wife over the phone, 'If God wills us, we will meet again.'"

Nico Smith, personnel manager for Gulf Catering, which employed the men, denied exploiting them. He told the *New York Times*, "The passports are kept only for safekeeping. When they wanted to resign, we never said they can't go."

In a July 1, 2004, article, the *Washington Post* described a similarly intricate recruiting scheme involving dining service workers from India. Dharmapalan Ajayakumar was recruited by Subhash Vijay Associates in India to work for Gulf Catering Company of Riyadh, Saudi Arabia. Gulf Catering was subcontracted to Alargan Group of Kuwait City, which was subcontracted to the Event Source of Salt Lake City, which in turn was subcontracted to Halliburton/KBR. "I cursed my fate—not having a feeling my life was secure, knowing I could not go back, and being treated like a kind of animal," for less than $7 a day, Ajayakumar told the newspaper.[19]

POOR WAGES AND WORKING CONDITIONS

Ramil Autencio, Karanpal, and Abdul Aziz Hamid's complaints were not unique. Jing Soliman, a thirty-five-year-old father of two, who signed up with PPI in the Philippines as a warehouse worker at Anaconda, says he was promised $615 a month, including overtime. For a forty-hour work week that would be just over $3 an hour. But for the twelve-hour day, seven-day week that Soliman says was standard for him and many contractor employees in Iraq, he actually earned $1.56 an hour.

Soliman planned to send most of his $7,380 annual pay home to his family in the Philippines, where the combined unemployment and underemployment rate tops 28 percent. The average annual income in Manila in 2004 was $4,384, and the World Bank estimated that nearly half of the nation's eighty-four million people live on less than $2 a day. "I am an ordinary man," said Soliman during a telephone interview with David Phinney, from Soliman's home in Quezon City near Manila. "It was good money." His ambitions, like the U.S. civilians working in Iraq, were similar. "I wanted to save up, buy a house, and provide for my family," he says.[20]

Once in Iraq he discovered that many PPI managers were foul-mouthed and verbally abusive. The company restricted employees to two five-minute phone calls home a month and deducted the cost from their paychecks. "[The calls] were $10 more expensive than at the PX [the retail store on the military base], but if they see you making a call at another location, they would send you home," Soliman said.

Lack of access to phones was the least of their troubles. Soliman and his fellow TCNs got very different amenities than their U.S. supervisors. They lived in crowded trailers, were not given adequate medical care, nor were they allowed to eat in the very dining facilities that they themselves had built, and were not allowed to eat the salad, pizza, sandwich, and ice cream bars that they served the U.S. troops. Instead they would often have to wait outside in line in 140-degree-plus heat to eat "slop."

Rory Mayberry, a former Halliburton/KBR contractor who worked at the dining facilities at Camp Anaconda, from February to April 2004, says that Halliburton/KBR was supposed to feed six hundred Turkish and Filipino meals. "Although KBR charged for this service," Mayberry said, "it didn't prepare the meals. Instead, these workers were given leftover food in boxes and garbage bags after the troops ate. Sometimes there were not leftovers to give them. . . . Iraqi drivers of food convoys that arrived on the base were not fed. They were given Meals Ready to Eat [U.S. military prepackaged rations], with pork, which they couldn't eat for religious reasons. As a result, the drivers would raid the trucks for food."

Another TCN supervisor in Baghdad described how her workers had to stand in line with plates and were served "something like curry and fish heads from big old pots. It looked like a concentration camp."[21]

MORTARITAVILLE

The TCNs not only did much of the dirty work, but like others working for the U.S. military, they risked and sometimes lost their lives. Few received proper workplace safety equipment or adequate protection from incoming mortars and rockets. When frequent gunfire, rockets, and mortar shell from the ongoing conflict hit LSA Anaconda, which was dubbed "Mortaritaville" by the U.S. soldiers, the TCNs were typically shielded only by the shirts on their backs and the flimsy trailers they slept in, often on the perimeter of the camps. "They didn't have personal protection equipment to wear when there was an alert," said Sharon Reynolds of Kirbyville, Texas, a Halliburton/KBR administrator, who spent eleven months in Iraq until April and was responsible for processing timesheets for 665 TCNs employed by PPI at Camp Victory, near Baghdad. "Here we are, walking around with helmets and vests because of an alert, and they are just looking at us, wondering what's going on."[22]

Her partner, Randy McDale—a Halliburton/KBR foreman for heavy construction equipment at Camp Victory and other installations near the Baghdad International Airport, who spent fifteen months in Iraq before returning home in April 2005—agreed. "Some were wearing sandals, walking in the mud when it was winter and forty degrees," he said of the Indians, Sri Lankans, and Filipinos he worked with. "One guy didn't even have a coat."[23]

And if they got sick, tough luck. "They don't get sick pay, and if PPI had insurance, they sure didn't talk about it much," Reynolds recalls. "TCNs had a lot of problems with overtime and things. I remember one time that they didn't get paid for four months. . . . I had to go to bat for them to get shoes and proper clothing,"

Many TCNs were killed in mortar attacks; some were taken hostage before meeting their death. Exact numbers are hard to come by because the Pentagon keeps no comprehensive record of TCN casualties. But the Georgia-based nonprofit, Iraq Coalition Casualty Count, which tallied media reports of deaths, estimated that TCNs make up more than 176 of the 437 reported civilian fatalities by mid 2008.[24] The actual number of unreported fatalities could be much higher, while unreported and life-altering injuries are legion.

In a particularly gruesome set of murders on August 30, 2004, the captors of twelve Nepalese cooks and cleaners who worked for a Jordanian construction company beheaded one worker and posted a video of the execution on the Internet with the following message: "We have carried out the sentence of God against twelve Nepalese who came from their country to fight the Muslims and to serve the Jews and the Christians . . . believing in Buddha as their God."[25]

Soliman barely escaped death on the night of May 11, 2004, when his trailer at Camp Anaconda was blown apart by a bomb attack. That night, three others were injured along with Soliman. One roommate—twenty-five-year-old fuel pump attendant Raymund Natividad—was killed. Days later, Soliman was flown home to the Philippines in a wheelchair because he wanted medical treatment in his own country. But even after surgery and skin grafts, he still sometimes feels a nagging pain in his leg, he says. Doctors tell Soliman he will walk with a piece of shrapnel lodged in his left leg for the rest of his life. "It was too deep" to remove, he explained.[26]

The attack ignited shock waves of fear among the thirteen hundred Filipino workers at Camp Anaconda. Some six hundred PPI employees immediately quit over safety concerns. "Filipinos don't want to work anymore in the mess halls, laundry, and fuel depot," a Filipino embassy official in Baghdad said at the time. "There's a paralysis of work."

The largest number of TCN casualties occurred on January 9, 2007, when an Antonov-26 plane chartered by TCN subcontractor Kulak Construction Company of Turkey crashed while landing at LSA Anaconda. The plane had taken off at 6 a.m. from the city of Adana, home to the Incirlik airbase, with thirty-five passengers, most of whom were Turkish construction workers but also included Ismail Kulak, one of the founding partners of the company. The plane belonged to Moldova's Aerian Tur Airlines. Official military reports suggest that the plane crashed because of weather conditions, but an insurgent group—the Islamic Army in Iraq—claimed that it had "opened fire on a plane trying to land at an American base near Balad from different directions, using medium-range weapons. . . . With the help of God, they were able to shoot it down," the statement said.[27]

Another horrific incident involving a TCN took place just over a month later, on February 15, 2007, at Al Asad Airbase, when Aaron Bridges Langston, a thirty-year-old KBR worker from Snowflake, Arizona, stabbed Gaddam Narayana, an Indian worker, in the throat in a dispute, cutting her internal jugular vein. The U.S. Naval Criminal Investigative Service (NCIS) conducted an investigation, and Langston was charged on February 23. He was indicted by a federal grand jury in Phoenix on March 1, 2007.[28]

"LABOR STRIKE, YOU'RE OUT"

TCNs who dared to stage labor strikes and sickouts to protest their treatment at military camps faced immediate dismissal. In May 2005, at Camp Cook, three hundred Filipinos went on strike against PPI and Halliburton/KBR. The workers were soon joined by five hundred others from India, Sri Lanka, and Nepal to protest working conditions and pay, according to the *Manila Times*.[29] The dispute was settled with intervention from the Philippines Department of Foreign Affairs.

At the time of the strike, the Filipinos offered the strikers free flights back to the Philippines. Other strikes have gone unreported, recalls former Halliburton/KBR employee Paul Dinsmore. Hired as a carpenter, he later changed jobs to become a heavy truck driver at Camp Speicher, a sprawling twenty-four-square-mile installation near Tikrit in northern Iraq. Dinsmore says the work crews he supervised at the former Iraqi airbase were made up of Indians, Pakistanis, Nepalese, and Filipinos working for First Kuwaiti.[30]

Working at Camp Speicher for seven months before returning home in May 2005, Dinsmore said he knew of three different instances of TCN construction workers who outright refused to work or showed up only to sit out most of the day. Asked what was going on, TCNs told him that First Kuwaiti had not paid them for several months and that they didn't want to be treated that way. "I heard that several hundred Filipinos were fired in September 2004 before I got there because of labor problems," Dinsmore said. After discovering that the TCN assistants were not paid any overtime, Dinsmore was careful to get them back to their compound after their ten-hour day.

Dinsmore also recounted dismal working conditions. His workers told him that they were treated "like human cattle by some of the Western employees" and were not provided with adequate health care. Many times, Dinsmore said, he would buy non-prescription drugs from the PX for his crews, especially when a very bad virus was going around during the winter of 2004–2005. If the case was bad enough, he would take the workers to the Halliburton/KBR employee clinic. His supervisor and the clinic medics told him that treating TCNs violated company policy. "We were told that First Kuwaiti was supposed to take care of them," Dinsmore said.

Dinsmore also turned to the army for food. He says the food First Kuwaiti served was so poor, that he and other Halliburton/KBR employees would hand out military field rations—known as "meals ready to eat" or MREs. "When the army stopped that practice, many of us KBR people would pick up 'to go' plates from the DFAC (dining facilities) and hand them out to the TCNs we were responsible for. If you want them to work well, you've got to feed them."

First Kuwaiti manager Wadi al-Absi insists that his company provides the same quality of living and food that the U.S. Army provides for its soldiers and that the company has received commendations from the army. "We have no problems with our employees; they get excellent care," he told David Phinney.[31]

"WILLING TO RETURN"

Despite complaints about First Kuwaiti, Ramil Autencio said he would return to Iraq if he had guarantees for proper food and pay. "I would take my chances abroad if I couldn't find a decent job here," he said during an interview at his home in Pasig City, an urban area in metropolitan Manila. "But I'd take any job here that pays enough to buy me a secondhand car and start my own business."[32]

Also back in the Philippines, Soliman had no job; he and his wife were on the verge of splitting up, and so his plans for providing a new home to his family had to be put on hold. He doubted that PPI will be sending money for his final medical checkup or even the several months' salary he said he was still owed. But those things didn't matter so much to him anymore—what really mattered was finding another job. "If you hear of anything, let me know," Soliman said at the end of the interview with Phinney. "I would even go back to Iraq."

His sentiments are shared by many. Maita Santiago, secretary-general for Migrante International, an organization that defends the rights of more than one million overseas Filipino workers, says that many workers "believe it is better to work in Iraq with their lives in danger rather than face the danger of not having breakfast, lunch, or dinner in the Philippines."[33]

NO COMMENT?

Asked about the disparity in wages based on nationality—that Halliburton/ KBR paid in Iraq—company spokesperson Melissa Norcross wrote in an e-mail: "We will not discuss our specific wage structures. Our compensation packages and the compensation packages provided by our subcontractors are based on a wage scale that was recommended by the Coalition Provisional Authority in Iraq and are competitive in terms of the local market."[34]

Halliburton/KBR also denies any mistreatment of workers. "KBR operates under a rigorous code of ethics that describes not only its standards of integrity, but its commitment to treat all of its employees and subcontractors with dignity and respect," Norcross wrote. The company "is aware of past disagreements between subcontractors and their employees, and KBR has interjected itself into the situation as appropriate and worked with the subcontractors to address these concerns."[35]

Wendy Hall, another Halliburton/KBR spokesperson, added that the company would aggressively investigate any trafficking. "KBR has a policy to terminate any and all subcontractors if we know of mistreatment of employees. Under KBR policies our employees are allowed to quit and leave the sector at their choosing."[36]

PPI in Dubai refused to talk with me about the accusations of mistreatment. "I don't think anyone will want to comment," said a representative who answered the phone when I called.[37]

MILITARY RESPONDS

But when I posed the same question to Army Corps spokesperson Richard Dowling, he yielded a more revealing answer. "These workers consider themselves fortunate to have jobs, even if it means them traveling somewhere else. There is an army of companies that move from conflict to conflict with experience in setting up chow halls from an empty field to a thousand army camps in a matter of days. It's not an easy job, and these guys are good at it. They bring their own people with them—people with experience in other military locations. . . . The (salary) decision is not based on the value of his life but on the cost of training and equipping the workforce. Nor would it be right for the U.S. Army to enforce U.S.-based salaries where no one else could match it. Life sometimes isn't fair."[38]

The Pentagon took the issue of trafficking more seriously. Margaret Browne, spokesperson for the Army Materiel Command in Rock Island, says that the subcontractors are expected to fulfill health, security, and life support requirements for their employees in the LOGCAP agreement. "We are concerned about employment conditions for all employees. . . . These are serious issues, and we are presently investigating the specific incidents," Browne said in an e-mail.[39]

In April 2006, General George Casey, the top U.S. commander in Iraq, issued an order titled "Prevention of Trafficking in Persons in MNF-I"—Multinational Forces-Iraq—which noted that the military confirmed a number of human rights abuses on U.S. military bases. They included deceptive hiring practices, excessive fees charged by overseas job brokers who lure workers into Iraq, substandard living conditions once laborers arrive, violations of Iraqi immigration laws, and a lack of mandatory "awareness training" on U.S. bases concerning human trafficking, according to a copy of the memo summarized in the *Chicago Tribune*.[40]

Casey ordered that contractors be required by May 1, 2006, to return passports confiscated from workers. Companies that failed to do this could be blacklisted from future work, and commanders could physically bar them from bases, according to his order. The contractors were also required to meet "measurable, enforceable standards for living conditions (e.g., sanitation, health, safety, etc.) and establish fifty feet as the minimum acceptable square footage of personal living space per worker."

A number of South and Southeast Asian governments have also taken action, notably after several drivers were kidnapped and killed. In 2004, India, Nepal, and the Philippines passed laws that made it illegal to work in Iraq. In an attempt to prevent workers from going to Iraq, all new Filipino passports are now stamped with "Not Valid for Travel to Iraq."[41]

By contrast, the management team of PPI has been able to travel and take luxurious holidays in Southeast Asia. In May 2005, Toby O'Connell was joined by Neil Helliwell, his boss, and three other co-workers, on the holiday island of Koh Samui in Thailand, where the former university champion sailor captained them on a yacht race in his newly purchased boat, *Yo!*. With the profits from PPI's Iraq contracts rolling in, O'Connell continued to compete in the annual race with a Firefly 850 boat named *Dhevatara Frog*, which by 2008 took third place overall.[42]

10

Keep on Truckin'

ON APRIL 9, 2004, the first anniversary of the occupation of Iraq, nineteen men left LSA Anaconda to drive a convoy of Halliburton/KBR trucks laden with fuel to deliver to the military at Baghdad International Airport.[1] It was, quite possibly, the most dangerous day to date to travel because Moqtada al-Sadr, the fiery young Shia leader, had ordered his militia to attack anyone who left their homes.

In the capital city, numerous extra armored tanks had been deployed near the Palestine and Sheraton hotels, where many Halliburton/KBR employees were stationed. I was in a hotel next door to those that very day. When I woke up, I discovered miles of razor-sharp concertina wire and barbed wire had been wrapped around every road intersection overnight to block anyone from coming within half a mile of the hotels. Every half hour loudspeakers would warn people to stay indoors all day.[2]

Indeed, the U.S. military had officially declared that all roads were too dangerous for civilian convoys to travel that day. It used a color-coded system that defines the threat levels in Iraq: "black" meant that all traffic on all roads is prohibited, "red" meant that a convoy can be deployed in the event of an emergency, "amber" meant that the road was clear, and "green" indicated that there was no threat at all. The previous day, a Halliburton/KBR convoy had been attacked and two convoys had already turned back because of the violence on the road. Despite the fact that the threat level had been raised to black that weekend, Halliburton/KBR officials ordered the uneasy men to take to the road.

The men left LSA Anaconda at about 10:40 a.m. They knew the drill: drive only in daylight, stay close together, and whenever possible try to drive in the center of the road—the better to avoid any ambushes from the side of the road; don't allow any unknown motorists to pull up alongside, but run them off into the ditch; and expect locals, especially children, to pelt their vehicles with stones.

Shortly after noon the convoy arrived in the vicinity of the Abu Ghraib prison, where they were attacked. Ray Stannard, a former marine from El Paso, Texas, said that they could see trucks from the previous convoy still burning up ahead, but it was too late to turn back. When the shooting began, he ran into a group of soldiers who were furious that the convoy was driving through the area and were yelling at him, "What the hell are you doing here? We have been under heavy attack for forty-eight hours!"

In the ensuing gun battle, six truckers were killed, one disappeared, and one was kidnapped by a group called Mujahideen Group-Kidnappings.[3] The remaining eleven men made it to the airport after suffering severe injuries, making it the single deadliest incident involving U.S. contractors in the war in Iraq to date.

Thomas Hamill, the leader of the convoy, was captured and escaped almost a month later, returning to the United States a hero—he and his son threw the first two pitches at a Houston Astros baseball game. Hamill became a poster boy for Halliburton/KBR and published a book about his exploits titled *Escape in Iraq: The Thomas Hamill Story*.[4] The other survivors were not given the red carpet treatment; instead they were flown to Kuwait to a fancy, private dinner with Tom Crum, KBR's chief operating officer, and awarded specially inscribed gold coins and asked to keep the matter quiet.[5]

But ten of the men who made it back alive struck a deal among themselves that they charged one of their number with: to have Stannard fight for justice for themselves and their fallen comrades, whom they believed were victims of a negligent employer. Unknown to them, half a world away, in Riverside County, California, April Johnson, a grieving twenty-three-year-old hairdresser who last saw her father, Tony, when she dropped him off at Los Angeles International Airport on New Year's Eve 2003 before he went to work at Camp Anaconda and died in the April 9 ambush, made the same decision soon after she saw him return in a coffin.[6] At the funeral, a stranger in a business suit arrived and handed her a check for $50,000 "no strings attached" but with an unspoken message from the company—Halliburton/KBR—who issued the check: Keep it quiet.[7]

April and her mother, Kim, noticed that there was something odd about the check—it was from the Halliburton asbestos workers' compensation fund. They decided not to cash the check immediately but to contact the families of the men who had died, hire a lawyer, and take on the company. Almost seven months after the massacre, the two groups—the truckers and the families of the dead and missing men—came together in Houston, to plan their strategy.

Facilitating them was Ramon Lopez, a short, energetic, and friendly Latino trial lawyer, grew up in the San Francisco Bay Area but migrated to Southern California where he ran a five-office, dozen-partner, trial law practice named Lopez, Hodes, Restaino, Milman & Skikos, on Fashion Island, which is a well-heeled neighborhood of Newport Beach along the Pacific Ocean. It is in Orange County, one of those places that seem to bask in eternal summer, which maybe explains why 1 percent of the population of the United States lives in the county.[8]

Lopez is a hearty man who loves to tell stories about his co-workers and himself. He's accompanied by Vince Howard, a handsome, crew-cut, African American lawyer from Tennessee who had served in the military at the Sierra Depot in northern California as well as in South Korea; Jack Pentecost, a private investigator and a former quarterback for the '49ers; and Michael Heaviside, a lawyer from Brooklyn who's made a living suing the Pentagon. The law firm has sued many multinational companies like Pfizer and Monsanto over defective products such as silicone breast implants and diet pills, taking doctors and hospitals to court for the failure to diagnose medical problems like cancer. And it represented a successful lawsuit for the families of the people who died in the Pam Am plane crash in Lockerbie, Scotland.[9]

Lopez's strategy was simple. Alliances among the plaintiffs have been particularly successful in recent multidistrict litigation, which compiles hundreds to thousands of tort actions filed at the federal level under one judge. The judge appoints plaintiff and defense committees that review discovery documents and assemble "generic" witnesses whose testimony can be submitted in each individual case. For the Halliburton/KBR truck drivers, Lopez intended to do the same—start with one case in California federal courts, follow-up rapidly with a dozen cases across the country in the states where the drivers or the families live, and then attempt to consolidate them all in California, where he could get the best judgment.

TONY JOHNSON

Tony Johnson was born in Indiana but lived most of his life in Riverside, California. When he was fifteen, he learned the masonry trade, and at the age of twenty-two he met his future wife, Kim, through a common friend. She was eighteen, from Long Beach, and had graduated from high school in nearby Irvine. "He was very shy but very honest, and, I can say, he had the most incredible work ethic of any man I have ever known," Kim said.[10]

She fell in love. Eight months later, the two got married, and their daughter April was born just a few months later. They saved $10,000 and put a down payment on their first house in Riverside in 1981. While Tony worked days as a mason, Kim worked as a waitress at night. Then, in 1988, Kim returned to school and became a nurse. "He was so proud of me," she recalls. Soon, Tony became a contractor and started his own business, Johnson Masonry, Inc. "We never even advertised the business. He did the most beautiful work with integrity and passion, so he always had work."

In 1998, the couple grew apart, and Tony moved out. At the same time, he decided he needed a new career. He went to truck driving school and then got several jobs driving for commercial truck companies. In 2002, his scrupulous attention to safety won him an award as Driver of the Year for a company called Martin Transportation.

In late 2003, Tony made a deal with April. If she moved in with him and took care of his house, he would pay the mortgage and bills, so she could save money. When she saved $10,000, he said he would match the money so that she could make a down payment on a place of her own. Then, in early December, Tony e-mailed his résumé to a woman named Nicky Williams at Halliburton/KBR. At 7 o'clock the next morning he got a call from the company, offering him a job, so he made immediate plans to leave.

April recalled, "In early December, we went to the Olive Garden [a restaurant chain] to make plans for me to move back in [she had planned to take care of his house in his absence]. While we were eating, he said he was planning to go to Iraq. He was very excited; he'd always wanted to be in the military, and he kept talking about how he'd be able to stay in the barracks. . . . I was in shock. But I could see how much he wanted it, so I didn't talk him out of it."

April moved back to her father's house, and the two of them spent fifteen days together, making plans. For the first time in five years, father and daughter shared Christmas. Over the next few days, April was as supportive as possible, helping him pack and buying him supplies for his trip.

On Sunday morning, December 28, April drove Tony to LA/Ontario International Airport just outside Los Angeles. He flew to Houston for two weeks for training, where he talked to his daughter and ex-wife every day. At first, Kim says she was happy for him, but by time day he left for Kuwait, she started to worry. "He was very nervous," she remembered. "He tried to keep his nose clean, so he could pass all the tests and go to Iraq." She spoke to him as he was heading to the airport.

April spoke to her dad a couple of times over his next eleven weeks in Iraq during snatches of conversation that lasted only a couple of minutes each. On April 8, they had a good twenty-minute conversation. She says he played down the danger. She asked him if he could hear bombs going off. He said, "Occasionally."

The next time the phone rang, it was Jenny Brooks, who said she was from KBR. April was puzzled at first; she'd never heard of KBR. Brooks asked her for Tony's social security number and date of birth, which puzzled April also. "Shows how incompetent they were," Kim said of KBR.

Two days later, Brooks called again with bad news, saying Tony was definitely missing. The next two weeks were agony for April and Kim. Then, on April 22, Brooks asked April to give a DNA sample. On April 26, a man named David Coles arrived from Halliburton/KBR with the bad news. They had found four vertebrae and a piece of muscle that matched April's DNA. Tony was definitely dead.

Today, April still cannot remember her dad without choking up. "I was Daddy's girl. I always wanted to be with him. I remember our river trips, the jet skis, the water skis, and tubing, dirt bike rides, off-roading in his truck."

On March 29, 2005, April brought a federal lawsuit in Santa Ana, California, against Halliburton/KBR, seeking redress for the wrongful death of her father. "What Halliburton did was criminal, and the public needs to know," her mother, Kim, told me. "They took good, honest Americans and didn't tell them that if they didn't do a mission, they would lose their job. They were told that at the slightest hint of danger, they could leave and come home."

"It is our opinion," said Lopez, "based on our investigations, that Halliburton's management has systematically, intentionally, and fraudulently misrepresented the true nature of its civilian employees' duties. . . . Simply put, Halliburton intentionally placed its employees in harm's way and received lucrative payment for a private, unarmed military force."

RAY STANNARD

Ray Stannard is a quiet, friendly sort of guy from El Paso, Texas. He is a former marine with a tattoo of "U.S.M.C." on the inside of his right forearm. You'd never spot him in a room because he would sit in the back and try to disappear into the background. But if you approached him, he would smile in a shy sort of way and eventually open up.[11]

Stannard told us that when he attended the Halliburton/KBR orientation in Houston, they were informed that they were being sent to Iraq for the rebuilding effort, and that it was a relatively safe environment. The company said that only two civilians had died so far, and that it was due to their own tomfoolery and not Halliburton/KBR. Halliburton/KBR also told them to recognize local customs in Iraq and to not discuss what it is that they do there. They were also told not to curse or get angry when they left the base and not to give candy or food to the kids or stop for them—they were told that kids are used as bait to lure the drivers out in the open so they could be shot.

Stannard remembers every single detail of the incident, down to the amount of jet fuel they had to deliver, which was one hundred twenty-five thousand gallons. Personally, he felt that the group was very poorly organized that day. They were driving unarmored military vehicles rather than their usual white civilian trucks, making them an open target. And none of the men was familiar with the route.

A military investigation into the incident released in March 2005 to the survivors and the families of those killed concurs with many of his memories. The 280-page document, written by Colonel Gary Bunch, the commander of the 172nd Corps Support Group, which escorted the Hamill convoy, suggests that the military and Halliburton/KBR failed to communicate properly. "If the information was properly sent to subordinate units, actions could have been taken to potentially minimize impact of hostile engagement," the report states.[12]

PRIOR ATTACK IN FALLUJAH

Halliburton/KBR managers were not taken unawares. Days before the April 9 massacre, a private security detail from Blackwater Security that was working for Halliburton/KBR had come under a fatal and gruesome attack. The task that the four men—Wesley Batalona, Scott Helvenston, Michael Teague, and Jerko Zovko—had been dispatched on was mundane. A Kuwaiti business called Regency Hotel and Hospital Company had been hired by Halliburton/KBR to transport kitchen equipment, and their job was to protect the convoy.[13]

The men got lost on the way and ended up driving through the town of Fallujah on the morning of Wednesday, March 31, 2004, where they got stuck in traffic. Several armed men approached their vehicles and opened fire from behind, shooting the men repeatedly at point-blank range. The bodies of the men were burned, dragged through the streets, and strung from a bridge.

Later, Halliburton/KBR managers would internally acknowledge that they never should have hired Blackwater. In a June 2004 internal e-mail, James Ray, the company's lead administrator for the contract, told other company officials, "Our contract states that the government provides us with force protection. . . . We should not attempt to effect a material change in our contract with the government by hiring a company that we know uses armed escorts. That company is an agent of KBR, and if anything happens, KBR is in the pot with them. Even with lipstick, a pig is a pig. This decision is something to address squarely. . . . I do not recommend proceeding with this option without senior management's approval."[14]

Private Security Endangers Clients

One of Halliburton/KBR's private security subcontractors is Triple Canopy of Virginia. While the trucks lack sufficient protection, these private security guards have allegedly targeted Iraqi civilians for sport, attempting to kill them, while doing work for Halliburton/KBR. A lawsuit filed in Virginia in late 2006 by two former security guards, Shane B. Schmidt and Charles L. Sheppard III, alleged that their boss, Jacob C. Washbourne, fired at Iraqis on the afternoon of July 8, 2006.[15]

Washbourne, a twenty-nine-year-old ex-marine, led one of two teams on Triple Canopy's "Milwaukee" project, a contract to protect Halliburton/KBR executives on Iraq's dangerous roads. He was paid $600 a day to command a small unit of guards armed with M-4 rifles and 9mm pistols—the same caliber weapons used by U.S. troops, according to an investigation conducted by the *Washington Post*.[16]

Washbourne's leadership was already under question before the shooting incident. His former co-workers accuse him of heavy drinking at the Gem, the company bar in Baghdad.

He has also been accused of previous shootings. On June 2, Washbourne was leading a convoy to a state department compound in Hilla, about sixty miles south of Baghdad. The Suburban, in which he was a passenger, jumped a curb at a high rate of speed, shattering the axles and halting the exposed SUV in the middle of the highway. When a blue civilian truck headed toward the convoy, Washbourne fired more than a dozen rounds into the oncoming truck with his M-4, wounding the driver.

The July incident was more deliberate, say co-workers. Washbourne, as team leader, led a pre-mission briefing in the parking lot that morning, they said. As the briefing concluded, according to a witness, Washbourne cocked his gun and said, "I want to kill somebody today." When a Fijian co-worker asked why, the *Washington Post* quotes Washbourne reportedly saying, "Because I'm going on vacation tomorrow. That's a long time, buddy."

On the way to the airport, according to Schmidt and Sheppard, Washbourne remarked, "I've never shot anyone with my pistol before." In witness statements provided to the military, Schmidt and Sheppard wrote that as the convoy passed the taxi, Washbourne pushed open the armored door, leaned out with his handgun, and fired "seven or eight rounds" into the taxi's windshield.

"From my position as we passed I could see [from spidering of the glass that] the taxi had been hit in the windshield," Schmidt wrote. But because of the "pace we were traveling, I could not tell if the driver had been hit. He did pull the car off the road in an erratic manner."

Sheppard said Washbourne was laughing as he fired.

Washbourne denies the allegations. "They're all unfounded, unbased, and they simply did not happen," he told the *Post*, during an interview near his home in Broken Arrow, Oklahoma. Lee Van Arsdale, Triple Canopy's CEO, told the *Post* that Triple Canopy was unable to determine the circumstances behind the shootings, especially since no deaths or injuries were recorded by U.S. or Iraqi authorities.

FAULTY DECISIONS

On Monday, April 5, with the security situation worsening around the country, Halliburton/KBR decided to stick to using military escorts for its equipment, and restrict decisions on whether convoys should be put on the road or not to two people in senior management: General Manager Craig Peterson, a former U.S. Army general who had commanded Task Force Falcon in Kosovo in 1999; and Keith Richard, chief of the trucking operation. Peterson wrote in an e-mail that day, "It was reiterated that only the army leadership can stop convoys" and that it was necessary "to team our way into decisions. We cannot unilaterally decide these things on our own."[17]

"Yeah, well I have been authorized for a year now to stop convoys, now all of a sudden Keith [Richard] . . . is the only one who can . . . well partner believe me the ball is in his court," wrote one angry security advisor.

There was even alarm among the senior brass at the Kuwait Hilton. "We cannot allow the army to push us to put our people in harm's way," wrote Tom Crum, KBR's chief operating officer. "We need to work with the army without a doubt relative to stopping the convoys. But if we in management believe the army is asking us to put our KBR employees in danger that we are not willing to accept, then we will refuse to go."

Richard himself was dismayed. He argued that the truckers were not soldiers. "Our drivers did sign up with the understanding of some level of hostility, but they did not expect to be in the middle of a war," he said in an e-mail.

One of Peterson's aides disagreed firmly. "[Peterson] says that if the client pushes, then we push," the message said. It also specified that convoys should stop only if security was not adequate and "doesn't pass the Common Sense Safety Test."

"Who in the hell determines adequate security . . . ? This is a roll of the dice. None of this passes any of these tests, if you ask me," said a furious Richard in a follow-up e-mail. "With this decision I cannot continue my employment with KBR. . . . I cannot consciously sit back and allow unarmed civilians to get picked apart. Putting civilians in the middle of a war is not in any contract, policy, or procedure. I will not allow this to happen."

On Wednesday, April 7, two days before the massacre, Richard wrote: "One of my convoys was hit with fourteen mortars, six RPGs, five IEDs, and small arms fire."

On Thursday, April 8, the day before the convoy, KBR regional security chief George Seagle noted that he was under pressure from the military to keep the convoys on the road: "Big politics and contract issues involved."

"Things started early this a.m., and it hasn't been good," a trucking project manager wrote that day. "Gentlemen . . . HOT!!! We have a convoy . . . that is in direct engagement at this time . . . and pleads for immediate assistance," e-mailed another.

"We are taking on gun fire, mortar, rocket launch, small arms fire, you name it, we got it, we are losing trucks one by one . . . my driver and I were lucky to get out alive," one convoy member wrote in.

One Halliburton/KBR driver was killed on Thursday and more than seventy were attacked. Down in Baghdad, it was clear to me and my colleagues at the Al Fanar Hotel that the following day, which was the first anniversary of the fall of Baghdad, was going to be brutal. One guest in the hotel, staying three doors down from me, was Nicholas Berg, a U.S. businessman who specialized in building and fixing communication towers. Berg decided to venture out on his own that day and was kidnapped and killed a month later.[18]

"I say we halt them for a day at least and consider it a safety/security stand-down, and mental health day," security chief Seagle wrote Thursday. "There is tons of intel stating tomorrow will be another bad day."[19]

Keith Richard wrote back, "Another day like today and we will lose most of our drivers. I cannot consciously sit back and allow unarmed civilians to get picked apart."

On Friday morning, General James E. Chambers, the head of the army's 13th Corps Support Command, sent out orders to his officers: "Not moving critical support is not an option," he wrote in an e-mail before dawn. "We just have to figure out how to mitigate the risks." The message was dispatched to convoys in Anaconda: "Note the statement about convoys. They move."

Not everyone agreed. Colonel Ray Josey, head of operations for Chambers told him it that it was a bad idea. "We should just stand down," Josey says he told Chambers.

The military order issued on the morning of the convoy's departure recommended a minimum ratio of one army soldier to accompany every two trucks. The Hamill convoy had just six soldiers among nineteen trucks.

Richard tried to stop the convoys one last time. Almost an hour after Chambers sent his e-mail, at 6:44 a.m., Richard sent a message to all drivers: "No convoys are to move" between Anaconda and the military bases south of Baghdad. At 7:14 a.m., a new command was issued: "Per Keith Richard, project manager, all traffic is to proceed as normal. All . . . traffic lanes are open in all directions."

Another error took place lower down in the chain of command. At 9:54 a.m.—less than an hour before the convoy departed—Lieutenant Colonel James Carroll, a reservist from Missouri who was working at 13th Coscom, initially confirmed orders on the convoy route. Three minutes later, Carroll changed his mind and sent out a second e-mail: "Sorry. It looks like [the route] is closed until further notice."

But by mistake, Carroll sent the second message to himself, and no one else ever saw it. "When I saw that I sent the e-mail to myself, I did everything I could" to reach them, Carroll told the *Los Angeles Times*. "It was the worst day of my life. You can't believe how much I second-guessed myself . . . [but] I firmly believe that I did everything I could."[20]

When the massacre took place hours later, there was an immediate backlash. "Can anyone explain to me why we put civilians in the middle of known ambush sites?" wrote one security advisor. "Maybe we should put body bags on the packing list for our drivers." A second advisor wrote: "I cannot believe this has happened; the ones responsible should be held accountable for this."

Peterson realized he had made a mistake. "No KBR convoys will move tomorrow, 10th April 04. I will inform the military chain of command," he wrote in an e-mail. Richard was beside himself. "I thought the man was going to break down and cry after he found out he sent all those people out there," Stephen Pulley, KBR's senior security advisor at Camp Anaconda, said in a court deposition. "He was very upset with himself."

Both Richard and Peterson quit Halliburton/KBR. Peterson took up a job with Neffgen as senior vice president at IAP Worldwide Service, the company that would later be accused of neglecting veterans at the Walter Reed hospital.

HALLIBURTON/KBR REFUSES TO TAKE BLAME

"Nearly a year later, KBR remains deeply saddened by this tragedy," wrote Beverly Scippa, a company spokesperson, in an e-mail response to my queries about the lawsuit in 2005. "KBR has cooperated fully as the army has spent the past year investigating these attacks, and we will continue to do everything we can to help piece together the events of April 9." She continued, "KBR representatives met face-to-face with the next of kin of those employees who were killed to advise them of their loved one's death, and the KBR representatives stayed with the families while they gathered other supportive resources around themselves."[21]

Scippa blamed the U.S. military: "It is not unusual for the military to change a route several times before a convoy departs, based on the best and most current information available from its own intelligence briefings and assessments.

"KBR does have the right to refuse a mission and, because KBR's primary concern is for the safety and security of all personnel, we have exercised that right on numerous occasions, both before and after April 9. KBR can refuse a mission if a convoy is improperly constructed, if the security provided by the military does not meet the established criteria, or if route conditions are not within guidelines. When KBR expresses concern with a mission, we work with the military until we are satisfied that the level of security is appropriate to meet the threat conditions so that convoys can proceed."

Scippa also noted that following the April 9, 2004, attack, Halliburton/KBR and the army jointly agreed to suspend convoy movements until the security requirements could be reassessed and additional security measures enacted. "To avoid jeopardizing future convoys, we will not detail the specific security measures that are currently in place," she wrote.

SECOND AMBUSH

Yet seventeen months after the first attack, on September 20, 2005, another Halliburton/KBR convoy was ambushed soon after it departed Camp Anaconda, which resulted in the deaths of three truckers: Keven Dagit, Sascha Grenner-Case, and Christopher Lem.[22]

The incident occurred after the military commander took a wrong turn, and the convoy ended up in an unfamiliar neighborhood. One of the surviving truck drivers, Preston Wheeler, says that Halliburton/KBR did not provide any of the drivers with maps or even rudimentary drawings of the location. He says that when he was hired, Halliburton/KBR promised the trucks would be equipped with bulletproof glass and armed guards on every third truck. "That's a lie; it's a gimmick, a sales pitch," Wheeler told *ABC World News Tonight.*[23]

A video of the ambush recorded by a camera installed in Wheeler's truck shows the convoy entering tiny Iraqi towns along the highway where children begin throwing rocks at the trucks. The Halliburton/KBR drivers are heard on the radio communicating with each other: "KBR just took two rocks [on the] right side, no glass broke," said one driver.[24]

"We made a wrong turn. Our military took us the wrong way," Wheeler tells his camera. A soldier is heard on the radio saying, "My map is evidently wrong." So, the convoy was forced to turn around and head back through the same town that only a few minutes earlier had greeted it with "raining rocks." "We're going back through hell," Wheeler laments.

Suddenly, a bomb explodes and a bullet hole is seen in Wheeler's windshield. "God damn, IED on the left side!" he reports on the radio, using military jargon—improvised explosive device—to refer to a bomb. Small arms fire is heard again. "Jesus Christ!" Wheeler cries. "Help us all, Lord!"

Soon after, the truck ahead of him overturns. "I am down!" Wheeler screams into the radio. Small arms fire continues. "Truck Five cannot move!" he says. "Please help me! I'm taking fire!" As the military fails to offer aid, Wheeler angrily screams into the radio for help: "I'm fixing to get killed, God dammit! I cannot move! Truck Five cannot move! Copy? I am getting shot! Someone get their ass back here now, please!"

"Sir, I have no gun back here and . . . I am by myself," Wheeler, hoping the military will hear his plea, reports into the radio. (Halliburton/KBR employees are forbidden to carry weapons.)

Three drivers were executed in front of Wheeler, who was rescued by U.S. Army helicopters that arrived forty-five minutes later. When he returned, a Halliburton/KBR security guard wanted to delete the video of the ambush so that it would not become public, Wheeler told reporters later.

LAWSUIT REJECTED AND APPEALED

In September 2006, U.S. District Judge Gray H. Miller, a Bush appointee, threw out the April Johnson wrongful death lawsuit. "The contracts show that the army, not the defendants, was responsible for the security of the convoys," Miller wrote. "Is it wise to use civilian contractors in a war zone? Was it wise to send the convoy along the route [to Baghdad airport] on April 9, 2004? Answering either question and the many questions in between would require the court to examine the policies of the executive branch during wartime, a step the court declines to take."[25]

T. Scott Allen Jr., a Houston lawyer who worked with Ramon Lopez to represent the plaintiffs, says that logic gives Halliburton/KBR carte blanche in Iraq. "The way I read this decision, anything Halliburton does in Iraq is not subject to oversight or review," Allen said.[26]

The truckers and the families appealed the verdict, and on May 28, 2008, the fifth U.S. Circuit Court of Appeals in New Orleans gave them leave to proceed. The appeals court, though, found that "the plaintiffs have presented a plausible set of facts as to the fraud and misrepresentation claims" against Halliburton/KBR "without questioning the army's role." The court agreed that the army was responsible for assessing contractor safety, but noted that Halliburton/KBR's contract doesn't put it under the army's supervision. The court also ruled "that these tort-based claims of civilian employees against their civilian employers can be separated from the political questions that loom so large in the background." [27]

"They're trying to hide behind the army's skirt, and the opinion says you can't do that," said a jubilant Allen. "Liberal or conservative, Republican or Democrat, for the war or against it, when you see what they did that day, it will shock your conscience." [28]

The court decision allows the plaintiff's lawyer to depose Halliburton/KBR officials and present previously unheard evidence about what went wrong that day in April 2004.

GHOST TRUCKS

As the work got more dangerous and truckers started to get injured or killed, some quit when they discovered that they were risking their lives for literally, nothing. In May 2004, a dozen current and former truckers who regularly made the three-hundred-mile supply run from Camp Cedar in southern Iraq to Camp Anaconda near Baghdad told a *Knight Ridder* reporter that as many as one in three trucks they drove was completely empty.[29]

Much of the time, drivers would drop off one empty trailer and pick up another empty one for the return trip. "There was one time we ran twenty-eight trucks, one trailer had one pallet [a trailer can hold as many as twenty-six four-foot-square pallets] and the rest of them were empty," said David Wilson, who was the convoy commander on more than one hundred runs. Four other drivers who were with Wilson confirmed his account, including one who videotaped fifteen empty trailers on the road in January 2004 and narrated what he was seeing. "This is just a sample of the empty trailers we're hauling called 'sustainer.' And there's more behind me. There's another one right there. . . . This is fraud and abuse right here."

"It was supposed to be critical supplies that the troops had to have to operate," said Wilson, who returned to his home in southwest Florida after being fired by Halliburton/KBR. "It was one thing to risk your life to haul things the military needed. It's another to haul empty trailers."

In testimony submitted to the Government Affairs Committee in July 2004, Wilson also described what appeared to be a complete lack of cost controls and systems to maintain equipment properly. "When I arrived at Camp Arifjan in Kuwait last November, I noticed fifty to one hundred brand new trucks sitting there unused," Wilson remembered.

"Five months later, when I came home," he wrote, "a large number of trucks were still there, not being used. These are $85,000 [or more] Mercedes and Volvo trucks. As every other trucker working on those convoys will tell you, KBR had virtually no facilities in place to do maintenance on these trucks. There were absolutely no oil filters or fuel filters for months on end. I begged for filters but never got any. I was told that oil changes were out of the question. KBR removed all the spare tires in Kuwait. So when one of our trucks got a flat tire on the highway, we just had to leave it there for the Iraqis to loot, which is just crazy. I remember saying to myself when it happened, 'You just lost yourself an $85,000 truck because of a spare tire. . . . We lost a truck because we didn't have a $25 hydraulic line to assist the clutch.'[30]

Another Halliburton/KBR convoy truck driver, James Warren, testified that "KBR didn't seem to care what happened to its trucks." He said Halliburton/KBR would strip the spare tires from brand new Mercedes and Volvo trucks. As a result, flat tires meant abandonment, not repair, of the trucks. He said, "It was common to torch trucks that we abandoned . . . even though we all carried chains and could have towed them to be repaired" to prevent them from being stolen by "insurgents."[31]

Both Wilson and Warren also said that U.S. Army soldiers would regularly steal items from the trucks at night. Since there was no manifest showing the contents of the trucks, it was impossible for Halliburton/KBR to document how many items were stolen. Warren's convoy commander said, "Don't worry about it. It's the army stealing from the army." Warren called Randy Harl, the head of KBR, to complain. Harl expressed dismay. Halliburton/KBR appeared to take no action. Instead, Halliburton/KBR fired Warren a few weeks later, saying he violated company policy by running civilians off the road. "I felt like I was being pushed out the door because they just wanted me gone," he said.

Halliburton/KBR executives, who testified at the same July 2004 hearing, claimed that trucks were routinely supplied with oil filters and spare tires and that no trucks had been abandoned because of maintenance problems. They said only the military, not Halliburton/KBR, could order abandoning trucks.[32]

Six of the twelve who testified had been fired by Halliburton/KBR for allegedly running Iraqi drivers off the road when the latter attempted to break into the convoy. In his defense, Wilson said that "KBR and the military made clear to everyone that this was what we were supposed to do" if convoys were attacked by insurgents.

Linda Theis, a spokesperson for the Army Materiel Command in Rock Island, confirmed that military commanders and company officials might choose to run empty trucks as a security measure, assuming perhaps that the attackers were just highway robbers who might give up if they thought they was wasting their time. This diversionary tactic of empty trailer runs in Iraq was at its highest in January, February, and March of 2004, but as the attacks on the convoys increased exponentially, the military decided that the ploy was not working.[33]

Halliburton/KBR officials added that empty runs resulted from a lack of cargo at one depot—the company sent extra trucks so they'd be available to pick up cargo for the return trip—but drivers said that explanation wasn't true either. "Sometimes we would go with empty trailers; we would go both ways," said one driver who went by the nickname Swerve and asked not to be named for fear of retribution. "We'd turn around and go back with empty trailers."[34]

In November 2006, Wilson and Warren filed a lawsuit against Halliburton/KBR, alleging that the company overcharged the military by $30 million as a consequence of its failure to maintain the trucks properly. The suit also alleges that the company unlawfully fired the two men to silence them.[35]

The lawsuit was filed under the False Claims Act (often called a "qui tam" lawsuit), a federal law giving employees authority to sue employers who defraud the government. The plaintiff-employee's incentive for blowing the whistle is that they receive a fifth of any damages awarded, which can sometimes run into the millions. The U.S. Justice Department has the option of joining lawsuits based on the False Claims Act, but declined to join this one.

On February 6, 2007, the court threw the lawsuit out of court and ordered Wilson and Warren to take up their dismissal with arbitrators, as specified in their contract.[36]

INSULT TO INJURY

Halliburton/KBR jobs in Iraq were much sought after because of the rumors of salaries ranging from $80,000 to $120,000 annually for unskilled or semi-skilled labor. Many of those applying for the jobs were aware that the job came with significant personal risk from the ongoing war, but what not many knew was that the high salaries were accompanied with dismal rights and benefits.

Few realized that they are actually contracted to a Cayman Islands subsidiary of Halliburton/KBR named Service Employees International, which meant that once their employment ended, the workers would not be entitled to collect unemployment benefits under Texas law. In one typical case, the Texas Workforce Commission ruled against a former Halliburton/KBR employee by concluding, "The claimant is not entitled to unemployment benefits because [Halliburton/KBR's foreign subsidiary] does not satisfy the definition for an 'American employer' under the [Texas] statute."[37]

Then there is the matter of health and accident insurance. Mark Baltazar, a thirty-two-year-old father of five, who was raised in Odessa, Texas, discovered the downside to working for Halliburton/KBR, when he was seriously injured in late 2004.[38]

He was between jobs operating heavy construction equipment when he heard he could make $84,000 doing the same work in Iraq. Less than two months after he started work in Iraq, when he had just finished lunch at the sprawling Halliburton/KBR dining facility at Camp Merez near Mosul on December 21, 2004, a suicide bomber launched one of the bloodiest attacks on U.S. forces since the invasion began. The explosion swept through the tent, hurled Baltazar into the air, and sent him crashing down over the back of a chair. A total of sixty-nine people were wounded, including Balthazar and twenty-four other civilian contractors. Seven of the twenty-two left for dead were Halliburton/KBR employees and subcontractors. One was a co-worker of Baltazar's who had just got up from the table to get some ice cream. It was the last time Baltazar saw him alive.

Six months later, like many civilian workers injured in Iraq, Baltazar was still battling with Halliburton/KBR's insurance adjusters. Instead of saving for a new home, which was his reason for taking a job in Iraq, Baltazar found himself back in Houston worse off than when he started—jobless because of his injuries, and relying on a $368 disability check every two weeks. "You make more money working at McDonald's," he told David Phinney of CorpWatch.

As a Service Employees International employee, he was not eligible for Texas unemployment insurance. Gary Pitts, his Houston-based lawyer, said Baltazar was denied full insurance coverage worth more than $1,000 a week as outlined in the 1941 Defense Base Act (DBA). (The DBA requires businesses working overseas under U.S.-funded contracts to provide insurance coverage for injuries and disabilities of all employees. Subcontractors are responsible for providing similar coverage to their workers. A DBA policy entitles the contract workers to reasonable and necessary health care for the rest of their lives, free access to an attorney, and weekly compensation for the time doctors' orders prevent them from working.).

Immediately after the bombing, Halliburton/KBR medics X-rayed Baltazar's back. They gave him morphine and said he was fine. But after spending two days resting in his trailer, Balthazar told his supervisors he wanted medical leave to go back to the United States and see a doctor of his choice. "I wanted to return to work after some medical leave," Baltazar told David Phinney of CorpWatch. "They said my injuries weren't severe enough to send me home, so I either had to stay in Iraq or quit."

Back in Houston, in January 2005, Baltazar needed spinal injections and had to go to physical therapy three times a week to help ease the pain of the back injury he sustained when he landed on the chair. He also suffered from hearing loss and blurry eyesight because of the blast and had to get psychological counseling for post traumatic stress disorder (PTSD), a temporary psychological condition that can also last a lifetime. "I wake up with nightmares, sometimes four times a night, sweating and yelling," he says.

PTSD symptoms include major depression and anxiety that can lead to suicidal behavior. The disorder haunts an estimated 15 to 17 percent of soldiers who return from Iraq, according to a study published by the *New England Journal of Medicine*.[39] Little data is available on just how widespread the problem may be among civilian workers. According to Dr. Charles Figley—director of the Psychological Stress Research Program at Florida State University and one of the country's most prominent PTSD experts—the number of contractors suffering from the disorder will likely remain an estimate. "No one is counting, no one is noticing, and no one cares," said Figley, a former marine and Vietnam veteran.[40]

Like Baltazar, another Halliburton/KBR employee, Samuel Walker of Augusta, Georgia, says the company denied him medical leave after he was injured in the Camp Merez bombing. His only options at that point were to quit or stay in Iraq. Walker, an army veteran of twenty-four years, worked for Halliburton/KBR for more than a year in Iraq as a fitness and recreation supervisor at the camp.[41]

He recalls that he was eating French fries when the explosion blasted through the mess tent. "Body parts were flying all over and pieces of flesh were flying in my face," Walker says. When it was over, the former contractor was drenched in the blood of the victims around him, and rescue workers took him for dead. "I was so close to the bomber," he adds. "There was copper wire from the bomb embedded in my jacket." Walker took a full blast to the side of his head, and shrapnel pitted his body. But when Halliburton/KBR medics treated him following the bombing, he says they merely rubbed petroleum jelly on his burns and gave him ibuprofen. "For two days I told them my side was hurting, but they said I would be okay and wouldn't give me medical leave," Walker says.

A week and a half later, like Baltazar, Walker quit and headed home to Houston. Months after the bombing, he still had ringing in his ears and migraines and had to get physical therapy for his neck, back, and right knee. Walker also believes he suffers from PTSD. Questions about his work in Iraq, scenes from the TV news, even French fries, all bring back the moment when the bomb flashed before him. "I can't even walk into a restaurant without remembering the screaming, the hollering, the yelling, and everyone thinking I was dead," Walker said. Like Baltazar, he was waiting on his claim for disability and medical bills. "I haven't gotten one red cent from them," Walker said in May 2005.

Pitts was fighting to get weekly compensation for both of them, for as long as they were unable to work, plus pay for their medical bills. He also wants the company to pay two-thirds salary for clients who are permanently out of work once everything medically possible had been completed. Pitts estimates that life-long disability claims for a widow/er and the family that lose their primary income provider could reach $2 million.

Baltazar and Walker are just two of some two hundred claimants who Pitts is helping to fight Halliburton/KBR's insurer, American International Group (AIG). "People are often stuck in Iraq, unaware of any entitlement," said Washington, DC, attorney Mark Schaffer, who represents other victims, adding that the prospect of continuing work outside the United States also tempts employees to keep mum about their injuries. "Sometimes people are afraid to go to the doctor because they will get sent home. And if you don't stay 330 days, you lose your tax-free salary. Everyone is over there to make money, and I haven't seen anyone turn down a paycheck yet."[42]

Halliburton/KBR insists that it is committed to ensuring its employees receive quality medical treatment. "As KBR's history of contracting for the U.S military in remote environments continues, the company remains committed to ensure[ing] its employees receive quality medical treatment and care, either locally or by means of evacuation to a more advanced medical facility as dictated by the nature of the situation," said Cathy Gist, a Halliburton/KBR spokesperson.[43]

Incidentally, Halliburton/KBR also offers injured U.S. workers the opportunity to apply for the Pentagon's Defense of Freedom medal, a seemingly honorable recommendation for those returning home with medical injuries. The worker is asked to sign a release form so Halliburton/KBR can provide the Pentagon with all the personal medical records needed for the award consideration process. But less conspicuous on the form is paragraph number nine that absolves Halliburton of all legal liability and forbids the worker from suing, even if the company's criminal negligence caused the injury.

A U.S. House of Representatives Committee on Oversight and Government Reform hearing in May 2008 revealed that insurance carriers like AIG and

Halliburton/KBR were making a huge profit out of the Defense Base Act scheme. At the hearing Congressman Henry Waxman's staff displayed a chart that showed that of the $284 million paid out by the government for worker's compensation coverage, the bulk was pocketed by the company. "Out of this amount, just $73 million actually goes to injured contractors, and AIG and KBR pocket over $100 million as profit," charged Waxman.[44]

An AIG spokesperson said that the company had to protect itself from future claims. "AIG is confident that we price our DBA coverage as accurately and fairly as possible, given the inherent high risks of this insurance line in these regions, the uncertainties concerning the frequency and severity of future claims, and the obligation to pay claims for many years after the losses occur, including lifetime death and disability benefits," the company wrote in an e-mail.[45]

INSURANCE WAIVERS

For non-U.S. truck drivers, the situation is much worse because many Halliburton/KBR subcontractors don't bother to get insurance so that they can keep costs down and maximize profit. In December 2006, investigative reporter David Phinney uncovered an internal Halliburton/KBR memo dated November 26, 2002, that was signed by none other than Tom Crum, KBR's chief operating officer; John Downey, project general manager (LOGCAP) project; Bob Herndon, vice president, operations maintenance and logistics; and Tod E. Nickles, senior procurement and materials manager. It reads as follows:

"Currently numerous subcontracts are being issued in remote locations worldwide. . . . Procurement personnel consistently make attempts to have subcontractors provide the minimum coverages . . . however in the event the subcontractors are unable to provide insurance or provide the minimum coverages or endorsements, this document shall act as a blanket waiver and allow procurement to proceed with subcontract award at all LOGCAP project locations."[46]

Halliburton/KBR spokesperson Cathy Gist confirmed the waiver: "KBR's standard commercial terms and conditions for subcontracts include a requirement to demonstrate that the vendor maintains appropriate commercial insurance. Understandably, most standard insurance policies contain war risk exclusions. Accordingly, due to the war-zone conditions in Iraq at the time, most insurance carriers would not extend coverage under their insurance policies to cover the work of the subcontractors in Iraq. In accordance with our established procurement procedures, KBR needed to waive this requirement to award the subcontracts to support the troops."[47]

TCNS TAKE THE WHEEL

With all the lawsuits and insurance claims flying around, Halliburton/KBR appears to have made a decision to reduce the numbers of U.S. drivers it puts on the road. When I visited Iraq for the fourth time in April 2008, most of the convoys on the road were being driven by TCNs from Egypt, Fiji, Nepal, Sri Lanka, and the Philippines. The company thus saved a bundle on wages: the Filipinos earn $4,500 a year and the Sri Lankans and Indians make barely $3,000, plus free accommodation in Kuwait (but no food or accommodation on the road where they are expected so sleep in their trucks).[48]

Tenison Perera, a forty-four-year-old Sri Lankan driver, operates an eighteen-wheeler that has neither bulletproof glass nor armor-plated doors or cabin. The gas tank is fully exposed and easy to target and blow up. An *Ottawa Citizen* article in April 2008 described how he "frantically ducks his head behind the dashboard of his truck, mimicking how he narrowly averted death. Gripping the wheel, he explains nervously how a sniper's bullet recently pierced through his truck's cabin and zipped by his head before exiting out the front window." Perera says he was given no war-zone training, just casual instructions. "Our company says to go fast," Perera explains. "They say if we go slowly, we will die."[49]

"If [U.S. drivers] can drive a big truck, we can also. If they can drive fifteen hours, we can also. What is the difference?" asks Joel, a Filipino driver who did not want give out his last name. He worked at Kuwait-based Jassim Transport and Stevedoring Company—one of the country's largest transport companies—and a Halliburton/KBR subcontractor. "The difference is that they are white and we are Asians."

The *Ottawa Citizen* reporters met with Syed Shaheen Naqvi, Jassim's business development executive, who admitted keeping driver passports, despite this being illegal. "If you subcontract with us, your work will be done. How we do it is our headache," he said. "I'll do whatever I have to do; that's my headache."

Naqvi said that his company had multiple contracts with Halliburton/KBR, and now has six hundred trucks driving through Iraq every day. He said 70 percent of the company's convoys are attacked by insurgents and also confirmed that drivers are given no special protection. When asked what happens to them when a convoy is attacked, he laughed hesitantly and said, "I don't know; the drivers are lucky." A Halliburton/KBR employee Jose Maldonado was more blunt: "If you put the music loud, you won't hear the gunfire. You need that kind of music in Iraq."

Part 3

The Whistle-blowers

GEORGE MILLER, A DEMOCRATIC MEMBER of Congress from Martinez, California, recalls his first encounter with Henry Waxman's determination to root out corruption. "When I first came on the Budget Committee, I thought Henry's first name was 'Sonofabitch.' Everybody who had to deal with the committee kept saying, 'Do you know what that sonofabitch Waxman wants now?'"[1]

Born nine days after Britain declared war on Germany in 1939, Henry Arnold Waxman grew up in Los Angeles, where he studied political science at the University of California and took a law degree.[2] He joined the U.S. House of Representatives in 1975, and after a quarter century of tirelessly leading battles in the U.S. Congress on health and environmental issues, he decided to take on Halliburton/KBR soon after the company started work in Iraq in 2003.

With the help of whistle-blowers in the Pentagon, former workers in Iraq, embittered subcontractors, and business rivals, his staff started to build a case against the company. Every week, he fired off memos to the Pentagon, asking for detailed information on payments to Halliburton/KBR, drafted diligently by his legal staff led by Jeff Baran and David Rapallo. His staff also released many of the documents that they obtained to the press and put together scathing analyses of what they had discovered.

As the ranking minority member on the Committee on Oversight and Government Reform in the U.S. House of Representatives, Waxman also tried to hold hearings on waste, fraud, and abuse among the contractors. Unfortunately for him, the chairman of the committee was Tom Davis from Virginia, the state where most military contractors have their headquarters. Davis initially agreed to a couple of hearings on war profiteering but soon tired of the subject or decided it was politically expedient to deny Waxman any opportunity to browbeat the companies.

Unable to find a committee in the House to challenge the company while the Republicans were in the majority, Waxman teamed up with Byron Dorgan, the chair of the U.S. Senate Democratic Policy Committee, to help him present the evidence on Capitol Hill. When the Republicans lost control of the house in 2006, Waxman became chairman of the Committee on Oversight and Government Reform, but the Democratic control of the House was so slender that he still had a hard time pursuing matters aggressively, particularly when the Bush administration often refused to let government officials testify and thumbed its nose at subpoenas. On the other hand, the Democratic Policy Committee—as the only official U.S. Congressional committee wholly controlled by party officials—was able to hold more hearings on military contracting waste, fraud, and abuse. Although it has no subpoena power at all and definitely no rule-making authority, its hearings have served as a way to put pressure through the media spectacle created by holding official hearings in the U.S. Congress.

BYRON DORGAN

Byron Dorgan, the junior Senator from North Dakota, was a twenty-two-year veteran of the U.S. Congress who started as a member of the U.S. House of Representatives at age thirty-eight in 1981. A progressive politician with a record of opposing "liberalization" of trade and sanctions on Cuba, he recently published a book titled *Take This Job and Ship It: How Corporate Greed and Brain-Dead Politics Are Selling Out America.*[3] He is the assistant Democratic Floor Leader in the U.S. Senate to Harry Reid, the senior senator from Nevada, and had the good fortune to be chair of the only committee in the U.S. Congress that was not controlled by the Republicans in 2003 and 2004. (Any member of Congress can hold meetings on the Hill, but official hearings can be called only by the party in power, with the sole exception of the party policy committees in the Senate. Unlike other committees, these party committees have no power to subpoena nor can they make law. Also it is rare, although not unknown, for members of the other party to attend such hearings.)

In the five years following the invasion of Iraq, the Democratic Policy Committee held well over a dozen hearings on Halliburton/KBR and related war contracting issues, presenting to the public numerous whistle-blowers for the first time. Initially, the hearings drew a lot of press, but as the war dragged on, the media slowed down a little bit.

Tim Gaffney, Neal Higgins, Leslie Gross-Davis, and Holly Teliska—the staff members who organized the hearings—tried to raise questions at important political moments (such as elections) and dramatically changed the nature of the debate by directing a media spotlight onto whistle-blowers who were otherwise easily dismissed by Pentagon brass and Halliburton/KBR itself, who repeatedly refused to testify.

HENRY BUNTING

The very first whistle-blowers to come forward, long before Bunny Greenhouse or Marie deYoung, were two contract managers at the Khalifa Resort in Kuwait: Henry Bunting, of Houston, Texas, and John Mancini, of Surprise, Arizona, who spoke up in February 2004, before the first anniversary of the invasion.

Bunting, a Vietnam veteran who worked as a purchasing and planning professional for a number of companies such as Hewlett-Packard, Tyco, and the Houston Metropolitan Transit Authority, went to work for Halliburton/KBR at the Khalifa Resort in early May 2003, staying on until mid-August of that year, and leaving before the Tiger Team arrived.

Bunting says he never saw any oversight auditors while he was stationed in Kuwait. Workers were told that if they spoke to an auditor or the media, they would be sent home, he added. Eventually he quit because he was "completely worn out" from working twelve- to sixteen-hour days, but, as he stresses, he was not fired.[4]

On February 13, 2004, Bunting testified before the U.S. Senate Democratic Policy Committee, bringing with him an embroidered orange towel, purchased by Halliburton/KBR for a Morale, Welfare, and Recreation facility for U.S. troops in Baghdad, as evidence of the company's practice of overcharging the taxpayer. Halliburton/KBR insisted on buying the embroidered towels for $5 each, he said, rather than ordinary towels for $1.60 each.

Bunting explained to senators that there are three levels of procurement staffing at Halliburton/KBR: buyers, followed by procurement supervisors, and the Procurement, Materials & Property Manager who was at the top. "A list of suppliers was provided by the procurement supervisor. It was just a list of names with addresses and telephone numbers. We were instructed to use this preferred supplier list to fill requisitions. As suppliers were contacted, commodities/product information was added. However, we found out over time that many of the suppliers were noncompetitive in pricing, late quoting, and even later in delivery."

Bunting also noticed that for purchase orders under $2,500, buyers needed only to solicit one quote from one vendor. To avoid competitive bidding, requisitions were quoted individually and later combined into purchase orders under $2,500. "About 70 to 75 percent of the requisitions processed ended up being under $2,500. Requisitions were split to avoid having to get two quotes," he told the committee. "For purchase orders above $2,500, buyers were required to obtain two quotes. The buyer would select a high-quoting supplier and a more moderate preferred-quoting supplier. Thus, the buyer would be able to place the purchase order with a preferred supplier, as he or she knew that the quote submitted by the preferred supplier would be lower."

To illustrate the system, he used the example of furniture supply. "The preferred supplier had provided office furniture almost from the beginning of Halliburton's time in Kuwait. No one questioned pricing. We simply called, furniture was delivered, and paperwork was completed. The comment by both Halliburton buyers and management was, 'It's cost plus; don't waste your time finding another supplier.' Most requirements for office furniture were filled without competitive quotes."

Bunting says he took it upon myself to find a second source for the furniture requirement. "I received quotes from several suppliers, resulting in cost savings of $30 per office desk and $10 per office chair. I estimate these savings as $5,000 to $6,000 per year. The point is that competitive pricing is available in Kuwait. But the preferred supplier list is questionable. Halliburton could reduce costs," he said.

In response to Bunting's charges, Halliburton/KBR spokesperson Cathy Gist defended the company to the media, saying that although the company had requested the towels, they cost just $3 each and were embroidered in an attempt to prevent pilferage.

After Bunting testified in the U.S. Congress, he returned to Iraq to work for another contractor.

JOHN MANCINI

The story of John Mancini, who joined Bunting as the first whistle-blower to agree to testify about Halliburton/KBR, is a sadder one. Initially, Mancini reached out to a number of reporters, including myself, to tell his story, on condition that his identity was not revealed, although eventually he changed his mind. When Bunting was asked to testify, Mancini agreed to talk to the Congressional staffers and issued an anonymous statement to back him up.[5]

Like Bunting, Mancini had a long history in procurement. He started working at Loral Electronics, which rebuilt worn circuit boards on F-16 fighter planes in the 1970s. He moved to Arizona in the 1980s where he worked for Motorola and Sperry Space Systems, buying equipment for Ronald Reagan's Star Wars program and surveillance satellites launched from the space shuttle. He also worked briefly for American Express. In 2001, Mancini took advantage of one of those travel opportunities, moving to Kuwait and working for

Combat Support Associates, a major contractor on Camp Doha. One of his jobs was finding cheaper ways to repair military equipment. "I cut the time from nine months to three months, and cut 50 percent of the costs," he boasted.[6]

In February 2003, Mancini returned to Kuwait where he, too, worked out of the Khalifa. There were hardly any computers; most records were kept on scraps of paper. Mancini says the managers told employees not to worry about the price of whatever they were buying, that it was "cost-plus," and that the company would be reimbursed by the government.

According to Mancini, Halliburton/KBR routinely insisted that the buyers use suppliers that had worked for them in the past, even if they weren't the cheapest. While it is common for companies to use reliable suppliers rather than the cheapest provider, the buyers quickly discovered that the suppliers weren't reliable. "Often these were favors to suppliers that Halliburton had used in Bosnia," said Mancini.[7]

Among the people whom Mancini felt was doing a bad job was Jeff Mazon, who was using a Kuwaiti middleman to secure cell-phone services and charging a 10 percent markup. With just a few phone calls, Mancini discovered that this was unnecessary. When he pointed this out to a supervisor, Mancini was taken off the contract.

Pretty quickly, Mancini made friends with Bunting, who shared his misgivings about the chaos and the corruption around them. Then his Bosnian supervisor told him that they would transfer him to a new office inside Iraq. Mancini refused to go. "I said, 'Fuck you, I ain't leaving.'" In midsummer 2003, Mancini quit and got on a plane home to Phoenix.

But Mancini needed another job. So in March 2004, he signed up to handle contract administration for CACI, the company that was later implicated in the Abu Ghraib torture scandal (for more on CACI, see *Iraq Inc.*). Then Mancini jumped ship for a company named Procurement Services Associates (PSA). Bad luck struck on September 23—a car carrying a Kuwaiti woman and six children slammed into the back of his Land Rover at seventy-five miles an hour, knocking him unconscious. When he woke up, he was in a Kuwaiti hospital being treated for a broken ankle, a broken wrist, and contusions to his ribs.

Within days, he was put on a flight back to the United States to avoid being asked any difficult questions. When he got back, his injured foot had turned stone cold from not getting proper circulation on the plane. Susan Mancini, his ex-wife who has worked as a surgical technologist for twenty-five years, realized that Mancini might get gangrene from his injuries unless he was treated right away. She took him to a hospital, but when the nurse asked Mancini how he was going to pay, he realized that PSA had lied about his health insurance. (Technically this is illegal, although fairly common, as under the federal

Defense Base Act all civilians working overseas for the military are supposed to have health insurance.)

Unable to walk, Mancini moved back home and kept up a series of calls to the reporters he had helped out over the years like myself. He was alternately helpful and alternately abusive. Eventually, he barricaded himself in his house and in early October he made a call to 911 emergency services and started insulting them. Later that day the Surprise police came over to his house, found eighteen thousand rounds of ammunition in the house, in addition to his dog, which had been shot and injured. Mancini was taken to prison.[8] When he was released after six months, he failed to reconnect his phone or e-mail and dropped out of sight.

TRUCKERS TESTIFY

In June 2004, another group of whistle-blowers came forward to testify before the Committee on Oversight and Government Reform at the U.S. House of Representatives, but Tom Davis refused to allow them to speak, so Waxman placed the testimony on his Web site.

One testimonial came from Mike West, who said that prior to Halliburton/KBR, he had been working as an area manager for Valero Energy with a yearly salary of $70,000. "When I heard about a chance to earn more with Halliburton, I called them up," he said. "After just a few minutes, the woman said I was hired as a labor foreman at a salary of $130,000. I didn't even have to send in a résumé." [9]

When he arrived, West explained he was paid despite the fact that he had no work. "I worked only one day out of six in Kuwait," he explained. "That day, a supervisor told me to operate a forklift. I explained that I didn't have a license, or any experience, to operate a forklift. The response was: 'It's easy and no one will know.'"

When West got to Camp Anaconda in southern Iraq, he says that he didn't have any work to do. Nor did most of the other thirty-five workers. The supervisors told them to walk around and look busy. Then they went to a camp in Al Asad, where they had only one day of work out of five days. They were told to bill for twelve hours of labor every day. From there, his group was sent to Fallujah for six weeks, where once again he had almost no work to do except help with security and follow Iraqi workers around to make sure they cleaned the toilets properly.

"One day, I was ordering some equipment," West said. "I asked the camp manager if it was okay to order a drill. He said to order four. I responded that we didn't need four. He said: 'Don't worry about it. It's a cost-plus contract.'

I asked him, 'So basically, this is a blank check?' The camp manager laughed and said, 'Yeah.' He repeated this over and over again to the employees. . . . As a Halliburton employee, I was disappointed by all of the company's lies and disorganization. As a taxpayer, I'm disgusted by all of the money spent by Halliburton to pay employees to do nothing." [10]

SPOILT FOOD

Rory Mayberry, a former Halliburton/KBR contractor who worked at the dining facilities in Camp Anaconda from February to April 2004, provided a videotaped deposition on June 27, 2005, to the U.S. Senate Democratic Policy Committee that the company often provided rotten food to the troops and often charged the army for twenty thousand meals a day when it was serving only ten thousand. At the time, he was working at First Kuwaiti where he was medical supervisor for the TCNs building the new U.S. embassy. [11]

"The first contractor that supplied food to KBR was Tamimi of Saudi Arabia," whom Mayberry says charged fair prices. Fairly soon after he arrived, PWC took over food supply, and prices skyrocketed to "almost triple. For example, tomatoes cost $5 a box, locally, but PWC prices were $13 to $15 per box. The local price of a fifteen-pound box of bacon was $12 compared to PWC's price of $80 per box," said Mayberry.

Mayberry claims that food items were being brought into the base that were outdated or expired as much as a year. "We were told by KBR food service managers to use these items anyway. This food was fed to the troops—a lot of these frozen foods, chicken, beef, fish, and ice cream. The trucks that were hit by convoys, firing, and bombings—we were told to go into the trucks and remove the food items and use them after removing the bullets and any shrapnel from the bad food."

He says that the switch to PWC made the situation worse because it took longer for the food items to get to the base as they were shipped from the United States to a warehouse in Kuwait. "When Tamimi dropped off food, there was often no place to put it into the freezers or refrigeration. Food would stay in the refrigeration and freezing trucks until they ran out of fuel. KBR wouldn't refuel the trucks, so the food would spoil. This happened quite a bit."

Mayberry says he was warned against speaking out. "Government auditors would have caught and fixed many of the problems, but KBR managers told us not to speak with the auditors," he told the committee. "The managers themselves would leave the base or hide from the auditors when they were on the base and not answer the radios when they were called for them. We were told to follow instructions or get off the base. The threat of being sent to a camp under fire was their way of keeping us quiet. I, personally, was sent to Fallujah for three weeks. The manager told me I was being sent away until the auditors were gone because I had opened my mouth to the auditors."

This testimony added fuel to a previous firestorm that was ignited when *NBC News* reported in December 2003 that a Pentagon report alleged that the food Halliburton/KBR served to U.S. troops in Iraq was "dirty," as were as the kitchens it was served in.[12]

The Pentagon report said that it found "blood all over the floor," "dirty pans," "dirty grills," "dirty salad bars," and "rotting meats . . . and vegetables" in four of the military messes the company operates in Iraq, including two in Tikrit and one in Baghdad, as well as the mess hall where President Bush served troops their Thanksgiving dinner, which was reported dirty in August, September, and October.

In response, Gist noted that the company was not responsible for purchasing food to serve at dining facilities throughout Iraq. (The food supply contract, which is called Prime Vendor, is separate from the LOGCAP contract.) "KBR's dining facilities are thoroughly inspected every month by the army's Preventive Medicine Services division, and one of the main things they check is the expiration dates on various food products. If at any point food is deemed unfit to serve, KBR follows the government-approved processes and procedures to destroy it," said Gist. "KBR's priority has always been providing the troops the best possible food, shelter, and living conditions while they serve in Iraq."[13]

RECREATION FACILITIES OVERCHARGES

Halliburton/KBR billed millions to U.S. taxpayers for nonexistent recreational activities in Iraq, charged Julie McBride, who worked for Halliburton/KBR in 2004 as a morale, welfare, and recreation (MWR) coordinator at a marine base in Fallujah, Iraq. She filed a *qui tam* lawsuit in 2005, which was made public in 2006. And she testified before the U.S. Senate Democratic Policy Committee on September 18, 2006.[14]

McBride's lawsuit says the military was billed according to the number of marines who used the MWR facility, but that the company deliberately and falsely inflated that figure. For example, a person who used a computer in the recreation center was counted as one customer, yet that same person was counted a second time when using the weight room. The center included a weight room, video games, Internet cafe, a library, and a phone bank.

"I was present in Iraq on February 27, 2005, when the 'Boots in the Door' count at the MWR facility in Fallujah was about 330," she told the U.S. Senate Democratic Policy Committee. Yet, she added, these totals were then combined for a fitness center head count "in excess of sixteen hundred, or five times the actual number of troops who came into the facility."[15]

McBride also claims that Halliburton/KBR charged U.S. taxpayers for a 2005 Super Bowl party meant for the troops, but that the company employees absconded with the food and widescreen television and launched their own private football party. "McBride witnessed [the disappearance of] a large amount of food that was ordered specifically for a Super Bowl party for the military," the suit says. "About ten large, metal tubs full of tacos, chicken wings, [and] cheese sticks were taken from the military party site to a KBR camp for a KBR Super Bowl Party for KBR employees."

"It wasn't double-dipping, but triple-dipping, or even quadruple billing," the suit claims. McBride was fired for lodging several complaints about Halliburton/KBR's accounting practices and was kept under guard until she was escorted to an airplane and flown out of the country, the lawsuit adds.

"The claims included in this lawsuit clearly demonstrate a complete misinterpretation of facts as well as a lack of understanding of KBR's contractual agreements with its customer, the U.S. Army," Halliburton/KBR spokesperson Melissa Norcross says. Halliburton/KBR's official annual report states, "Our investigation is ongoing. However, we believe the allegations to be without merit, and we intend to vigorously defend this action."[16]

WATER CONTAMINATION

Ben Carter, the owner of a water testing laboratory named Air & Water Technologies—where he designed and analyzed water purification systems (including on federal contract)—testified before the Democratic Policy Committee on January 23, 2006, about his experiences working for Halliburton/KBR. From January 2005 through early April 2005, Carter worked for Halliburton/KBR at Camp Ar Ramadi in Iraq, also known as Junction City, which is home for five to seven thousand U.S. troops, before returning to the United States and moving to Cedar City, Utah.[17]

He was hired as acting foreman of the Reverse Osmosis Water Purification Unit (ROWPU), which he described as a "standard piece of equipment, roughly the size of two shipping containers that purifies water by separating out any dissolved solids and other impurities." His job was to decontaminate the polluted water from the Euphrates River for both potable (cooking and drinking purposes) and non potable uses (bathing, showering, shaving, laundry, and cleaning).

On March 23, 2005, a fellow employee reported to him that he had discovered worms swimming in a toilet bowl, leading him to suspect that the chlorination system was not working [which would have killed any insects]. When

Carter tested the system, he discovered that the water was not being chlorinated. "Until that point, I had assumed that we were experiencing a temporary equipment malfunction or human error or something had just gone wrong temporarily," Carter told the committee members. "In fact, I was told that they had never chlorinated the water [despite the fact] that it was KBR's responsibility to test the water quality three times a day to confirm the presence of chlorine."

When Carter informed his immediate superiors about this, he was approached by Harold "Mo" Orr, who was the Halliburton/KBR health, safety, and environment coordinator, and asked to send in a detailed report. Carter's superiors, notably Suzanne Raku Williams, the Halliburton/KBR site manager, told him not to send any e-mails to anyone outside the military base.

At that point Ken May, from Louisville, Kentucky, who worked as an operations specialist with Halliburton/KBR at the same site over the same period of time, forwarded a report from Will Granger, Halliburton/KBR's Iraq water quality manager, that stated, "No disinfection to non potable water was occurring [at Camp Ar Ramadi] for water designated for showering purposes. This caused an unknown population to be exposed to potentially harmful water for an undetermined amount of time."[18]

"This event should be considered a 'NEAR MISS,'" the Granger report warned, "as the consequences of these actions could have been VERY SEVERE resulting in mass sickness or death" (emphasis in the original). The report added, "The deficiencies of the camp where the event occurred is [sic] not exclusive to that camp; meaning that countrywide, all camps suffer to some extent from all or some of the deficiencies noted."

Carter spoke to Granger, who told him that he had been contacted by Halliburton Watch. "KBR lawyers grilled [Granger] about our communications and threatened to hold him personally liable for any damage the company incurred."

Meanwhile Orr, who shared Carter and Granger's concern, decided to resign, and sent his bosses the following e-mail: "There are still possible health issues, and this has been confirmed through Charlie Med, and I am trying to make sure we do all that is possible to prevent health risks to our employees."

"This behavior has been going on for a long time, and I no longer feel that I want to work for an environment where deception and fraud are commonplace when no recourse or disciplinary action are taken. I am resigning now, as of this e-mail to all pertinent parties, and will copy H. R. to ensure that this is recorded for all."

Carter and May also resigned from their jobs.

Senior management reacted to try and staunch any negative publicity. Jennifer Dellinger of Halliburton/KBR's public relations sent out an e-mail on July 14 that stated: "I've spoken with Faith [Sproul], and she does not have much more information at this time. However, she does believe that initial tests showed some contamination to be present. Can you please run some traps on this and see what you can find out? I don't want to turn this into a big issue right now, but if we end up getting some media calls, I want to make sure we have all the facts."

Shortly after the January 23 hearing, Halliburton/KBR issued a statement saying that they had found neither contaminated water nor medical evidence to substantiate reports of illnesses at the base. The Pentagon referred the matter to its inspector general and said, "The allegations appear to have no merit."

These denials were simultaneously contradicted by military personnel. Captain Michelle Callahan, MD, a U.S. Army surgeon in Iraq with the 101st Sustainment Brigade, e-mailed the U.S. Senate Democratic Policy Committee in April 2006 to say that water containing human fecal matter and other human waste was being recirculated by Halliburton/KBR employees back into the non potable water supply used by the troops for showering, brushing teeth, shaving, washing clothes, and preparing food and coffee at a second location in Iraq. According to Callahan, "concentrate reject was being used to fill the water tanks."[19]

After finding coliform bacteria and e-coli in the water, Callahan said a Halliburton/KBR official informed employees that "there's not a problem with it."

Callahan also stated that, after discovering Halliburton/KBR was filling the water with waste water concentrate, the same official informed employees, "This was the way KBR always treated the water."

"I had a sudden increase in soldiers with bacterial infections presenting to me for treatment," Callahan told the committee in her e-mail. "All of these soldiers live in the same living area (PAD 103) and use the same water to shower. I had four cases of skin abscesses, one case of cellulitis, and one case of bacterial conjunctivitis."

After reviewing the Granger report, Jeffrey Griffiths, MD, professor of public health and medicine at Tufts University School of Medicine, testified to the committee in April 2006 that the source water used at Ar Ramadi was "highly polluted" and "highly likely to make [the troops] sick." "Everyone knows that drinking, or washing with poop is bad for you. The reasons are so obvious we consider them common sense," he said.[20]

Dr. Griffiths said the troops "would have been better off with water [taken] directly out of the Euphrates River," which the doctor described as an "open sewer." That's because Halliburton/KBR's non potable water was not chlorinated or filtered to remove parasites, amoebas, and viruses that cause various illnesses, including dysentery—an inflammatory disorder of the lower intestinal tract that causes fever, severe diarrhea, vomiting, and often "pooping of blood." Dr. Griffiths pointed out that "in many if not most wars, dysentery has killed more soldiers than has combat." He also noted that showering with untreated water is still dangerous because ingestion of diseases can occur through the mouth and skin.

Anticipating that Dorgan's criticism could create a public relations problem, Halliburton/KBR attempted to deter the senator by sending a second internal report to his office the night before the hearing, which contradicted the first internal on-site report and purportedly "exonerates" (as Dorgan put it) the company. But this second report admits that Halliburton/KBR "lacked an organizational structure to ensure that water was being treated in accordance with army standards in its contractual requirements."[21]

ELECTROCUTIONS

On January 2, 2008, Staff Sergeant Ryan Maseth, of Shaler Township, Pennsylvania, a former Green Beret, was electrocuted to death while showering in his barracks at the Radwaniyah Palace Complex in Iraq.[22] Just over two years before Maseth died, Staff Sergeant Christopher Lee Everett from Huntsville, Texas, was killed on September 7, 2005, at Camp Taqaddum in Iraq, while he was power washing sand from the underside of a Humvee.[23] The two men were among a dozen fatalities from such electrical accidents since the March 2003 invasion.

On July 11, 2008, Cheryl Harris and Larraine McGee, the mothers of the two of the victims, testified before the Democratic Policy Committee. Maseth's mother, Cheryl Harris, says she discovered later that KBR, which hired the company that installed the wiring, had been notified of problems at that very same location eleven months before the accident.[24] The Pentagon was also well aware of the issue—indeed in October 2004, the army issued a report titled, "Electrocution: The Unexpected Killer."[25]

Debbie Crawford of Battle Ground, Washington, a licensed journeyman electrician with nearly thirty years experience in the trade, worked for Halliburton/KBR in the Green Zone in Iraq from July 2004 to July 2006. She told the hearing that the lack of proper tools and material was a consistent problem. "Even the most basic material such as electrical tape and wire nuts were at times scarce," she said. "This lack of tools and material forced work to be done in a less than professional manner."[26]

Her complaints were backed up by Jefferey Bliss, a licensed electrician at the Davis-Besse Nuclear Power Station in Oak Harbor, Ohio, who worked for

Halliburton/KBR in Afghanistan as a field combat electrician from 2005 until 2006. "The carelessness and disregard for quality work at KBR was pervasive," said Bliss. "For one thing, the company did not provide electricians with the tools they needed to do the job properly. On my first assignment, I was given a pair of lineman's pliers and a screwdriver. No meter, no other tools. I would have been happy to bring tools myself, but was specifically told not to. I was told I would find what I needed in the field from other KBR workers or U.S. soldiers." (Bliss also said that he was sent to a base for two and a half months with no assignments, where he was expressly told not to do any electrical maintenance. Eventually, he was assigned the task of building a doghouse.)[27]

RAPE ALLEGATIONS: JAMIE LEIGH JONES

In July 2007 four female employees of Halliburton/KBR filed lawsuits alleging sexual harassment and two cases of rape while working in Iraq. One plaintiff said she needed surgery after being drugged and raped by male coworkers in Baghdad in 2005.[28]

In December 2007, Jamie Leigh Jones, a former Halliburton/KBR employee from Houston, Texas, came forward to tell *ABC News* that she was the woman who had been drugged and gang-raped on July 28, 2005, at Camp Hope, Baghdad, after she accepted an invitation to have a drink from a group of Halliburton/KBR firefighters a few days after she arrived in Iraq. Jones also alleged that she had moved to Iraq, after previously having been forced into a sexual relationship with Eric Iler, her immediate supervisor, while working in Houston.[29]

On December 19, 2007, she testified before the House Judiciary Committee's subcommittee on Crime, Terrorism, and Homeland Security. Jones alleged after she took one or two sips from the drink, she lost consciousness. "When I awoke the next morning, I was extremely sore between my legs, and in my chest," she told the committee. "I was groggy and confused, but did not know why at that time. I tried to go to the restroom, and while there I realized that I had bruises between my legs and on my wrists. I was bleeding severely between my legs. At that point in time, I suspected I had been raped. When I returned to my room, a man [whom I now know to be Charles Bortz], was lying in the bottom bunk of my bed. . . . I asked him if he 'had sex with me,' and he said that he did. I asked if it had been protected, and he said 'no.' I was still feeling the effects of the drug from the drink and was now very upset at the confirmation of my rape.

"I dressed and went out. I reported this incident to Pete Arroyo [whom I had known by phone and e-mail from Houston], who took me to the KBR clinic. The clinic then called KBR security, who took me to the army CASH

[Combat Army Support Hospital]. There, a rape kit was performed by the army doctor, Jodi Schultz, M.D. . . . Dr. Schultz confirmed that I had been penetrated both vaginally and anally, and that I was 'quite torn up down there.' She indicated that based upon the physical damage to my genitalia that it was apparent that I had been raped. She stated that she didn't know if I wanted to hear it or not, but that I had 'also been sexually assaulted anally.' Dr. Schultz took photographs, and completed a form that indicated the bruising on my inner thighs and stomach, and on my wrists. She also took swabs, vaginal combings, and scrapings from under my fingernails (on a blue sheet) as well as my panties and bra, and then put the entire kit together in a small, white box. I watched her give this box to the KBR security personnel as I was again turned over to these men."[30]

Jones was then taken to a trailer and locked up, where she was denied food, water, and medical treatment. After about one day, says Jones, a sympathetic guard gave her a cell phone, and she called her father, Tom, who in turn contacted Ted Poe, a Republican Congressman from Texas who contacted the State Department, who in turn dispatched agents from the U.S. embassy in Baghdad to rescue her.

In May 2007, a State Department diplomat recovered the rape kit from Halliburton/KBR, but the notes and photographs taken by Schultz were missing.

When Jones returned home, she sought psychiatric and physical attention, with Halliburton/KBR's help. "I was originally sent to a psychiatrist of Halliburton's choosing. The first question asked was 'Are you going to sue Halliburton?' So my mother and I walked out," Jones said. 'At some point, Halliburton also required me to undergo a 'psychological evaluation' by Dr. Stuart Meisner, whom they hired for the purpose of disproving my case. He was abusive and insensitive and made it very clear that his intention was to disprove the facts of my case."

Department of Justice officials were invited to the hearing but did not attend. When Senator Bill Nelson wrote to the Pentagon Inspector General Claude Kicklighter to ask him to investigate, he declined to do so. "The U.S. Justice Department has issued a statement that they are investigating the allegations," wrote Kicklighter's office. "No further investigation by this agency into the allegations made by [Jones] is warranted."[31]

Soon after Jones returned, she set up a foundation to support other women who had been raped in Iraq. She says that by the early 2008 some forty women had contacted her organization.[32]

On May 9, 2008, Keith Ellison, a federal judge in Texas, ordered that Jones could bring her case to court instead of being involved in secretive arbitration proceedings with Halliburton/KBR, as provided under the terms of her original employment contract. Ellison, however, said that Jones's claims of sexual assault, battery, rape, false imprisonment, and others fall beyond the scope of her employment contract. "The court does not believe that plaintiff's bedroom should be considered the workplace, even though her housing was provided by her employer," Ellison wrote.

The company announced that it would "review the judge's opinion and will continue to vigorously defend itself, which may include an appeal."[33]

DAWN LEAMON

In April 2008, Dawn Leamon (who initially used the pseudonym, Lisa Smith) told the *Nation* magazine that she, too, had been raped by KBR coworkers in Iraq in January when she was working there as a paramedic at Camp Harper, a military base near Basra in southern Iraq. In an interview on *Democracy Now!*, she said she had also been invited to have a drink with coworkers. "Shortly after consuming part of that drink, I have very little memories of any activity after that," Leamon said. "I also woke up in another location and had been assaulted. There was blood and feces in the room, and there was a military person in the room. And the camp management, from what I found out through the investigation and what the investigators have told me, the camp management actually was in the room during the assault several times."[34]

Leamon called her son, who was serving as a soldier. "'Of course you're going to talk to CID [the criminal investigation division], Mom. Of course you are,'" she says he told her. "He doesn't think people should be allowed to wear this uniform and act like that. He's been in the war, too, and says it's no excuse. They're better trained than that. That's what my son thought. And he's not angry at his mom."

Leamon says that she reported it immediately to "DJ"—the military's Special Forces liaison on the base, as well as to her KBR supervisors. "[DJ] told me not to speak of this to anyone and that he would take care of it," Leamon says.

But there was no investigation of her case for five weeks. Leamon was also discouraged by her KBR coworkers from taking it to higher authorities. As the only medical staffer on the site, she had to treat herself with doxycycline, and even treat one of her alleged assailants for a minor injury. When she finally submitted her complaint to authorities in the United States, she says her computer was confiscated as "evidence" by other KBR staff. Others were barely helpful. "Someone from KBR Employee Assistance gave me a flier to call someone in Houston," she says. The person who answered the phone referred her to a Web site. "I'm nine thousand miles away in Iraq and the Web site says, 'Please put in your zip code, and we'll refer you to a rape crisis counselor in your zip code area.'"

Shortly after that, Leamon returned to the United States on a routinely scheduled vacation. As soon as she arrived home from Iraq, she heard that her husband had been rushed to the hospital earlier that day after suffering a partial stroke. She faced a dilemma: "Human Resources made me sign statements saying that I'm supposed to be back in Dubai on April 7 at 10 p.m., and if I'm not there I will not be reimbursed my $1,600 airfare for my two weeks' vacation."

Heather Browne, the KBR spokesperson, issued a statement about the complaint: "The safety of all employees remains KBR's top priority. The company in no way condones or tolerates any form of sexual harassment. Any allegation of sexual harassment or sexual assault is taken seriously and thoroughly investigated. In no way are the allegations publicized recently, an indication of KBR's treatment of women. The company's zero tolerance policy towards sexual harassment is unwavering."[35]

In reply to a letter from Leamon's lawyer, KBR attorney Celia Ballí, wrote that Leamon had been "afforded with counseling and referral services through the Company's Employee Assistance Program." But Ballí noted there are "inaccuracies" in the description Leamon made of her treatment after the alleged sexual assault. "Therefore, the Company requests that you fully investigate all the facts alleged by Ms. Leamon as the Company intends to pursue all available remedies should false statements be publicized."[36]

LAVENA JOHNSON

Another case linked circumstantially to KBR surfaced in July 2008. On July 19, 2005, army Private First Class LaVena Johnson of the 129th Corps Support Battalion was found dead at LSA Anaconda in a tent belonging to KBR that had been set on fire.[37] No allegations have been made about the company's role in the affair.

Dr. John Johnson and Linda Johnson, her parents who live in St. Louis, Missouri, say that her body had numerous abrasions, a broken nose, a black eye, burned hands, loose teeth, acid burns on her genitals, and a bullet hole in her head. They think that she was raped and murdered.

"I had just spoken with my daughter on Sunday, July 17, and everything was fine," her mother told the radio show *Democracy Now!* "There was no distress, no sadness. She was her bubbly self. We talked, we laughed, and we were making plans. She was telling me how she would be coming home sooner than she expected and certainly would be home for Christmas, which was her favorite time of the year."

Her father examined the body and noticed a hole on the left side of her head near the temporal lobe. "And so, I went to the news media the next day, and I said, 'They said my daughter shot herself in the head. She's right-handed, and the bullet hole was on the left side of her head,'" he told *Democracy Now!*

A pathologist from Dover Air Force Base called Dr. Johnson to tell him that what he saw was an exit wound. "And we got into a debate over what that was an exit wound from, and he finally said it was from an M-16 rifle. And I thought that was ridiculous because I'm a veteran, and I'm very familiar with that M-16 rifle and its capacity. And first of all, my daughter was five feet one inch, and that weapon is forty inches long. And let's say if she did manage to get it into her mouth, then the recoil from that weapon would have blown her face off. Let's say, if she was tall enough, and she got it in her mouth pretty well, when that bullet pops out of that barrel, it starts tumbling all over the place. So when it exits, it exits in a straight line, and it tears a huge hole in one's head. This bullet hit at the temporal lobe, bounced, and ended up going two-and-a-quarter inches toward the temporal lobe, and popped out. And that is a hand revolver and not an M-16 rifle."

Dr. Johnson said that her nose had been broken because plastic surgery had been done. "Even though she had makeup on, I could see an abrasion up under her eye. I could see that her lips had been busted because right on the edges, right near the edges of both lips, I could see what looked like a cut. And her gloves were glued on her hands, and I thought that was peculiar. So I was pretty confident she had been beaten."

On July 31, 2008, a hearing on the issue of sexual assault in the U.S. military was held by Congressman Henry Waxman in the Oversight and Government Reform Committee of the House of Representatives. Dr. Kaye Whitley, the senior civilian in charge of its Sexual Assault Prevention and Response Office (SAPRO) was asked to testify about a number of cases, including that of LaVena Johnson. Instead, Principal Deputy Undersecretary of Defense Michael Dominguez appeared and said that he had ordered the chief of SAPRO to refuse to honor the subpoena issued by the subcommittee for her appearance.[38]

12

Investigation and Punishment

WHEN STUART BOWEN, AN EX-AIR FORCE CAPTAIN who had joined George Bush's campaign team in his successful run for governor of Texas in 1994, was appointed by the president to run an independent investigative agency named the Special Inspector General for Iraq Reconstruction (SIGIR)—with a wide remit to audit the $18.7 billion requisitioned for the rebuilding of Iraq, most Bush administration critics assumed Bowen would just toe the party line.

After all, when Bush became governor of Texas, Bowen had been assistant general counsel and then deputy general counsel under Alberto Gonzales, who later became the U.S. attorney general. The *Wall Street Journal* credited Bowen with crafting some of Governor Bush's most controversial legal decisions, such as ousting a Democratic judge and dismissing widespread questions about the guilt of a death-row inmate. Bowen also spent thirty-five days in Florida, helping Bush during the infamous 2000 election recount and had lobbied USAID for Iraq contracts. (The company Bowen was helping, URS, ultimately won a series of CPA contracts valued at as much as $30 million to oversee reconstruction projects.)[1]

Yet the critics wound up being pleasantly surprised when Stuart Bowen decided to follow up on some of the allegations against Halliburton/KBR.

One SIGIR report, issued in July 2004, faulted Halliburton/KBR for not being able to locate a third of its assets in Iraq. An audit of the 20,531 items valued at $61.1 million that they were in charge of showed that they could not locate 34 percent of randomly selected sample objects, including a giant generator costing: $734,863. (The missing generator was eventually found.) In November 2004, SIGIR issued a report, recommending that the Pentagon withhold money from Halliburton/KBR for missing receipts.[2]

SIGIR's reports were received with dismay, even anger, by Paul Bremer, the ambassador in charge of Iraq for the first year of occuption. Bremer criticized Bowen for "misconceptions and inaccuracies" and for expecting the CPA to follow accounting standards that "even peaceful Western nations would have trouble meeting." [3] Newt Gingrich, the former House speaker, said that SIGIR was "dramatically out of touch with the practical realities of waging war and setting up a new government in a war-torn country."[4]

(In late 2006, Congressional staff members working for Duncan Hunter, a California Republican who was the chairman of the House Armed Services Committee at the time, inserted a clause into a Congressional bill that would have terminated SIGIR. In a demonstration of how much credibility Bowen had built, former skeptic Henry Waxman sprang to SIGIR's defense. "It appears to me that the administration wants to silence the messenger that is giving us information about waste and fraud in Iraq," he told the *New York Times*. "I just can't see how one can look at this change without believing it's political." [5] The termination clause was dropped.)

THE PENTAGON WATCHDOGS

The SIGIR reports and the whistle-blowers from Halliburton/KBR brought much-needed public attention to the waste, fraud, and abuse in Iraq that they had personally witnessed. Even more important however, was the fact that there were plenty of internal Pentagon audits that backed up their charges, though initially most seemed unlikely to see the light of day. These audits were typically done by the Defense Contract Audit Agency (DCAA), which was headquartered at Fort Belvoir, Virginia. The four-thousand-member staff of this agency provided standardized audit services over all military expenditures, including the records of the LOGCAP contract that was being managed out of Army Materiel Command in Rock Island, Illinois.[6]

(The sheer number of military agencies involved in the military contracting process is dizzying. As noted before, the master LOGCAP contract and "administrative task orders" were issued by the Army Corps in Washington, DC, and the day-to-day management of individual subcontracts are handled in regional offices like Camp Arifjan or LSA Anaconda with the help of the Defense Contract Management Agency at the Pentagon. But the payments for work done by Halliburton/KBR are handled out of Rock Island. DCAA checks up on the paperwork and often issues recommendations on how to better manage the process.)

In addition to the DCAA audits, there are a couple of independent agencies that can investigate problems, such as the General Accounting Office (GAO), the Congressional Research Service, and of course the Pentagon's own inspector general. In addition, there are criminal investigators who can be called in such as the Defense Criminal Investigative Service (DCIS) and the Federal Bureau of Investigation (FBI).

COOKING THE NUMBERS?

In February 2004, whistle-blowers at the Pentagon handed Neil King of the *Wall Street Journal* some tantalizing memos: Halliburton/KBR may have overcharged taxpayers by more than $16 million for meals served in Iraq during the first seven months of 2003. Another showed that in July 2003, alone, Halliburton/KBR billed for 42,042 meals a day at Camp Arifjan in Kuwait, even though only 14,053 meals were served daily.[7] (An internal Halliburton/KBR memo, dated January 8, 2004, directed Tamimi to charge "for the projected number of meals or the actual head count—whichever is greater.")

The newspaper also published a story that KBR was abusing the $2,500 threshold for competitive bidding. For example, the Al-Hasawi Industrial Group received an order for five hundred sleeping bags to be delivered to a military base one night, chopped into four separate orders for 125 sleeping bags, with each order right at the $2,500 threshold.[8]

At the same time, Rock Island said that it had rejected two huge, proposed invoices from the company, including one for $2.7 billion, because of myriad "deficiencies."[9] On February 13, Waxman's office released another memo describing a briefing given to his staff by the GAO. In the briefing the GAO reported that some of the contract monitoring of the LOGCAP work was being done by military reservists with only two weeks' training.

Further, the memo said, the GAO found that a $587 million contract had been approved in ten minutes based on six pages of documentation. Reportedly, there was a single $700 million "discrepancy" between Halliburton/KBR's estimate of $2.7 billion to provide food and other logistics services to the government, and the company's own line-by-line breakdown of the estimated expenses. After the Defense Department's questioning, the company slashed its estimate for the work to $2 billion—though it never fully explained how it had reached the new figure, the memo said.[10]

In mid-May 2004, the Pentagon suspended another $159.5 million payment to Halliburton/KBR after incomplete files and bills were found to have been submitted by the company. A Pentagon spokesperson said in a statement that a "Tiger Team" of investigators and auditors, appointed by Halliburton/KBR to look for possible problems, had calculated excess meal costs (overbilling) that amounted to more than 19.4 percent of the actual price charged for meals.[11]

In June 2005, Waxman released another report with new information from the DCAA. His report says that the military auditors found $813 million in "questioned costs" (expenses that military auditors consider "unreasonable" because they "exceed that which would be incurred by a prudent person") and $382 million in "unsupported costs" (expenses that do not contain any documentation or verification) for the LOGCAP projects.[12]

DCAA auditors said Halliburton/KBR often offered cost estimates that were several times higher than that of the government. For example the Pentagon estimated that it would cost $1.9 million for operations and maintenance support at the Baghdad International Airport while Halliburton/KBR's estimate for the same task order was $12.8 million. Likewise, operations and maintenance support at Camp Arifjan in Kuwait, the Pentagon estimate was $2.8 million, while Halliburton/KBR's estimate was $10.8 million. The Pentagon typically accepted Halliburton/KBR's estimate and threw away the one prepared by its staff.

The Waxman report says that DCAA discovered that Halliburton/KBR had overpriced and double-billed on a number of items, including soft drinks, movie rentals, tailoring services, tractors, trailers, and other heavy equipment. In one task order, Halliburton/KBR charged $2.31 for towels and $300 for video players. But in other task orders, Halliburton/KBR charged $5 for towels and $1,000 for video players.[13]

Another example that the Waxman report gave was a Halliburton/KBR request to be paid $2.2 million for leased cargo aircraft as well as $7.6 million for freight costs that "appeared to be duplicate costs." Halliburton/KBR also asked for $1.4 million to pay 146 personnel to provide electrical, plumbing, and cleaning services at a facility, but "the contractor had only sixty-two personnel on hand."

Halliburton/KBR, it seems, was one of the few contractors in Iraq with such problems. Most of the audits of the Pentagon's seventy-seven contractors in Iraq have "found only minor cost" problems, reported the DCAA in its audit, and "the majority of these problems have been resolved by the contractors." But this is not the case with Halliburton/KBR. According to DCAA "major contract audit issues" are "limited to [the] largest Iraqi reconstruction contractor," which is Halliburton/KBR.[14]

Halliburton/KBR responded by saying that many of these problems were caused by the unexpected and rapid expansion of its responsibilities. For instance, with little advance warning the company was asked to feed one hundred thirty thousand troops in July 2003, nearly triple the fifty thousand troops it fed in June 2003. "I don't think people appreciate the real-time nature of the work we're doing. This is not, 'Can you do this in two months?'

This is, 'Can you do this by the morning?'" David Lesar, Halliburton CEO told the *Wall Street Journal.*[15]

Melissa Norcross, the Halliburton/KBR spokesperson, defended the company's practices: "For example, commanders do not want troops 'signing in' for meals due to the concern for safety of the soldiers; nor do they want troops waiting in lines to get fed." Norcross also claimed that the "dirty kitchen" problems have been taken care of, and the facilities have since passed subsequent inspections.[16]

"Keep in mind that serving food to more than one hundred thirty thousand patrons daily in a hostile war zone is not easy. And it's worth noting that although there are many challenges involved in supplying food to more than one hundred thirty thousand patrons every day, there are also accounts of wonderful things our employees do," said Norcross.

She quoted a note from a Halliburton/KBR client in Tall Afar, Iraq: "The commander gave kudos to the staff for the Thanksgiving Meal served. He said it was the best he had ever seen, and I told him that it was the best that I have seen anywhere in twenty-three years of government service."

Even though the allegations of food overcharges by Halliburton/KBR died down by late 2004 and early 2005, other revelations continued to come out: The company had overcharged for ice-making, idle trucks, and most significantly, a refusal to share basic information about what it was charging for in Iraq.

ICE MACHINES

The company was given a priority order to provide troops in Kuwait and Iraq with ice every summer. The order stated, "The contractor shall produce or subcontract and make available potable ice." So Halliburton/KBR built a plant in southern Kuwait with a walk-in freezer and delivery dock and imported two industrial-sized ice makers from east Texas that could churn out forty tons of ice a day. Halliburton/KBR hired twenty-eight people to run the plant around the clock. And it stamps every bag of ice produced "KBR Iceworks Inc. Serving the U.S. Military."

"The deluxe ice service shows how KBR has made the most of its unique and powerful role as the sole provider of many support services to the military. KBR's contract with the military contains big incentives to deliver goods and services in a hurry to keep army brass happy—with little attention to the cost or efficiency of the solution," wrote Russell Gold, a *Wall Street Journal* reporter, who was astonished when he accidentally stumbled upon the ice factory, while being given a routine tour of the base.[17]

In addition, Marie deYoung testified to the U.S. Congress that she found paperwork that suggested that Halliburton/KBR had received two bids for ice factories—one for $450,000 and another for $3.4 million. The company chose the higher bidder, and paid another $900,000 in shipment fees to import the factory.[18]

IDLE TRUCKS

Halliburton/KBR charges millions of dollars to U.S. taxpayers for Mercedes trucks that sit idle and unused in the Iraqi desert, an internal Pentagon memo obtained by HalliburtonWatch revealed.[19] The memo, written on September 16, 2004, by the Baghdad branch manager of the DCAA, reported that Halliburton/KBR "procures and retains excess vehicles" under its troop support contract with the Army Corps. The memo concludes that the excess vehicles result in "increased costs to the government."

The total value of the vehicles under review was $300 million and included both purchased and leased vehicles. HalliburtonWatch obtained a digital photograph from a source inside the federal government showing dozens of these Mercedes trucks parked permanently at Camp Anaconda, Iraq (with an average cost of $85,000 each).

It's unclear how many idle or under-utilized Halliburton/KBR trucks are stored in Iraq because Halliburton/KBR "does not have an adequate system for determining the utilization of vehicles," the DCAA memo states, noting however, that existing records appear to indicate "low utilization of vehicles." Auditors specifically requested the mission control logs to reveal how often each truck is used. But Halliburton/KBR balked. The memo reveals that it would cost 750 labor hours to compile the data for twenty-nine of the trucks under review.

As an alternative, Halliburton/KBR offered the "vehicle dispatch records." But, again, this proved insufficient since, as the memo states, Halliburton/KBR "provided only dispatch records for twenty-two of the twenty-nine selected vehicles, and six of the records provided were maintenance logs, not dispatch logs, with no mileage or other utilization information." Other dispatch logs requested by the DCAA "would require a manual search" at several locations and "would take time," Halliburton/KBR is quoted in the memo as saying.

The DCAA official to whom the memo was addressed, Bill Daneke, told HalliburtonWatch he was not authorized to comment on the issue, so he referred the inquiry to Lieutenant Colonel Rose-Ann Lynch in the Office of the Assistant Secretary of Defense for Public Affairs. Lynch referred HalliburtonWatch to Art Forster in the Congressional and Public Affairs Office of DCMA, who was not able to answer any questions and suggested a Freedom of Information Act (FOIA) request would be required to determine how the military concluded the issue. To date the military has not provided a response to the FOIA request.

Halliburton/KBR spokesperson, Melissa Norcross, did not specifically deny the allegations in the memo. In an e-mail response to HalliburtonWatch, she said, "For more than two years KBR has been involved in numerous government audits relating to our work in Iraq, and we continue to cooperate with our customer and the appropriate government agencies to demonstrate that our work has been performed at a fair and reasonable cost and within the appropriate bounds of government contracting."

Another internal DCAA memo, first publicized by HalliburtonWatch, alerted the Pentagon that Halliburton/KBR's proposed purchase of 106 postal vehicles, for a total of $12.6 million, "was supported only by a memorandum" that contained "apparent math errors." It concluded that "the proposed quantities for some of the equipment purchases were not supported by an adequate analysis of the requirement." The memo, written on May 28, 2004, by the branch manager of the Iraq Branch Suboffice at Camp Arifjan, Kuwait, was also addressed to Daneke.[20]

Halliburton/KBR confirmed to the DCAA that thirty-four of the 106 postal vehicles were needed only for a "temporary surge" in troop numbers. The memo chided the company for failing to consider leasing, rather than buying, the vehicles. Halliburton/KBR also agreed that temporary surges in troop numbers occur only once or twice per year. "Based on our discussion, he stated he would consider leasing the surge vehicles and revising the proposed quantities accordingly," the memo concludes.

PUBLIC INTEREST DATA STAMPED "PROPRIETARY"

SIGIR released a report in October 2006 saying that Halliburton/KBR was withholding information from federal investigators.[21] Halliburton/KBR claimed the data were proprietary—meaning they would unfairly help competitors—and therefore protected by the Federal Acquisition Regulations (FAR). These "trade secrets" included such mundane items as how many people Halliburton/KBR fed each day in its dining facilities and how many gallons of fuel it delivered.

SIGIR says that Halliburton/KBR routinely stamped nearly all of the data it collects on its work as proprietary. "The use of proprietary data markings on reports and information submitted by KBR to the government is an abuse of the FAR and the procurement system," wrote the investigators. "KBR is not protecting its own data but is in many instances inappropriately restricting the government's use of information that KBR is required to gather for the government."

The investigators also noted that Halliburton/KBR deliberately slowed down their work by releasing data in gigantic tables rather than in the kind of commonly used database programs that allow auditors to check the numbers. This was not the first time the company has come under fire for using the "proprietary" label to hide information. (see Collecting the Money in Chapter 7) Not surprisingly, in an e-mail response to SIGIR, Halliburton/KBR said it "has encountered situations in the past where extremely competition-sensitive data has found its way to the press and/or to the Internet. As a result, this data is being properly protected." It justified the unusual step of marking nearly all of its information as "proprietary" on grounds that "disclosure would cause a foreseeable harm" to operations.

Halliburton/KBR spokesperson Cathy Gist told the *New York Times*, "KBR has included proprietary markings on the majority of its data and property in support of its government contracts for the U.S. Army for at least the last decade." [22]

CHARLES SMITH

In June 2008, the *New York Times* dropped a bombshell on the overcharging debate. Charles Smith, the former head of Field Support Contracting at the Army Materiel Command, in Rock Island, who had recently retired after thirty-one years in the military, went on record to say the Pentagon had ignored DCAA reports on $1.8 billion in "unsupported costs" on the LOGCAP contract. He says he personally found "over $1 billion worth of unsupported charges to the government." [23]

On July 9, 2008, Smith testified before the U.S. Senate Democratic Policy Committee. Smith said that the years that he spent overseeing the LOGCAP contract were initially the most fulfilling of his career "because I felt that the services provided under the contract were a key component to the well-being of U.S. troops during wartime." However, he says, he found it extremely difficult to oversee the $5 billion annual contract with a staff of a two-and-a-half people (the number typically assigned to a $100 million per year project). [24]

Smith gave examples of what he found: "$1 billion in Dining Facility Costs were converted from a cost-type contract to fixed-price. DCAA had questioned over $200 million of these costs as unreasonable due to poor subcontracting. This resulted in the government paying for thousands of meals that were never served to troops. The profit on this contract was set at 3 percent, the maximum fee KBR would receive on a cost contract."

Initially, the Pentagon held off on sanctions because they realized that there had been a lot of changes to contract requirements. But by the summer of 2004, DCAA had endorsed withholding 15 percent of payments to Halliburton/KBR until the company reconciled its unsupported charges to the government. This, he says, was standard contracting practice and a method for encouraging contractors to give an accurate description of costs.

Smith says that, at the time, the company was having problems with cash flow and needed to get paid. "I believe such action would have significant harm to KBR and threatened the existence of the company. Halliburton, the KBR parent, had provided the government with financial guarantees of performance during the solicitation phase, so they would have been involved in government litigation by such an action."

In June 2004, the Army Sustainment Command (ASC) Commander, Major General Wade Hampton McManus Jr., retired and was replaced by Brigadier General Jerome Johnson. Smith was asked to meet with General Johnson at Halliburton/KBR's offices in Washington, DC. "In a morning session with KBR, I reviewed our position and noted that KBR was not making the necessary progress to provide me with government proposals," Smith recounted. "In an afternoon session, General Johnson attacked me over the issue of locating our contracting staff in [the] theater. This was rather strange behavior in a government/contractor meeting, more appropriate to a government-only setting."

Following this meeting, Smith traveled to Iraq, Kuwait, and Qatar and returned in time for a major session with Halliburton/KBR and all of the government participants in contract administration, including DCAA. The next day when he showed up for a meeting with Halliburton/KBR officials, he found a colleague in his place and was told that he had been replaced.

In February, the Pentagon abruptly announced that it would pay all the disputed costs. Jeffrey Parsons, executive director of the Army Contracting Command, later told the *New York Times* that circumstances were such "we could not let operational support suffer because of some other things."[25]

Next, the Pentagon essentially hired RCI, a private contractor that was later acquired by Virginia-based Serco, to do oversight. The Pentagon also waived its normal 15 percent withholding of payment prior to negotiation of estimated costs. "The whole process was irregular and highly out of the ordinary," said Smith. "The interest of a corporation, KBR, not the interests of American soldiers or American taxpayers, seemed to be paramount. In thirty-one years of doing this work, I have never seen anything like the way KBR's unsupported charges were handled by the Department of Defense."[26]

KBR spokesperson Heather Browne issued a response to Smith's testimony. She wrote, "KBR conducts its operations under LOGCAP III in a manner that is compliant with the terms of the contract. We take exception to any inference that the company engaged in any improper behavior."[27]

Late Payments

In March 2004, in response to a criminal investigation launched by the DCIS,[28] Halliburton/KBR announced it would suspend billing the government as a gesture of good faith. But concurrently the company froze payments to its subcontractors to the tune of $500 million in outstanding invoices. The biggest invoices were owed to Tamimi for $136 million, Kuwait-based La Nouvelle Trading for $76 million, and Event Source of Salt Lake City, which claimed it was owed $87 million.[29]

The Wall Street Journal interviewed Ahdy Boutros, managing director of Idris National Trading Company, in April 2004, who says he called Halliburton/KBR after a bill for leased generators wasn't paid within thirty days. He eventually got his money but it was five months late. Worse off was Jason Varghese, general manager of Fitco Technical Services, a computer- and electronics-supply company, who was owed about $730,000, including past-due invoices that were as much as nine months old. "We're already neck-deep in the mud. We have to keep the relationship to get the money out," he told the reporter.[30]

Another company that says it was stiffed by Halliburton/KBR was Morris Corporation, of Queensland, Australia—the company that provided Thanksgiving dinner to President Bush when he made a surprise visit to Baghdad in 2003, appearing in front of the cameras and offering U.S. troops a plastic turkey on a tray.[31]

Morris was hired in June 2003, in partnership with KCPC, a Kuwaiti company, to supply meals to eighteen thousand troops at three bases in northern Iraq for $100 million. Six weeks later Halliburton/KBR canceled the contract saying that Morris and its Kuwaiti partner had not met their obligations. A whistle-blower told the Sydney Morning Herald that the Australian-Kuwaiti joint venture was approached by a U.S. Halliburton/KBR employee, seeking kickbacks worth up to $3 million during the contract negotiations. "We're not talking about a paper bag. This guy was after a percentage of your sales every month. They wanted kickbacks of 3 percent to 4 percent, which pushed up the prices because then the subcontractors would add the price of the kickbacks to their costs."[32]

BREAKING UP THE CONTRACT

In order to deal with the DCAA audits, General Jerome Johnson first turned to a company based in Vienna, Virginia, named RCI, to check up on the company, as noted earlier. A management consulting company that provided services to the Pentagon, RCI was bought up by Serco, a company out of Hampshire, England. Both companies had some work in Iraq already—Serco managed air traffic control at two airports and RCI employed in human resources and recruiting. Serco was also employed to recruit teenagers into the military.[33]

Serco was adamant that it was not actually overseeing KBR. Serco spokesperson Steve McCarney told the *Houston Chronicle.* "We simply provide independent economic cost analysis to our client, which is the U.S. Army. But as Lee Thompson, the executive director of LOGCAP, would put it, "It didn't take a rocket scientist to figure out we were getting beat up by the Hill."[34]

In July 2006, the Pentagon took the next step: it announced that the ten-year LOGCAP III contract issued in December 2001 was being canceled (technically it was a one-year contract with nine extra option years that the Pentagon opted not to exercise after the first five years) Instead a brand new competition was to be held for LOGCAP IV.[35]

The new contract was to be divided into two: a planning contract, which would have a contractor drawing up plans for supporting future contingencies and exercises; and a separate execution contract, which would be actually providing services at U.S. military facilities, including in war zones. To make it even more competitive it would hire three prime contractors that would compete among themselves for awards to perform individual task orders—for instance, running dining facilities or providing cargo transportation services (sort of like having three finalists on hand who would run a race every time the Pentagon wanted something done).[36]

In February 2007, the Pentagon announced that Serco had won the first planning contract, with a potential value of $225 million over five years. In June 2007, the Pentagon selected the three finalists: KBR, Fort Worth, Texas-based DynCorp International (in a consortium with PWC/Agility and CH2M Hill) and Fluor Intercontinental of Greenville, South Carolina (in a consortium with ITT's Systems Division). The indefinite quantity and indefinite delivery contract had a one-year base period with nine option years that could be worth up to $150 billion. Each company was capped at $5 billion per year.[37]

Not surprisingly, there was an immediate protest by the contractors who lost. (This is very common on military contracts.) One protest was launched by a consortium led by IAP, and the second was launched by a group called

Contingency Management (AECOM Government Services, Shaw Group, and PAE Government Services). The Pentagon finally resolved the matter on April 28, 2008, with a new deal that essentially split the work up between KBR, Dyn-Corp, and Fluor.[38]

Henry Waxman was deeply skeptical. "The army can say that they are retaining the final say, but when they outsource this much work on contract management, they really are outsourcing oversight," he said. Byron Dorgan was equally critical. "This is just another verse in the same old song. It appears to me that this is a broken process."[39]

WANTED: FIVE NEW GENERALS

The Pentagon also came up with a new plan to solve the problems with the pervasive fraud. It would appoint five new generals and issue contracts from headquarters. It's not as simplistic as it seems, and it may not be as clever as one might hope.

On September 12, 2007, Pete Geren, the secretary of the army, asked Dr. Jacques Gansler, an undersecretary of defense for acquisition, technology, and logistics under President Clinton, to head up a blue-ribbon panel to figure out what to do. Seven weeks later Gansler came up with a set of recommendations.[40] First, shut down the contracting at Camp Arifjan in Kuwait. Second, move the decision-making to Fort Lee in Virginia. And, third, hire new generals. "It's sort of like an assembly line for cars and having more checkers at the end of the line when the people aren't building the cars right," Gansler told the *Associated Press*. "What we really need to eliminate the abuse is people doing it right in the first place." Wes Kilgore, director of the Major Procurement Fraud Unit, agreed. "There's obviously more going on out there today than there was five years ago, but I have the same number of people," he said.[41]

The argument was simple: As of 2007, the U.S. Army had employed approximately one hundred sixty thousand contract personnel and spent more than $112 billion in taxpayer dollars on those personnel in the war on terror, principally in Iraq. The result, according to Army Criminal Investigation Command, was 168 investigations related to $6 billion in contract fraud, resulting in indictments of nearly a dozen military and civilian army personnel; and more than $15 million in bribes had been confirmed. The problem was that the army had just seventy-five contracting personnel at Camp Arifjan overseeing the tens of billions of dollars being spent in Iraq. (By comparison, the Pentagon has a total of ten thousand contracting officers to oversee annual expenditures of roughly $400 billion. The Gansler panel recommended hiring another two thousand.[42])

At first the White House balked. The army already has 310 generals, and the cost of five more generals was estimated at $1.2 million a year. But the Pentagon supported the plan. Nelson Ford, assistant secretary of the army for financial management, wrote in a response to the Senate Armed Services Committee, "The key question is, given the current (operational tempo) and the stress on army leadership, both military and civilian, does the army need more general officers to meet the leadership demands of the force?"[43]

He was backed up by U.S. Senator Bob Casey, a Democrat from Pennsylvania: "I cannot understand why a plan developed by the U.S. Army itself to combat waste, fraud, and abuse and improve the future oversight of contracts has been blocked by the Office of Management and Budget."[44]

The White House approved the request on July 2, 2008. The Pentagon now expects to hire two major generals and three brigadier generals. One of the major generals, who wear two stars, plus two brigadier generals, would run the newly established Army Contracting Command at Fort Lee, while the second two-star general would work at the Pentagon. The third brigadier general would become chief of contracting at the Army Corps.[45]

GETTING OUT WHILE THE GOING IS GOOD

It hardly seems coincidental that shortly after the DCAA began its investigations into Halliburton/KBR overcharging in the summer of 2004, CEO David Lesar announced on September 23, 2004, that Halliburton was considering spinning off KBR as a separate company, stating that the company had become part of a "vicious campaign" of political attacks and that the company's employees "don't deserve to have their jobs threatened for political gain."[46]

It took more than two years for the spin-off to take place, but on November 16, 2006, KBR was floated on the New York Stock Exchange at $21 a share. By mid-April 2007, the spin-off was complete—KBR was an entirely separate company with its own institutional shareholders like Barclays Global, Goldman Sachs, Fidelity Mutual, Jana Partners (a hedge fund from San Francisco), and corporate raiders like New York–based Jeffrey L. Gendell.[47]

Just before KBR's annual meeting in Houston, on March 11, 2007, Lesar made another surprise announcement. He told the regional energy conference in Bahrain that the company would move its corporate headquarters to Dubai, in the United Arab Emirates, to strengthen the company's activities in the region.[48] The company says it will still be incorporated in the United States but may seek an additional listing on a Middle Eastern stock exchange.[49]

Industry experts say the move makes sense. "There's not much oil in Texas any more," Dalton Garis, a U.S. energy economist at the Petroleum Institute in Abu Dhabi, told the Associated Press. "Halliburton is in the oil and gas industry, and guess what? Sixty percent of the world's oil and gas is right here. If they didn't move now, they'd have to do it later."[50]

Oil analysts noted that despite the fact that Halliburton generated about 38 percent of its $13 billion oil field services revenue in the region, it wasn't doing as well as its chief competitor, Schlumberger, which earned more profit outside North America. Chinese oil field services competitors are also swiftly moving into the Middle East.[51]

Halliburton has maintained several offices in the region for years, but why in Dubai? Well, it is the busiest port in the region, and it is the main hub for companies setting up business in the Middle East. But there are other obvious advantages. Martin Sullivan, contributing editor at the nonpartisan *Tax Notes* magazine, said relocating to the no-tax jurisdiction of Dubai would change Halliburton's tax situation "significantly," even though the company would still be registered in the United States. By relocating its top executives to Dubai, Halliburton can argue that a portion of its profits should be attributed to the no-tax jurisdiction, he said.[52]

Senator Hillary Clinton, a Democrat from New York, was among several Congress members who issued a statement in response to the Halliburton announcement. "I think that raises a lot of serious issues we have to look at," she said. "Does this mean they are going to quit paying taxes in America? They are going to take all the advantage of our country but not pay their fair share of taxes? . . ."[53] They get a lot of government contracts. Is this going to affect the investigations that are going on? Because we have a lot of evidence of misuse of government contracts and how they have cheated the American soldier and cheated the American taxpayer. They have taken the money and not provided the services, so does this mean that we won't be able to pursue these investigations?" (Charlie Cray, co-director of HalliburtonWatch and director of the Center for Corporate Policy, also notes that the United States has no extradition treaty with the United Arab Emirates.[54])

When I met David Lesar at the company's annual meeting in Houston, I asked him if the company was going to tackle the multiple investigations that were ongoing in Iraq, and he looked me squarely in the eye and said, "That question is really best addressed to KBR. We no longer speak on behalf of KBR."[55]

He also said that both he and Halliburton would continue to be U.S. tax residents. "Halliburton has been, and will continue to be, a U.S. company and therefore a U.S. taxpayer," he told me. "I, personally, will remain a U.S. citizen and a U.S. taxpayer."

CONCLUSION

Revisiting the Revolution in Military Affairs

THE LOGISTICS OF WAR have always been half the battle, if not more than that. Napoleon Bonaparte once said that an army marches on its stomach to underscore the importance of the supply line—getting food, clothes, and spare parts to the front—and it is often what makes or breaks a conflict.[1]

This truism has been repeated by many a general throughout history. General Matthew B. Ridgway, who helped plan the airborne invasion of Sicily in July 1943, once said, "What throws you in combat is rarely the fact that your tactical scheme was wrong . . .but that you failed to think through the hard, cold facts of logistics."[2]

But what is harder yet is recruiting the people to carry out those less-glamorous tasks. In 1904, U.S. Secretary of War Elihu Root warned, "Our trouble will never be in raising soldiers. Our trouble will always be the limit of possibility in transporting, clothing, arming, feeding, and caring for our soldiers. . . ."[3]

If JFK had a hard time dispatching a draft army to do these tasks in Vietnam, George Bush faced a far tougher task convincing twenty-first-century U.S. teenagers to volunteer to peel potatoes, dig ditches and clean toilets in the desert for months, even years, at a stretch.

Complicating matters further was the fact that Secretary of Defense Donald Rumsfeld asked General Tommy Franks to draw up plans for a small force that would use "shock and awe" for the invasion of Iraq, rather than the five hundred thousand troops that Franks estimated would be needed for a conventional war. Likewise, in February 2003, when army chief of staff General Eric Shinseki publicly stated that several hundred thousand troops would be needed to sustain an occupation, he was rebuked by Rumsfeld's deputy, Paul Wolfowitz.

So Franks followed up on Rumsfeld's suggestion of September 10, 2001, to outsource anything that was not inherently military to contractors. Paul Cerjan, then director of Halliburton/KBR's worldwide military logistics operation, explained what was outsourced and why in a *Frontline* interview, "I would put it in terms of what used to be a three-tier definition for military forces. One was combat forces—infantry, armor, artillery, and such; one's combat support forces, which essentially were MPs [military police] and other activities that supported the war fighter; and then the third one is combat service support forces, which is the tails. And so the tail lends itself to contracting; there's no question about it. It's a mission-critical function when you're supplying food for troops. Without full bellies, they can't fight."[4]

Globalization made it easy to find migrant labor to do this work even during a dangerous and unpopular war. An even greater benefit of contracting out these logistical jobs was that this dedicated work force was able to go beyond the traditional army chow to provide a dazzling array of creature comforts that convinced reluctant U.S. soldiers to continue to sign up to fight in Iraq—from all-you-can-eat dinner buffets to Burger King and Pizza Hut on demand, as well as hot showers and an endless supply of video games—mimicking their lifestyles back at home, except that in Iraq, the soldiers didn't even have to clean up after themselves.

HALLIBURTON'S ARMY

The Fahaheel Expressway shoots like an arrow out of Kuwait's city center, bearing southeast toward Saudi Arabia, until it merges with King Faheed Bin Abdul Aziz road on the way to Camp Arifjan, which is the biggest U.S. military base in Kuwait. A modern, six-lane highway that was completed more than a decade ago, the highway connects to the booming new neighborhoods of Fintas, Mahboula, Mangaf, and Fahaheel that together make up a spanking new city that rivals the country's somewhat old and decrepit capital. These four new and adjoining neighborhoods, each with its own unique off-ramp, represent the present and the future of Kuwait's economy. Originally ignored because of pollution caused by the three refineries that dot the beach, these desert backlots sprang to life only after the U.S. invasion in March 2003. With Hussein gone, Kuwaiti investors who had previously invested abroad returned to put money into their own economy.[5]

If you wander through the unpaved dusty backstreets of Mahboula, you will run into thousands of Egyptians, Fijians, Indians, Filipinos, and U.S. citizens who are flocking to live in the small apartments that make up the highrise residential complexes that are growing like mushrooms around the area. What draws them are the jobs on the military bases like Camp Arifjan, as well as the new refineries and related industries planned. KBR and PWC are household names here, as are a host of other U.S. military contractors like CSA, IAP, and ITT.

Not far from Mahboula is Mangaf, where the wealthy executives of KBR make their home at the Hilton. It is here that Tom Crum, KBR's chief operating officer, once demanded that hotel staff get his wife a diamond-encrusted Cartier watch in the middle of the night, when hers mysteriously disappeared. ("Get off your f&^%ing ass, put my wife in a car, and go get her a watch," Crum is alleged to have told Camille Geha, the Egyptian sales manager at the Hilton in Kuwait, in early 2004. Aware that the company was spending up to millions at the hotel, Geha is said to have told an unnamed hotel worker to have a jewelry store at the Marina Mall down the road opened in the middle of the night to get a new watch.)[6]

Outside of the near ubiquitous presence of KBR workers on U.S. military bases in Iraq—these fast-growing suburbs from Mahboula to Mangaf are the most visible presence of Halliburton's Army.

As noted previously, Halliburton/KBR estimated that by April 2008 their 50,000 workers in Central Asia and the Middle East had cooked more than 720 million meals, driven more than 400 million miles in various convoy missions, while providing 12 billion gallons of potable water and more than 267 million tons of ice. By the time this book is published in 2009, the revenue that will have accrued to Halliburton and its former subsidiary KBR for this work will have exceeded $30 billion, a huge increase over the meager $1.2 billion in government contracts it completed over a period of five years in the early 1990s.[7]

David Lesar, the CEO of Halliburton once told *Fortune* magazine that what the company created in 2003 was tantamount to "creating a Fortune 270 company in eighteen months." He says, "In any other context, it would be, 'Zero to forty-six thousand [employees]!'—this wonderful entrepreneurial success story!"[8]

"Of course, a company that grew that fast is going to have growing pains," Lesar told the magazine. But "every little stumble is held up and magnified in the political process. If you look at what we've done on the ground, it's a pure miracle. What we've done in Iraq is good—to the third power!"

By and large, the military top brass is also delighted with what Halliburton/KBR has achieved by providing them with fifty thousand workers or the equivalent of a hundred battalions. Without KBR, the occupation of Iraq would have been a total, unmitigated disaster. (There are many who believe that the situation in Iraq is a disaster, but I'm simply discussing military logistics here.)

In my visits and interviews with Pentagon officials on military bases in Afghanistan, Iraq, Turkey, Kosovo, and in the United States, I found that Pentagon staff were firmly convinced that outsourcing was one of the most useful new trends in supporting the troops in the last few years. "Civilian contractors are meeting the army's changing needs. Today we are able to deploy private companies at seventy-two-hours notice, while in the past it could take 120 to 180 days to get permission for such operations," Mike Noll, chief for plans and operations for the LOGCAP contract explained to me in a telephone interview from the U.S. Army Operations Support Command in Alexandria, Virginia.[9]

THE WINNERS

Today Halliburton CEO David Lesar, who sold his modest million-dollar home in Plano, Texas, and moved out of the condominium at Four Leaf Towers on San Felipe and Post Oak Boulevard in Houston, commutes to work on Sheikh Zayed Road in Dubai, which is the equivalent of New York's Fifth Avenue (or the closest counterpart to the Fahaheel Expressway in Kuwait, linking Deira to the new suburbs in Jebel Ali).[10]

In mid-July 2008, David Lesar owned 961,003 shares in Halliburton, worth just shy of $50 million. Over the last few years, Lesar has sold more than half a million shares, collecting tens of millions in cash—indeed, at one point his holdings in the company were valued at $129.4 million (in early September 2005, shortly after Hurricane Katrina hit).[11] Factoring in his stock options, *Forbes* magazine's April 2008 CEO compensation report calculated that Lesar made an average of $20 million a year over the last five years.[12]

There is no doubt that this astronomical salary is linked to the company's soaring revenues. In 2004 some $7.1 billion, a third of Halliburton's revenue, was generated by the LOGCAP and RIO contracts. In 2004 the company generated $75 million in profits, swelling to $172 million in 2005 on revenues of $5.4 billion, dropping slightly to $166 million in 2006. The company's share price has also risen exponentially from a low of $4.98 on January 18, 2002 (it was $14.36 on September 10, 2001). Ever since it started to collect LOGCAP dollars, Halliburton's share price has inched upward until it hit $32.51 on the day it finally spun off KBR in mid-April 2007 (which was effectively worth $65.02 as the company had created a two-for-one stock split). By July 2008, Halliburton's stock price had reached $50 a share (or $100 for the original shares), reflecting the boom in oil prices. KBR's shares were stuck at a respectable $30 (up from the $21 when they were first issued in November 2006).[13]

To most investors, Halliburton and KBR are both doing well, particularly in light of the fact that they had hit rock bottom at the dawn of the new century. Halliburton/KBR lost nearly $2 billion in the five years after Lesar replaced Dick Cheney as CEO in August 2000, mostly because Cheney saddled the company with a mammoth $5.1 billion asbestos liability problem when he bought Dresser Industries. (Lesar also made some terrible financial decisions such as a $2.5 billion construction project in Brazil's Barracuda and Caratinga oil fields, one hundred miles out in the Atlantic, which also lost tens of millions of dollars.)[14]

William Utt, who is Lesar's CEO colleague over at KBR, made a much more modest sum of $3.29 million in 2007 and owned 257,426 shares worth approximately $7.7 million in mid-July 2008.[15]

Halliburton/KBR continues to win major government contracts. When Hurricane Katrina hit the Gulf Coast in August 2005, Halliburton/KBR was tasked with the reconstruction of several naval stations and the Stennis Space Center on the Mississippi/Louisiana border. "Due to the magnitude of Hurricane Katrina and the urgent requirements for emergency response, the corps was authorized to tap into the existing contracts of sister services," said Army Corps spokesperson Carol Sanders. The main contracting vehicle used was CONCAP (Construction Capabilities), issued by the Naval Facilities Engineering Command, the very same contract used to build prisons in Guantánamo Bay, Cuba. Under this navy contract, Halliburton/KBR was also awarded an early contract to pump water from Plaquemines Parish in Louisiana and set up a temporary morgue, which is not normally a military job.[16]

In January 2006, the Army Corps awarded the company a contract worth up to $385 million to build temporary detention centers in the event of an immigration crisis at the border.[17]

The list of winners from LOGCAP would hardly be complete without including the businesses that blossomed overnight, initially with subcontracts from Halliburton/KBR, then with independent contracts from the U.S. government. At least two companies have racked up well over a billion dollars in business: Agility/Public Warehousing Corporation and First Kuwaiti Trading Corporation. Others like IAP, La Nouvelle, and Tamimi have also done well, while yet others such as Prime Projects International and Butch Gatlin's GKL were created solely to serve the military after the invasion of Iraq.

Not every new business succeeded; some, like Terry Hall's businesses in Georgia, were caught for bribery. A number of investigations remain open, and a handful of smaller business owners and ex-military have gone to jail— like Stephen Seamans and Shabbir Khan—or remain under indictment like Jeff Mazon.

THE LOSERS: TAXPAYERS

Tales of fraud and abuse worth millions of dollars of taxpayer money in the Halliburton/KBR contract started to surface within a few months of the 2003 invasion. Whistle-blowers came forward to report allegations of overcharges for everything from towels to trucks while internal Pentagon numbers presented by Congressman Henry Waxman suggested that billions of dollars worth of invoices could be missing.

The slew of investigations that have been detailed in the previous chapters suggests that at the very least, the company was simply not prepared to set up for anything on the scale of the job General Tommy Franks handed them in 2003. Marie deYoung told a Senate Democratic Policy Committee hearing that even the company's "manual accounting system" was obsolete, despite the fact that she says that there was "no reason in the world why Halliburton can't do real time data management."[18]

There is no doubt it was a much tougher job than in the Balkans where Halliburton/KBR was allowed to build up slowly, starting with providing truck drivers and eventually building entire bases after the peace was won. This time, the company was asked to lay the basic foundation of a major invasion in just six months and do so quietly. In desperation, the contract managers hired whomever they could find, rarely checked invoices, and sometimes pocketed money on the side. (It is worth remembering that Halliburton/KBR contract manager Stephen Seamans agreed to accept a secret payoff from Shabbir Khan of Tamimi Corporation, three days before the Senate even voted on war with Iraq.)

Lax oversight at Halliburton/KBR allowed some procurement staff to take advantage of the situation. Whistle-blowers have testified that Halliburton supervisors routinely announced, "Don't worry about price. It's cost-plus."[19] This in turn encouraged fleet managers to import unnecessary quantities of expensive vehicles, and companies like Altanmia and managers like Jeff Mazon to charge several times the going rate for fuel.

If that wasn't bad enough, as the disaster in the Iraqi oilfields indicates, Halliburton/KBR also failed in certain crucial areas despite its technological expertise, because of the lack of independence and oversight. A Pentagon order to fix broken pipelines with bad technology simply wasn't possible just because the order was issued. A system of checks and balances could have allowed experienced engineers to veto bad plans and suggest alternatives that would have solved that matter quicker and more cheaply.

Halliburton/KBR officials wave away these allegations of fraud and abuse as either inaccurate or the normal cost of doing business. When I brought the allegations of waste, fraud, and abuse up with David Lesar, Halliburton CEO, at the company's annual meeting in 2006 and asked him what he had to say about the canceled contracts and overcharges, he replied: "I've been to Iraq a number of times, and it's a tough place to do work. I'm proud of our folks there and . . . we will continue to support the troops. I think we're just going to respectfully disagree with each other on the rest of your comments."[20]

Cerjan freely admits that the company has employed bad apples who have since been convicted of fraud. "When you have a contract this size, I don't care what company you are, you still run the same potential when you run a contingency. We need to do it fast. You'll run that potential. And by the way, this is the Mideast, and part of it is cultural also, . . ." Paul Cerjan told *Frontline*. "But I think when you start taking a look at the fact that we have been accused of overcharging for food, okay—when the military moved forward, the government said to us, 'Prepare to feed at locations five thousand at a meal.' If three thousand showed up, we're still prepared or bought food for five thousand. The government came back with the audit agency and said, 'No, you pay for boots through the door.' Now, you as a civilian, if you had a daughter and you married that daughter off, and you'd hired a catering hall and hired it for five hundred people and only 450 showed up, how many would you pay for? . . . So the bottom line is, when you're told in a contingency operation, 'Be prepared,' you're prepared. You're not going to turn away a brigade at the door because you plan only for thirty-five hundred and they brought five thousand through the door when they told you to prepare for five thousand."

"Do I think that we ought to be audited? Absolutely. I don't have any problem with that at all. None whatsoever," said Cerjan. "The only thing we can do is stand up and give a true and honest evaluation of what we've done, show the documentation and why we arrived at those conclusions, and let whoever is making the assessment make the assessment. We are not afraid of that process. We are not afraid of that process at all. I welcome it because I'm a taxpayer, too, and one thing I try to be constantly on the lookout for is fraud, waste, and abuse."[21]

A LACK OF QUALIFIED PROFESSIONALS

Whether the fraud is incidental, as Halliburton/KBR claims, or pervasive as Henry Waxman alleges, why did it occur? Well, most soldiers and contractors went to Iraq simply because they needed money. While initially many soldiers who were sent overseas joined the military for the many reasons that people have always signed up: the idea of serving their country, the thrill of handling weapons or simply the opportunity to get a college scholarship; the realities of suicide bombing have whittled down the volunteers to those who have few other career choices.

And the same goes for contractors; few qualified managers and engineers are willing to work in Iraq, apart from the early days after the invasion when Iraq was seen as an exciting place to be. A Republican staffer who spent considerable time in Iraq once told me: "Do you know what every American contractor I have ever met in the Green Zone shares? A broken marriage." While his statement was a bit of a generalization, it was true: hardship at home was what made most people sign up to work for Halliburton/KBR—mortgages, college debt, absent spouses and empty nests. Those with good jobs and career prospects in the U.S. did not sign up.

"The top LOGCAP managers were crying for people," a former Halliburton/KBR executive in Iraq told *Fortune.* "Two or three times a day we would call, asking for procurement people, IT help, finance people to keep the books. Houston couldn't get them to us. The company did not throw enough resources at the problem soon enough. There comes a point where you lose control. People started talking shortcuts—'We'll do it verbally, and we'll document tomorrow.' Well, tomorrow you have more work."[22]

But paying higher salaries did not ensure that the company got the best people or the best results. After all, unqualified professionals will work for higher pay and even the most qualified personnel can be tempted to cheat if vast amounts of money are left lying around unsupervised.

Yet the idea persists that a workforce from the private sector would perform miracles that the government bureaucracy could not. Is it even possible that the highly experienced retired military managers who run Halliburton/KBR would be able to do what they could not do when they were in the army? Laszlo Tibold once told me: "If the military can't do it, how do you think we can? They make the rules and they can break them if they want. We are bound by our contracts in addition to having to comply with the military rules which makes it that much harder."

LABOR EXPLOITATION

One major argument that military officials make is that outsourcing should be cheaper—and it rings true. "[It's] not immediately evident to somebody listening to you because they're going to see that a truck driver, for instance, who is brought over here from the States [is] paid much more than anybody who was driving a truck for the armed services in the past was getting. How is it cheaper?" says Cerjan. "Because we increased the number of soldiers who can go out on patrol. And when you look at the cost of that soldier and a lifecycle environment, the dollars just show up. It's more cost-effective to outsource some of those activities, those functions, outside of the military. I didn't do the numbers, but I'm telling you, it's cheaper. You're paying some people more money. You're talking about expatriates who come over here. There's an American truck driver who gets more money, but you don't take into account the third-country nationals we hired at less wage because they can come over here and do it cheaper."

Titoko Savuwati, the Fijian truck driver in Kuwait, who lives basically from paycheck to paycheck, sending the bulk of his earnings back to his family in Totoya Lau, can testify to the fact that the Halliburton/KBR and PWC are saving a bundle. When I last saw Savuwati in the spring of 2008, PWC had suspended him from driving into Iraq for no apparent reason, although he guessed it was probably because of his injured foot, so his modest hazard bonus of KWD 50 (US$183) has disappeared. Making matters worse, he says that the company failed to pay him for the several months that he was in Kuwait. His bank balance was zero.[23]

Savuwati is just one of dozens of Fijian truck drivers who claim that PWC often shortchanges them on their meager monthly salaries of KWD 175 (US$640). They have clubbed together and pooled their money to hire a local lawyer—Abdul Majeed Khuraibet, a former Kuwaiti police officer, whose office is on the sixth floor of the Al-Saleh building, opposite the Maghreb mosque in the heart of Kuwait city—to fight on their behalf. The problem is that they never bothered to keep their pay stubs, so their claims are hard to document.

"Why do these companies cheat these men?" Majeed asked me, when I interviewed him about their prospects. "They do all their dirty work and they cannot even go home."[24]

The answer is simple: The low salaries and lack of benefits for migrant workers is one of the principal ways that Halliburton/KBR generates profits and the Pentagon and U.S. taxpayer save money. The salaries are not the only way that the Pentagon is saving money compared to previous wars; it no longer has to recruit new soldiers, pay for training (which exceeds $100,000), or pay for the benefits package that soldiers expect when they leave the military for things like college tuition, healthcare, and pensions, a package which generally adds up to tens of thousands of dollars per soldier. In extreme cases disability may be as high as $5 million.

The U.S. citizens who work as truckers and supervisors are much better off than Savuwati and are paid salaries that are much higher than the average U.S soldier, but even they do not run up training costs or veteran benefits. Even if they worked for four years straight in Iraq, which is rare, they would still cost the taxpayer less than an ordinary recruit.

I asked the commanders I met at LSA Anaconda in Iraq and Camp Arifjan if they were worried about the low wages and lack of human rights for workers. The answer was almost always a shrug. When I brought up the many examples of petty fraud and waste, they were only mildly worried, but they pointed out that most of the examples I was citing dated back to 2004, which they claim to have resolved today.

Ultimately, several senior military officers told me, their duty was to "defeat the bad guys" and help liberate Iraq and everything else was incidental. Young soldiers paid just as little attention to the men and women that supported them. On my last day at LSA Anaconda, in April 2008, I asked a young California National Guardsman whether he thought Iraqis supported the U.S. troops. "Yes, of course," he said. "All the Iraqis on the base are very happy." I asked him where he met Iraqis inside the wire. "The men who cook the food and clean the floors. They seem happy," he told me. I was puzzled for a moment, and then I realized who he was talking about: the Halliburton/KBR workers from South and Southeast Asia who cooked and cleaned for him while he was out on patrol.[25]

What is perhaps more disturbing is that the labor practices in Iraq are now becoming commonplace on domestic U.S. military bases. In late October 2005, federal immigration officials conducted two surprise raids at Belle Chasse Naval Base near New Orleans and processed fourteen undocumented people who worked for Halliburton/KBR subcontractors doing Hurricane Katrina reconstruction.[26]

The National Committee of La Raza (NCLR) also found multiple abuses by Halliburton subcontractors. On November 18, 2005, NCLR staff visited a "tent city" of Latino workers in Gulfport. They reported, "Workers repeatedly complained about contractors who hired them for long periods of time and then refused to pay them for their labor. For example, Esteban J., a Mexican worker who left behind a wife and four children in Veracruz, Mexico, was recruited in North Carolina by a subcontractor hired by Halliburton/KBR to perform debris removal with 105 other workers.

"The subcontractor promised an hourly wage of $13, along with food, lodging, and overtime pay; yet, after several weeks, the subcontractor had not paid any of them, and many of the men were forced to sleep outside. After making several demands, Esteban was finally paid a week's worth of wages with little for him to send back home to his family," reported NCLR. Esteban estimated that the contractor owed him two hundred hours worth of wages and consequently filed a wage-and-hour claim with the Department of Labor. The agency ruled favorably in the case and ordered Halliburton/KBR to pay $141,887 in back wages to Esteban and his fellow workers.[27]

At the KBR annual meeting in April 2008 at the Houstonian hotel in Texas, I asked William Utt, the KBR CEO, why his company paid his South and Southeast Asian workers so badly and what they intended to do about the trafficking allegations. "We react to all those inquiries very quickly, very thoughtfully," said Utt. "They do concern us when an employee feels their rights have been violated, and we take the appropriate action with immediate investigation. But we pay world-scale wages."[28]

ST. MICHAEL'S, MARYLAND

I began this book with the stories of Dick Cheney and Donald Rumsfeld, the two men who created Halliburton's Army of migrant labor and forged the revolution in military affairs to allow the United States to pursue its Global War on Terror. While these two men have been outspoken on "defeating terrorism," neither of them have chosen to say a word about the company in the last several years, and it may fall to the next generation of politicians, in 2009, to hold them accountable for the waste, fraud, and abuse, including human right abuses, in executing this war. Should one want to track them down, they will probably be found in the quiet resort town of St. Michaels, on Chesapeake Bay, in Maryland, just about an hour's drive from Washington, DC.

There, in late 2005, Cheney sat down to a lamb dinner, along with Donald Rumsfeld and their wives, at a high-end restaurant named Talbot. They dined just as they had when they first vacationed together in Eleuthera in January 1977, away from the pop of media flashbulbs.[29] High on the list of subjects on both occasions were their plans for the future, after they would leave the world of politics behind.

The vice president wanted to buy Ballintober, a nine-acre lot that includes extensive gardens, ornamental pools, and spectacular views from a large, glass-walled waterside room.[30] Most importantly it adjoined Rumsfeld's $1.5 million retreat on the bay, a former bed-and-breakfast that had been named Mount Misery and was built by Edward Covey—a notorious slave owner who beat up the abolitionist Frederick Douglass.[31] Cheney eventually paid $2.6 million for his property.

Today, the two men are often spotted in St. Michael's: Cheney cruises around in a convoy of black SUVs shopping for shotgun shells at Albright's Gun Shop to go duck hunting, while Rumsfeld buys ice cream at Justine's and drives around in a Volkswagen Jetta.[32]

Houston, We Have a Problem

One of the thorniest problems Halliburton/KBR has had to face has been unruly protests of antiwar activists, particularly in its hometown of Houston. In May 2004, across the street from the Four Seasons Hotel in downtown Houston where company executives were scheduled to meet for the shareholders' annual general meeting, some three hundred protestors showed up with a twenty-five-foot inflatable pig, arranged by a group from San Francisco named the Ronald Reagan Home for the Criminally Insane. Jazz music played, and local activists dressed up with

George Bush and Dick Cheney masks and were offering fake one hundred dollar bills to everybody. Among them was Bob Buzzanco, a history professor from the University of Houston, who was dressed up as a "Billionaire for Bush."[33]

Another group of protestors led by Jodie Evans of Code Pink booked themselves into a suite on the top floor of the hotel and dropped a ten-by-thirty-foot pink banner out of the window, just as the meeting was to begin, that read, "Cheney's in bed with Halliburton, but we got screwed." Another group of five attempted to blockade the meeting by shackling themselves to brass banisters in front of the security checkpoint on the third floor, while chanting, "Halliburton, Kellogg, Brown, and Root—go to Iraq to loot, loot, loot." They also shouted, "Oil is not worth human blood!" and then squirted fake blood on themselves that was made out of corn syrup and red dye. Angry police officers used bolt cutters to remove their handcuffs and arrested them.[34]

The protests were organized by a group called the Houston Global Awareness Collective (HGAC) and were led by Scott Parkin, a local activist, who continued to put together protests against the company. For months his group of half-a-dozen activists regularly showed up outside the Houston headquarters of the company, handing out leaflets to Halliburton/KBR employees as they left work.[35]

The protests continued at the shareholder annual general meeting the following year. Instead of a giant pig, a local carpenter named David Graeve built a twenty-foot wooden cow with cash-filled udders. Also at the protest were a corporate crime-fighting dog, a Dick Cheney flasher with an oil rig and two oil cans as his private parts, and Code Pink women in pink shrouds with the names of dead Iraqis.

Once again, a dozen protesters who had rented a hotel room spewed into the lobby and the entrance to the meeting itself, shouting "No War for Profits," "Stop War Profiteers," and "Halliburton Cooks the Books." Eleven protesters were dragged out of the hotel and arrested after refusing to move. "We are engaging in civil disobedience to demand justice for Halliburton workers who have been injured and killed in Iraq, and for the American people, who have been defrauded and fleeced by the company's greedy overcharging on their no bid contracts," said Maureen Haver of HGAC who was among those arrested.[36]

In 2006, Halliburton decided to move its annual meeting to a quieter locale. Instead of the Four Seasons Hotel, they decided to move it to the town where Erle Halliburton first set up the company—Duncan, Oklahoma—and invited local employees to the meeting. To little avail, a group of protestors drove up from Houston, and others came from Dallas, on a gaily painted, antiwar bus and camped out in a local park.[37]

More than one hundred demonstrators set up outside the meeting, where they strummed guitars, chanted "No war for oil," and carried banners questioning Halliburton's billing practices in Iraq and its human rights track record. Sixteen of the protesters were arrested when they rushed a plastic fence perimeter in an attempt to get inside the meeting to question executives.[38]

In 2007, Halliburton moved its meeting back to Houston but decided not to hold it in downtown. Instead it booked a basement conference room at the privately owned Woodlands Resort and Conference Center about twenty-five miles north of the city center. HGAC and the Ronald Reagan Home for the Criminally Insane continued their merry pranks outside the meeting but toned down the angry messages. Instead they threw a farewell party for the CEO David Lesar. Wearing red party hats and blaring the song "Take the Money and Run," some two dozen protestors partied on the grassy median just outside the resort, while bemused police officers looked on, unsure what to do with this change in tactics.[39]

In 2008 the protest numbers dwindled further. This time the company held its annual meeting at the Houstonian Hotel. About five protestors held signs outside while David Graeve attended the meeting as a proxy shareholder where he read a statement on behalf of the KBR rape victims.

NOTES

Introduction

1. Tim Sander, "VP Cheney Makes Surprise Visit to Troops at LSAA," *Anaconda Times* (U.S. Army newspaper), March 26, 2008.

2. Base details are derived from author visit to LSA Anaconda in April 2008—two weeks after the Cheney delegation had departed. Additional details from Global Security Web site, http://www.globalsecurity.org/military/world/iraq/balad-ab.htm, was accessed on September 20, 2008.

3. "Vice President Cheney's Remarks in Rally with Troops," White House press release, March 18, 2008.

4. Breakfast details derived from photos by Julianne Showalter and video footage from Multi-National Corps Iraq Public Affairs, LSA Anaconda.

5. "Cheney Makes First Trip to Iraq's Kurdish Region," Associated Press, March 18, 2008.

6. Deb Riechmann, "Cheney's on the Road: Pack Diet Sprite, Switch on Fox News," Associated Press, March 31, 2008.

7. Rick Atkinson, *The Day of Battle* (Henry Holt and Co., October 2007).

8. "Halliburton KBR Wins Logistics Civil Augmentation Contract from U.S. Army," Halliburton press release, December 17, 2001.

9. "KBR Awarded Logistics Civil Augmentation (LOGCAP) IV Contract from U.S. Army," KBR Press Release, April 18, 2008. Revenue numbers were derived from Halliburton Annual report in 2005 and 2006 and the KBR Annual Report in 2006 and 2007.

10. Molly Moore, "U.S. Boosting Efforts to Draw Kurds Into Iraq; Cheney Says Security Zones Focus of Plan," *Washington Post*, May 7, 1991.

11. "Feeding the Troops," *Los Angeles Times*, February 19, 1991; "Pentagon; Chow; Approval," *Newsday*, February 20, 1991.

12. Alfredo Jimenez, Jr., "A Taste of History," *Freedom Watch* (U.S. Army newspaper), November 29, 2002.

13. Estimates of the precise number of contractors in the 1991 Persian Gulf War vary, depending on definitions. The generally accepted number is one contractor for every one hundred soldiers. A good guide to the role of contractors in the 1991 Persian Gulf War is John A. Brinkerhoff, "External Support for the Army in the Persian

Gulf War," Institute for Defense Analysis, November 1997. Current numbers are also somewhat vague, but the generally accepted one-to-one ratio is cited in a blue-ribbon commission report requested by Secretary of the Army Pete Geren. Jacques Gansler, et al., "Urgent Reform Required: Report of the Commission on Army Acquisition and Program Management in Expeditionary Operations," report from a blue ribbon panel, October 31, 2007.

14. Michael R. Gordon, "The 1991 Budget: Armed Forces; Cheney Would Cut Divisions in Army But Maintain B-2," *New York Times*, January 30, 1990.

15. Jeffrey L. Rodengen, "Legend of Halliburton," Write Stuff Enterprises, December 1996.

16. "DOD Acquisition and Logistics Excellence Week Kickoff-Bureaucracy to Battlefield," remarks as delivered by Secretary of Defense Donald H. Rumsfeld, the Pentagon, Monday, September 10, 2001.

17. Author interviews in March and April 2008.

18. Garrison History & About Us, U.S. Army Rock Island Arsenal. See http://www.ria.army.mil/, accessed on September 20, 2008. J. B. Patterson, editor, and Antoine LeClair, interpreter, *The Autobiography of Black Hawk* (Oquawka, Illinois, 1833).

19. Ann McGlynn, "Judge Rules Mistrial in Federal Fraud Case," *Quad City Times*, April 30, 2008. Biography of Joe Billy McDade available at Judges of the United States courts Web site. See http://www.fjc.gov/servlet/tGetInfo?jid=1540.

20. "Former KBR Employee and Subcontractor Charged With $3.5 million Government Contract Fraud in Kuwait," Department of Justice press release, March 17, 2005.

21. Ann McGlynn, "Iraq Fraud Case Goes to Jury," *Quad City Times*, April 29, 2008.

22. David Jackson and Jason Grotto, "Inside the World of War Profiteers: From Prostitutes to Super Bowl Tickets, a Federal Probe Reveals How Contractors in Iraq Cheated the U.S." *Chicago Tribune*, February 21, 2008.

23. Testimony of Robert Gatlin, court transcript, U.S. District Court, Central District of Illinois, April 15, 2008.

Chapter 1

1. Author visit to LSA Anaconda, April 2008.

2. Sandra Jontz, "Getting Americans into the Skies and Away from Iraq's Dangerous Roadways," *Stars and Stripes*, April 24, 2005. Steven J. Schneider, "'Catfish Air' Provides Space-A Travel in Iraq," U.S. Army News Service, November 16, 2004. Judith DaCosta, "Catfish Air Gets a PAX Terminal Facelift," *Anaconda Times*, June 4, 2006.

3. Robert Hodierne, "Rhinos Offer Safety on Dangerous Highway," *Army Times*, May 30, 2005. See also blog item by Christian Lowe, "Road of Death's Bad-Ass Bus," at http://www.defensetech.org/archives/001612.html, accessed September 20, 2008.

4. Ibid.

5. Author visit to Baghdad Victory Complex, April 2008.

6. Author visit to LSA Anaconda, April 2008.

7. Sarah Stillman, "Bloated in Baghdad," TruthDig, http://www.truthdig.com, accessed April 28, 2008.

8. Author visit to U.S. military base in Kuwait, April 2008.

9. Author visit to LSA Anaconda, April 2008.

10. "Logistics Civil Augmentation Program Overview," from http://www.army reserve.army.mil/USARC/OPS/USARRC/LSU-LOGCAP/default.htm. See also "About Us" at Army Materiel Command Web site, http://www.amc.army.mil/pa/about.asp, and LOGCAP article at Global Security Web site, http://www.globalsecurity.org/military/agency/army/logcap.htm, accessed September 20, 2008.

11. Pat Royse, "Crystal Underground Opens," *Washington Post*, Sept. 30, 1976. See also "About Us," Smith Managament Construction, Inc., http://smconst.com/subframes/about.htm, accessed September 20, 2008.

12. "About Crystal City," from http://www.commuterpage.com/art/villages/crystalcity2.htm. See also "Crystal City Business Improvement District," http://www.crystalcity.org/default.asp?PageId=2, and http://crystalcity.com/, accessed September 20, 2008.

13. Tim Mazzucca, "Halliburton's KBR Leases 125K s.f. in Crystal City," *Washington Business Journal*, August 26, 2005.

14. *Frontline* interview with Paul Cerjan, "Camp Victory in Iraq," on April 13, 2005.

15. Author interview, April 2008.

16. Fox TV report by Gregg Kelly, April 27, 2005. See "Fox News Produces Video Valentine for Halliburton," Halliburton Watch, http://www.halliburtonwatch.org/news/fox.html, April 27, 2005, accessed September 20, 2008.

17. E-mail from KBR worker to author, September 6, 2005.

Chapter 2

1. Biography of Lyndon B. Johnson, White House Web site, http://www.white house.gov/history/presidents/lj36.html, accessed September 20, 2008. The best histories of Johnson are Robert A. Caro's three-volume biography *The Years of Lyndon Johnson*, which include *The Path to Power* (New York: Knopf, 1982), *Means of Ascent* (New York: Knopf, 1990), and *Master of the Senate* (New York: Knopf, 2002).

2. Caro, *The Path to Power*, op. cit.

3. Transcript of Lady Bird Johnson interview with Christopher Castaneda, November 15, 1990. Located in Oral History of George and Herman Brown collection, Woodson Research Center, Rice University.

4. Caro, *The Path to Power*, op. cit.

5. Dan Briody, *The Halliburton Agenda* (New York: John Wiley & Sons, 2004).

6. Hal K. Rothman, *LBJ's Texas White House* (College Station, TX: Texas A&M University Press, 2001).

7. Ronnie Dugger, *The Politician: The Life and Times of Lyndon Johnson* (New York: W. W. Norton, May 1984). Ronnie Dugger, "The Texafication of the USA," *Texas Observer*, December 3, 2004.

8. Briody, op. cit. See also Fran Dressman, *Gus Wortham: Portrait of a Leader* (College Station, TX: Texas A&M University Press, 1994). Robert Bryce, *Cronies: Oil, the Bushes, and the Rise of Texas, America's Superstate* (New York: Public Affairs, 2004).

9. Rodengen, op. cit.

10. Briody, op. cit.

11. Caro, *The Path to Power*, op. cit. 2007, value calculated at http://www .measuringworth.com/calculators/uscompare/ September 20, 2008.

12. Transcript of George R. Brown interview with Michael L. Gillette, July 11, 1977, Lyndon B. Johnson Library, Austin, Texas

13. Briody, op. cit.; Rodengen, op. cit.

14. Caro, *The Path to Power*, op. cit.

15. George R. Brown letter to Lyndon B. Johnson, May 2, 1939, Lyndon B. Johnson Library, Austin, Texas.

16. George R. Brown letter to Lyndon B. Johnson, October 27, 1939, Lyndon B. Johnson Library, Austin, Texas.

17. Lyndon B. Johnson letter to George R. Brown, February 27, 1940, Lyndon B. Johnson Library, Austin, Texas.

18. Caro, *The Path to Power*, op. cit.

19. Briody, op. cit.

20. Joseph A. Pratt and Christopher J. Castaneda, *Builders: Herman and George R. Brown* (College Station, TX: Texas A&M University Press, 1999).

21. Joseph A. Pratt and Christopher J. Castaneda, *From Texas to the East: A Strategic History of Texas Eastern Corporation* (College Station, TX: Texas A&M University Press, 1993).

22. William Lambert and Keith Wheeler, "The Man Who Is the President," *Life*, August 21, 1964.

23. Caro, *The Path to Power*, op. cit.

24. Briody, op. cit.

25. Drew Pearson, "The Washington Merry-Go-Round," *Washington Post*, March 26, 27, and 28, 1956.

26. Robert Bryce, "The Candidate from Brown and Root," *Texas Observer*, October 6, 2000.

27. Caro, *Means of Ascent*, op. cit.

28. Ed Clark interview with Christopher Castaneda, August 15, 1990. Located in Oral History of George and Herman Brown collection, Woodson Research Center, Rice University.

29. Caro, *Master of the Senate*, op. cit.

30. Rodengen, op. cit.

31. History of Halliburton Services, undated manuscript from Halliburton Archives. Cited in Rodengen, op. cit.

32. "A Quarter Century of Progress," *The Cementer* (Halliburton internal magazine), July–August 1949.

33. Halliburton company Research Library documents: Rex Hudson, "A Brief History of Halliburton Services"; Earl Babcock, "The Good Old Days at Halliburton"; J. Evetts Haley, "Erle P. Halliburton: Genius With Cement," 1959. Rodengen, op. cit.

34. History of Halliburton Services, cited in Rodengen, op. cit.

35. Ibid.

36. *Duncan Daily Banner*, October 14, 1957. cited in Rodengen, op. cit.

37. Rodengen, op. cit.

38. Pratt and Castaneda, op. cit.

39. Pratt and Castaneda, op. cit.

Chapter 3

1. The description of the Congressional delegation is derived from an interview with one of the participants—former Congressman David S. King—conducted by the author in May 2005. Many specific details were obtained from the schedule and itinerary prepared for Foreign Operations and Government Information Subcommittee, House Committee on Government Operations located in the papers of David S. King, University of Utah libraries.

2. Leo Rennert, "Obituary: John E. Moss," *Sacramento Bee*, December 6, 1997.

3. Biography of Secretary of Defense Donald Rumsfeld, http://www.white house.gov/government/rumsfeld-bio.html, accessed September 20, 2008.[i] "An Investigation of the U.S. Economic and Military Assistance Programs in Vietnam," Report from the Committee on Government Operations, House of Representatives report number 2257, 1966.

4. "Cam Ranh Bay," *Encyclopædia Britannica* (Chicago: Britannica, 2008).

5. Detailed daily descriptions of what work was done each day were recorded by A. H. Lahlum, in *Diary of a Contract*, July 1967, Washington Group International corporate archives. See also James Carter, *Inventing Vietnam* (New York: Cambridge University Press, 2008).

6. "Viet Nam: Building for Battle, Building for Peace," *Em-Kayan* (RMK-BRJ internal magazine), September 1966. Lahlum, op. cit.

7. Cheng Guan Ang, *The Vietnam War from the Other Side* (New York: Routledge, 2002).

8. John F. Kennedy Inaugural Address, January 20, 1961.

9. Lyndon B. Johnson biography at the Lyndon B. Johnson library Web site, http://www.lbjlib.utexas.edu/johnson/archives.hom/biographys.hom/lbj_bio.asp #1960, accessed September 20, 2008.

10. Lahlum, op. cit.

11. A detailed chronology of Gulf of Tonkin incident can be found on the National Security Archive Web site together with redacted transcripts of the actual radio conversations. See http://www.nsa.gov/vietnam/, accessed September 20, 2008. See also Lyndon B. Johnson biography. op. cit.

12. Southeast Asia Resolution, Public Law 88-408, August 10, 1964. See also Lyndon B. Johnson's message to the U.S. Congress, August 5, 1964.

13. The tapes can be listened to at the Web site of the Presidential Recordings Program of the Miller Center of Public Affairs at the University of Virginia http://tapes.millercenter.virginia.edu/exhibits/tonkin/. Michael R. Beschloss, *Reaching for Glory: Lyndon Johnson's Secret White House Tapes, 1964–1965* (New York: Simon & Schuster, 2002).

14. "Colin Powell on Iraq, Race, and Hurricane Relief," *ABC News*, September 8, 2005.

15. John Morocco, *Thunder from Above* (New York: Time Life Education, 1984).

16. Hearings before the Committee on Armed Services and the Subcommittee on Department of Defense of the Committee on Appropriations, United States Senate, 89th Congress, 2nd Session, January–February 1966.

17. Carter, op. cit. See also James M. Carter, "The Vietnam Builders: Private Contractors, Military Construction and the 'Americanization' of United States Involvement in Vietnam," *Graduate Journal of Asia-Pacific Studies*, November 2004.

18. Paul D. Harder, "Vietnam Paradox of Construction and Destruction," *Power Parade*, Volume 20, Number 2, 1967.

19. "Construction of Military Facilities Br RMK-BRJ Is Changing the Face of South Vietnam," *The Em-Kayan*, August 1966. "Subject: Impressive Achievements in South Vietnam," *The Em-Kayan*, December 1966.

20. Supplemental Agreement Number 3 to Contract NBy44105, May 25, 1966, RMK-BRJ Papers.

21. Eric Wentworth, "Plan to Help Vietnam Feed Self Fails," *Washington Post*, January 21, 1967. Samuel Huntington, "Political Stability and Security in South Vietnam," December 1967 (study prepared for the Policy Planning Council, U.S. Department of State). Marylyn Young, *The Vietnam Wars* (New York: HarperCollins, 1991).

22. "Civilian Casualty, Social Welfare, and Refugee Problems in South Vietnam," Hearings before the Subcommittee on Refugees and Escapees, Senate Judiciary Committee, May 10–October 16, 1967.

23. "Investigation of the U.S. Economic and Military Assistance Programs in Vietnam" op. cit.

24. The Carter calculation was based on the supplemental bill on "Military Procurement and Construction Authorizations" for 1966 and a publication titled "U.S. Apparatus of Assistance to Refugees Throughout the World," Hearings before the Subcommittee to Investigate Problems Connected with Refugees and Escapees, Senate Judiciary Committee, 2nd Session of the 89th session of Congress, 1966.

25. Congressional Record, August 30, 1966.

26. William V. Shanon, "The President's Club Is Too Clubby, Says the G.O.P.," *New York Times*, September 4, 1966.

27. "Investigation of the U.S. Economic and Military Assistance Programs in Vietnam," op. cit.

28. Pratt and Castaneda, op. cit.

29. Descriptions of Rumsfeld's early life are derived from Midge Decter, *Rumsfeld* (New York: ReganBooks, 2003); Rowan Scarborough, *Rumsfeld's War* (Washington,

DC: Regnery Publishing, 2004); and Jeffrey A. Krames, *The Rumsfeld Way* (New York: McGraw Hill, 2002).

30. Ibid.

31. Ben McGrath, "Rummy Meets His Match," *New Yorker*, April 14, 2003.

32. Ibid.

33. David Hiller, "Rumsfeld Was My Squash Partner," *Los Angeles Times*, November 12, 2006.

34. David S. Cloud, "Rumsfeld Also Plays Hardball on Pentagon's Squash Courts," *New York Times*, September 24, 2006.

35. Jacob Heilbrunn, "Hawk on the Wing," *Los Angeles Times*, October 5, 2003.

36. The best and most-detailed biography of Cheney is by Stephen Hayes, *Cheney* (New York: Harper Collins, 2007). Hayes reconstructed Cheney's time at Yale by interviewing his friends: Dennis Landa, Jim Little, Rees Jones, Ned Mason, and Peter Cressy.

37. Copies of the arrests can be seen at http://www.thesmokinggun.com/archive/cheneydwi1.html and http://www.thesmokinggun.com/archive/cheneydwi2.html, accessed September 20, 2008.

38. Katharine Q. Seelye, "Cheney's Five Draft Deferments During the Vietnam Era Emerge as a Campaign Issue," *New York Times*, May 1, 2004.

39. Dick Cheney speech, "Government Must Help Business Flourish," *American Business and the Quest for Freedom, Ethics and Public Policy* Essay 62, (Ethics and Public Policy Institute publication) 1986.

40. James Mann interview with David Gribben, December 17, 2001. Cited in James Mann, *The Rise of the Vulcans* (New York: Penguin, 2004).

41. The meeting is described in detail by Stephen Hayes who interviewed both Rumsfeld and Cheney, op. cit.

42. John Nichols, *Dick: The Man Who Is President* (New York: The New Press, 2004).

43. "The Steel Seizure Case of 1952 and Its Effects on Presidential Powers," Donald Rumsfeld senior thesis, Yale 1954.

44. Stephen Hayes interview with Donald Rumsfeld, June 1, 2006. Cited in Hayes, op. cit.

45. Stephen Hayes interview with Richard Cheney, April 27, 2006. Cited in Hayes, op. cit.

46. Hayes, op. cit.

47. Hayes, op. cit.

48. Stephen Hayes interview with Richard Cheney, August 31, 2005. Cited in Hayes, op. cit.

49. Aaron Latham, "The Sunday Morning Massacre, A Murder-Suicide?" *New York Times*, December 22, 1976. Stephen Hayes interview with Richard Cheney, April 27, 2006. Cited in Hayes, op. cit.

50. Interview with Richard Cheney, "Face the Nation," *CBS News*, January 4, 1976.

51. Stephen Hayes interview with Richard Cheney, August 9, 2006. Cited in Hayes, op. cit. Island details from Darwin Porter, *Caribbean For Dummies* (New York: John Wiley & Sons, 2006).

52. Pentagon biography of Richard B. Cheney posted at http://www.defense link.mil/specials/secdef_histories/bios/cheney.htm, accessed September 20, 2008.

53. Alison Mitchell, "Voting Record Dogs Cheney as G.O.P. Team Campaigns," *New York Times*, July 27, 2000,

54. Joseph E. McCann, "Sweet Success: How NutraSweet Created a Billion Dollar Business," *Irwin Professional*, 1990. See also Decter, op. cit. Scarborough, op. cit. and Krames, op. cit.

55. Thomas C. Hayes, "Searle's Enriching Sweetener," *New York Times*, July 17, 1981.

56. *Food Chemical News*, June 12, 1995. "Aspartame Alert," *Flying Safety*, U.S. Air Force 1992. See also Barbara A. Mullarkey, "Bittersweet Aspartame: A Diet Delusion," *Health Watch Book*, 1992.

57. Andrew Cockburn, *Rumsfeld: His Rise, Fall, and Catastrophic Legacy* (New York: Scribner, 2007). See also Decter, op. cit., Scarborough, op. cit., and Krames, op. cit.

58. Richard Cheney remarks at Pentagon briefing on January 29, 1990.

59. Stephen Hayes interview with Richard Cheney, August 9, 2006. Cited in Hayes, op. cit.

60. Jane Mayer, "Contract Sport," *New Yorker*, February 10, 2004.

61. Robert Bryce, "Cheney's Multimillion Dollar Revolving Door," *Mother Jones*, August 2, 2000.

62. Colin Powell, *My American Journey* (New York: Ballantine Books, 1996).

63. Josh Getlin and Scot J. Paltrow, "Paper Blizzard Welcome Gulf Troops in N.Y.," *Los Angeles Times*, June 11, 1991. Robert D. McFadden, "As Operation Get Ready Comes to an End, Operation Welcome Home Begins," *New York Times*, June 9, 1991.

64. Stephen Hayes interview with Richard Cheney, August 31, 2005. Cited in Hayes, op. cit.

65. Nicholas Lemann, "The Quiet Man," *New Yorker*, 2001.

66. Stephen Hayes interview with Thomas Cruikshank, December 4, 2006. Cited in Hayes, op. cit.

67. Stephen Hayes interview with Richard Cheney, August 22, 2006. Cited in Hayes, op. cit.

Chapter 4

1. Author visit, May 2004.

2. Details of the purchase can be seen in Stephen E. Jones, Linda D. Lydia, and Caroline Franco vs. Governor George W. Bush and Richard B. Cheney, Civil Action Number: 300CV2534D. A copy is located at http://election2000.stanford.edu/jones-v-bush.pdf, accessed September 20, 2008.

3. Author visit, May 2004.

4. Marego Athans and Ann LoLordo, "Cheney profited richly from his time in office: His D.C. connections served business well," *Baltimore Sun*, August 16, 2000.

5. Sanctions were imposed by the U.S. on Azerbaijan in 1992, under the "Freedom Support Act" (Public Law 102-511).

6. Remarks by Richard Cheney delivered at "Azerbaijan: From Communism Towards Democracy and Oil," conference held at U.S.-Azerbaijan Chamber of Commerce, February 18, 1997.

7. Lawrence F. Kaplan, "From Russia with Loans," *New Republic*, August 7, 2000.

8. "Defending Liberty in a Global Economy," remarks by Richard Cheney, delivered at the Collateral Damage Conference, Cato Institute, June 23, 1998.

9. National Energy Policy (NEP) paper, May 17, 2001. Available at http://www.energy.gov/about/nationalenergypolicy.htm, accessed September 20, 2008. See also Michael Abramowitz and Steven Mufson, "Papers Detail Industry's Role in Cheney's Energy Report," *Washington Post*, July 18, 2007.

10. Transcript of press conference held by Steven Mann, special advisor to the secretary of state on Caspian Energy Diplomacy, United States Embassy, Baku, Azerbaijan, June 6, 2001.

11. "Bush Lifts Azerbaijan Sanctions," *Oil Daily*, January 31, 2002.

12. "Cheney Asks about Aliyev's Health," Interfax News Agency, February 22, 2002.

13. Andrei Sitov, "US-Azerbaijan meeting held in warm, cordial atmosphere," *Tass*, February 27, 2003.

14. "Human Rights on the Line: The Baku-Tbilisi-Ceyhan (BTC) Pipeline Project," Amnesty International, May 20, 2003. "Some Common Concerns: Imagining BP's Azerbaijan-Georgia-Turkey Pipelines System," published by Campagna per la Riforma della Banca Mondiale, CEE Bankwatch Network, The Corner House, Friends of the Earth International, The Kurdish Human Rights Project, and PLATFORM. Final project approval details can be seen at http://www.ifc.org/btc, accessed September 20, 2008.

15. "US, Azerbaijan signed bilateral agreement for immunity from the ICC," *Tass*, February 27, 2003.

16. Aram Roston, "The Cheney Loyalty Test," *Mother Jones*, March–April, 2003. Knut Royce and Nathaniel Heller, "Cheney Led Halliburton to Feast at Federal Trough," Center for Public Integrity, August 2, 2000.

17. Rostom, op. cit.

18. "Azerbaijan: From Communism Towards Democracy and Oil," speech, op. cit.

19. Richard Cheney interview with Nine Network's Business Sunday, April 19, 1998. Daniel Morrissey, "BHP Should Be Allowed in Iran, Says Dick Cheney," Australian Associated Press, April 19, 1998.

20. Halliburton Oil Well Cementing Company Annual Report, 1957, Cited in Rodengen, op. cit.

21. Richard Cheney interview with "This Week," *ABC News*, July 30, 2000.

22. "Doing Business With the Enemy," CBS *60 Minutes*, January 25, 2004. The report can be seen at http://www.cbsnews.com/stories/2004/01/22/60minutes/main 595214.shtml.

23. Peter Wallsten and T. Christian Miller, "Grand Jury Steps Up Inquiry into Possible Halliburton Ties to Iran," *Los Angeles Times*, July 21, 2004.

24. "Halliburton completes oil field projects in Iran," Associated Press, April 10, 2007.

25. "Chevron Awards $200 Million Contract for Multiple Services in Cabinda," Halliburton press release, October 19, 1995. For Angola oil imports to the U.S. see http://tonto.eia.doe.gov/dnav/pet/pet_move_impcus_a2_nus_ep00_im0_mbbl _m.htm, accessed September 20, 2008.

26. Federal Document Clearing House transcript of Madeleine Albright, remarks at Chevron's Takula Oil Drilling Platform, December 12, 1997.

27. Justin Pearce, "Poverty and War in Cabinda," BBC, October 27, 2002.

28. Katherine Pfleger, "U.S. Embassies Assisted Cheney Firm," Associated Press, October 26, 2000.

29. Ibid.

30. An excellent chronology of the TSKJ consortium can be found at http://www.halliburtonwatch.org/about_hal/nigeria_timeline.html, accessed September 20, 2008. See also Russell Gold and Charles Fleming, "Out of Africa: In Halliburton Nigeria Probe, a Search for Bribes to a Dictator," *Wall Street Journal*, Sept. 29, 2004.

31. *Middle East Economic Digest*, April 9, 1999.

32. "Halliburton 'Backed' Bribes Probe Agent," *Financial Times*, September 16, 2004.

33. "Halliburton and KBR Ending Relationship with Jack Stanley," Halliburton press release, June 18, 2004.

34. Halliburton Annual Report, 2006.

35. Russell Gold, "Halliburton Ex-Official Pleads Guilty in Bribe Case," *Wall Street Journal*, September 4, 2008.

36. David Ivanovich, "KBR inquiry broader: Federal bribery investigation goes beyond single case in Nigeria," *Houston Chronicle*, September 4, 2008.

37. Bill Hemmer, Charles Zewe, and Daryn Kagan, "Gallup Poll: Cheney's V.P. Selection Draws 55 Percent Favorable Reaction," CNN, July 25, 2000.

38. Ed Timms, "GOP Donor, Texas Resident Buys Cheney's House," *The Dallas Morning News*, December 8, 2000.

39. Transcript of news conference with GOP Vice Presidential Candidate Richard Cheney, Federal News Service, November 29, 2000.

40. Share price values obtained from Yahoo! finance at http://finance.yahoo.com/ q/hp?s=HAL, accessed September 20, 2008.

41. An excellent analysis of the financial impact of Cheney's decisions can be found in Peter Elkind's article: "The Truth About Halliburton," *Fortune*, April 18, 2005.

42. Royce and Heller, op. cit.

43. Lowell Bergman, Floyd Norris, and Diane B. Henriques, "Cheney Is Said to Be Receiving $20 Million Retirement Package," *New York Times*, August 12, 2000.

44. "Senator Frank Lautenberg Releases CRS Report Confirming Cheney's Deferred Salary and Stock Options Constitute a 'Financial Interest' in Halliburton," Press Release from Senator Frank R. Lautenberg's office, September 25, 2003. The report maybe downloaded at http://www.giveitupcheney.org/crs.pdf, accessed September 20, 2008. "Vice President Cheney and Mrs. Cheney Release 2003 Income Tax Return," Office of the Vice President press release, April 13, 2006; "Vice President Cheney and Mrs. Cheney Release 2004 Income Tax Return," Office of the Vice President press release,

April 15, 2005; "Vice President Cheney and Mrs. Cheney Release 2005 Income Tax Return," Office of the Vice President press release, April 14, 2006.

45. For details on the 2005 sale, see http://www.giveitupcheney.org/disclosure .html, accessed September 20, 2008.

46. Dan Eggen, "Bush May Have Lost Wealth During Presidency," *Washington Post*, May 16, 2008.

47. Lautenberg press release, op. cit.

48. Richard Cheney interview with NBC television's *Meet the Press*, September 14, 2003.

49. Mary Williams Walsh, "Shriveling of Pensions after Halliburton Deal," *New York Times*, September 10, 2002. Mary Williams Walsh, "Halliburton violated pension Laws," *New York Times*, November 10, 2005.

Chapter 5

1. Richard Cheney, Foreword to Jeffrey L. Rodengen, *Legend of Halliburton*, op. cit.

2. Fred Hiatt, "Improved Economy Fails to Stem Military Recruiting," *Washington Post*, March 10, 1984.

3. George J. Church and Bruce W. Nelan, "How Much Can America Do?; Its power is vast, but its global commitments are breathtaking," *Time*, November 7, 1983.

4. Richard Halloran, "U.S. Forces May Lack Resources for Sustained War, Officers Say," *New York Times*, May 13, 1984. Richard Halloran, "Army Plans for 'What If' Latin War," *New York Times*, May 4, 1985. Michael Gordon, "The Charge of the Light Infantry—Army Plans Forces for Third World Conflicts," *National Journal*, May 19, 1984. Michael Gordon, "Army's Third World Strike Force Finds a Home—in Alaska, of All Cold Places," *National Journal*, April 6, 1985.

5. "Logistics Civil Augmentation Program (LOGCAP)," Army Regulation 700–137, December 16, 1985.

6. George C. Wilson, "General Sees Army Short of Supplies, U.S. Industrial Base Concerns Wickham," *Washington Post*, June 17, 1987.

7. U.S. Navy Support Facility, Diego Garcia at http://www.dg.navy.mil/web/2007/html/island_history.htm, accessed September 20, 2008.

8. John Pilger, "Paradise cleansed," *The Guardian*, October 2, 2004. Ian Williams, "Marooned by the special relationship," *The Guardian*, February 25, 2008. See also the Web site of Le Comité Suisse de Soutien aux Chagossiens, http://www.chagos .org/home.htm, accessed September 20, 2008.

9. T. R. Reid, "Big Bucks," *Washington Post*, September 1, 1981. Written answers provided by the UK Secretary of State for Foreign and Commonwealth Affairs to Dale Cambell-Savours, member of Parliament, June 3, 1986. History of Vinnell Brown & Root, http://www.vbr-turkey.com/mainpages/history.htm, accessed September 20, 2008.

10. A history of operations based out of Diego Garcia is available at the Global Security Web site, http://www.globalsecurity.org/military/facility/diego-garcia.htm, accessed September 20, 2008.

11. A history of Incirlik is available at the Global Security Web site, http://www.globalsecurity.org/military/facility/incirlik-history.htm, accessed September 20, 2008.

12. Vinnell, Brown & Root Web site, http://www.vbr-turkey.com/mainpages/ index.htm, accessed September 20, 2008.

13. Kim Willenson, Nicholas C. Profitt, and Lloyd Norman, "This Gun for Hire," *Newsweek*, February 24, 1975. Henry Weinstein, "Vinnell," *New York Times*, February 24, 1975. Charles J Hanley, "Royal Family Gets Quiet Help from U.S. Firm with Connections," Associated Press, March 22, 1997.

14. Toni Kemper interview with Sasha Lilley, January 3, 2003.

15. S. J. B. Bryant, "Taking Care of Incirlik Airmen on All Levels," U.S. Air Force in Europe News Service, February 28, 2006.

16. Alex Daniels interview with Sasha Lilley, January 3, 2003.

17. Author visit, December 2002.

18. Ahmet Balan, "U.S. Businessman Slain; Terror Group Claims Responsibility," *New York Times*, March 22, 1991

19. Author interview, December 23, 2002.

20. Lilley interview, op. cit.

21. "Turkish Workers to Protest Layoffs in U.S. Bases," *Xinhua*, December 23, 1989.

22. Author interview, December 23, 2002.

23. Lilley interview, op. cit.

24. Mehmet Bonuck, "Strike at Incirlik Air Base," *Firatta Yasam Weekly*, December 8, 2002.

25. Colonel Timothy R. Reese with the Contemporary Operations Study Team, "On Point II: Transition to the New Campaign," U.S. Army Combined Arms Center, Fort Leavenworth, Kansas, June 2008.

26. Ibid.

27. Bryce, "Cheney's Multimillion Dollar Revolving Door," op. cit.

28. A history of Force Provider is available at the Global Security Web site, http://www.globalsecurity.org/military/systems/ground/force-provider.htm and

http://www.globalsecurity.org/military/systems/aircraft/systems/harvest-eagle.htm, accessed September 20, 2008.

29. Ibid.

30. "Base camps provide creature comforts for soldiers in austere environments," AccessNorthGa.com, February 10, 2002.

31. Robin Estrin, "Army designs chapel to serve troops overseas," Associated Press, January 31, 2000. Thanassis Cambanis, "Army Has Chapel-To-Go for All Faiths," *Boston Globe*, October 25, 2001

32. "Owner's Manual for the LOGCAP contract," LOGCAP Support Unit, Fort Belvoir, VA. Available at http://www.jmc.army.mil/lsu/LOGCAP_101.doc.

33. United Nations Mission in Somalia backgrounder. http://www.un.org/Depts/DPKO/Missions/unosomi.htm, accessed September 20, 2008.

34. Briody, op. cit.

35. "Somalis Protest Dismissals by a U.S. Company," Reuters, November 5, 1994.

36. Victoria Greenfield, "Risk management and performance in the Balkans support contract," Rand Corporation, 2005.

37. James P. Herson, Jr., "Road Warriors in the Balkans," *Army Logistician*, March–April 1997.

38. Anthony H. Kral and Drefus Lane, "Food for Operation Joint Endeavor," *Army Logistician*, November–December 1996.

39. Tim Lindsay, James J. McLaughlin, and Norm Bruneau, "Force Provider Deploys to Bosnia," *Army Logistician*, May 1997.

40. Michael J. Jordan, "Settling in for a Long Kosovo Run," *Christian Science Monitor*, November 22, 1999.

41. A profile of Camp Bondsteel is available at the Global Security Web site, http://www.globalsecurity.org/military/facility/camp-bondsteel.htm, accessed September 20, 2008.

42. Steven Komarow, "Army Base Being Built In Kosovo," *USA Today*, August 26, 1999.

43. George Cahlink, "Army of Contractors," *Government Executive*, February 1, 2002.

44. Ibid.

45. Ibid.

46. "Army Should Do More to Control Contract Cost in the Balkans," United States General Accounting Office Report NSIAD-00-225, September 2000.

47. Bob Burtman, "Down the Drain," *Houston Press*, May 23, 1996. Bill Dawson, "A Biological Island: Urbanization threatens Sheldon Lake," *Houston Chronicle*, May 14, 1996. Bill Dawson, "Suit Looms as Lake Jackson Golf Course Approved," *Houston Chronicle*, February 10, 1996.

48. Kevin Dougherty, "Bondsteel Battles Skepticism of Local Water with Sophisticated Purification Plant," *Stars and Stripes*, May 23, 2001.

49. "Army Should Do More to Control Contract Cost in the Balkans," op. cit.

50. David Gallay and Charles Horne, "Feasibility of a Joint Engineering and Logistics Contract: LOGCAP Support in Operation Joint. Endeavor," Logistic Management Institute, 1996.

51. Author interview, May 2003.

52. "Contingency Operations: Opportunities to Improve the Improve the Logistics Civil Augmentation Program," United States General Accounting Office Report NSIAD-97-63, February 1997.

53. "Army Should Do More to Control Contract Cost in the Balkans," op. cit.

54. Griff Witte, "Halliburton Unit to Pay $8 Million for Overbilling: KBR Settlement Ends Kosovo Case," *Washington Post*, November 30, 2006.

55. Briody, op. cit.

56. LOGCAP Battle Book, available at http://www.afsc.army.mil/gc/files/battle book.pdf, and accessed September 20, 2008.

57. Denny Walsh, "Construction Company to Pay $ 2 Million to Federal Office in Sacramento, Calif.," *Sacramento Bee*, February 8, 2002.

58. Ibid.

59. Author interview, April 2003.

60. Halliburton annual report, 2001.

Chapter 6

1. Author visit, August 2008. Halliburton lobbying reports in compliance with the Lobby Disclosure Act of 1995 for the years 1999–2008, available at http://www.opensecrets.org, accessed September 20, 2008.

2. Charles Dominy's retirement from the U.S. Army was announced on March 28, 1995. "General Officer Announcement No. 158-95," Department of Defense. Jim Snyder, "Charles Dominy answers critics of Halliburton firm," *The Hill*, February 24, 2004.

3. Halliburton quarterly report filed with the Securities & Exchange Commission, September 30, 1996, announcing David Gribbin's appointment on August 20, 1996. See also "DC Mormons: The Players," *Salt Lake Tribune*, April 10, 2005.

4. "Former Four-Star Navy Flag Officer Admiral 'Joe' Lopez Joins Halliburton Business Unit," Halliburton press release, July 20, 1999. James Risen, "Gulf War Led Cheney to the Oil Boardroom," *New York Times*, July 27, 2000.

5. John Burnett, "Halliburton's Military Contract Connections Before and After the Tenure of Dick Cheney as CEO," *All Things Considered*, National Public Radio, December 23, 2003

6. Snyder, op. cit. Records of the Savannah District Corps of Engineers, 1983, Missouri Savannah District Corps of Engineers, 1986.

7. Gribbin early political career derived from Bob Woodward, *The Commanders* (New York: Touchstone Press, 1991). Hayes, op. cit. Nichols, op. cit.

8. Amy Keller, "Hill Climbers," *Roll Call*, August 29, 1996.

9. Woodward, *The Commanders*, op. cit.

10. Lance Cheung, U.S. Air Force file photo, September 9, 1996.

11. Transcript of News Conference with GOP Vice Presidential Candidate Richard Cheney, Federal News Service, November 29, 2000.

12. "Gribbin Joins Clark & Weinstock," *National Journal*, June 22, 2001.

13. Halliburton lobbying reports in compliance with the Lobby Disclosure Act of 1995 for the years 2000–2008, available at http://www.opensecrets.org, accessed September 20, 2008.

14. Ibid.

15. Army Contracts, Department of Defense, December 14, 2001, archived version available at http://web.archive.org/web/20011214233034/http://www.defenselink .mil/news/Dec2001/c12142001_ct635-01.html, accessed September 20, 2008.

16. Soledad O'Brien, "Halliburton Under Fire," Charles Dominy interview with CNN, December 18, 2003.

17. Steve Kroft, "All In The Family," *60 Minutes*, CBS News, April 27, 2003.

18. Snyder, op. cit.

19. Kroft, op. cit.

20. Khanabad profile at Global Security Web site http://www.globalsecurity.org/ military/facility/khanabad.htm, accessed on September 20, 2008.

21. David Cintron, "MTMC Surface Shipments Sustain Troops in Afghanistan," *Army Logistician*, September–October 2002. See also U.S. Army Transportation Museum exhibit on Operation Enduring Freedom http://www.transchool.eustis .army.mil/Museum/Afghanistan.htm, accessed September 20, 2008.

22. "Logistics Civil Augmentation Program-Camp Stronghold Freedom, Uzbekistan," U.S. Army Audit Agency Report A-2003-0110-IMU, December 21, 2002.

23. Author interview with Defense Contract Management Agency source, March 2002. Author interview with Mike Noll, chief for plans and operations for LOGCAP at U.S. Army Operations Support Command May 2002.

24. Noll interview. op. cit.

25. Fariba Nawa interview with Rick Scavetta, Camp Bagram, Public Affairs Officer, December 2005.

26. "Military Operations: DOD's Extensive Use of Logistics Support Contracts Requires Strengthened Oversight," U.S. General Accounting Office Report GAO-04-854, July 2004.

27. Greg Heath, "Food for Thought: What It Takes to Feed an Army," Department of Defense "Defend America" Web site, August 11, 2003; http://www.defendamerica .mil/articles/aug2003/a081103k.html, accessed September 20, 2008.

28. Alfredo Jimenez, Jr., op. cit.

29. E-mail from Fariba Nawa to author, December 6, 2005.

30. CONCAP profile at Global Security Web site http://www.globalsecurity.org/ military/agency/navy/concap.htm, accessed September 20, 2008

31. "Brown & Root Services Receives US Navy CONCAP Contract," Halliburton press release, May 22, 2001. "Radio Range Fact Sheet," U.S. Naval Station, Guantánamo Bay, Cuba, http://www.nsgtmo.navy.mil/JTF-160/Facts/factsheet _radio.htm, accessed April 2002. Fact sheet no longer available on the Internet.

A July 2002 CONCAP contract for $9.7 million can be seen at http://www
.defenselink.mil/contracts/contract.aspx?contractid=2315, accessed September
20, 2008.

32. Briody, op. cit.

33. Rick Rocamora, "Made for Al-Qaeda," *Newsbreak* (Philippines), August 5, 2002.

34. Author interview with Laszlo Tibold, July 2005. Jim Spore's résumé available
at the Web site of the Princetek-Peregrine Group. http://www.ppgfirst.com/down-
loads.htm, accessed September 20, 2008.

35. Ibid.

36. Vanessa Blum, "U.S. Building New Prisons for Terrorists," *Legal Times*, October 4, 2004. David Ivanovich, "Halliburton to Build $30 Million Prison at Guantá-
namo Bay," *Houston Chronicle*, June 17, 2005

37. Ibid.

38. The details of how the invasion of Iraq were planned were first laid out in Bob
Woodward's book *Plan of Attack* (New York: Simon & Schuster, 2004). See also
Michael Gordon and General Bernard Trainor, *Cobra II* (New York: Pantheon,
March 2006).

39. Bob Whistine, "Tent Cities Spring Up Across Kuwait," U.S. Army News Ser-
vice, February 25, 2003. "Operation Iraqi Freedom—It Was a Prepositioned War,"
Logistics Issues Research Memoranda issued by U.S. Army Materiel Command
(AMC) Historical Office. Document no longer appears to be available online.

40. Woodward, op. cit.

Chapter 7

1. Events recounted by Bunnatine Greenhouse. See also Michael Shnayerson,
"The Spoils of War," *Vanity Fair*, March 7, 2005. Neely Tucker, "A Web of Truth,"
Washington Post, October 19, 2005.

2. "On Third Anniversary of Global Protest Against Iraq War, a Look at Challenging Empire: How People, Governments, and the UN Defy U.S. Power," *Democracy
Now*, February 15, 2006.

3. Carl Strock résumé available at http://www.hq.usace.army.mil/cepa/strock
.htm, accessed September 20, 2008.

4. "The Corps of Engineers Responds," pamphlet available at http://
www.usace.army.mil/publications/eng-pamphlets/ep870-1-50/c-2.pdf, accessed
September 20, 2008.

5. National Situation Update, Federal Emergency Management Agency, February
26, 2003, as well as historical National Oceanic & Atmospheric Administration data
from the Weather Underground Web site, http://www.wunderground.org.

6. Neela Banerjee, "3 Get Top Posts to Revive Iraqi Oil Flow," *New York Times*,
May 4, 2003. Dean Calbreath, "A Blueprint for a Nation," *San Diego Union-Tribune*,
July 4, 2004.

7. "Profile: Clarke Turner, RMOTC," *In Touch*, U.S. Department of Energy Fossil
Energy's newsletter, Summer 2003.

8. Stephen Browning profile, Service to America medals. See http://service toamericamedals.org/SAM/recipients/profiles/iam04_browning.shtml, accessed September 20, 2008.

9. Barbara Glotfelty résumé available at http://www.dau.mil/conferences/presentations/2000/Agenda/glotfeltyBio.pdf, accessed September 20, 2008.

10. "1991 Kuwait Oil Fires," NASA fact sheet available at http://www.nasa.gov/centers/goddard/news/topstory/2003/0321kuwaitfire.html, accessed September 20, 2008.

11. Katherine Griffiths, "Oh What a Lovely War on Terror It's Been for Halliburton," *The Independent*, March 27, 2005.

12. Shnayerson, op. cit.

13. Bunnatine Greenhouse testimony at U.S. Senate Democratic Policy Committee Hearing, June 27, 2005.

14. L. Paul Bremer, "The Top Officials During My Time at the Coalition Provisional Authority," *Wall Street Journal*, November 2, 2006. Hans Greimel, "Will Iraq Have to Import Oil?," Associated Press, April 28, 2003. Transcript of Iraq Reconstruction Seminar hosted by Trade Partners UK in London, May 23, 2003.

15. Minutes of Program Review Board held on September 1, 2003, in Baghdad. Available at http://www.cpa-iraq.org/budget/PRB/archive/index.html, accessed September 20, 2008.

16. U.S. Senate Democratic Policy Committee hearing, op. cit. Erik Eckholm, "Army Contract Official Critical of Halliburton Pact Is Demoted," *New York Times*, August 29, 2005.

17. Jeremy Kahn, "Will Halliburton Clean Up?" *Fortune*, March 30, 2003.

18. Ibid. Testimony of Alfred V. Neffgen to U.S. House of Representatives Committee on Oversight and Government Reform, hearing on "U.S. Effort To Rebuild Iraq," July 22, 2004.

19. Minutes of the Defense Energy Support Center Quality conference no. 4, Defense Energy Support Center, October 20–21, 1999. Available at http://www.desc.dla.mil/DCM/Files/minu.doc, accessed September 20, 2008.

20. E-mail to author from Kuwait Oil Corporation source in April 2003.

21. Chip Cummins, "Fighting Oil Fires in Iraq Rekindles Desert Rivalry," *Wall Street Journal*, March 28, 2003.

22. Ibid.

23. Neffgen testimony, op. cit.

24. Memo from unknown U.S. Army Corps of Engineers staff. Redacted original may be viewed at http://www.judicialwatch.org/archive/2004/030503.pdf, accessed September 20, 2008.

25. "Frequently Asked Questions, Engineer Support to Operation Iraqi Freedom," http://www.hq.usace.army.mil/cepa/iraq/faq.htm, U.S. Army Corps of Engineers, January 20, 2004, accessed September 20, 2008.

26. Chip Cummins, "British and U.S. Oil Firms Give Advice to Troops: Employees Show How Oil Fields Operate and Help to Draw Up Emergency Plans," *Wall*

Street Journal, March 27, 2003. Sal Ruibal, "Much Depends on Restart of Refinery," *USA Today*, May 2, 2003.

27. Chip Cummins, op. cit.

28. Gordon, op. cit.

29. Jackie Northam, "Slow Pace of Efforts to Revive Oil Production in Southern Iraq," *All Things Considered*, National Public Radio, May 7, 2003.

30. T. Christian Miller, *Blood Money* (New York: Little, Brown and Co., August 2006).

31. Strock and Crear continued to work together for the summer of 2003. See minutes of Program Review Board held on August 30, 2003, in Baghdad. Available at http://www.cpa-iraq.org/budget/PRB/archive/index.html, accessed September 20, 2008.

32. Neffgen testimony Op.Cit.

33. "The Corps of Engineers Responds," op. cit.

34. Dan Baum, "Nation Builders for Hire," *New York Times Magazine*, June 22, 2003.

35. Peter S. Goodman, "At Oil Plant, Bitterness and Idleness," *Washington Post*, April 30, 2003.

36. Ibid.

37. "Kirkuk to Beiji Pipeline and Canal Crossings," Special Inspector General for Iraq Reconstruction, Report # PA-06-063, July 31, 2006.

38. Sheryl Tappan, "Shock and Awe in Fort Worth: How the U.S. Army Rigged the 'Free and Open Competition' to Replace Halliburton's Sole-Source Oil Field in Iraq," *Pourquoi Press*, July 2004, "March 2003 Contract Obligation Status Task Orders," U.S. Army Corps of Engineers, October 7, 2004.

39. Tappan, op. cit.

40. David Streitfeld, "New Iraq Contracts Offer Just 'Scraps,'" *Los Angeles Times*, August 14, 2003.

41. Author interview, September 2005.

42. Erik Eckholm, "A Watchdog Follows the Money in Iraq," *New York Times*, November 15, 2004.

43. Timothy J. Burger and Adam Zagorin, "The Paper Trail," *Time*, May 30, 2004. "Justification and Approval (J&A) for other than Full and Open Competition for the Execution of the Contingency Support Plan," signed by Claude Bolton, secretary of the army, dated February 28, 2003.

44. Charles Dominy biography at IAP Web site, http://www.iapws.com/who/leadership.aspx, accessed September 20, 2008.

45. Eckholm, op. cit.

46. Author interview November 2004.

47. U.S. Senate Democratic Policy Committee hearing, op. cit.

48. Shnayerson, op. cit.

49. Eckholm, op. cit.

50. Shnayerson, op. cit.

51. Tucker, op. cit.

52. Wendy Hall e-mail to David Phinney, September 2004.

53. Sheryl Tappan testimony at U.S. Senate Democratic Policy Committee Hearing, September 10, 2004.

54. "Task Order 0044 of the Logistics Civilian Augmentation Program III Contract," Special Inspector General for Iraq Reconstruction (SIGIR) Audit Report, 05-003, November 23, 2004.

55. Testimony of Alfred V. Neffgen and Charles "Stoney" Cox testimony, U.S. House of Representatives, Government Reform Committee, July 22, 2004

56. "Halliburton's Questioned and Unsupported Costs in Iraq Exceed $1.4 Billion," report prepared for Representative Henry Waxman and Senator Byron Dorgan, June 27, 2005.

57. "Review of Administrative Task Orders for Iraq Reconstruction Contracts," Special Inspector General for Iraq Reconstruction Report # PA-06-028, October 23, 2006.

58. Ibid.

59. James Glanz, "Idle Contractors Add Millions to Iraq Rebuilding," New York Times, October 25, 2006.

60. "Halliburton's Performance under the Restore Iraqi Oil 2 Contract," report prepared for Representative Henry Waxman by Minority Staff Special Investigations Division, March 28, 2006.

61. Author trip to Al Zubayr in December 2003.

62. "Project Al Fatah River Crossing," undated video produced by Maria Or for the gulf Region division of U.S. Army Corps of Engineers provided to author in April 2004.

63. T. Christian Miller, "Missteps Hamper Iraqi Oil Recovery," Los Angeles Times, September 26, 2005.

64. Ibid.

65. Ibid.

66. Ibid.

67. "Al Fatah Horizontal Directional Drilling (HDD) Pipe Crossing," Special Inspector General for Iraq Reconstruction Report # SA-05-001, January 27, 2006.

68. James Glanz, "Rebuilding of Iraqi Pipeline a Disaster Waiting to Happen," New York Times, April 25, 2006

69. Glanz, op. cit.

70. SIGIR Report SA-05-001, op. cit.

71. Glanz, op. cit.

72. Glanz, op. cit.

73. Glanz, op. cit.

74. "Kirkuk to Baiji Pipeline Project," Special Inspector General for Iraq Reconstruction Report PA-06-063, July 31, 2006

75. Edward Lundquist, "Crude Terminals: Platforms for Iraqi Recovery," Maritime Reporter and Engineering News, September 8, 2008. Sandra Jontz, "Sailors

Pump Up Iraq Oil Terminal," *Stars and Stripes*, March 3, 2007. See also Michael Yon's blog: "Walking the Line II," 25 June 2005 at http://www.michaelyon-online.com/index.php?option=com_content&view=article&id=121:walking-the-line-ii&catid=61:archive-2005&Itemid=106, accessed September 20, 2008.

76. Joseph Ebalo, "Iraqi Marines Prepare to Take Over Oil Platform Security," U.S. Navy Public Affairs press release, June 15, 2005.

77. Faleh al-Khayat, "Iraqi Statistics for 2005 Leave 60 Million Barrels Unaccounted For," *Platts Oilgram News*, May 9, 2006.

78. Christian Parenti, "Who Will Get the Oil?" *The Nation*, March 1, 2007.

79. Jontz, op. cit.

80. Robert Riggs, "Meters Cost Iraq Billions In Stolen Oil," KTVT (CBS), in Dallas, February 8, 2007.

81. Pratt and Castaneda, op. cit.

82. "Parsons Wins Iraq Oil Contract," Parsons press release, January 19, 2004. "Foster Wheeler awarded oil sector program management contract In Iraq," Foster Wheeler press release, March 12, 2004.

83. Robert Bryce, "America's Achilles' heel," Salon.com, August 16, 2004. Pratt and Castaneda, op. cit. Rodengen op. cit.

84. Pratt and Castaneda, op. cit. Rodengen op. cit.

85. Pratt and Castaneda, op. cit. Rodengen op. cit. James Glanz, "15 Miles Offshore, Safeguarding Iraq's Oil Lifeline," *New York Times*, July 6, 2004.

86. Colum Lynch, "Firm's Iraq Deals Greater Than Cheney Has Said," *Washington Post*, June 23, 2001.

87. For a detailed explanation of flow meters, see http://www.flowmeter directory.com/, accessed on September 20, 2008.

88. "Al Basra Oil Terminal Metering," U.S. Embassy Baghdad press release, December 23, 2006.

89. Author interview with Saybolt staff, April 2007.

90. E-mail to author September 29, 2007.

91. Minutes of Program Review Board in Baghdad. Available at http://www.cpa-iraq.org/budget/program_review_board.html, accessed September 20, 2008.

92. Chip Cummins, "U.S. Officials May Have Steered Halliburton to Kuwaiti Supplier," *Wall Street Journal*, December 15, 2003.

93. Ibid. "Dollars, not Sense: Government Contracting under the Bush Administration," report prepared for Representative Henry Waxman by Minority Staff Special Investigations Division, June 2006.

94. Ibid.

95. Don Van Natta, Jr., "High Payments to Halliburton for Fuel in Iraq," *New York Times*, December 10, 2003.

96. Ibid.

97. "Dollars Not Sense," op. cit.

98. "Halliburton Confirms It Received Fuel Waver from U.S. Army Corps of Engineers," Halliburton press release, January 6, 2004.

99. Minutes of the Program Review Board, op. cit.

100. The full resolution can be viewed at http://www.globalpolicy.org/security/issues/iraq/document/2003/0522resolution.htm or downloaded from http://www.iamb.info.

101. "Rebuilding Iraq: U.S. Mismanagement of Iraqi Funds," U.S. House of Representatives, Committee on Government Reform, Minority Staff, June 2005.

102. Minutes of the Program Review Board, op. cit.

103. Minutes of the Program Review Board held on July 12, 2003, in Baghdad. Available at http://www.cpa-iraq.org/budget/PRB/archive/index.html, accessed September 20, 2008.

104. Ibid.

105. Ibid.

106. Ariana Eunjung Cha, "$1.9 Billion of Iraq's Money Goes to U.S. Contractors," *Washington Post*, August 4, 2004.

107. "Big Spender: What Happened to $20bn of Iraqi Funds?," *Financial Times* editorial, December 10, 2004.

108. James Glanz, "Army to Pay Halliburton Unit Most Costs Disputed by Audit," *New York Times*, February 27, 2006.

109. Ibid.

110. Letter from Congressman Henry Waxman to Congressman Tom Davis, chairman of the U.S. House of Representatives Committee on Government Reform, February 27, 2006.

111. "Defense Contract Audit Agency Audit Report No. 3311-2004K17900055," October 8, 2004. A copy with the redacted sentences highlighted in yellow may be found at http://www.halliburtonwatch.org/news/conceal_overcharges.html, accessed September 20, 2008.

112. Ibid.

113. A history of the International Advisory and Monitoring Board may be found at its Web site, http://www.iamb.info, accessed September 20, 2008.

114. "Interim Update—External Audit Services to the Development Fund for Iraq. KPMG Ref: DABV01-04-R-0015." This report was first obtained by Iraq Revenue Watch and a copy can be found on IRW's Web site at http://www.iraqrevenuewatch.org, accessed September 20, 2008. A good summary of the problems faced by the International Advisory and Monitoring Board can be found in "Disorder, Negligence and Mismanagement: How the CPA Handled Iraq Reconstruction Funds," Iraq Revenue Watch, September 2004.

115. Transcript of press conference held by Jean-Pierre Halbwachs, chairman of the International Advisory and Monitoring Board at the United Nations in New York on December 28, 2005.

116. "Updated Report of Agreed-Upon Procedures Regarding the Settlement Between U.S. Army Corps of Engineers and Kellogg Brown & Root," prepared for U.S. Defense Reconstruction Support Office and International Advisory and Monitoring Board, Crowe Chizek and Company LLC, November 16, 2006.

117. "DOD's Lack of Adherence to Key Contracting Prinicples on Iraqi Oil Contract Put Government Interests at Risk," U.S. General Accounting Office Report #07-839, July 31, 2007. See Greenfield for details on Balkans award fees.

118. Testimony of Alan Waller, U.S. Senate Democratic Policy Committee Hearing, June 27, 2005.

119. Ibid.

120. Author interview with Alan Waller, June 27, 2005.

121. Testimony of Alan Waller, op. cit.

122. E-mail from Cathy Gist to author, June 27, 2005.

Chapter 8

1. Nate Orme, "Catamaran Hauls Equipment Double-time," American Forces Press Service, September 8, 2003.

2. "Operation Iraqi Freedom—It Was a Prepositioned War" op. cit.

3. Ibid.

4. Frank N. Pellegrini, "Supporting Gulf War 2.0," *Army Magazine*, September 1, 2003.

5. Testimony of Robert Gatlin in the trial of *USA v. Mazon et al.* in U.S. District Court, Rock Island, Illinois, April 15, 2008.

6. Baum, op. cit.

7. Ibid.

8. Whistine, op. cit.

9. Web site of the Khalifa Resort, http://www.jfkw.com/english/khalifa-e.html, accessed October 5, 2008.

10. Author interviews with Laszlo Tibold and Marie deYoung, July 2005.

11. Brochure and Web site of the Kuwait Hilton, http://www.hiltonworld resorts.com/Resorts/Kuwait/index.html, accessed on October 5, 2008. Author interviews with sources who asked to remain anonymous in Kuwait, April 2008.

12. Author interviews with Kuwait residents April 2006, January 2007, and April 2008.

13. "Charges of KBR Improprieties," undated U.S. Embassy, Kuwait, memo provided to Defense Contract Audit Agency on December 19, 2003. Copy in author's possession provided by staff of Representative Henry Waxman's office.

14. Testimony of Stephen Lowell Seamans in the trial of *USA v. Mazon et al.* in U.S. District Court, Rock Island, Illinois, April 21, 2008.

15. Web site of the Tamimi of Saudi Arabia, http://www.altamimi.com, accessed October 5, 2008.

16. Plea Agreement of Mohammad Shabbir Khan in U.S. District Court, Rock Island, Illinois, March 22, 2006.

17. Author visit to LSA Anaconda, April 2008.

18. Plea Agreement of Stephen Lowell Seamans in U.S. District Court, Rock Island, Illinois, February 23, 2006.

19. Author interviews with Kuwaiti sources who asked to remain anonymous, April 2006.

20. Shnayerson, op. cit.

21. David Phinney, "Halliburton Hit with Multiple Lawsuits," CorpWatch, October 27, 2004, http://www.corpwatch.org/article.php?id=11613, accessed October 5, 2008.

22. Seamans plea, op. cit.

23. Criminal Complaint against Mohammad Shabbir Khan in U.S. District Court, Rock Island, Illinois, March 22, 2006

24. Ann McGlynn, "Humanitarian Faces Prison Time for Bribe," *Quad City Times*, November 29, 2006.

25. Seamans plea, op. cit. Author interview with Nelson Chase, Stephen Lowell Seamans's attorney, July 2008. Khan plea agreement, op. cit.

26. Testimony of Anthony J. Martin in the trial of *USA v. Mazon et al.* in U.S. District Court, Rock Island, Illinois, April 17, 2008.

27. Plea Agreement of Anthony J. Martin in U.S. District Court, Rock Island, Illinois, May 9, 2007.

28. Martin testimony, op. cit.

29. David Phinney, "Baghdad Embassy Bonanza: Kuwait Company's Secret Contract & Low-Wage Labor," CorpWatch, February 12, 2006, http://www.corpwatch.org/article.php?id=13258, accessed October 5, 2008.

30. Web site of First Kuwaiti Trading Company, http://www.firstkuwaiti.com/history.php, accessed October 5, 2008.

31. Martin testimony, op. cit.

32. Martin plea agreement, op. cit.

33. Martin testimony, op. cit., Martin plea agreement, op. cit.

34. First Kuwaiti contracts available at the company Web site, http://www.firstkuwaiti.com/projects/index.php, accessed October 5, 2008.

35. Phinney, op. cit.

36. Sentencing agreement of Anthony J. Martin in U.S. District Court, Rock Island, Illinois, June 6, 2008.

37. Pete Yost, "Embassy Builder Linked to Kickbacks," Associated Press, September 20, 2007.

38. Warren P. Strobel, "Government Reviews Ties with Firm Criticized for Iraq Embassy Flaws," McClatchy-Tribune News Service, October 26, 2007.

39. "Former KBR Employee and Subcontractor Charged With $3.5 Million Government Contract Fraud in Kuwait," Department of Justice press release, March 17, 2005. Gatlin testimony, op. cit.

40. David Phinney, "Halliburton Bribery Scandal Deepens: Former Kuwait Manager Indicted for Million Dollar Payoff," CorpWatch, March 29, 2005, http://www.corpwatch.org/article.php?id=12011, accessed October 5, 2008.

41. Martin testimony, op. cit.

42. Gatlin testimony, op. cit.

43. Ibid.

44. Ann McGlynn, "KBR sent former cop to question fraud suspect," *Quad City Times*, April 22, 2008.

45. Pratap Chatterjee, *Iraq, Inc: A Profitable Occupation* (New York: Seven Stories Press, 2004).

46. Ann McGlynn, "E-mails Come Up in Iraq Fraud Case," *Quad City Times*, April 24, 2008.

47. "Government's Proffer Regarding Admissibility of Co-Conspirator Declarations," Documents submitted in *USA v. Mazon et al.*, U.S. District Court, Rock Island, Illinois, August 3, 2007.

48. Ann McGlynn, "Illinois Man's Trial on Iraq Fraud Set to Begin Later This Month," *Quad City Times*, September 3, 2007

49. McGlynn, "KBR sent former cop to question fraud suspect," op. cit.

50. Government's Proffer documents, op. cit.

51. McGlynn, "KBR sent former cop to question fraud suspect," op. cit.

52. Author interview with Ali Hijazi, January 2007.

53. Ann McGlynn, "Accused Kuwaiti Asks Feds to Dismiss Charges," *Quad City Times*, December 26, 2007.

54. Ibid.

55. Ibid.

56. Ann McGlynn, "Judge Rules Mistrial in Federal Fraud Case," *Quad City Times*, April 30, 2006.

57. Eric Rosenberg, "Despite Warnings, KBR Got Contract," Hearst News Service, May 15, 2004.

58. KBR internal memo from T. Joe Lopez dated December 3, 2003. Notes from copy reviewed by author in July 2005.

59. Author interviews with Marie deYoung, July 2005.

60. Brian Hickey, "Ms. deYoung Goes to Washington," *Philadelphia City Paper*, July 28–August 3, 2005.

61. Testimony of Marie deYoung, U.S. Senate Democratic Policy Committee Hearing, September 10, 2004.

62. Shnayerson, op. cit.

63. Testimony of Marie deYoung, U.S. House of Representatives, Government Reform Committee hearing, July 22, 2004.

64. Ibid.

65. Statement of Marie deYoung, June 6, 2004, placed on the Web site of the Committee on Government Reform Minority Committee, http://www.house.gov/reform/min/inves_admin/admin_contracts.htm, accessed October 5, 2008.

66. Author interviews with Marie deYoung, April 2006 and December 2007.

67. Gatlin testimony, op. cit.

68. Internal e-mails from Robert Gatlin to Tom Crum, February 15, 2004, and April 10, 2004, with subject line: Resignation. Copy in author's possession.

69. Gatlin testimony, op. cit.

70. Chris Heinrich memo dated April 12, 2004, with subject line: RE: Resignation. Copy in author's possession.

71. Gatlin testimony, op. cit.

72. "Civilian Contractor Indicted for Allegedly Soliciting Bribes While Working at Camp Arifjan in Kuwait," Department of Justice press release, November 20, 2007. Guillermo Contreras, "Former Sergeant Caught in Bribery Probe," *San Antonio Express-News*, November 16, 2007.

73. Guillermo Contreras, "Contractor Is Indicted in Bribery," *San Antonio Express-News*, November 20, 2007.

74. Contreras, "Former sergeant caught in bribery probe," op. cit.

75. "Three Defendants Indicted in Case Involving Bribery, Conspiracy, Money Laundering, And Obstruction Offenses Related to Contracts in Iraq And Kuwait," Department of Justice press release, August 22, 2007.

76. Ginger Thompson and Eric Schmitt, "Graft in Contracts Spread From Kuwait Base," *New York Times*, September 24, 2007

77. Ibid. Contreras, "Former sergeant caught in bribery probe," op. cit.

78. Testimony of Alfred Neffgen, U.S. House of Representatives, Government Reform Committee hearing, July 22, 2004.

79. Dana Priest and Anne Hull, "Soldiers Face Neglect, Frustration at Army's Top Medical Facility," *Washington Post*, February 18, 2007; Steve Vogel and Renae Merle, "Privatized Walter Reed Workforce Gets Scrutiny: Army Facility Lost Dozens of Maintenance Workers," *Washington Post*, March 10, 2007.

80. Justin Rood and Anna Schecter, "Waxman to Force Walter Reed Ex-Chief to Talk About Problems, Contract," *ABC News*, March 2, 2007.

81. Vogel and Merle, op. cit.

82. IAP senior management biographies available at IAP Web site, http://www.iapws.com/who/leadership.aspx, accessed September 20, 2008.

83. "Army Officer Pleads Guilty to Conspiracy, Bribery and Money Laundering Scheme Involving Department of Defense Contracts at U.S. Army Base in Kuwait," U.S. Department of Justice press release, June 24, 2008.

84. Eric Schmitt and James Glanz, "U.S. Says Company Bribed Officers for Work in Iraq," *New York Times*, August 30, 2007.

85. Web site of Sultan Center, http://www.sultan-center.com/Default.aspx?pageId=10 and http://www.sultan-center.com/Default.aspx?pageId=12, accessed October 5, 2008.

86. Author visits, April 2006, January 2007, and April 2008.

87. Web site of Sultan Center, op. cit.

88. Cam Simpson and Glenn R. Simpson, "How Iraq Conflict Rewards a Kuwaiti Merchant Family: Sultans' Supply Deals Bring Rapid Growth but Trigger U.S. Probes," *Wall Street Journal*, December 17, 2007.

89. Author interviews with multiple former PWC employees who asked to remain anonymous, January 2007, April 2008.

90. Simpson and Simpson. op. cit.

91. Author interviews with multiple former PWC employees who asked to remain anonymous, January 2007 and April 2008.

92. "Supply Corps Birthday Celebrations," U.S. Navy Supply Corps newsletter, May 1, 2003.

93. Author interviews with multiple former PWC employees who asked to remain anonymous, January 2007 and April 2008.

94. Transcript of the sentencing hearing for Peleti Peleti, Jr. in U.S. District Court, Rock Island, Illinois, February 20, 2008.

95. "PWC Logistics Wins Exclusive Prime Vendor Contract," Public Warehousing Corporation press release, March 31, 2003.

96. Author interviews with Kamal Sultan, January 2007 and April 2008.

97. "PWC Logistics Awarded Contract to Assist in Iraq Reconstruction," Public Warehousing Corporation press release, June 25, 2004.

98. "PWC Logistics Wins Largest-Ever Heavy-Lift Contract," Public Warehousing Corporation press release, June 17, 2005.

99. "PWC Logistics Buys Taos," *Traffic World*, October 5, 2006.

100. Author interviews with multiple former PWC employees who asked to remain anonymous, January 2007 and April 2008.

101. Ibid.

102. Glenn R. Simpson, "Food Companies Face U.S. Probe over Iraq Deals," *Wall Street Journal*, October 17, 2007.

103. Author interview with Jim Cox, September 2008.

104. Simpson and Simpson, "How Iraq Conflict Rewards A Kuwaiti Merchant Family," op. cit.

105. Simpson, "Food Companies Face U.S. Probe over Iraq Deals," op. cit.

106. Simpson and Simpson, "How Iraq Conflict Rewards a Kuwaiti Merchant Family," op. cit.

107. Glenn R. Simpson, "U.S. Rebuffed Food-Fraud Case," *Wall Street Journal*, October 22, 2007.

108. Testimony of Rory Mayberry, U.S. Senate Democratic Policy Committee Hearing, June 27, 2005.

109. "Interview with Sheikh Tariq A. Tamimi," *United World*, March 26, 2006. See http://www.unitedworld-usa.com/reports/saudiarabia/interview05.asp, accessed October 5, 2008.

110. Web site of Tamimi Global, http://www.altamimi.com/companies.asp, accessed October 5, 2008.

111. Clementine Owens, "Logistics Between the Gulf and Sand," *Army Logisitician*, September 1997.

112. Web site of Tamimi Global, http://www.altamimi.com/co_commercial.asp, accessed October 5, 2008.

113. Glenn R. Simpson, "Inside the Greed Zone," *Wall Street Journal*, October 20, 2007.

114. Ibid.

115. Ibid.

116. "Price of U.S. Army 'Confidentiality'; Leaked Information Sends Chilling Message to Contractors," *Kuwait Daily Star*, November 8, 2007.

117. Simpson, op. cit.

118. "Army Chief Warrant Officer Charged with Taking Bribe to Influence Food Services Supplies Contract," U.S. Department of Justice press release, January 25, 2007. Jackson and Grotto, op. cit.

119. "Agility—Announcing a New Logistics Leader," Public Warehousing Corporation press release, November 13, 2006.

120. "Agility top line grows over USD 6.2 billion for 2007," Agility press release, March 22, 2008

121. Evelyn Iritani, "Global Capital; Logistics Firm Staging Expansion," *Los Angeles Times*, December 16, 2006.

122. "Former EGL Houston Executive Admits Giving 'Perks' to KBR Employees and Lying to Federal Investigators," U.S. Department of Justice press release, July 20, 2007; "Former Air Freight Executive Pleads Guilty to Inflating Invoices for Baghdad Shipments," U.S. Department of Justice press release, February 16, 2006.

123. "Texas Man Pleads Guilty to Accepting $110,000 Kickback from KBR Subcontractor," U.S. Department of Justice press release, August 19, 2005.

124. "Former KBR Employee Sentenced for Scheme to Defraud the U.S. Department of Defense," U.S. Department of Justice press release, April 11, 2008.

Chapter 9

1. Author interview with Laszlo Tibold, July 2005.

2. Tom Sawyer, "Iraqi Firms Win Work at Base Near Balad," *Engineering News-Record*, February 2, 2004.

3. Spore résumé, op. cit.

4. David Ivanovich, "Halliburton Employees Coping with Tedium, Terror," *Houston Chronicle*, April 5, 2004.

5. David Phinney, "Blood, Sweat & Tears: Asia's Poor Build U.S. Bases in Iraq," *CorpWatch*, October 3, 2005, http://www.corpwatch.org/article.php?id=12675, accessed October 5, 2008.

6. "Defense Base Act Insurance: Review Needed of Cost and Implementation Issues," U.S. General Accounting Office report GAO-05-280R, April 29, 2005.

7. E-mail from Lee Wang to author, October 30, 2005.

8. Russell Gold, "The Temps of War: Blue-Collar Workers Ship Out for Iraq," *Wall Street Journal*, February 25, 2004.

9. Author visits to Dubai January 2006, April 2006, and April 2008.

10. Criselda E. Diala, "22 Stranded Filipinos Still Waiting for Deportation," *Khaleej Times*, December 18, 2005.

11. Pia Lee-Brago, "88 Iraq-Bound OFWs Stranded in Dubai," *Philippine Star*, December 14, 2005.

12. Transcribed from video broadcast of Second International Employer Awards at Malacanang Palace, November 10, 2005.

13. Amrita Chaudhry, "Eight Boys Return from Iraq to Tell the Tale of Horror," Ludhiana Newsline, December 20, 2005; "Laborers Claim U.S. Held Them Captive on Base," Associated Press, May 6, 2004. Siddharth Srivastava, "Lured by Dollars Indian Soldiers Are in Iraq," Asia Times Online, May 1, 2004.

14. Phinney, "Blood, Sweat & Tears," op. cit.

15. Ibid.

16. Rupak D. Sharma, "A Nepali Worker's Plight in Kuwait," *Kathmandu Post*, September 6, 2004.

17. Testimony of Rory J. Mayberry to the Committee on Oversight and Government Reform Subcommittee on National Security and Foreign Affairs, in the U.S. House of Representatives, July 26, 2007.

18. David Rohde, "Exploited in Iraq, Indian Workers Say," *New York Times*, Friday, May 7, 2004.

19. Ariana Eunjung Cha, "Underclass of Workers Created in Iraq; Many Foreign Laborers Receive Inferior Pay, Food, and Shelter," *Washington Post*, July 1, 2004.

20. Phinney, "Blood, Sweat & Tears," op. cit.

21. Ibid.

22. Ibid.

23. Ibid.

24. Numbers obtained on July 1, 2008. Latest figures may be seen at the Web site of the Iraq Coalition Casualty Count, http://icasualties.org/oif/Contractors.aspx.

25. Karl Vick, "12 Nepalese Hostages Are Slain in Iraq: First Mass Killing Displayed on Web," *Washington Post*, September 1, 2004.

26. Phinney, "Blood, Sweat & Tears," op. cit.

27. "Turkey: Iraq Plane Crash Kills 30," *CNN*, January 9, 2007. Maamoun Youssef, "Islamic Army in Iraq Claims Responsibility for Downing," Associated Press, January 13, 2007. "Turkish Plane Crash in Iraq Reportedly Due to Bad Weather," Anatolia News Agency, January 9, 2007.

28. "Military Contractor Charged with Assaulting Woman on U.S. Military Base in Iraq," U.S. Attorney's Office for Arizona press release, March 1, 2007.

29. Christine O. Avendaño and Jerome Aning, "Filipino Labor Dispute 'Temporarily Resolved,'" *Philippine Daily Inquirer*, May 28, 2005.

30. Phinney, "Blood, Sweat & Tears," op. cit.

31. Ibid.

32. Ibid.

33. Ibid.

34. E-mail to author from Melissa Norcross, February 9, 2004.

35. Phinney, "Blood, Sweat & Tears," op. cit.

36. Rohde, "Exploited in Iraq, Indian Workers Say."

37. Phone call by author to PPI headquarters in Dubai, October 2005.

38. Richard Dowling interview with author in Baghdad, December 2003.

39. Phinney, "Blood, Sweat & Tears," op. cit.

40. Cam Simpson, "Iraq War Contractors Ordered to End Abuses," *Chicago Tribune*, April 23, 2006.

41. "Philippine Embassy Kuwait Takes Steps to Enforce Travel Ban to Iraq," Philippine Department of Foreign Affairs press release, November 30, 2005.

42. Report from fourth and seventh Koh Samui International Regatta, available at http://asianyachting.com/news/KoSamui05.htm and http://asianyachting.com/news/KohSamui08.htm, accessed October 5, 2008.

Chapter 10

1. Events of the day reconstructed from author interviews in November 2004 with Ray Stannard and Keith Stanley, truck drivers on the April 9, 2004, convoy, as well as family members of other truck drivers who were killed that day.

2. Author visit to Iraq, April 2004.

3. Paul Von Zielbauer, "Hostage Was Working in Iraq to Aid His Struggling Family," *New York Times*, April 12, 2004.

4. Thomas Hammill, Paul T. Brown, and Jay Langston, *Escape in Iraq: The Thomas Hamill Story* (Accokeek, MD: Stoeger Publishing, 2005).

5. Author interview with Ray Stannard, November 2004.

6. Author interviews with April Johnson, November 2004 and March 2005.

7. Author interviews with Michael Heaviside, Vince Howard, Ramon Lopez, and Jack Pentecost in November 2004 and March 2005.

8. Author visit to Lopez, Hodes offices in Newport Beach in March 2005.

9. Web site of Lopez, Hodes at http://www.lopezhodes.com/, accessed October 5, 2008.

10. Author interviews with Kim Johnson, November 2004 and March 2005.

11. Author interviews with Ray Stannard, November 2004 and May 2005.

12. Excerpts from Colonel Gary Bunch's report provided to the author by Lopez, Hodes lawyers.

13. Jeremy Scahill, "Blood Is Thicker than Blackwater," *The Nation*, April 19, 2006.

14. E-mail from James Ray of KBR dated June 3, 2004, provided by Congressman Waxman at U.S. House of Representatives Committee on Oversight and Government Reform, hearing on February 6, 2007.

15. "Contractor's Boss in Iraq Shot at Civilians, Workers' Suit Says," by C. J. Chivers, *New York Times*, November 17, 2006.

16. Steve Fainaru, "A Chaotic Day on Baghdad's Airport Road," *Washington Post*, April 15, 2007.

17. A detailed account of e-mail and phone conversations related to the April 9, 2004, attack under court seal were reviewed by T. Christian Miller who transcribed

them in "Iraq Convoy Was Sent Out Despite Threat," *Los Angeles Times*, September 3, 2007.

18. Author visit to Iraq, April 2004 and interview with Michael Berg—Nicholas Berg's father—in April 2006.

19. Miller, "Iraq Convoy Was Sent Out Despite Threat," op. cit.

20. Miller, "Iraq Convoy Was Sent Out Despite Threat," op. cit.

21. E-mail to author from Beverly Scippa, March 28, 2005.

22. Author interviews in November 2005 with one member of the truck convoy who survived and the family of one who was killed. Both interviewees asked not to be identified.

23. Brian Ross and Rhonda Schwartz, "U.S. Troops Abandoned Me, Says Convoy Driver," *ABC World News Tonight*, September 27, 2006.

24. Transcript of Preston Wheeler videotape, recorded September 20, 2005. Original available at http://www.halliburtonwatch.org/news/ambush.html, accessed October 5, 2008.

25. Brian Ross and Rhonda Schwartz, op. cit.

26. Griff Witte, "Judge Dismisses Halliburton Suit," *Washington Post*, September 23, 2006.

27. Brett Clanton and David Ivanovich, "Ruling Revives KBR Case: Court Sees Way Lawsuits Over Workers' Deaths Could Be Resolved," *Houston Chronicle*, May 30, 2008. Loren Steffy, "KBR Workers Caught Up in Quagmire," *Houston Chronicle*, May 30, 2008. Author interview with T. Scott Allen, June 2008.

28. Ibid.

29. Seth Borenstein, "Trucks Made to Drive Without Cargo in Dangerous Areas of Iraq," Knight Ridder Newspapers, May 21, 2004.

30. David Wilson testimony at U.S. House of Representatives Committee on Government Reform hearing on July 22, 2004.

31. James Warren testimony at U.S. House of Representatives Committee on Government Reform hearing on July 22, 2004.

32. Testimony of Alfred V. Neffgen, op. cit.

33. Borenstein, Op. Cit

34. Ibid.

35. *U.S. v. Kellogg Brown & Root, Inc.*, US4th No. 07-1516.

36. KBR quarterly report filed with the Securities & Exchange Commission, May 4, 2007.

37. Texas Workforce Commission Unemployment Claim memo. Redacted original may be viewed at http://www.halliburtonwatch.org/images/twc.jpg.

38. David Phinney, "Adding Insult to Injury: Halliburton Contractors Denied Insurance Benefits," CorpWatch, May 24, 2005, http://www.corpwatch.org/article.php?id=12286, accessed October 5, 2008.

39. Charles W. Hoge, Carl A. Castro, Stephen C. Messe, Dennis McGurk, Dave I. Cotting, and Robert L. Koffman, "Combat Duty in Iraq and Afghanistan, Mental

Health Problems, and Barriers to Care," *New England Journal of Medicine*, July 1, 2004.

40. Phinney, "Adding Insult to Injury" op. cit.

41. Ibid.

42. Ibid.

43. Ibid.

44. U.S. House of Representatives Committee on Oversight and Government Reform hearing, Thursday, May 15, 2008,

45. Andrew G. Simpson, "House Panel Hits Defense Department, Insurers Over War Zone Insurance Costs," *Insurance Journal*, May 16, 2008.

46. The memo may be viewed on David Phinney's blog at http://www.david phinney.com/pages/2006/12/insurance_waive.php, accessed October 5, 2008.

47. Ibid.

48. Author visit to Iraq and Kuwait, April 2008.

49. Craig Kielburger, Marc Kielburger, and Chris Mallinos, "U.S. Subsidiary Tricks Migrant Workers into Delivering Supplies on Iraq's Highway of Death," *The Ottawa Citizen*, April 6, 2008.

Chapter 11

1. Robert Scheer, "Henry Waxman: In the Eye of the National Health-Insurance Storm," *Los Angeles Times*, October 10, 1993.

2. Ibid. See also Web site of Congressman Henry Waxman at http://www.house .gov/waxman/bio.htm, accessed October 5, 2008.

3. Biography of Senator Byron Dorgan at http://dorgan.senate.gov/about/biogra-phy/, accessed October 5, 2008.

4. Testimony of Henry Bunting, U.S. Senate Democratic Policy Committee Hearing, February 13, 2004.

5. Author interview with John Mancini, February 2004.

6. Chris Thompson, "Soldiers of Misfortune," *East Bay Express*, October 4, 2006. Author interview with John Mancini, February 2004 and September 2006.

7. Author interview with John Mancini, September 2006.

8. Author interview with John Mancini, September 2006 and April 2007. Interview with Susan Mancini, November 2006.

9. Statement of Robert Michael West, June 6, 2004, to the U.S. House of Representatives Committee on Government Reform. Web version available at http:// www.halliburtonwatch.org/news/west_testimony.pdf, accessed October 5, 2008.

10. Ibid.

11. Testimony of Rory Mayberry, U.S. Senate Democratic Policy Committee Hearing, June 27, 2005. See also David Phinney, "A U.S. Fortress Rises in Baghdad: Asian Workers Trafficked to Build World's Largest Embassy," CorpWatch, October 17, 2006. http://www.corpwatch.org/article.php?id=14173, accessed October 5, 2008.

12. *NBC Nightly News*, December 12. 2003. "Contractor Served Troops Dirty Food in Dirty Kitchens," Agence France Press, December 14, 2003.

13. E-mail from Cathy Gist to author, June 27, 2005.

14. Deborah Hastings, "Whistle-blower Lawsuit: Halliburton Subsidiary Overcharged, Took Food Meant for U.S. Troops," Associated Press, September 8, 2006.

15. Testimony of Julie McBride, U.S. Senate Democratic Policy Committee Hearing, September 18, 2006.

16. T. Christian Miller, "Halliburton Fraud Lawsuit Details Super Bowl Party," *Los Angeles Times*, September 9, 2006; Halliburton Annual Report 2006.

17. Testimony of Ben Carter, U.S. Senate Democratic Policy Committee Hearing, January 23, 2006.

18. William Granger, "KBR: Report of Findings & Root Cause, Water Mission B4 Ar Ramadi," Halliburton Report, May 13, 2005. http://www.halliburtonwatch.org/reports/granger_water.pdf , accessed October 5, 2008.

19. E-mail of Capt. Michelle A. Callahan to the U.S. Senate Democratic Policy Committee, March 31, 2006. http://www.halliburtonwatch.org/reports/callahanemail.pdf, accessed October 5, 2008.

20. Testimony of Jeffrey K. Griffiths, U.S. Senate Democratic Policy Committee hearing, April 7, 2006.

21. Statement of Senator Byron Dorgan, U.S. Senate Democratic Policy Committee hearing, April 7, 2006.

22. Testimony of Cheryl Harris, U.S. Senate Democratic Policy Committee hearing, July 11, 2008.

23. Testimony of Larraine McGee, U.S. Senate Democratic Policy Committee hearing, July 11, 2008.

24. Harris testimony, op. cit.

25. James Risen, "Despite Alert, Flawed Wiring Still Kills G.I.'s," *New York Times*, May 6, 2008.

26. Testimony of Debbie Crawford, U.S. Senate Democratic Policy Committee hearing, July 11, 2008.

27. Testimony of Jefferey Bliss, U.S. Senate Democratic Policy Committee hearing, July 11, 2008.

28. "Female Ex-employees Sue KBR, Halliburton: Report," Reuters, June 29, 2007.

29. Brian Ross, Maddy Sauer, and Justin Rood, "Victim: Gang-Rape Cover-Up by U.S., Halliburton/KBR," *ABC News*, December 10, 2007.

30. Jamie Leigh Jones testimony to the House of Representatives Judiciary Committee's subcommittee on Crime, Terrorism, and Homeland Security, December 19, 2007.

31. Justin Rood, "Pentagon Won't Probe KBR Rape Charges," *ABC News*, January 8, 2008.

32. James Risen, "Limbo for U.S. Women Reporting Iraq Assaults," *New York Times*, February 13, 2008. See also the Jamie Leigh Foundation at http://www.jamiesfoundation.org/, accessed October 5, 2008.

33. Maddy Sauer, "Halliburton Rape Claim Goes to Court," *ABC News*, May 12, 2008

34. "In Their First Joint Interview, Two Ex-KBR Employees Say They Were Raped by Co-Workers in Iraq," *Democracy Now!*, April 8, 2008. Karen Houppert, "KBR's Rape Problem," *The Nation*, April 18, 2008.

35. Risen, "Limbo for U.S. Women Reporting Iraq Assaults," op. cit.

36. Houppert, op. cit.

37. "Suicide or Murder? Three Years After the Death of Pfc. LaVena Johnson in Iraq, Her Parents Continue Their Call for a Congressional Investigation," *Democracy Now!*, July 23, 2008.

38. Trasncript of U.S. House of Representatives Oversight and Government Reform Committee hearing on July 31, 2008. See also Ann Wright, "Sexual Assault in the Military: A DoD Cover-Up?" *Truthdig*, August 1, 2008. http://www.truthdig.com/report/item/20080801_sexual_assault_in_the_military_a_dod_cover_up/, accessed October 5, 2008.

Chapter 12

1. Yochi Dreazen, "Digging In Former Bush Aide Turns Tough Critic as Iraq Inspector Mr. Bowen Finds Poor Controls, Waste in Reconstruction; Seeking Missing Millions Harsh Rebuke From Bremer," *Wall Street Journal*, July 26, 2005.

2. "Audit of the Accountability and Control of Materiel Assets of the Coalition Provisional Authority in Baghdad," Special Inspector General for Iraq Reconstruction (SIGIR) Audit Report, 04-011, July 26, 2004.

3. Dreazen, op. cit.

4. Ibid.

5. James Glanz, "Congress Tells Auditor in Iraq to Close Office," *New York Times*, November 3, 2006.

6. Defense Contract Audit Agency website: http://www.dcaa.mil, accessed October 5, 2008.

7. Neil King, "Halliburton Hits Snafu on Billing in Kuwait," *Wall Street Journal*, February 2, 2003.

8. Russell Gold, "Halliburton Unit Runs into Big Obstacles in Iraq," *Wall Street Journal*, April 28, 2004.

9. Neil King, Jr., "Halliburton Tells Pentagon Workers Took Kickbacks to Award Projects In Iraq," *Wall Street Journal*, January 23, 2004.

10. T. Christian Miller, "Contract Flaws in Iraq Cited," *Los Angeles Times*, March 11, 2004.

11. Sue Pleming, "U.S. Questions More Halliburton Bills," Reuters, May 17, 2004.

12. "Halliburton's Questioned and Unsupported Costs in Iraq Exceed $1.4 Billion," op. cit.

13. Ibid.

14. Ibid.

15. Gold, "Halliburton Unit Runs into Big Obstacles in Iraq," op. cit.

16. E-mail from Melissa Norcross to author, February 9, 2004.

17. Ibid.

18. Testimony of Marie deYoung at U.S. Senate Democratic Policy Committee hearing, September 10, 2004.

19. The truck photos can be seen at the Web site of HalliburtonWatch, http://www.halliburtonwatch.org/news/idletrucks.html, accessed October 5, 2008.

20. Ibid. The memo is available at http://www.halliburtonwatch.org/news/trucks _postal.pdf, accessed October 5, 2008.

21. "Interim Audit Report on Inappropriate Use of Proprietary Data Markings by the Logistics Civil Augmentation Program (LOGCAP) Contractor," Special Inspector General for Iraq Reconstruction, Report # 06-035, October 26, 2006.

22. C. J. Chivers, "Questions, Pledges, and Confrontations; Report Says Iraq Contractor Is Hiding Data From U.S.," *New York Times*, October 28, 2006.

23. James Risen, "Army Overseer Tells of Ouster Over KBR Stir," *New York Times*, June 17, 2008.

24. Testimony of Charles Smith before U.S. Senate Democratic Policy Committee, July 9, 2008.

25. Risen, "Army Overseer Tells of Ouster Over KBR Stir," *op. cit.*

26. Smith testimony, op. cit.

27. Ed Tibbetts, "Ex-Arsenal Exec Says He Was Reassigned After Standing Up to KBR," *Quad-City Times*, June 21, 2008.

28. Russell Gold and Christopher Cooper, "Pentagon Weighs Criminal Charges Of Halliburton Arm," *Wall Street Journal*, January 23, 2004.

29. Greg Jaffe and Neil King, Jr., "U.S. General Criticizes Halliburton," *Wall Street Journal*, March 15, 2004.

30. Gold, "Halliburton Unit Runs Into Big Obstacles in Iraq," op. cit.

31. Nick Grim, "Queensland Company Loses Lucrative Iraq Contract," *The World Today*, Australian Broadcasting Corporation, May 21, 2004.

32. Marian Wilkinson, "Corruption Stench as Company Loses Iraq Contract," *Sydney Morning Herald*, May 21, 2004.

33. U.S. Department of Defense Contract Awards press release, June 22, 2007; Renae Merle, "Army Tries Private Pitch for Recruits," *Washington Post*, September 6, 2006.

34. James Risen, "Controversial Contractor's Iraq Work Is Split Up," *New York Times*, May 24, 2008.

35. Griff Witte, "Army to End Expansive, Exclusive Halliburton Deal: Logistics Contract to Be Open for Bidding," *Washington Post*, July 12, 2006.

36. LOGCAP IV Pre-Proposal Conference, PowerPoint presentation by Susan McKinnis and Valliant Duhart, August 29, 2006, available at http://www.afsc .army.mil/ac/aais/ioc/industryday/docs/LOGCAP_IV_Conference/63293670757176 3560.ppt, accessed October 5, 2008. Risen, "Controversial Contractor's Iraq Work Is Split Up," op. cit.

37. "Serco Selected for $225m US Contract to Oversee Key Defense Spending Programme," Serco press release, February 21, 2007; Dana Hedgpeth, "Army Splits Award Among 3 Firms," *Washington Post*, June 28, 2007.

38. Dana Hedgpeth, "Protest Leads Army to Reconsider Big Contract," *Washington Post*, October 31, 2007.

39. Risen, "Controversial Contractor's Iraq Work Is Split Up," op. cit.

40. Gansler et al., "Urgent Reform Required: Report of the Commission on Army Acquisition and Program Management in Expeditionary Operations," op. cit.

41. Richard Lardner, "Too Many Dollars, Too Few Army Investigators," Associated Press, June 12, 2008.

42. Ibid.

43. Ibid.

44. "Casey Disappointed After Bush Rejects Plan for More Contract Oversight," Press Release from the office of Senator Bob Casey, June 25, 2008.

45. Richard Lardner, "White House Fronts Army Request for More Brass," Associated Press, July 2, 2008.

46. Simon Romero, "Troubled Unit of Halliburton May Go on Block," *New York Times*, September 24, 2004.

47. Stock history and ownership obtained from Yahoo! finance at http://finance.yahoo.com/q/hp?s=HAL and http://finance.yahoo.com/q/hp?s=KBR, accessed October 5, 2008. See also KBR annual report 2006.

48. "Halliburton Opens Corporate Headquarters in the United Arab Emirates," Halliburton press release, March 11, 2007.

49. Clifford Krauss, "Halliburton Moving C.E.O. From Houston to Dubai," *New York Times*, March 12, 2007.

50. Jim Krane, "Halliburton's Dubai Move Draws Criticism in Congress, But Industry Experts Say it Makes Sense," Associated Press, March 13, 2007.

51. Russell Gold and Susan Warren, "Halliburton Looks to Dubai for Mideast Expansion," *Wall Street Journal*, March 12, 2007.

52. Stephanie Kirchgaessner, "Halliburton Under Fire Over Dubai Proposal," *Financial Times*, March 12, 2007.

53. Krauss, op. cit.

54. United Arab Emirates, International Narcotics Control Strategy Report: Volume I: Drug and Chemical Control, Bureau of International Narcotics and Law Enforcement Affairs, March 2004, http://www.state.gov/p/nea/ci/79207.htm.

55. Author interview with David Lesar, May 2007.

Conclusion

1. E. D. Hirsch, Jr., Joseph F. Kett, and James Trefil, *The New Dictionary of Cultural Literacy* (New York: Houghton Mifflin, 2002).

2. Beth F. Scott, et al., *The Logistics of War* (Darby, PA: Diane Publishing, 2000).

3. Charles R. Shrader, *U.S. Military Logistics, 1607–1991: A Research Guide* (Westport, CT: Greenwood Press, 1992).

4. *Frontline* interview with Paul Cerjan, op. cit.

5. Author visits, April 2006, January 2007, and April 2008.

6. "(Redacted) Wife's Watch," March 6, 2004, U.S. embassy Kuwait memo from "Costa" describing an incident in August 2003. Memo provided to Defense Contract Audit Agency. Copy in author's possession provided by staff of Representative Henry Waxman's office.

7. Estimated from Halliburton annual reports for 2003–2007 and KBR annual reports for 2006 and 2007. Also, 1990 estimates obtained from Royce and Heller, op. cit.

8. Elkind, "The Truth About Halliburton," op. cit.

9. Author interview with Mike Noll, May 2002.

10. Yazad Darasha, "UAE: Halliburton CEO to Move into Dubai HQ this Week," *Emirates Today*, May 13, 2007.

11. David Lesar's stock ownership obtained from Yahoo! finance at http://finance.yahoo.com/q?s=HAL, accessed September 5, 2005 and July 15, 2008.

12. CEO Compensation Report, *Forbes*, April 30, 2008.

13. Halliburton annual report 2004 and 2005. Share prices derived from Yahoo! finance charts, http://finance.yahoo.com/q?s=HAL and http://finance.yahoo.com/q?s=KBR, accessed July 15, 2008.

14. Elkind, "The Truth About Halliburton," op. cit.

15. CEO Compensation Report, Forbes, April 2008 and KBR major holders listed at http://finance.yahoo.com/q?s=HAL, accessed July 15, 2008.

16. Renae Merle, "4 Firms Hired to Clear Debris in Gulf Coast," *Washington Post*, September 16, 2005.

17. Rachel Swarns, "Halliburton Subsidiary Gets Contract to Add Temporary Immigration Detention Centers," *New York Times*, Feb. 4, 2006.

18. Testimony of Marie deYoung at U.S. House of Representatives Committee on Oversight and Government Reform, hearing on "U.S. Effort to Rebuild Iraq," July 22, 2004.

19. Testimony of Henry Bunting at U.S. House of Representatives Government Reform Committee hearing, June 6, 2004.

20. Author interview with David Lesar, May 2006.

21. *Frontline* interview with Paul Cerjan, op. cit.

22. Elkind, "The Truth About Halliburton," op. cit.

23. Author interview with Titoko Savuwati, April 2008.

24. Author interview with Adbul Majeed Khuraibet, April 2008.

25. Author interview at LSA Anaconda, April 2008.

26. Michael Getler, "What Did NOW Know," *PBS Ombudsman*, December 16, 2005, available at: http://www.pbs.org/ombudsman/2005/12/what_did_now_know.html, accessed October 5, 2008.

27. Brenda Muñiz, "In the Eye of the Storm: How the Government and Private Response to Hurricane Katrina Failed Latinos," National Committee of La Raza, February 28, 2006. Available at http://www.nclr.org/content/publications/detail/ 36812/, accessed October 5, 2008.

28. Author interview with William Utt, April 2008.

29. Dan Morse, "Where the Rumsfelds Retreat, the Cheneys Soon Could Follow," *Washington Post*, September 5, 2005.

30. Elisabeth Bumiller, "White House Letter; Top Hawks in Search of Their Own Peace," *New York Times*, December 19, 2005.

31. Ian Finseth, "Douglass and the Legacy of Mount Misery," *Baltimore Sun*, August 20, 2006. Al Kamen, "4 More Feet in the Ark of Operations?" *Washington Post*, January 14, 2004.

32. Bumiller, op. cit.

33. Author interviews with Andrea Buffa, Robert Buzzanco, Jodie Evans, Jeffery Grubler, and Scott Parkin at Halliburton annual meeting in Houston, May 2004. Shannon Buggs, "Protests Cause Stir at Annual Meeting," *Houston Chronicle*, May 20, 2004.

34. Ibid.

35. Author interviews with Scott Parkin, May 2005.

36. Author interviews with David Graeve, Jeffery Grubler, Maureen Haver, and Scott Parkin at Halliburton annual meeting in Houston, May 2005. Purva Patel and Paige Hewitt, "15 Arrested at Rowdy Halliburton Protest," *Houston Chronicle*, May 18, 2005.

37. Author interviews with Maureen Haver at Halliburton annual meeting in Duncan, May 2006. Lynn Cook, "Shareholders, Protesters Alike Bring Issues," *Houston Chronicle*, May 17, 2006.

38. Author interviews with Jeffery Grubler and David Graeve, at Halliburton annual meeting in Woodlands, May 2007. Brett Clanton, "Halliburton Meeting: Though CEO Leaving for Mideast, He Says City Is Still Key," *Houston Chronicle*, May 16, 2007.

39. Author interviews with David Graeve, at Halliburton annual meeting in Houston, May 2008. Brett Clanton, "Halliburton CEO Says Dubai Base the 'Right Decision,'" *Houston Chronicle*, May 21, 2008.

ACKNOWLEDGMENTS

This book came together because of the help that hundreds of people gave me over the last seven years, many of whom must go unnamed at their request. There were dozens of anonymous whistle-blowers at Halliburton/KBR and its subcontractors who risked their jobs to come forward to talk to me off the record. Others spoke to me despite their skepticism of my critical approach; I hope they will find that I have been fair and accurate.

At the top of the list of people that I can thank publicly for detailed research help are David Phinney who wrote numerous feature stories for CorpWatch, often convincing me to run stories that I was skeptical of, only to discover that he was right; David Martinez, who accompanied me on three of my fact-finding trips to Iraq; and Charlie Cray and Jim Donahue of Halliburton Watch.

I traveled to many places for this book and in each I was assisted by many people who did additional reporting, translation, and even opened up their homes to me: Fariba Nawa and Parwiz Hakim in Kabul, Afghanistan; Laszlo Tibold in Budapest, Hungary; Istifan Braymok in Erbil, Wada Qasimy and Salam Allawi in Baghdad, Iraq; Jackson Allers and Kata Mester in Pristina, Kosovo; Alan Waller and Titoko Savuwati in Kuwait city; Lee Wang and Howie Severino in Manila, the Philippines; Aaron Glantz and Sasha Lilley in Incirlik, Turkey; Mirza in Dubai and Sharjah in the United Arab Emirates; Mr Nam in Tashkent, Uzbekistan; Aaron Glantz and Ngoc Nguyen in Cam Ranh bay, Vietnam. In the United States, Bob Buzzanco, David Graeve, Jeffrey Grubler, Maureen Haver, Katie Heim, and Scott Parkin helped me over five years of visits to Dallas and Houston, Texas; while David Phinney, Michael Rios, Tabassum Siraj, and Anjali Thavendran graciously hosted me in Washington, DC, when I visited.

I was assisted also by a number of military public affairs officers, notably Tim Horton and David Zerbe in LSA Anaconda, Iraq; Richard Dowling at the U.S. Army Corps of Engineers in Baghdad; Maria Or at the Corps in Kirkuk; and Mary Hahn at Camp Bondsteel in Kosovo.

I was always accorded a quick and detailed reply to my questions by the public affairs staff at Halliburrton/KBR, despite the nature of my queries. For this I thank Zelma Branch, Heather Browne, Cathy Gist-Mann, Wendy Hall,

Melissa Norcross, Stephanie Price, and Beverly Scippa. I was pleasantly surprised to be approached directly by the CEOs of both Halliburton and KBR at their respective annual meetings and given short personal interviews: David Lesar of Halliburton on no less than three occasions and William Utt in 2008. Jim Dale, director of Halliburton corporate security and his staff, notably Tom Cochran and Randy Lawton were always accommodating.

I must also thank the many participant in the active list-serv of the private military contractors run by Doug Brooks, especially Nick Bicanic, David Isenberg, Robert Young Pelton, and Peter Singer. Thanks also to my long-standing colleagues and listeners at KPFA radio in Berkeley and *Democracy Now!* in New York who asked me to report back on what I had seen on the ground in Afghanistan and Iraq.

Every chapter of this book was inspired by the work of many others. Matt Armstrong introduced me to the Rumsfeld speech on September 10, 2001, which I used in the introduction. The detailed transcripts of the trial of Jeff Alex Mazon would not have been possibly if not for Nancy Mersot, court reporter for the federal court house in Rock Island, Illinois, and the reporting of Ann McGlynn of the *Quad City Times*.

The first chapter was a result of a detailed tour of the military logistics facilities in Iraq and Kuwait, coordinated by Tim Horton at LSA Anaconda and Mary J Constantino at Camp Arifjan in Kuwait. The history of Halliburton, Brown & Root, and Lyndon B Johnson in Chapter 2 owes much to three writers: Dan Briody, author of *The Halliburton Agenda*; the three-volume biography of LBJ by Robert Caro; and Jeffrey L. Rodengen, the author of *Legend of Halliburton*; as well as the work of Robert Bryce, Ronnie Dugger, Christopher Castaneda, and Joseph Pratt.

Chapter 3 owes its origins to the research of James Carter and Robert Buzzanco of the Department of History at the University of Houston and to David S. King, former Congressman from Salt Lake City in Utah, who traveled with Donald Rumsfeld to Vietnam in 1966. His travel documents were indispensable in reconstructing the period as well as James Carter's excellent book *Reinventing Vietnam*. The biography of Dick Cheney written by Stephen Hayes, the profile of the vice president by Nicholas Lemann in the *New Yorker*, and the three biographies of Rumsfeld by Midge Decter, Jeffrey A. Krames, and Rowan Scarborough, were essential reading to understand the two men.

The account of Cheney's days at Halliburton in Chapter 4 is derived from the work of Robert Bryce and Aram Roston at *Mother Jones* magazine, Knut Royce and Nathaniel Heller of the Center for Public Integrity, and the incredibly detailed profiles created by Jim Donahue at Halliburton Watch. Jim Vallette of the Institute for Policy Studies provided analysis of Halliburton's lobbying activities over the years. Back issues of *Army Logistician* and the reports of the General Accounting Office were invaluable in guiding me in my trips to Afghanistan, Kosovo, Turkey, and Uzbekistan for the material in chapters 5 and 6, in addition to the people who helped me in each country. Rick Rocamora's reporting was invaluable in understanding how the prison camps in Guantánamo Bay were built in the absence of an opportunity to visit Cuba. Bob Woodward and Michael Gordon's books on the Iraq invasion provided me with the background for some of the accounts of the Iraq invasion in 2003.

Bunnatine Greenhouse of the U.S. Army Corps of Engineers, Michael and Stephen Kohn of the National Whistle-blower Center, and Sheryl Tappan helped shed light on the secret contracts signed for Operation Iraqi Oil—as did Erik Eckholm of the *New York Times* and Adam Zagorin at *Time* magazine. Dan Baum of the *New York Times Magazine* aided me with detailed reports on the ground of the oil rehabilitation from Kuwait and Iraq for Chapter 7 of this book. T. Christian Miller of the *Los Angeles Times*, James Glanz of the *New York Times*, and of course the staff of Stuart Bowen at the Special Inspector General for Iraq Reconstruction (SIGIR), notably Jim Mitchell; the auditors at the Defense Contract Audit Agency (DCAA) and the investigators on Congressman Henry Waxman's staff dug up the real story of how the rehabilitation of Iraq's oil fields were botched and how the taxpayer was charged astronomical sums for shoddy work. The pressure to publish the internal workings of the Coalition Provisional Authority from Revenue Watch Institute and the audits of the International Advisory and Monitoring Board explained how the money was given to Halliburton/KBR. Alan Waller of Lloyd-Owen International took the trouble to personally escort me from Kuwait city to the Iraqi border so that I could better understand the fuel delivery system.

The detailed accounts of the shady deals that were cut in Kuwait by Halliburton managers and subcontractors came to light by many individuals in that country whom I cannot name, but the indictments issued by the Department of Justice as well as the court transcripts of the trials and sentencing hearings in federal courts in Rock Island help back up and flesh out what transpired during and after the build-up to the invasion that I describe in Chapter 8. Marie deYoung and Henry Bunting are two of the whistle-blowers who did come forward and speak on the record on these matters. Cam Simpson and Glenn R. Simpson of the *Wall Street Journal* and David Phinney's reporting for CorpWatch broke the first detailed reports on Public EWarehousing Corporation and First Kuwaiti, respectively.

Phinney was also the first to detail the labor conditions of Asian and U.S. workers in Iraq in his reporting for CorpWatch, which appears in chapters 9 and 10. Similar reporting by T. Christian Miller of the *Los Angeles Times*, David Rohde at the *New York Times*, Russell Gold at the *Wall Street Journal*, and Cam Simpson at the *Chicago Tribune* have provided more horror stories of workers trafficked to Iraq. Lee Wang brought me firsthand reports from Manila of the recruitment companies. The building of Camp Anaconda was recounted to me by Laszlo Tibold while the details of the deadly truck convoys that departed the base in April 2004 came from Ray Stannard and the family of Tony Johnson. Ramon Lopez, Vince Howard, and T. Scott Allen—the lawyers who brought suit against the company for wrongful death—arranged for me to track the case from its inception. Once again, T. Christian Miller's excellent reporting for the *Los Angeles Times* on the internal communications on the day of the attack of the convoy helped fill in missing details, as did Jeremy Scahill and Steve Fainaru's reports for the *Nation* magazine and the *Washington Post* on Blackwater and Triple Canopy respectively.

The list of Halliburton/KBR and military whistle-blowers that the staff of Senator Byron Dorgan and Congressman Henry Waxman arranged to testify at hearings on Capitol Hill is lengthy and impressive: Jefferey Bliss, Michelle Callahan, Ben Carter, Debbie Crawford, Dawn Leamon, Jamie Leigh Jones, Ken May, Rory Mayberry, John Mancini, Julie McBride, James Warren, Mike West, and David Wilson. The families of Wesley Batalona, Christopher Lee Everett, Scott Helvenston, LaVena Johnson, Ryan Maseth, Michael Teague, and Jerko Zovko also came forward to testify, which provided me with the material for Chapter 11. Alan Brayson, the lawyer for many of these whistle-blowers, who was elected to the House of Representatives in November 2008, deserves to be singled out for his one-man legal battles to combat fraud and corruption among military contractors.

The first reports of overcharging at Halliburton/KBR were broken by Neil King and Chip Cummins of the *Wall Street Journal*, after they obtained leaked information from the DCAA which I describe in Chapter 12. The full details were revealed by Charles Smith who came forward to James Risen of the *New York Times*. My understanding of Pentagon oversight was aided by an interview with Jacques Gansler, former undersecretary of defense. Reporting in the *Houston Chronicle* by Brett Clanton, Lynn Cook, Purva Patel, Loren Steffy, and their DC colleague David Ivanovich aided me greatly in understanding Halliburton/KBR's Houston operations.

If I have omitted any names or made any mistakes in this account, the fault is mine alone.

I could not have written this book if it had not been for the able support and staff of CorpWatch, namely Terry Allen, Jennifer Borden, Tonya Hennessey, Amelia Hight, Sasha Lilley, Joslyn Maula, and Sakura Saunders. The board of CorpWatch—Antonio Diaz, China Brotsky, Antonio Diaz, Josh Karliner, and Mele Lau Smith—guided us regularly. Thanks also to our funders: the Arca Foundation, Educational Foundation of America, the George

Washington Williams Fellowship of the Independent Press Association, the Jeht Foundation, the Lawson Valentine Foundation, Revenue Watch Institute, and the Wardlaw Foundation. The Fund for Investigative Journalism and the LEF Foundation provided me with the first funding for my trips to Iraq while the Lannan foundation provided me with the funding to take time off to write this book.

Much gratitude to the folks at Nation Books who patiently endured my many missed deadlines: Carl Bromley and Lori Hobkirk who edited the book; Claudia Dizenzo for publicity; and of course Sam Stoloff, my agent who shepherded my proposal from a hastily scribbled one-pager to getting me a real book contract.

In writing this book in Vancouver, British Columbia, in the summer of 2008, I had the daily support and encouragement of Lily Smith. Thanks also to Max Smith who understood why her daughter spent so much time away as well as the Boothroyd family who made sure I emerged from seclusion from time to time. The same goes to Ronald Nobuhisa Sakamoto and Malou and Mary Lou Babilonia at Pusod, in Berkeley, Calfornia, who kept the home fires burning as I traveled the world.

Last, but not least, my thanks goes to my parents, Gregoryne Olivemalar Chatterjee and Jayanta Chatterjee, who taught me right from wrong.

INDEX